AF575460

IF THESE APPLES SHOULD FALL

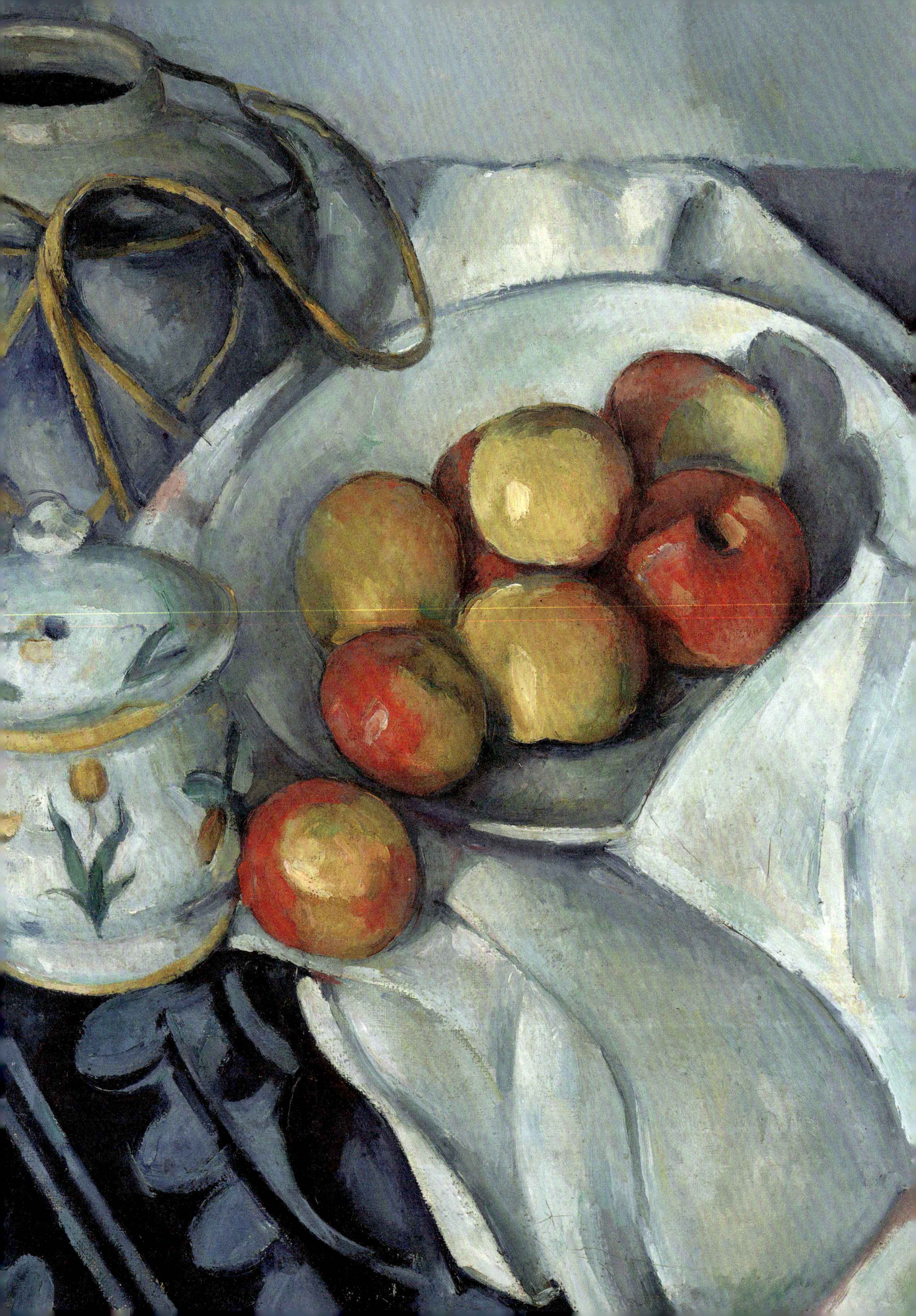

T. J. CLARK

IF THESE APPLES SHOULD FALL

CÉZANNE AND THE PRESENT

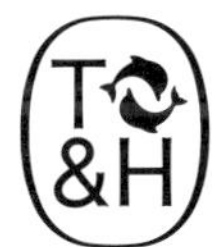

The apples of Cézanne are not fruit any longer,
nor fruit made over into paint;
instead all imaginable life is in them,
and if they should fall,
a universal conflagration would ensue.

Ernst Bloch, *Geist der Utopie*, 1916

Also by T. J. Clark

The Absolute Bourgeois: Artists and Politics in France, 1848–1851 (1973)

Image of the People: Gustave Courbet and the 1848 Revolution (1973)

The Painting of Modern Life: Paris in the Art of Manet and his Followers (1984)

Farewell to an Idea: Episodes from a History of Modernism (1999)

(with 'Retort': Joseph Matthews, Michael Watts, Iain Boal) *Afflicted Powers: Capital and Spectacle in a New Age of War* (2005)

The Sight of Death: An Experiment in Art Writing (2006)

(with Anne M. Wagner) *Lowry and the Painting of Modern Life* (2013)

Picasso and Truth: From Cubism to Guernica (2013)

Por uma Esquerda sem Futuro (2013)

(with Anne M. Wagner) *Pity and Terror: Picasso's Path to 'Guernica'* (2017)

Heaven on Earth: Painting and the Life to Come (2018)

CONTENTS

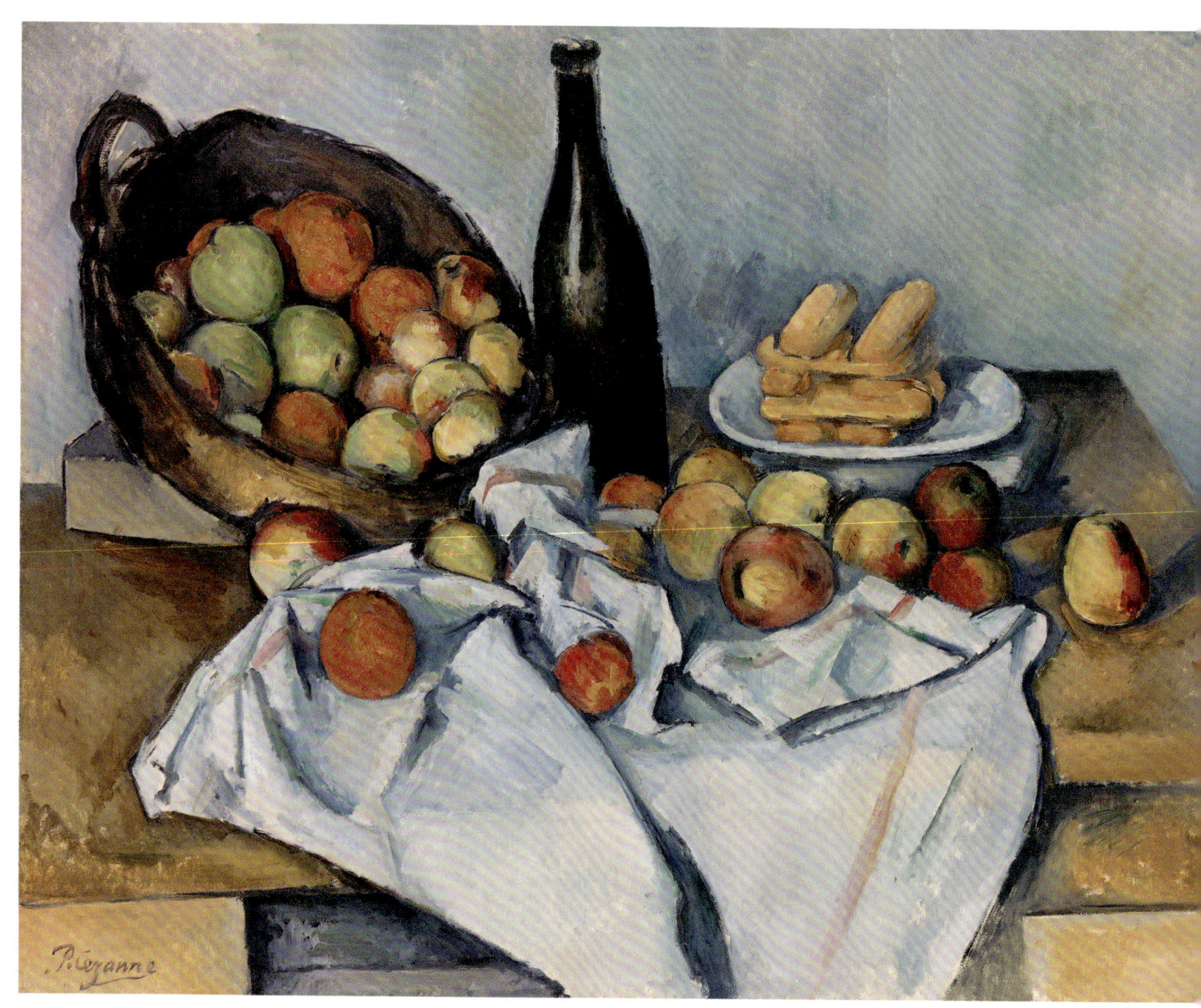

1. *The Basket of Apples*, *c.* 1893, 65 × 80 cm (25⅝ × 31½ in.). Art Institute of Chicago.

Introduction

I cannot remember the year I bought my first book on Cézanne – maybe it was 1958 – or what had led me to the artist previously. Cézanne was a value in those days: his name cropped up. Meyer Schapiro, the author of the Cézanne volume in the 'Library of Great Painters', was nobody I knew about, and only later did I begin to learn from his magnificent text. What I can remember is the feeling that came over me when I first looked at the painting on the book's dust jacket, *The Basket of Apples*.[1] I think I can retrieve the feeling even sixty years later, it was so powerful, so distinct. And if I hadn't had the feeling back then, and persisted in it (cultivated it) through the years, I reckon my life would have been immeasurably poorer. I wouldn't fully have known what it was to be modern.

Maybe that opening paragraph moves too far too fast: it seems to end up equating 'knowing what it is to be modern' with some special, indispensable intensity. Part of me recoils from just such an equation – I remain an 'anti-modern' through and through. (Of course, I know that this anti-modernity is part of the modern package.) But anyway I am over-reacting. For in fact the offending sentences don't say anything, positive or negative, about modernity itself: 'knowing what it is to be modern' is not the same as *being* modern. It's the knowing that is the value. Cézanne, for instance, may or may not have been a modern himself; he may or may not have valued modernity (very probably not, at least in terms of his conscious opinions and way of life); but what matters is that he knew – his painting was his knowing – what modernity felt like. And he understood that a very great deal – almost everything – about painting would have to be reconstructed if that knowledge was to be given form. And it had to be given form, whatever you thought of its object. The feeling, damn it, was the thing to be painted.

The Basket of Apples hates the object called modernity. It sets up a whole impossible anti-modernity to stave it off, to overwhelm it, to sing it to sleep – a peasant world, a natural world, a world of endurances and irremovables. The plain black bottle. The fruit in the folds of simple cloth. But not for a moment does the painting ask us to believe that its set-up will stave off the reality of the 1890s. Everything in the painting is falling – and where it falls to is where we are. I saw that immediately in 1958; or that's how I remember things.

'What modernity felt like…' The reader will see from the previous lines that the temptation in writing about Cézanne is to give that feeling a definite tonality, and almost inevitably an ominous one. If things are falling in a picture, isn't it always into an abyss? If the world isn't natural, doesn't that mean it is denatured? But the real difficulty, and splendour, of a characteristic painting by Cézanne has to do with its tonality – the feeling it is trying to give form to – *not* being definite. If things in modernity do not endure, or if those that do (the bottle, the apples) are powerless against the tipping and sliding, that does not seem to mean, in Cézanne, that the world we live in is unendurable; but equally, it isn't wonderful in its instantaneity, or thrilling in its ambiguity. The latter modern value in particular – the ambiguous as a realm of truth or an ethics of endless negotiation – is one that a Cézanne painting ironizes even as it brings on.

None of this adds up to saying that the ominous is simply absent in a Cézanne, or that ambiguity isn't often chilling – that it doesn't threaten to puncture the illusion. Look at the dark between the lowest folds of the tablecloth in *The Basket of Apples*. Think of the dark (or try to) in relation to the answering shadow underneath the tabletop, and the whole accompanying weird buildup of blocks and supports. Look at the tablecloth's pink stripe – the one heading off the table. Where is it? Where is it going? There is a nowhere-ness in Cézanne – an unmooring. It just refuses to be modernity's note.

The book that follows gathers together efforts, made over decades, to come to terms with the strangeness as well as the beauty of Cézanne's achievement. There are moments in one or two chapters that tip too much towards the minatory, I now think. But I have retained them, and not tried to lighten them much, because I believe they speak to the bewilderment

I felt looking at the 'Library of Great Painters' cover. The world I saw there was so entirely familiar and yet so distant – so unreachable, so unrecognizable. That's what had me transfixed. If a piece of writing stays true to that basic uncanny, it passes muster.

◆

Lately I've found myself writing one or two poems about paintings by Cézanne. ('Found myself writing' is no exaggeration. One of the poems cropped up on a bench in the French Nineteenth Century room at the National Gallery in London, looking at *Hillside in Provence* (FIG. 3) through a wall of selfies.) The first poem addresses a painting that lives in a less frantic place, the Norton Simon Museum in Pasadena – I've been back many times to see it there and it has never failed to look threatening, exquisite, unlikely (FIG. 2).

Tulips in a Vase

A terrible invention, the flower. Monster
Out of the mud and green mantle of the early Cretaceous,
Reaching up to the X-ray sun
And puffing scent, pollen, spores from its garish cheeks.

Just look at the agonized folds of the leaves in Cézanne
Supporting the flags above,
And the sadness of the glaze on the stoneware,
Trying so hard to be a rival, a representation, of the chaos
Coming out of its mouth – the vase hardly big enough
To hold the octopus, the base marooned on the table
Like a boulder downstream from a glacier
Or a chess piece in a game with no squares.

But here's where the picture gets difficult.
Because all this unfamiliarity on the edge of melodrama
(Of the kind that flowers regularly specialize in), all this existence

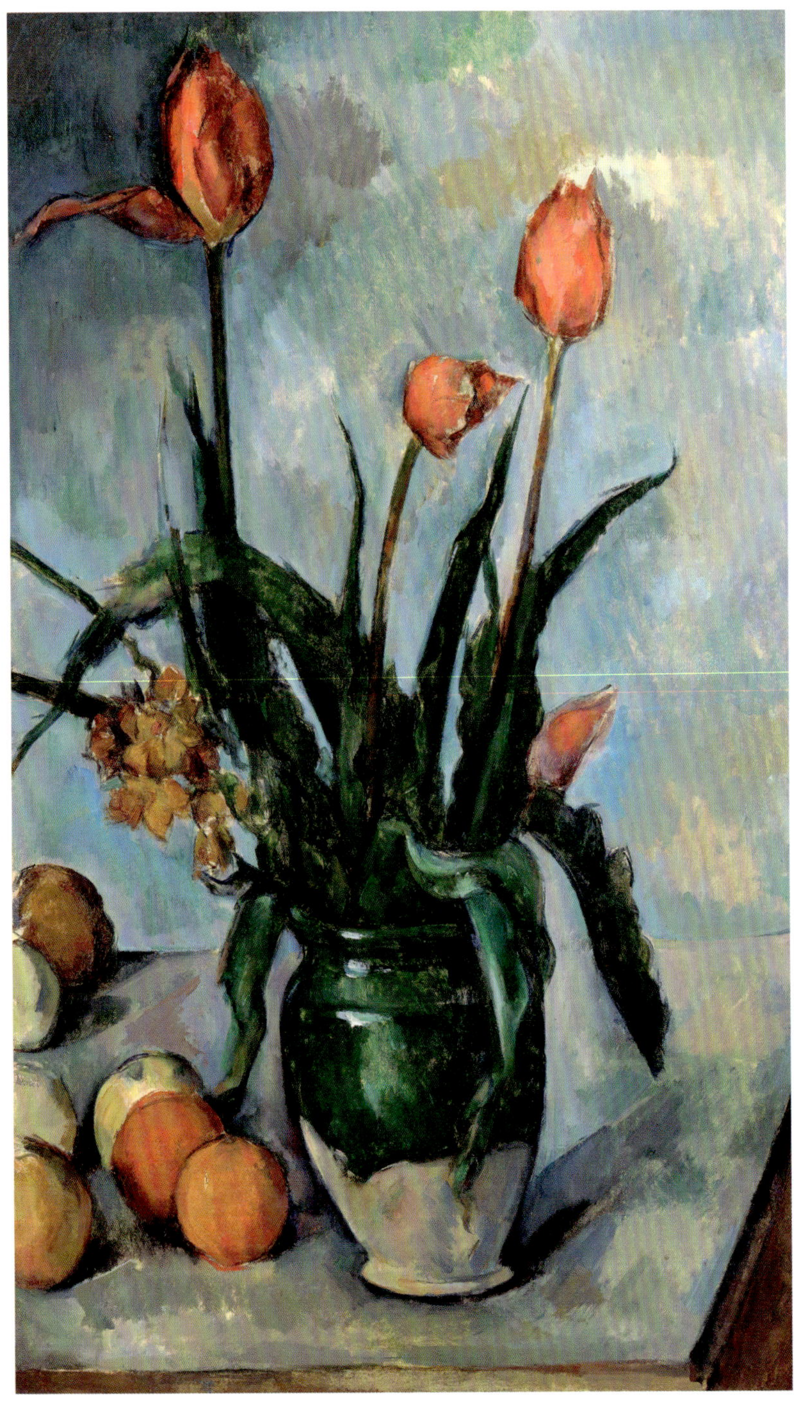

2. *The Vase of Tulips*, *c.* 1890, 72.5 × 42 cm (28½ × 16½ in.).
Norton Simon Museum, Pasadena.

In a space that's not yet a firmament (the tabletop as close
To a territory where water and air are still undivided
As painting has ever come) is also so gentle, so palpable, so plain –
The overweight leaves entirely happy with their twisting and bending and
almost breaking,
The flower heads in such harmony, such accommodation
To the wall and warmth of the room. These seem to be things
In need of protection, simple things.

Granted. But then look at the painting's shape,
Climbing and climbing to keep pace with the cultivars
And hacking off leaves at will. 'Picturing'
Isn't always a kindness.

They say that Cézanne in his older age dreamt
Of doing an Apotheosis of Delacroix, *his*
Hero carried heavenward on clouds. We have a sketch
In which the painter and his admirers are there in the rough,
Stubby, inept, touching.
The Apotheosis *never got done. But here it is, on the table,*
Delacroix's Liberty *raising the red white and blue,*
The studio ceiling hardly high enough to hold the tricolour,
Green fighters gathered at Lady Liberty's feet
Looking for a place among the cannon balls.

It is the Cézanne dilemma. The world rears up in its ordinary glory,
Vase and tulips placed in the centre of things, solid, maybe a touch
pedantic;
But the action on either side of the spine is
Crazily asymmetrical – the right edge of the painting empty,
The left seething with lines and breaks,
And we are invited to decide if what we are seeing
Has a touch of danger to it, leaves and flowers at war with the space
Meant to contain them, or is as harmless and beautiful as a set
Of tritons blowing water from shells
In a fountain in the park.

Hillside in Provence

Everything in a picture is turned to face us,
But in a good picture the turning is done with tact,
Almost reluctantly, so that we see a kind of shadow world –
Shadows softer and brighter than the things that cast them –
Standing next to the trees come forward to meet us, made from
Objects we sense as much as see, forms not belonging to the world we are part of,
Gradients (unfoldings) of infinite space. The rocks on the quarry wall.

How this other world takes place in us, and why we fear it,
Is Cézanne's subject.

Maybe the ivory road (or is it a riverbed?) in the foreground of Hillside
in Provence
Is intended to spell this out. It is the floor of the earth
Emerging after the flood, with colours stacked in a small neat pile to one side,
as if
Waiting to be used. The road is not ominous or remote, just not continuous
with the world
We know. It is the least anthropological ground plane ever painted.
But then why is the scene erected on top of it, with the road as
necessary footing,
So entirely alive? Why is its coldness a fire?

There is a poem by Ammons in which a blackbird 'shoots through
a vacancy
In the elm tree and bolts over the house'. The poet wants to show the way
the vacancy
Is full of the life passed through it. I don't think the emptiness
Appearing in the screen of leaves in Hillside*, like a window carved out of a*
green arc de triomphe, has anything to do with
A maker, a bird of passage. You sometimes can find yourself wishing for
a hawk or a hare
Or a woman at a cottage door in Cézanne, but the next moment you know
the rock face

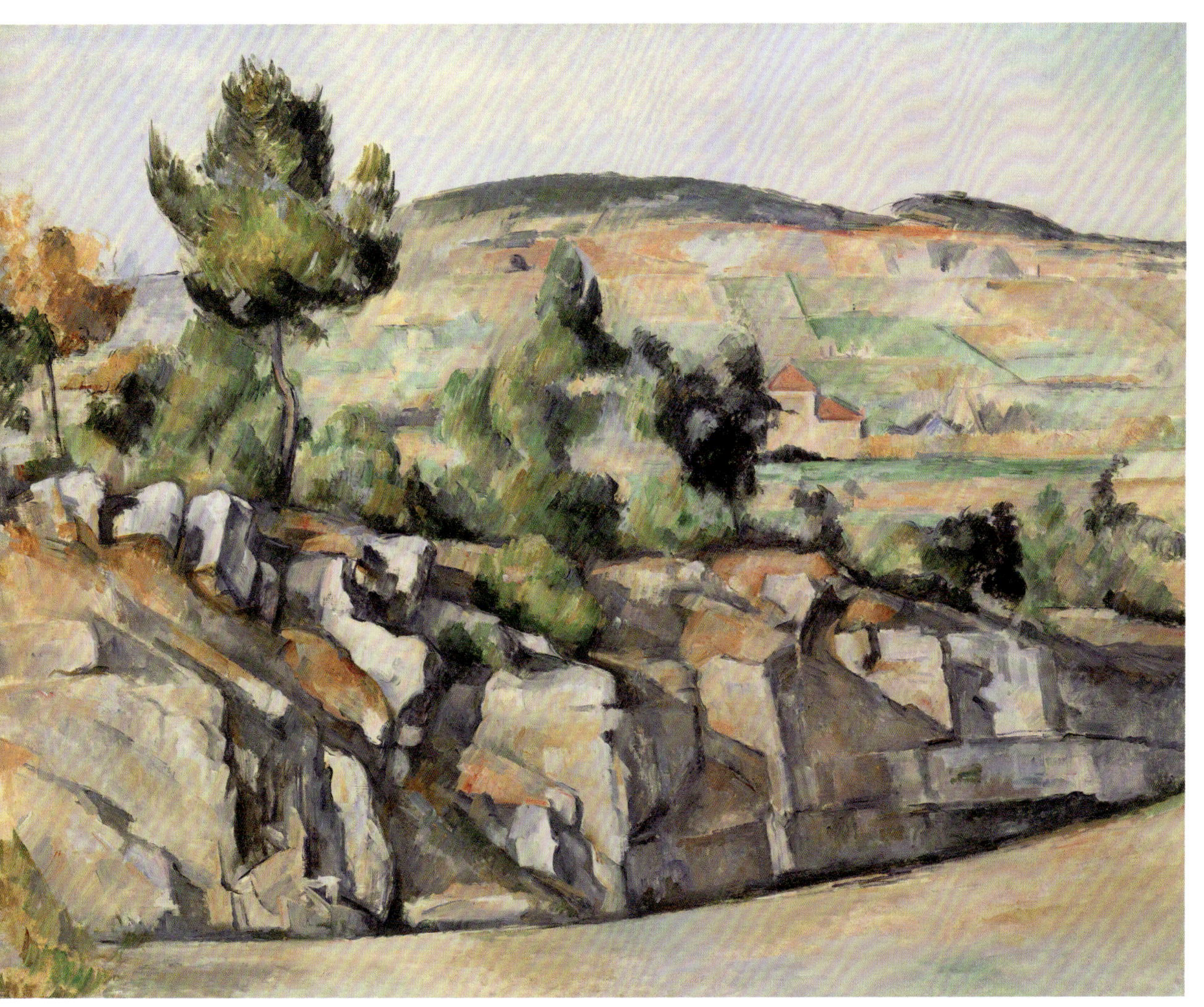

3. *Hillside in Provence*, 1890–92, 65 × 81 cm (25⅝ × 31⅞ in.). National Gallery, London.

And the windowless farm have to be as remote from our doings
As they are in Cézanne in order to be our representatives, us in the world,
us become colours.

Look at the playing card fields and the tallest tree, raising its stubby hands
In prayer or surrender. Look at the air blue as nothing. This is eternity
With just one blemish – a tiny dark oval high on the hill, rearing leftwards and
Toppling into its own shadow, like a tank at the battle of the Somme. I hear
The sound of artillery clattering in the rocks. The green is smoke
From a shell hole.

◆

The second poem is the one begun in the National Gallery. I think the two poems make an appropriate start to the book, above all because they try to suggest – almost to perform – the bewilderment of seeing a Cézanne for the first time. They go back to 1958. And what makes the shock so indelible – what makes it survive through subsequent viewings – is that it has so little to do with outlandishness or provocation. Cézanne as a young man in Paris had been a specialist in both strategies; but in the 1870s he left that idea of the modern in art (which persisted with others) definitively behind. My Chapter 1, on his apprenticeship with Pissarro, discusses why and how. And it is the idea that replaced the initial one – the amalgam of ordinariness and unfamiliarity in the mature Cézanne, of trust in the eye and admission of loss, of shock *and* objectivity – which shapes the rest of the book. There is a chapter on Cézanne's treatment of the objects we use and consume every day – the genre that in English is given the double-edged title 'still life' – and a following one on his unique approach to landscape. Whether the word 'landscape' really applies to his pictures is a question, for all their familiar scenes of the South. Still more the word 'rustic'. Cézanne was a proud native of Provence, at a moment when some of his greatest admirers were preaching a new ethnic and linguistic nationalism. But here too Cézanne's art – Cézanne's modernity – is impenetrable. A chapter on his paintings of *Card Players* tries to understand the artist's belonging and not-belonging to the peasant world surrounding him.

Lastly the book turns to a painting by Matisse. His *Garden at Issy* was painted in a Paris suburb in 1917, at a time of war and revolution (FIG. 75). The exchanges of fire at the front to the north could sometimes be heard in Matisse's studio. The world of Cézanne – the structure of belief and assumption that had made his kind of aesthetic concentration possible – was going down in flames. Matisse's *Garden* is full, I think, of a consciousness of that ending – Matisse, after all, was just as deeply a nineteenth-century man as the older artists he revered – and the painting struggles to decide what, if anything, from the past of French art might still be usable in the chaos. Cézanne is the presiding deity. The view taken of the master in *Garden* is ironic and unsparing – despair may be close – but Matisse's allegiance remains total.

◆

A last image to set the book in motion. Sometime in the late 1890s Cézanne painted in an abandoned quarry to the east of Aix-en-Provence. The canvases he did there are all astonishing, and several have viewpoints that cut the ground from underneath our feet. (Cézanne's dealer, Ambroise Vollard, even claimed not to know which way up one of them was meant to hang.) Perhaps the most extraordinary of the series – in its very simplicity of structure, the completeness of its disobedience to the world of up and down – is entitled *The Red Rock* (FIG. 4).

Red Rock has been written about excellently by others, and all I wish to add here is a plea to look again at the rectangle and submit to its unearthliness.[2] I know of no other pictorial order remotely like this one. (Maybe the previous *di sotto in su* conventions of ceiling painting occasionally threw up a view of the heavens, up past an angel looming in the foreground, that puts one in mind of the Cézanne. But the point of *Red Rock* is precisely that we're not looking upwards, any more than setting out bravely along the path.) No painter, I reckon, has ever risked conjuring space out of such a standoff between opposed realities. To call the realities in question – the bristle of green and blue and orange in the mid-ground, the Euclidean figure set apart from it to the right – 'organic' versus 'geometric', or 'animate'

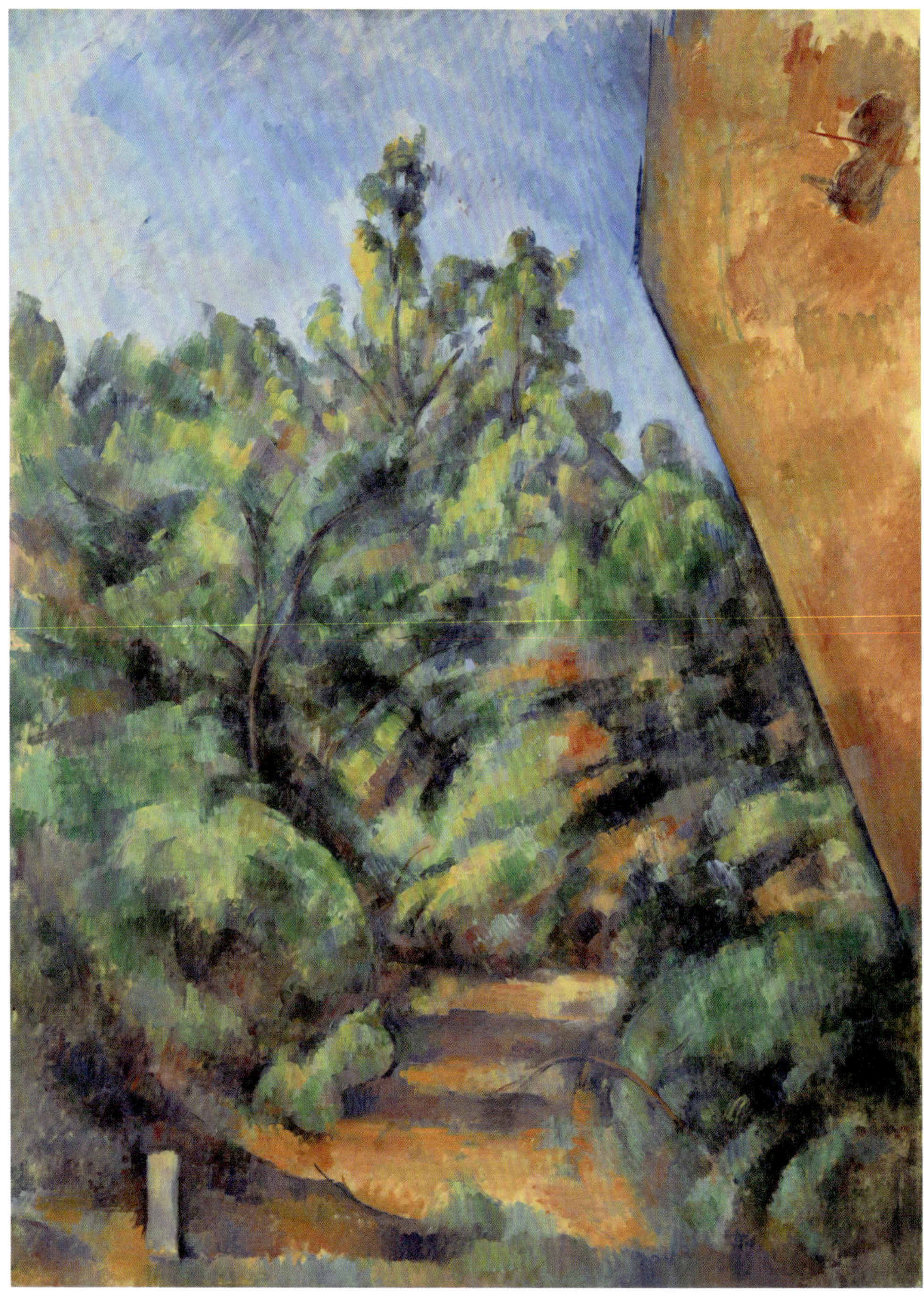

4. *The Red Rock*, 1895–1900, 91 × 66 cm (35⅞ × 26 in.). Musée de l'Orangerie, Paris, Jean-Walter and Paul Guillaume Collection.

versus 'abstract', or even 'perceived' as opposed to 'invented', seems to me to avoid the absoluteness of the to-and-fro, and the final effect of the absoluteness. All identities and categorizations are swallowed by the *machine* of depiction. The mid-ground foliage is a system of gears: objects are pulled into it as if into an abyss. The so-called rockface is facelessness immortalized – a sign come from elsewhere, fastened insecurely to the picture corner, saying 'here no picturing takes place'. This is a world – a set of antinomies – with no descriptions to match.

And the dead tree gives no shelter, the cricket no relief,
And the dry stone no sound of water. Only
There is shadow under this red rock,
(Come in under the shadow of this red rock),
And I will show you something different from either
Your shadow at morning striding behind you
Or your shadow at evening rising to meet you;
I will show you fear in a handful of dust.[3]

'Fear' is not right for *Red Rock*, we realize. Dust and dryness don't speak to the picture's vitality. The poet in *The Waste Land*, we might say, still wants his nature to have an overall tone – a humanness, even if a despairing and vestigial one. He looks out at a world from which the gods have departed. It is a desert for him. And the secret the desert is keeping is fear, the terror of homelessness and disbelief: the poet produces it finally, a note of grim triumph in his voice. But there are no secrets in Cézanne.

1. Pissarro and Cézanne

'What do you make of Cézanne?'
'I see him as being, in his own art, what Rimbaud was to literature.'
Paterne Berrichon (Rimbaud's first biographer), *Mercure de France*, 1905[1]

I begin with an old photograph and a fragment of reminiscence. The photo was taken probably in 1874 or 1875 in Auvers, and the two characters in light clothes, holding straw hats, are Cézanne and Pissarro. Cézanne is the one on the garden bench, pretending to be absorbed in thought.[2] The small boy sitting on the back of the bench, hands in lap, is Pissarro's beloved eldest son, Lucien: he can have been no more than eleven or twelve when the photo was taken. Nonetheless he retained strong memories of the time, and of slightly later moments when Cézanne came to visit, and many years later his brother Paul-Émile persuaded him to put them in writing:

> Cézanne lived in Auvers, and he used to walk three kilometres to come and work with father. They discussed theories endlessly, and one day bought palette knives to paint with. Several pictures remain of the work they did at this time. They are very similar in treatment, and the *motifs* are often the same. One morning, father was painting in a field, and Cézanne was sitting on the grass watching him. A peasant came along and said to father: 'Your workman over there isn't putting in much effort!'[3]

The final anecdote is good, and the fact that a peasant appears in it not incidental. But two phrases seem crucial: 'They discussed theories endlessly' and 'Cézanne was sitting on the grass watching him.' The first

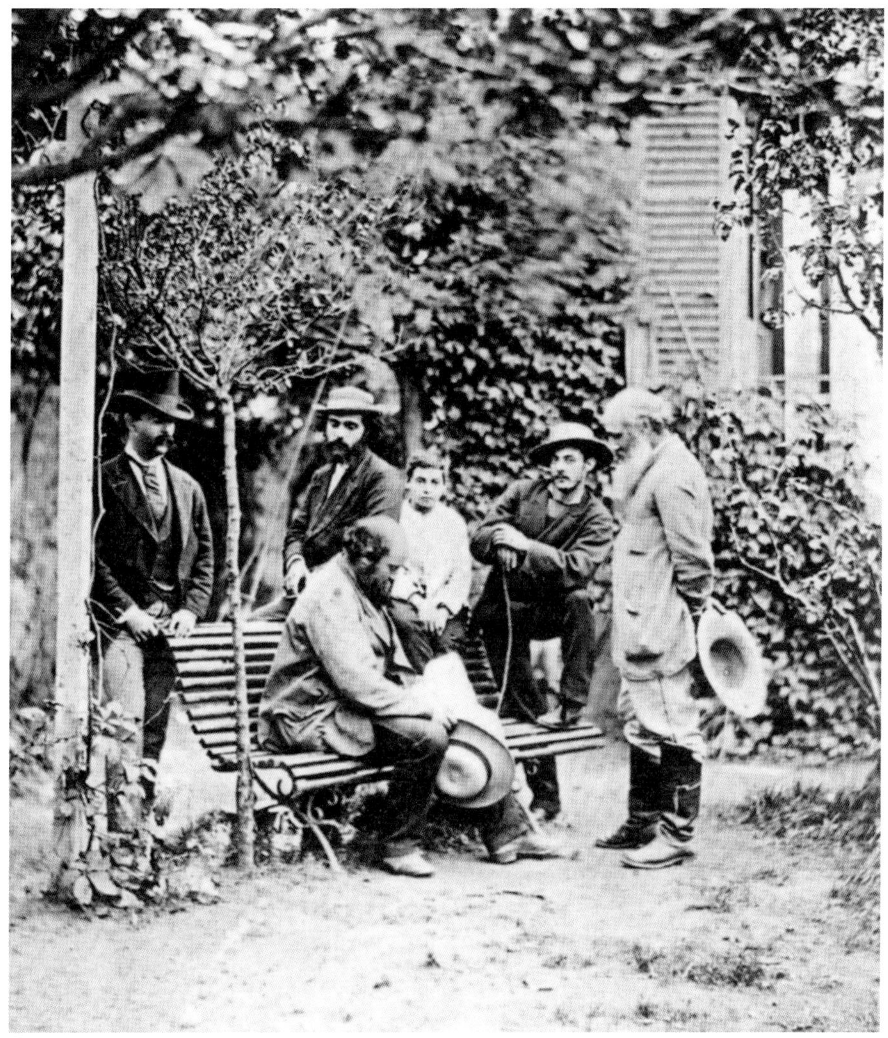

5. Nicolás Martinéz Valdivieso: *Pissarro, Cézanne and friends*, photograph, *c.* 1874–75. L&S Pissarro Archives

suggests that the interaction between the two painters was verbal as well as pictorial, and that the two of them were conscious that something intense and difficult – something that demanded verbal clarification as it happened – was at stake in the painting they did together. Theory came up, maybe concerning the nature of painting, even the nature of perception, and never seemed to stop. Looking back, this doesn't surprise us. We go on thinking in retrospect that in this 'working with father', Cézanne, and Pissarro himself, came to recognize certain features – certain ways of doing things, ways of understanding the world – that in due course determined the character of modern art. No wonder discussion had to be part of the process.

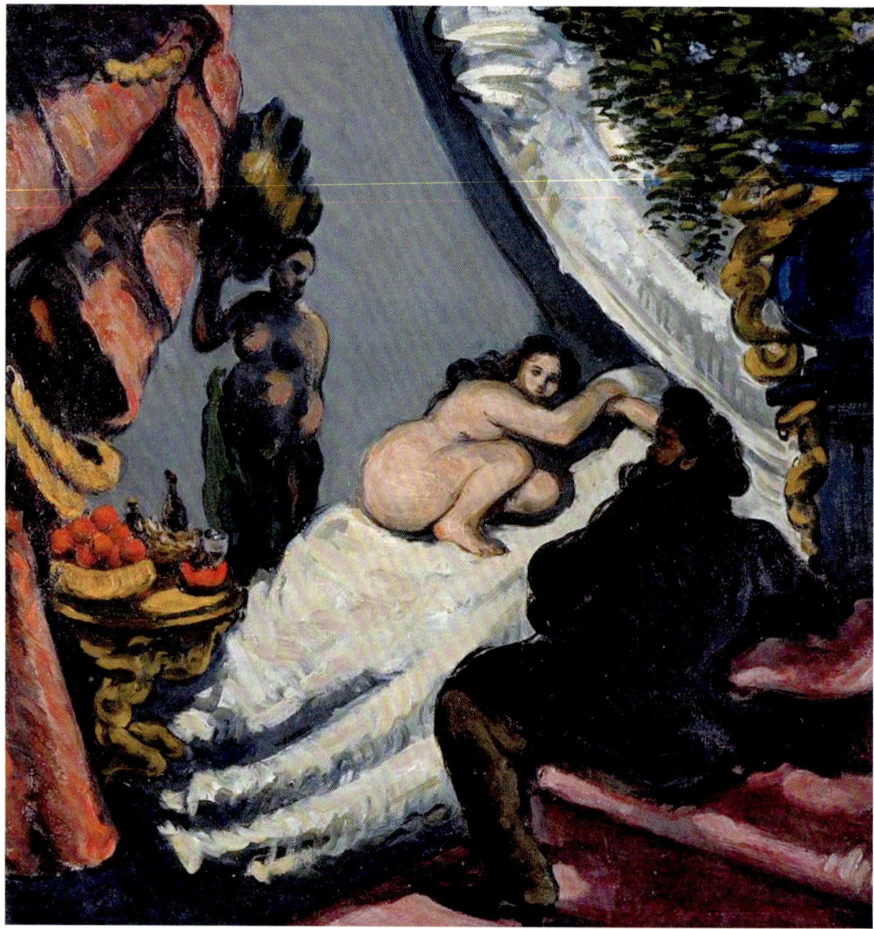

6. *A Modern Olympia*, *c.* 1872–73, 56 × 55 cm (22 × 21⅝ in.). Private Collection.

Theory is the first thing. But the second – the second phrase from Lucien's letter – goes in a different direction. 'Cézanne was sitting on the grass watching him.' It points to the fundamental wordlessness of painting, and how much, in this moment of apprenticeship to an older artist, had to be a matter of just looking, noticing how things were done, mulling over the meaning of procedure. The peasant was exactly wrong, we suspect, that this activity did not involve putting in much effort. Seeing Pissarro – seeing what Pissarro was doing – was a fiercely difficult business.

For a while in the 1870s – once, twice, maybe three times, each over a period of weeks and months – and then again briefly in the early 1880s, Cézanne and Pissarro painted together. Cézanne was younger than Pissarro: in early summer 1873, when the two of them most probably worked side by side for the first time, he was thirty-four and Pissarro forty-two. The age difference disguises a complex story. Cézanne was graceless, immature, belligerent, foolhardy in his early thirties, but when he went to work with the older man he had already built, in the previous five years, a tremendous way of painting: it seems best to call it his 'first style' rather than his early one, because the style's amalgam of Courbet's thick handling, Manet's aggression and Delacroix's cold lasciviousness clearly issued from half a lifetime of brooding on what French painting had been and might become. No one looking at Cézanne's *Portrait of Valabrègue*, for example, done around 1871, or his *A Modern Olympia*, which I think was painted a year or so later, could doubt that such paintings set forth a distinctive vision – preposterous and crude in the case of *Olympia*, but also subtle, compassionate, sardonic, decisive – and one that had found a means of expression to match (FIGS 6 & 7). Certainly Pissarro thought so. He seems to have admired Cézanne deeply, even if with a shake of the head at the young man's chutzpah.

Nonetheless, Cézanne came to Pissarro to unlearn his first style, and, seemingly, to change his mind about Courbet, Manet and Delacroix; or at least about what might be made from them, from their attitudes (their subjects, their stances) and their materials. Provocation in art would give way to patience, to exposure to optical events. The word 'humble', which Cézanne chose years later to characterize Pissarro – 'humble and colossal' he called him, and perhaps even 'justified in his anarchist theories' – sums up a lot of things. The way forward for French painting, Cézanne seems to have decided in 1873, was to be found in the style that Monet had built and to which Pissarro had given his distinctive stamp, in the very years Cézanne had built *his* – his massive first contrary to Monet's lightness and impersonality. ('Monet, around 1869, he struck the great blow': this was Cézanne's verdict in retrospect. 'Monet and Pissarro, the two great masters, the only two.'[4]) The Courbet, Manet and Delacroix in oneself, in other words – and no doubt the three remained heroes, exemplars – would have to be painted out. Sometime in the winter of 1872–73, we shall see, Cézanne borrowed a landscape Pissarro had done two years before, in the first heyday of Impressionism, and sat down to copy it stroke by stroke.

The coming together of Cézanne and Pissarro – their common cause, their peaceful coexistence, their rivalry, their contrariety – is a mystery. For me it is the deepest mystery of the nineteenth century; and I cannot escape the feeling that if we could unravel it we would have in our hands the key to French painting, in much the same way as the relation of Plato to Socrates, for example, still seems the key to the enigma called 'philosophy'. The comparison could be pursued further. Greek philosophy and French painting (meaning the line from Corot to Matisse, from *Sardanapalus* to *Ma Jolie*) may be seen as events of equal weight. They both, taken as a whole – the simple fact of them, their coming into being, their import, their purpose – are mysteries. Both, many have thought, speak to a fundamental change in the conditions of representation in the cultures that gave rise to them: some felt need for a different voicing or picturing of experience, at a turning point in history.

It may not be accidental that at such a turning point the discovery of an adequate new form for such recasting depends, for a moment, on the to-and-fro of contrary personalities: a suspension of personality for a while, an *im*personation, the creation of a double, all the better to magic into being a dreadful indispensable singularity.[5] The singularities in these two cases being 'Plato', whoever he may be in the dialogues he wrote, or 'Cézanne', as he finally emerges from his trying or pretending to be Pissarro.

What both Plato and Cézanne were ultimately in search of, to put it a little differently, was an authority, a voice, a viewpoint beyond the personal,

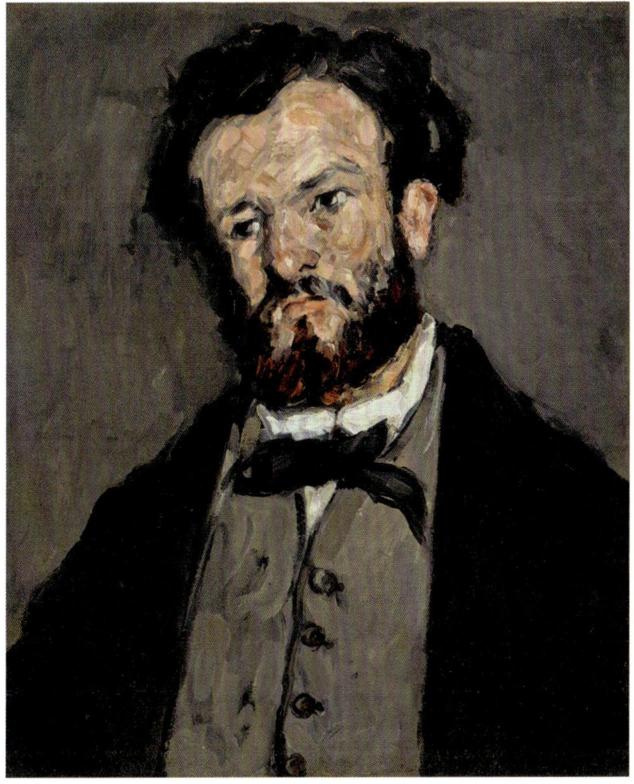

7. *Portrait of Valabrègue*, c. 1871, 60 × 50 cm (23⅝ × 19¾ in.).
The J. Paul Getty Museum, Los Angeles.

a high and irrefutable impersonality. No doubt in the end they found it. But finding it involved, first of all, *not* being impersonal, not being the Forms themselves speaking, but *being someone else* – experiencing a voice or a view that was not one's own.

◆

I need to put the case as strongly as I just have, but I know that doing so threatens to steer us back to a story – the story of the origins of modern art – from which I would like to escape. It may sound as if I think that the main difficulty in the modern art case turns on the identity called 'Cézanne', and how that identity's learning from Pissarro became part of a stronger and stranger account of visual experience – the account that made 'strangeness' (uniqueness) the marker of modernity. It is tempting,

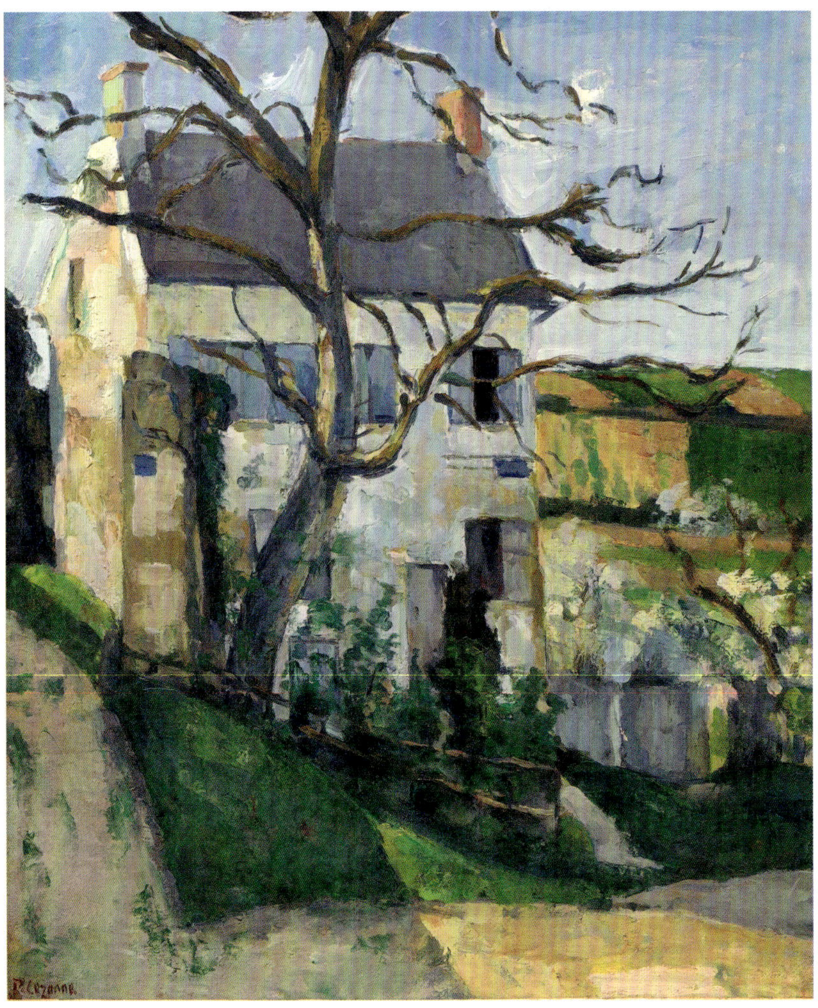

8. *House and Tree, L'Hermitage (La Maison Rondest)*, 1874–75, 65 × 54 cm (25⅝ × 21¼ in.). Private Collection.

for instance, to put side by side an unruffled late-afternoon Pissarro like *Bourgeois House at L'Hermitage*, dated 1873, and a bristling Cézanne from a year or so later, *House and Tree, L'Hermitage*, and declare the balance of risk and ambition in the two self-evident. Or to juxtapose two still lifes from the same decade – Cézanne's elaborate *Dish of Apples*, shown at the Third Impressionist Exhibition in 1877, and Pissarro's *Apples and Pears in a Basket* from 1872 – to similar effect (FIGS 10 & 11).

Comparisons of this sort have been the staple of art writing for a century. And of course the writers had a point. The style Cézanne can be seen to be building from 1873, out of the Pissarro materials, is in the end more turbulent and perplexing than the style he had set himself to master. And yes, in the end it may be more difficult to understand, more wonderful and baffling. But there is difficulty and difficulty – the difficulty of the 'difficult' and the difficulty of the 'humble and colossal'.

We are in uncharted territory. I do not mean to imply by my last aphorism, for example, that Pissarro's apparent simplicity – his evenness of tone, his straightforwardness, his aiming for the moment of mere disclosure – is deceptive. No doubt at some level it is. No doubt if we begin to look at the means of construction in a particular Pissarro case – at the balance of orientations in *Apples and Pears in a Basket*, say, or the line of the basket's ellipse in relation to the loop of its handle, or the tipping of the basket towards the picture plane, or the depth and non-depth of the

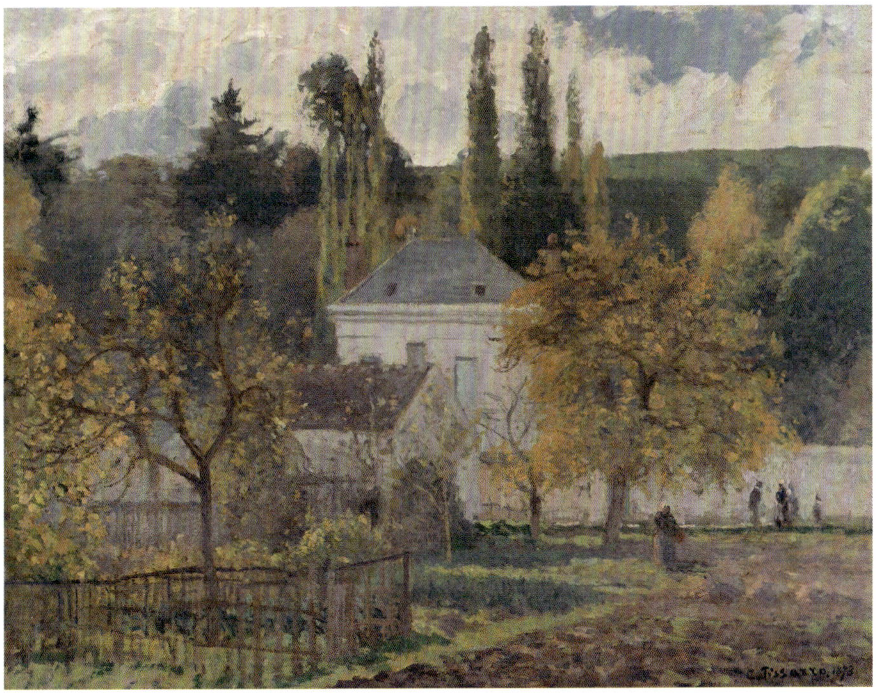

9. Camille Pissarro, *Bourgeois House at L'Hermitage*, 1873, 50.5 × 65.5 cm (20 × 25⅞ in.). Kunstmuseum, St Gallen, Switzerland.

tablecloth (transfixing, that light–dark contrast of the cloth's two knife-edge creases) – we soon come to see that simplicity (disclosure) is exquisitely fine-tuned. Flowers on wallpaper have never been more will o' the wisp. An apple in shadow never a cooler negation. The dialogue of background and foreground in Cézanne's *Dish of Apples*, when we turn back to it, can look even a little florid, a little evasive – decorative anecdote substituting for felt distinctions in space.

But to the extent that any such dismantling of the established opposition tends to make Pissarro more *like* Cézanne, it is fundamentally wrong – it misses the point. The difficulty with Pissarro – the difficulty *of* Pissarro – is his simplicity. 'Strangeness' is the last word that comes up in connection with him. The challenge Pissarro presents to interpretation has to do with the depth of his purposes in painting, and how and why they resulted in such simplicity. But that in turn depends on our seeing why and how

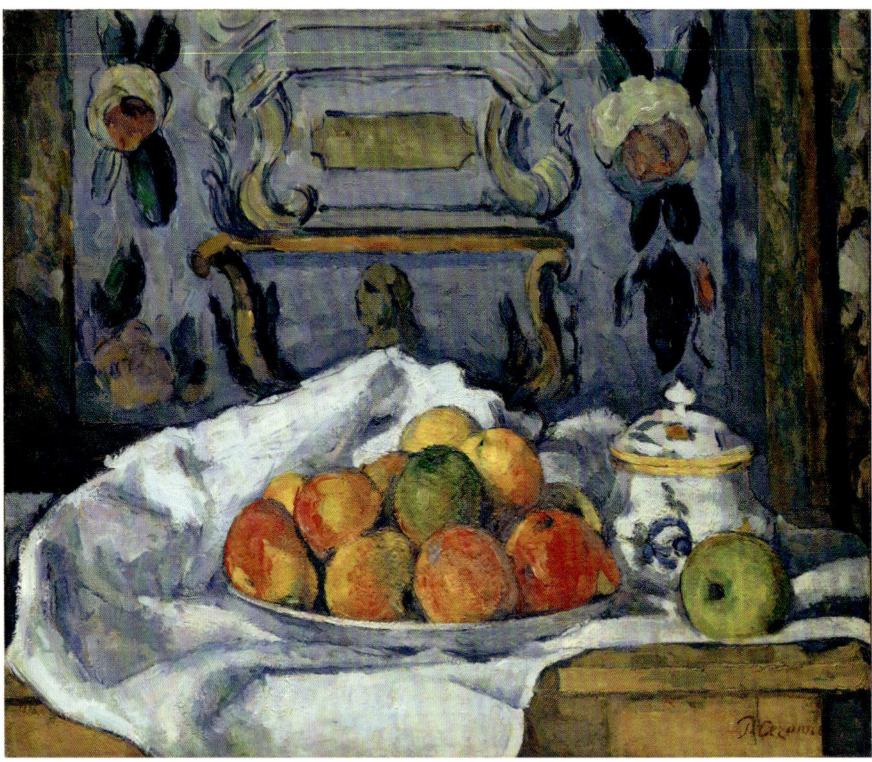

10. *Dish of Apples*, *c.* 1876–77, 46 × 55 cm (17⅞ × 21⅝ in.). Metropolitan Museum of Art, New York.

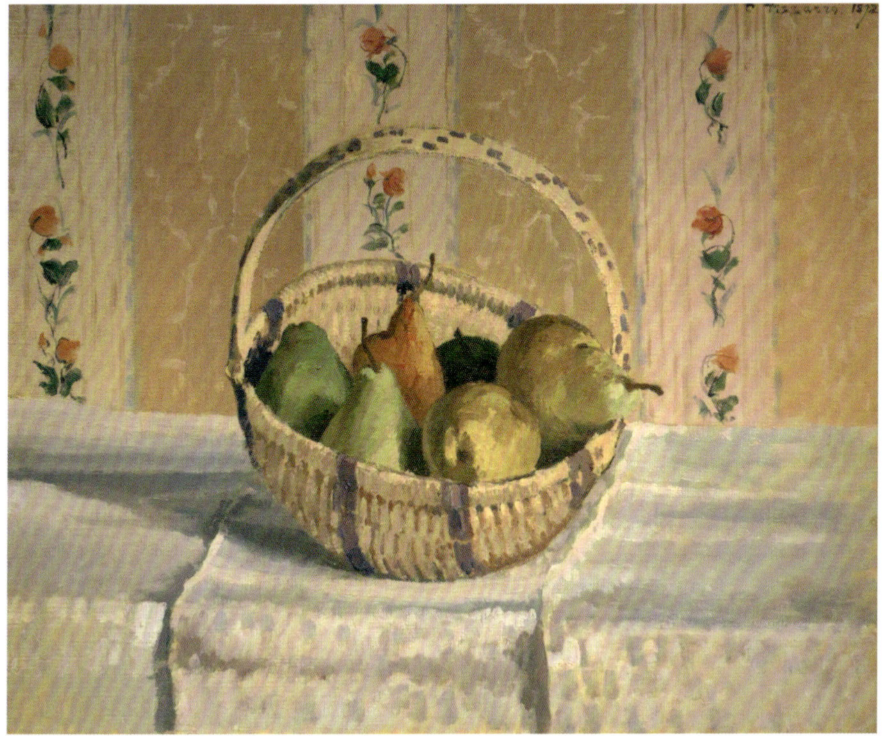

11. Camille Pissarro, *Apples and Pears in a Basket*, 1872, 46 × 55 cm (18 × 21¾ in.). Princeton Art Museum.

Cézanne understood the depth. For Cézanne is Pissarro's best viewer. The paintings he made from Pissarro's – and 'from' in this case, granting the point, must mean 'for and against' – are our best guide to the painter he was trying to learn from. *House and Tree* is the deepest meditation we have on *Bourgeois House*. Or maybe better, look at *Bourgeois House* alongside *The Garden of Maubuisson, Pontoise*, done four years after *House and Tree*, when Cézanne's means and insight were more fully in sync (FIG. 12). (The orchard in *Garden of Maubuisson*'s foreground lay directly behind Pissarro's house. Pissarro was the Cézanne painting's first owner.) What Plato is saying about Socrates in a case like this – how much of Socrates he impersonates in order to say something back to the master, to assume his 'own' voice – seems to me truly a hard question.

◆

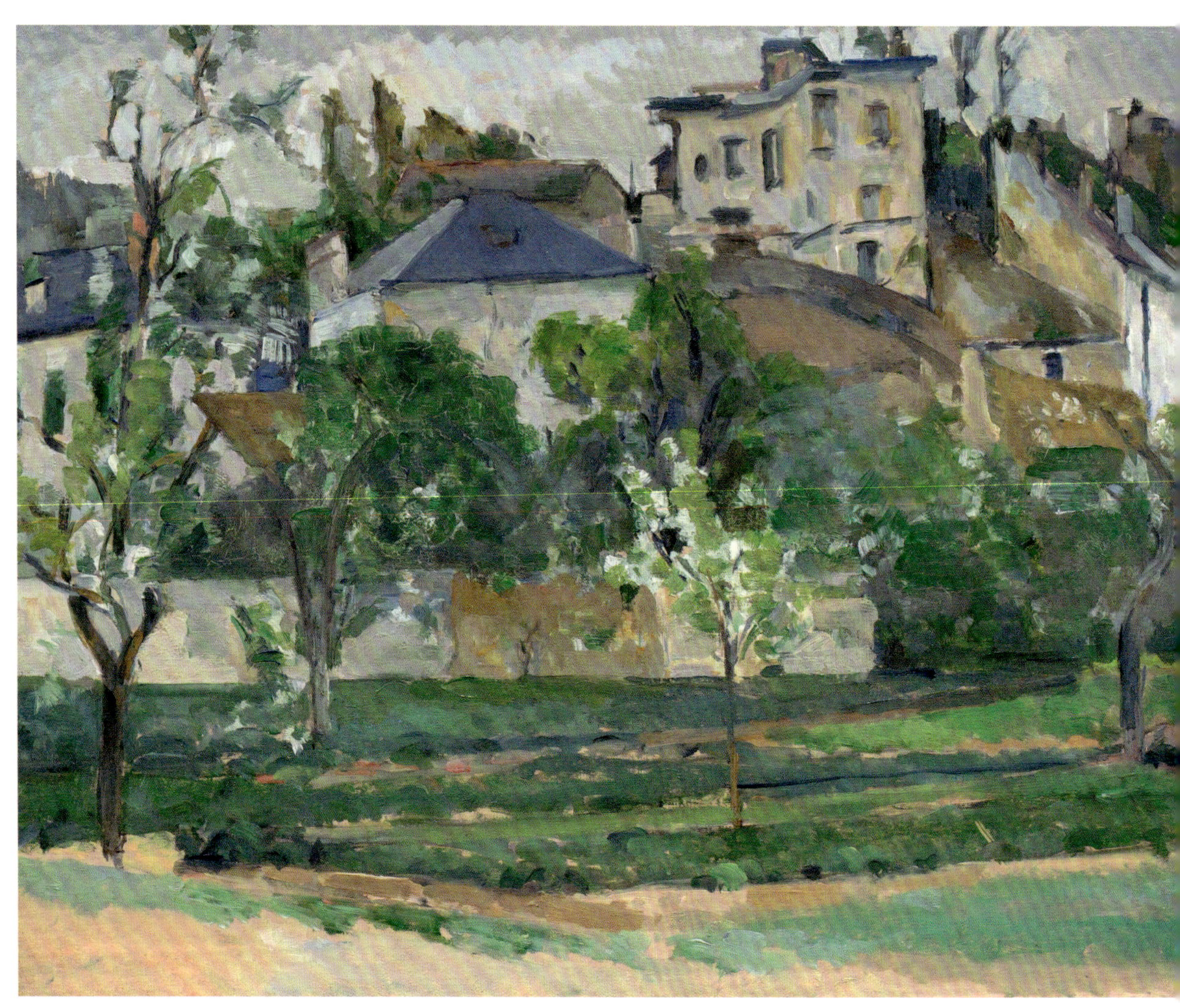

12. *The Garden of Maubuisson, Pontoise*, c. 1878–80, 50 × 60 cm (19¾ × 24 in.). Private Collection.

Pissarro's *Landscape near Pontoise* is dated 1872 (FIG. 13). 'I shall try a field of ripe wheat this summer,' Pissarro wrote in a letter the following year. 'The colourists get it entirely wrong: nature is coloured in winter and cold in summer, there's nothing colder than full summer sun.'[6] The remark is helpful, though clearly in *Landscape near Pontoise* the fields in the mid-distance are not sweating in full summer glory and the sun has gone behind clouds, beautifully rendered. So an outright coldness of colour has given way, as it regularly does in Pissarro's painting from this time, to something hovering between temperatures – and, even more, between intensities, between brightness and dullness. Any reproduction is bound to get this slightly wrong, since the dullness of the scene, and the *intensity* of that dullness, inheres in oil paint's opacity, its smeared matt surface, which the reproduction is bound to tune up a little and render more 'lit from within'. There is no inner light in Pissarro, no trace of the numinous.

I have found that each time I see *Landscape near Pontoise* again at the Ashmolean Museum – it belonged early on to Degas, was still in his hands at his death, and came to Oxford from a private collection in 1940 – there is at first a moment of disappointment. Is the world as we see it really as *unlit* as this one, as subdued, even on a good day? I said 'at first', but in a Pissarro of this kind the disappointment persists as we go on looking: it is part of the painting's disenchantment of its genre. Landscape, and the kinds of attention and distraction it fosters – the unfolding of a natural scene in front of us, the suspension of workaday time as we let the scene come forwards, the fact and feel of its surrounding us, containing us – no doubt became, in the nineteenth century, painting's prime resource. They were what art had left. But they had to disappoint. Resistance to human wishes and appetites – to our 'views' – is written deep into the landscape genre, if we take its ambitions at all seriously. 'Little we see in Nature that is ours,' to quote Wordsworth; but that is not a tragic condition, Pissarro replies, so much as a matter of fact, a maturity. There is a difference between 'scene' and 'scenery', and Pissarro is always out to strip what he sees of the final '-ry'.

Nature does not have high points, is one way of saying it. It is not picturesque. Or rather, looking now specifically at *Landscape near Pontoise*, the incidents and episodes it does possess – the hay cart, the horses, the brittle fence at the turn of the path, the poplars on the horizon – must cede to the overcast, the overall, the non-ominous totality.

So the true intensity of the new painting, Pissarro proposes, will inhere in its showing us what, after all, of beauty – of emphasis, of the suddenness of things seen – is there *in* the dullness... not punctuating it, not coming out of it. This is Pissarro's painting's triumph: the complete steadiness of its hold on a single plain state of the light; the subduing of every separate entity to that state; and the peculiar beauty of that submission. Granted, certain episodes in the scene are on the edge of becoming 'things in themselves'. The pale grey of the tree trunk at left is one such, done in a single smear. The path with its rustle of uncut dry grass, and then the path losing its way by the fence and going on into distance, across fields not yet harvested, as a tentative green smudge. The pale blotted saplings on the other side of the fence; the flattened horizon way off to the right; the small square darker cloud. These are astonishments – the mind and eye can feast on them. But they do not disturb the sense of the whole. They are fine-tunings of a single song.

This is true not only of the kind of small-scale incidents I've just pointed to. It seems to apply to the whole shape of the clump of trees at left and their relation to – their standing apart from – the painting's three great horizontal bands: the grey of the sky, the yellow and brown of the fields, the scuffed green and brown of the foreground. The clump of trees, to adopt the jargon of landscape painting, is a *contrejour*. It functions as a kind of anchor: a darkness against which a more distant light is silhouetted, in a to-and-fro that intensifies both parties, separating near from far. This silhouetting happens in the Pissarro, certainly, but in a way that somehow completely 'fits' within the picture's monotone. The smear of grey on the tree trunk, which looks to have come late, is the sign of that final pressing in place. But the fit derives, more deeply, from the character of the trees' drawing, so delicate and yet so sturdy, and the calling out of their colours to the painting's other greens: the hay cart and its half-dried load, the poplars in the distance, the un-mowed wedge of field floating forwards to the lower right corner.

Pissarro's paintings are unemphatic. It is hard to imagine their maker laying down the law. Nonetheless, his art is surely decided – implacable

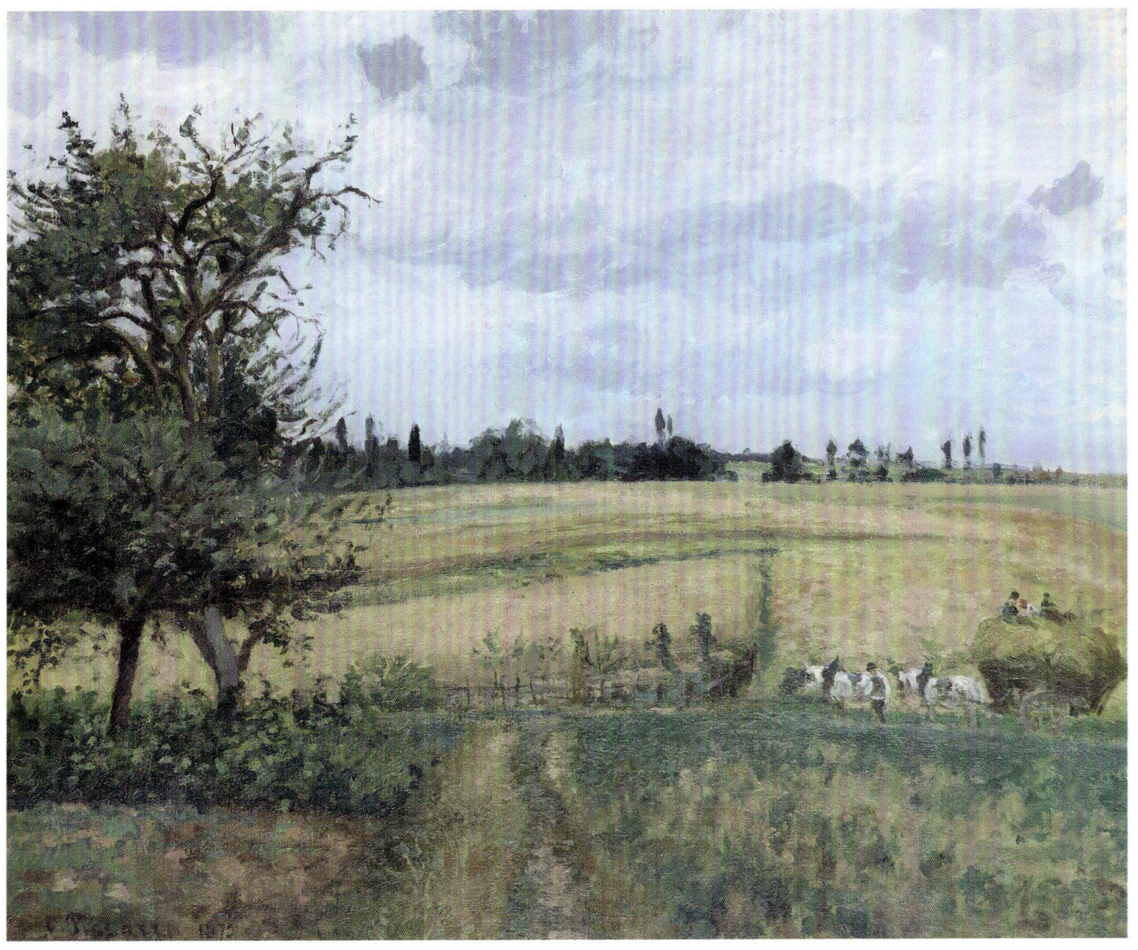

13. Camille Pissarro, *Landscape near Pontoise*, 1872, 46 × 55 cm (18⅛ × 21¾ in.). Ashmolean Museum, Oxford.

– about what painting should and should not be. So the following aphorisms may be in order. (I think of Lucien listening to his elders 'discussing theories endlessly'.) Space is not distance, says Pissarro, not a journey to a horizon: it is here where we are, an immense proximity, a total intuition of place and extent. And Time is not becoming, not endless contingency: it is a Now that goes on being Now as we live it, a unique kind of permanence, one we know we have only for an instant but which is not for that reason experienced as fleeting, or even transitory. Every instant deserves to be monumentalized. It is not a 'moment' fizzing by.

I'll come back to momentariness later. Let me concentrate first on space and colour. Colour may be the key to the mystery: Pissarro and Cézanne certainly agreed on this. We can say as a first approximation that what makes colour so endlessly absorbing for them both is its being somehow 'neither here nor there' in experience; but this does not mean – look back at *Landscape near Pontoise* – that the colours of things are unattached or insubstantial. Being neither here nor there is not the same floating in a void, or even in an atmosphere. Colour is not a false friend, says Pissarro. The yellows of the rutted fields are as solid as a rock. It is our bland established notions of 'here' and 'there' that need revising.

These are, as I've said, the aphorisms of an un-aphoristic art. They are never in Pissarro produced as surprises; they are always qualified, put forward tentatively, happened upon one quiet afternoon. The pace of the painting is that of the creaking cart. So the first assertion about space, to return to it – space not being a 'prospect', space being an immense proximity – has immediately to be robbed of its un-matter-of-factness. Should we not better say – I know, disappointingly – that space as we experience it is not *primarily* a reaching into distance, though near and far are aspects, unfoldings, of it? The qualifications, when they are put into words, may seem just to retreat from insight into banality. But here is the crux: in painting as Pissarro does it, qualification – the holding in balance of strong contrariety and careful admission of the obvious – is strength. In *Landscape near Pontoise*, for example, the balancing between space felt as a kind of charged proximity, pressing gently against the picture plane, and space as a path into distance, a petering out, a soft blur of shapes on a grey horizon (the poplars congealing the vapour of the clouds) – this putting together of such opposite intuitions ends up as definitive as ever a view can be. I like to think of Degas, that aphorist in paint, looking each morning at his Pissarro and smiling at its pretence of understatement. How could the painter have resisted making his path *perform* more – go off somewhere unexpected, more at an angle, inviting us to lose our way?

Paths are the lifeblood of Pissarro's art. And they take us back to the very nature of landscape as a form. Where does the world begin for us as we look at it? What is our proper way into it? Every square inch of the foreground and mid-ground in *Landscape near Pontoise* is 'cultivated', no doubt. But the word expresses the strangeness of the case. Everything is man-made, but out of a materiality that is not ours, not *us*, not anyone's property. The reality of the fields in the mid-distance – their leftover emptiness, the ruts and interruptions, maybe the stirring of a wind – is as impervious to our wishes, our understanding, as the wildest bleakest sea. The little dark square cloud at upper left may function as a kind of thumbprint, but it seals the skyscape only ironically.

Yes, says Pissarro, we have put our crude and subtle imprint onto nature. We have made it a home, a surrounding. But there is a side of it that has no place or time for us, that goes entirely its own way. Hence the painting's impenetrability. It is the business of trying to express the world's ordinariness *and* unfamiliarity that drives Pissarro on. 'Pissarro a été tres près de la nature,' Cézanne put it later.[7] But being near is not the same as taking possession.

◆

I turn to *Cabbage Field, Pontoise*, dated 1873, now hung in the Thyssen-Bornemisza Collection in Madrid (FIGS 14 & 15). I want to focus on one main aspect of it, which in treating *Landscape near Pontoise* has only barely been mentioned: namely, the character of time in a Pissarro of this type – the kind of duration and instantaneity Pissarro's painting aims to stop in its tracks. In practice this question can't be separated from another: the pace of actual painting in Impressionism, and the effect on our perception and understanding of the famously free fast handling that Pissarro learnt from Monet. Both things were recognized from the start as distinctive features of the new art, and no doubt they were partly what Cézanne came to Pontoise to learn. But what the focus on the moment and the new kind of touch truly were, as modes of understanding (the touch as a whole way of seeing, that is), seems to me still mostly a mystery.

Can we agree that the light in *Cabbage Field*, which is immediately breathtaking, is some kind of high-summer gloaming, maybe with moisture in the early evening air? (Of course, the painting is equivocal about clock time. It isn't a Monet sunset. It could be that the peasants are taking advantage of the coolness of morning. But the overall colour balance seems to look forward to dusk.) Light is coming down from a whitened

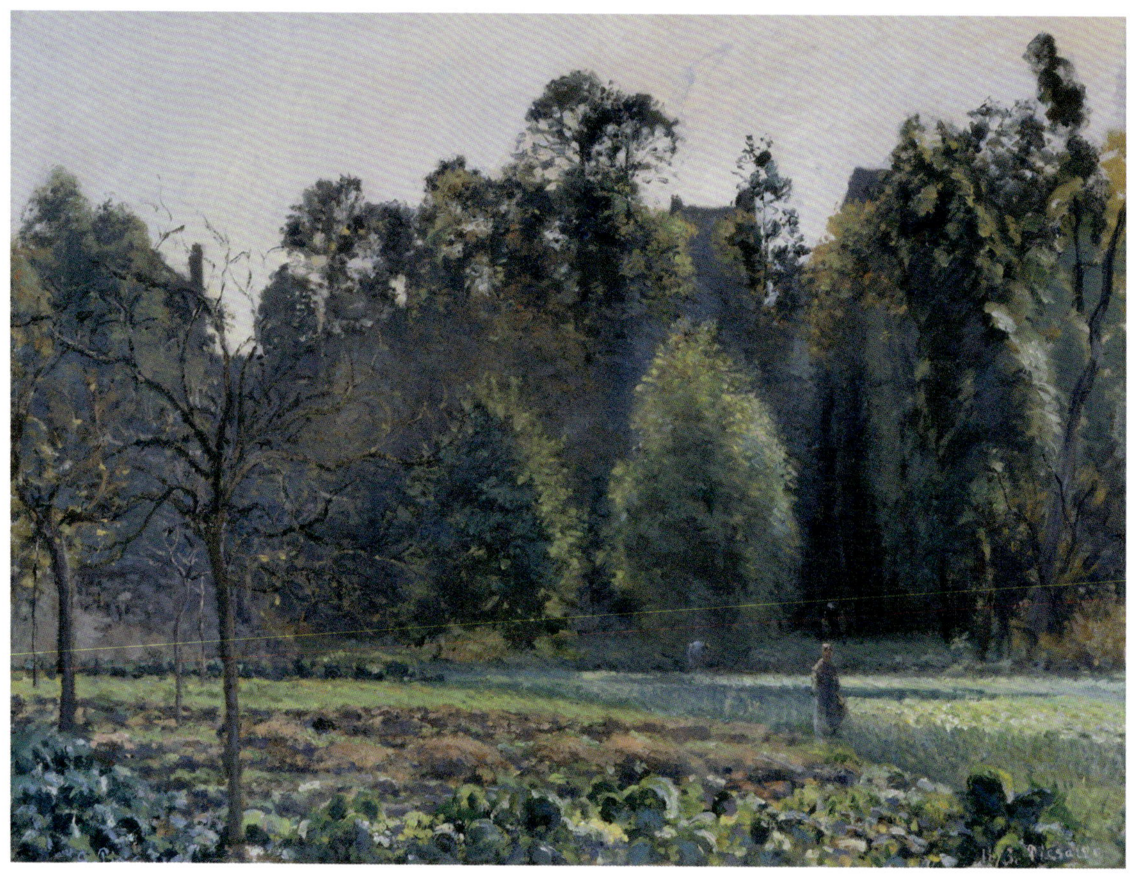

14. Camille Pissarro, *Cabbage Field, Pontoise*, 1873, 60 × 80 cm (23⅝ × 31½ in.).
Carmen Thyssen-Bornemisza Collection, Madrid.

sky, pink just beginning to appear in it – coming from behind the hill, so that the hill is silhouetted, but with light humming in the foreground, flooding everywhere, muting the high silhouettes, picking out feathery edges of foliage on the lower trees and the plump leaves in the cabbage patch. There are three peasants in the fields: a woman with a basket, a man in blue and a further faint figure far back to the right in a shadowed clearing. The emptiness of the air above the field closer to us – the coloured emptiness – is a tour de force of illusion. The man in blue alerts us to the presence of a haze, almost a ground mist, of very light blue-purple all round him, seeping towards the woman with the basket. And there is a ghostly blue halo behind the tree above him. The ruckus of cabbage leaves nearby is rhymed with the russet of new-turned earth. There are many such wonders.

Things emerge from the evening light only gradually: it is the light that is striking, not the ghosts of trees. The edge of visibility is a world of its own. Push towards the unnoticeable in vision, therefore, and if necessary the unpaintable: that seems to be Pissarro's self-instruction. Look at the leafless tree in the picture's left foreground, drawn dark on dark against the hill and a house on its crest. How did Pissarro do it? How did he see it as paintable in the first place? Or look at the light caught in the trees on top of the hill, and the final flourish of touches that establish the sparser tree standing on its own between the houses centre-right, its dark greens scrawled liquid on pink.

These are extraordinary feats of drawing; and they are all the more affecting in the painting because they are juxtaposed with areas of colour in which drawing, or even 'handling', seems to cede to a kind of disembodied appearance of light – light, in the almost dusk, everywhere and nowhere. Look closer, for instance, at the pile-up of trees towards top right. The paint is applied almost like photographic emulsion. Handling in this case – and of course one never quite loses the sense of the surface *as* handmade – is essentially a feat of equalization, of preventing identities from coming too far out of the half-light. The analogy that comes to mind is with a kind of late-nineteenth-century orchestral music, probably French, where detail is absorbed into an even, almost attenuated, texture of sound.

It is very early evening and there's still work to be done. We could say – I think it runs the risk of tying Pissarro's account of time too closely to a single set of class experiences, but he himself would probably have assented to it – that the character of time felt for in *Cabbage Field* is that of agriculture or peasant economy. Time passes in that economy, for sure; light thickens, bodies begin to ache from work, one day is replaced by another; but the passing away of any one moment is not what gives time its identity, its resonance. ('Away' in this context is a strange adverb.) Time is not endless becoming. And painting, notoriously, is the art that cannot show us time. Nothing happens in *Cabbage Field*, nothing changes. But for Pissarro that is the point. The *moment* in peasant society – that is to say, the kind of time lived by the great majority in Pissarro's world – is this unique, unnoticeable, difficult, unrepeatable persistence.

I do not think this experience of time is insignificant or lacking in grandeur – the picture is proof of that. But it is not portentous, not primordial. It does not have History written into it. The words that the language naturally provides tend to be heavy and ordinary: endurance, perseverance, long-standing, never-endingness. Words on stones in country churchyards. The equivalent of such a diction in Pissarro seems to me the refusal of emphasis that is his characteristic note: the evenness and solidity of colour in *Cabbage Field*, for instance, the filling of every inch of the canvas with light of the same character, the same saturation, the same coolness and steadiness. *Plein air* in Pissarro is always a strange reality. 'Open air' seems a poor way of putting it. Full sun similarly. The word Monet often turned to in his letters – 'l'enveloppe', the containing, encroaching presence of an atmosphere all round us as we look – gets close.

Long ago the critic Clement Greenberg had things to say about the dangers run by an art of Pissarro's kind – 'its tendency toward monotony, its frequent lack of incisiveness and motion'. No one had a surer sense than Pissarro of the picture as all one thing, Greenberg conceded, and a deeper and more justified contempt for oil paint trickery. 'But the total final effect of the flat rectangle was often a paralyzing obsession for him. He allowed his perception of the free atmospheric diffusion of light to hush and merge all salient features… and would mistake uniformity for unity.'[8] The criticism came from someone who admired Pissarro enormously, and it points to something important. There is a price to be paid for lack of emphasis in art, for constant hushing and merging; and the gloaming of *Cabbage Field*, we sense, is on the edge of tipping into indistinctness, indecisiveness. Many other paintings by Pissarro do tip. Art is obliged to run the risk of disappointing, for reasons already stated; but the risk is real. Nonetheless, I imagine Cézanne standing in front of *Cabbage Field* and I have no doubt he thought the risk worth running. This is what it took to put painting in touch.

◆

'Putting painting in touch.' This leads to the difficult – metaphysical – phrase that one witness has Cézanne producing later in life: 'Je vois. Par taches.'[9]

'I see in touches – patches – dabs – stains.' Or, I see *by* touches. I see by means of coloured marks: I see by making them. The phrase is a clue to the wider enigma of handling in Impressionism, and what the new speed and immediacy of the hand were supposed to make visible.

'Immediacy' is a treacherous word. It seems to have been the case that for much of the time painters in Pissarro's cohort did jab and jab at the canvas on the easel at speed, as if the look of a thing had to pass from eye to hand as fast as possible, before knowledge interfered. We have early newsreels of Renoir at work, for example, and whatever the untrustworthiness of frame speed in primitive cinema, there is no mistaking the nervousness, the staccato, the worrying of an optical retriever. And yet the *par* in 'Je vois. Par taches' speaks to the depth of the problem. Paint is a means. Painting is putting something wholly unlike seeing in seeing's place, to 'stand for it', maybe, but not to stand *still* for it; to have its *un*stillness lead back to the paradox of the eye – to the fact that the eye's restlessness and voracity are what give the onlooker access to the totality, the whole look of the evening, the hushing and merging that make everything clear, everything present.

Immediacy must therefore be itself a creation. I see nothing in the record that suggests the Impressionists were unaware of this. Pissarro, being the kind of quiet dogmatist he was, liked on occasion to give his viewers a specific stage direction. Down at bottom left in *Cabbage Field*, written across an area of green that is darker than the main plot of cabbages (have some of them been cut, perhaps, and put in a pile to go home?) is the painter's signature, 'C. Pissarro', done in a pale grey-blue. Over to the right, on top of the cabbages still in the ground, is a second bolder signing, '1873. Pissarro', written in a kind of peach pink. (There is showmanship in Pissarro. I think that in this case he is taking up a colour from the atmosphere behind the fruit trees.) The two signatures – there are other paintings from the 1870s with the same signing twice – speak to duration, to an action (a conclusion) occurring more than once. They put the moment in parenthesis.

Immediacy in a picture, then, is different from instantaneity. It has to do with the wholeness, the felt totality, of the moment on display. The ambiguity of the phrase 'all at once' in English is useful: it does not point necessarily to things taking place in a flash. It can be about simultaneity as much as suddenness. What marks off French landscape painting of the last thirty years of the nineteenth century from previous tradition is above all its conviction that the world in a picture – that is, the fact discovered about the world which could make a picture worth looking at – comes to us simultaneously or not at all. This was Impressionism's metaphysics. The world, says Pissarro, no longer offers itself in the form of a prospect or a view. Our entry into the picture's fiction is not by means of a way to be walked down step by step. Ruysdael and Claude are behind us. The world has to *happen to* a picture – the world's totality of light, in particular. Ask this question of a painting, then: Are you convinced in front of it that the pattern of touches filling the rectangle has been made by – or at least, to be more guarded about it, in some sense made for – a particular occurrence of sun and air? Ask this and you have the essential means to judge, as the painter did, whether the painting succeeds.

◆

'Je vois. Par taches.' I have still not quite faced the most obvious, and yet in the end most difficult, characteristic of Impressionism: namely, its pace and freedom of handling. Clearly pace and freedom in a painting like *Cabbage Field* don't have to do with approximation or not being sure of what you see. *Cabbage Field* is not preliminary to anything. It is not a sketch. But specific identities and incidents in it do come out of a looser and more ad hoc flow of touches than most previous painters would have allowed themselves. Each dab of pigment strikes hard for an equivalent of a perception, without apology or prevarication; but at the same time it declares itself – in its very form, its speed and abbreviation – ready to be interrupted or overtaken by another.

The question, again, is what this loosening and restlessness do to our understanding of the scene. I do not think, *pace* Meyer Schapiro, that in the end the new handling is essentially a means of insisting on the individuality of any one painter's apprehension.[10] Personal freedom is a given for Pissarro; but his anarchism does not seem to have been built around the idea of an irreducible ego. It was founded more on a confidence in commonality, in the world as a thing to be shared. The individual and the

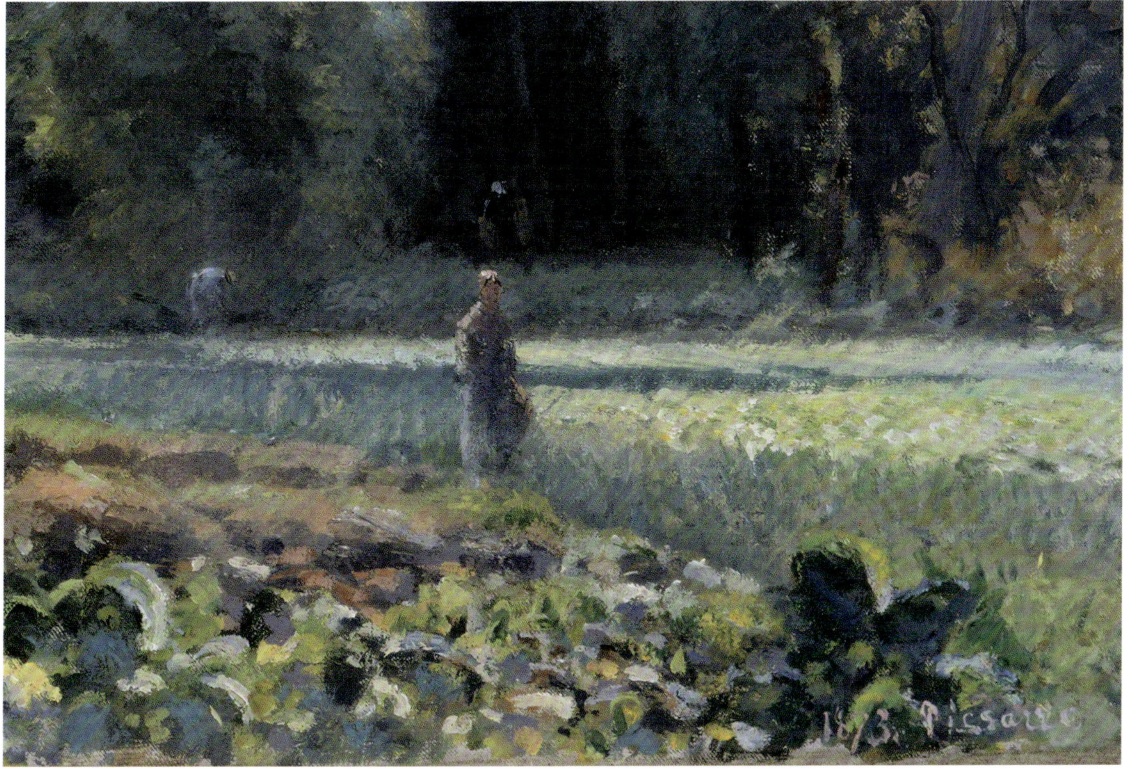

15. Detail from Fig. 14: Camille Pissarro, *Cabbage Field, Pontoise*, 1873. Carmen Thyssen-Bornemisza Collection, Madrid.

commonplace in experience go together: that is *Cabbage Field*'s message. Here is the world as we know it, ordinary through and through; and the world as it never has been before and never will be again.

I take it that Cézanne was right in believing that freedom and openness of handling in Pissarro were bound up with a theory of politics. 'Inquiry modifies our way of seeing', he wrote later, 'to such an extent that the humble and colossal Pissarro finds himself justified in his anarchist theories.'[11] ('L'étude modifie notre vision à un tel point que l'humble et colossal Pissarro se trouve justifié de ses théories anarchistes.') Sustained attention to anything, that is to say – let alone the kind of relentless concentration and elaboration of vision that comes from painting seriously – transforms the parameters of seeing. The human sensorium is plastic: it is changed by use – changed for the better. And what is true of the senses may be true of the instincts, and of our established patterns of knowing and being. We can but hope. Loosen the hold of likeness in painting, in the meantime, and wait for the moment at which the known disappears. Let the tree in the half-dark replace it.

I said that these painters believed that the world had somehow to *happen* to a picture – impinge upon it, touch it. This ultimately is the point of the 'tache'. It puts us back in the moment when the world occurs to the sensorium; and at that point it isn't clear to the painter whether the occurrence is something made by the mind – by the mind's eye – or entirely a material event, an actual unstoppable touch of light on the receptor evolved to receive it. Is the 'tache' transitive or intransitive, in other words? It is certainly a *made* thing, but made by what… by whom?

This brings us back to Schapiro and the question of individualism. Both Cézanne and Pissarro put their trust in the notion that painting like theirs would stay true to some basic irreducible 'petite sensation'. But what the 'petite sensation' was remained a mystery.[12] This was the great thing that painting was meant to find out. Yes, it was 'mine'; but as I made the actual marks that were my seeing, I came to understand that in some sense it did not belong to me at all – or not to the me of mind, of subjectivity. It, the sensation, was the contact – the deep structure of the contact – between sensorium and surrounding. Unique to each individual, doubtless, but full of a materiality, an exposure to the exterior, that put individuality at risk.

◆

Answering the question 'What was Cézanne looking at when he sat watching Pissarro paint?', the reader will gather, leads deep into philosophical territory. The Plato and Socrates comparison may be apt. And the question is shadowed by another. What did Cézanne *make* of what he was looking at? If what he made was *House and Tree, L'Hermitage* (FIG. 8) – a painting as strange and rebarbative as this, and several others just as difficult from around the same time – then had he simply missed Pissarro's point?

I shall tackle the problem two ways. First, and mainly, by attending to the matter of actual imitation: to the moment in 1872 or 1873 when Cézanne borrowed a painting Pissarro had done eighteen months or so earlier, in 1871, and copied it point by point (FIGS 16 & 17). And second, by setting out in bare outlines – schematically, more or less as a set of maxims – what Cézanne could and could *not* do with Pissarro's way of painting, and what else he put in its place. Inevitably some elements of the 'could and could not do' will emerge as we look at the process of copying; but I don't think it misrepresents the situation between the two artists to have the differences finally stated baldly, polemically. Cézanne was the strangest apprentice ever known. Lucien's memory is right. 'They discussed theories endlessly, and one day bought palette knives to paint with.' Painting together was self-denial, but also self-assertion. It was an argument. I wouldn't have wanted to be too close when the palette knives were on the go.

Cézanne's choice of the Pissarro he'd copy speaks immediately to the height of his ambition.[13] The 1871 picture – its title, *Louveciennes*, is the name of the village Pissarro lived in just before moving to Auvers – is slightly different from *Landscape near Pontoise* or *Cabbage Field*, or any other painting from the years 1872–75. It is larger. At three feet high by just under four feet wide, it is even a little larger than most of the palette knife pictures Pissarro had done a few years earlier, in 1867–68 – almost exactly the same size as the wonderful *Côte du Jallais* shown in the Salon of 1868, which seems to have still been in Pissarro's possession in 1871 – and larger than anything done since, or at least that survived the years of war and exile. (The exception is a picture dated 1870, *Landscape at Louveciennes, Autumn*, now hung in the Getty Museum, again of much the same dimensions (FIG. 18). It is splendid in its awkwardness, but still far from sure if Monet's way of handling could be made to work at such a scale.)

Maybe it is also worth pointing out that *Louveciennes* stood alone in Pissarro's work for many years to come. It was not till 1875 and 1876, hundreds of canvases later, that Pissarro painted another four-footer; and I would say that it was not till 1877, in *The Côte des Boeufs at L'Hermitage*, that Pissarro truly felt able to produce a monumental version of his Impressionist landscape manner – that is, to have largeness emerge from it as a genuine aesthetic possibility (FIG. 19). The dimensions he chose for *Côte des Boeufs* are very close to *Louveciennes*, turned ninety degrees. And this is another Pissarro painting that Cézanne seems to have studied (FIG. 20). He did his own version of the view up the slope.

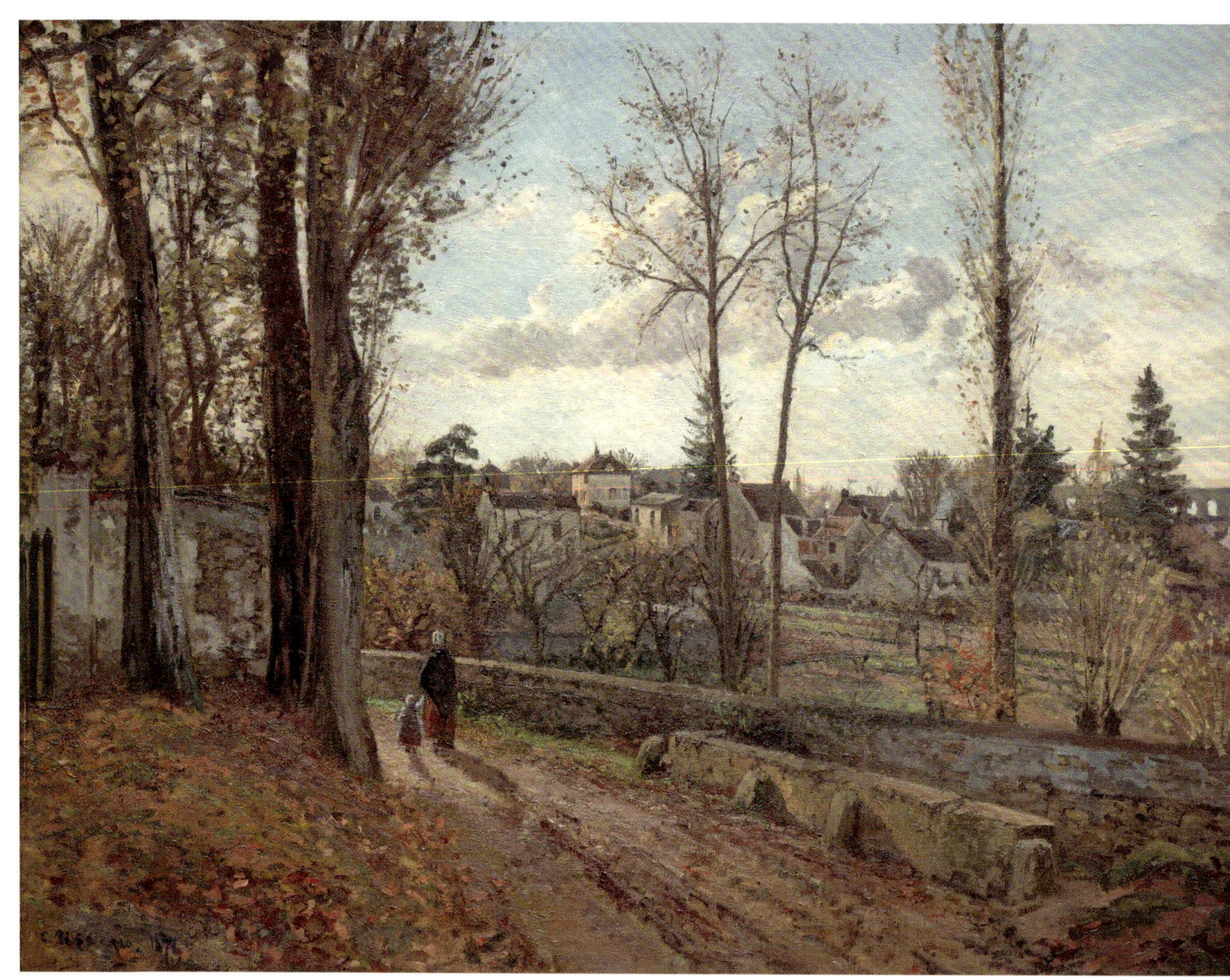

16. Camille Pissarro, *Louveciennes*, 1871, 90 × 117 cm (35½ × 46⅛ in.). Private Collection.

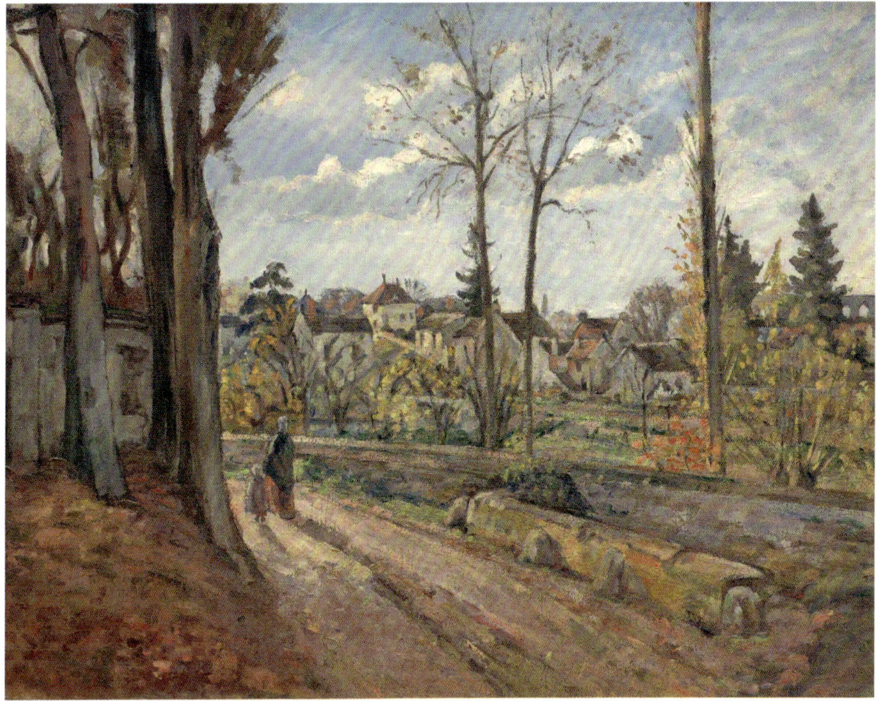

17. *Louveciennes, after Pissarro, c.* 1872–73, 73 × 92 cm (28¾ × 36¼ in.). Private Collection.

Could we say that Cézanne feels drawn above all to the potential or actual monumentality in Pissarro's anti-monumental style? This may be a clue to his future career. It seems he can see what Pissarro is doing most clearly, or see a way to work with what he sees, when Pissarro is painting big. Though again, Cézanne's version of *Côte des Boeufs* miniaturizes the monumentality he's looking at – just as his copy of *Louveciennes* does. Both his renderings of the master's big statements are decisively smaller than the paintings they hark back to. The four-footer of 1871 shrinks to three, and the four-footer of 1877 is done again more or less half-size. This too points forward to the mixture of massiveness and compression that makes a mature Cézanne unmistakable. (I said that Cézanne 'felt drawn' to the big Pissarro of 1877, but I'd be hard put to say when, exactly. We know that at least a year elapsed between original and reproduction in the *Louveciennes* case – most likely two. My hunch is that with *Côte des Boeufs* it was several more years than that.)

The moment of copying, then, is part of a complex – maybe impenetrable – story. But at least with the two *Louveciennes* paintings our questions can be specific. What was it, we want to know, on the evidence of his transcription, that Cézanne saw in Pissarro? What could he duplicate and what couldn't he (or wouldn't he)?

Louveciennes, as I've said, stands a little apart from the line of painting begun a year or so later: it is a little heavier, thicker, with an atmosphere fascinatingly close to *Cabbage Field* – the same late afternoon filling of the air, I think – but in the end more solid, more fixed in place by light. The world of the Getty *Landscape at Louveciennes, Autumn* is close. Nonetheless, the 1871 painting already turns, typically for Pissarro, on an unrepeatable charged emptiness. All of the painting's specific colours – and they are individually often pungent – are put down as inflections of the overall colour that is the work's real subject: the colour of the air at this hour in this light, the colour of our 'surroundings'.

Is this how Cézanne understood Pissarro's achievement? Perhaps – but he certainly could not repeat it. The changes from original to copy hardly need spelling out. Colour in the Cézanne is not primarily an aspect – a felt reality – of an atmosphere: it adheres somewhat perfunctorily to *things*. Look, for example, at the yellows and oranges on the bulwark at the side of the road, or the yellows and browns making the screen of trees to the right of the two figures, over the low wall. Equally, space in Cézanne's copy is not a filled emptiness. It is not something grounded and contained. It does not approach the viewer along the modest dirt road, across a solid proximity, offering us a way into the illusion. 'Way' is a notion foreign to Cézanne's vision. Where in general we might be in space is an enigma in the copy: the houses in the distance in the original enter a kind of non-distance, or anti-distance, when Cézanne redoes them – not that this means they are nearer, more tangible. The highest house is an epitome of this. Cézanne takes Pissarro's gentle indications of a road climbing the hill to the house and zigzagging left towards it, and turns the whole collocation into a crisp folding of edges and collision of overlapping planes. We are already in the world of *House and Tree, L'Hermitage* – no need to exaggerate the resemblance, but I think the way points forward. (*House and Tree* is difficult to date, but a reasonable guess is 1874.)

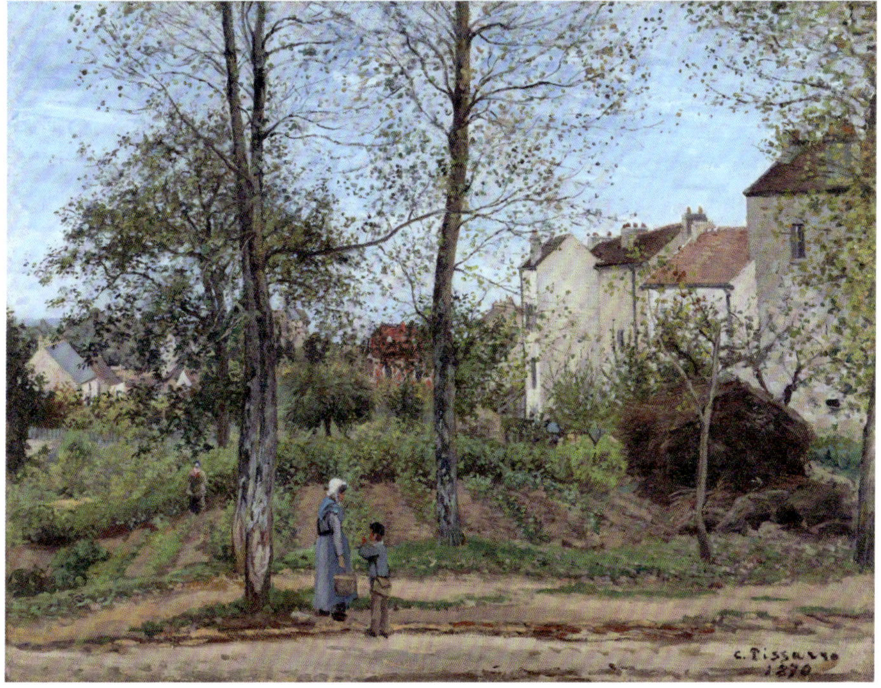

18. Camille Pissarro, *Landscape at Louveciennes, Autumn*, 1870, 89 × 116 cm (35⅛ × 45¾ in.). The J. Paul Getty Museum, Los Angeles.

The difference between the two *Louveciennes* pictures is summed up by what happens to the mother and child. Cézanne's human beings do not really cast shadows: the mother's shadow slides away from her, thick on the surface, and disappears into a rut. (In the Pissarro the rut carries a little rivulet of rainwater. Cézanne has no time for such traces of weather.) Space in Cézanne, we already begin to see, is not a reality inhabited by others besides ourselves, beings with an equal claim on the landscape. His two figures are groundless ghosts: they're about to go round the corner into the abyss. Space in Pissarro is essentially containment, a form of surrounding: it can in the end be metaphorized, as he dares do here, by a holding of hands, a reaching up of a child to its mother. In Cézanne the gesture is the first thing to go. There need be no green gate at far left in the copy, leading out to other people's property – marks of ownership are not part of seeing for Cézanne. No real light comes over the copy's horizon – just a theatrical backlighting, which splashes crudely against

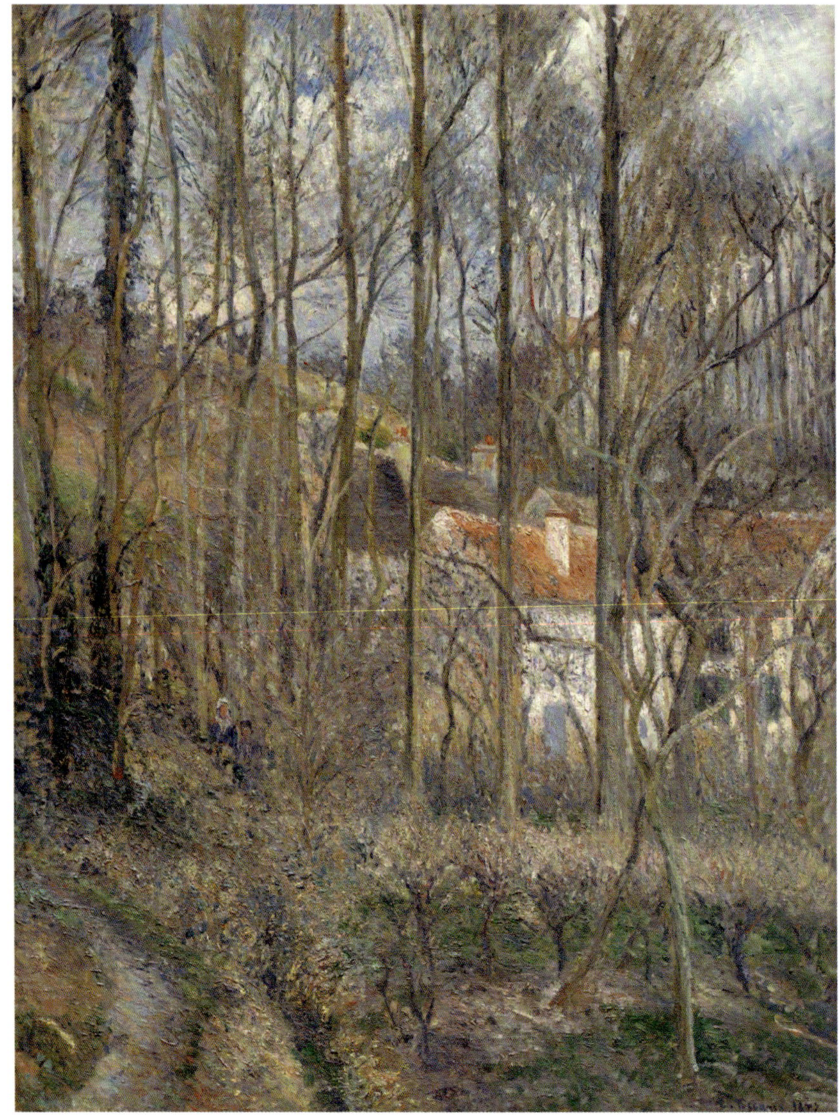

19. Camille Pissarro, *The Côte des Boeufs at L'Hermitage*, 1877, 115 × 88 cm (45⅜ × 34¾ in.). National Gallery, London.

the houses on the hill, breaking them into facets. There is no evening glow under the arches of the aqueduct. And of course no agriculture to speak of, no field system, no raked earth in peasant plots, no lines of new planting. Pissarro liked to call himself 'a painter of cabbages'. Cézanne's seeing in touches does not divulge identities of this kind.

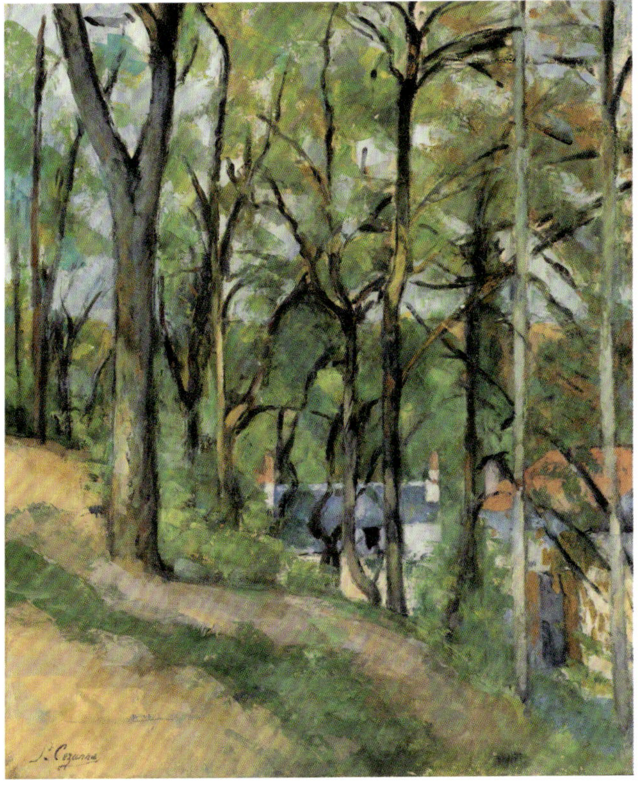

20. *The Côte des Boeufs at L'Hermitage*, c. 1880–82, 66 × 56 cm (26 × 21⅜ in.). Private Collection.

◆

Two things to add. First, it is true that many copies are never intended to be faithful: they are meant from the start as free translations, submitting someone else's vision to one's own. But I don't think this was the case with the Cézanne. It was a true act of submission: it wished to enter into Pissarro's way of seeing and doing things. And, second, that is what makes the divergences so telling. They assert themselves against Cézanne's will. They are the 'deep structure' of his vision taking hold of the picture as he works. So the interest of the copy lies not in the fact that Cézanne couldn't do these many things that Pissarro could, but that the failures turn out to have their own coherence, their own aesthetic dignity: they shadow forth the Cézanne we know. Plato, if you like, is already speaking through Socrates' mask.

I have inevitably dramatized the differences between the two paintings by putting them into words, and maybe I have made the Cézanne more a premonition of things to come than it is. And therefore, I realize, the various absences and negations I see taking over the Cézanne as it tries to reproduce Pissarro begin to turn – I feel it as I set them out – into positives, or at least into a set of negatives that enact a sense of things we might come to regard as closer, in their negativity, to the feel of the world we have, we moderns. The reader will have registered the familiars: groundlessness, airlessness, absence of contact, lack of distance but also of proximity, lack of the sense of a palpable shared world, uncertainty and a strange false vividness. Though perhaps the 'false' is wrong. Look again at *House and Tree, L'Hermitage* and talk instead of a vividness that is irresistible but puts one nowhere – that one clings to and strangely depends on because its nowhere-ness speaks to one's whole sense of life. This is the Cézanne who defined a century.

◆

There is, as I said, a story to be told about how long it took, in the to-and-fro with Pissarro through the 1870s, for this other apprehension to become a vision, a practice. The story is complex and too many of its elements strike me as still undecided – maybe undecidable – for it to be told properly here. But I owe the reader a glimpse of the problems.

Fifteen years ago in New York, the Museum of Modern Art mounted an exhibition entitled 'Pioneering Modern Painting: Cézanne and Pissarro 1865–1885'. If ever there was going to be a moment when the microstructure of modernism at its point of origin would be open to scrutiny, this promised to be it. And the exhibition was a triumph: Joachim Pissarro, its curator, put us all in his debt. But like many great exhibitions, this one proved as much bewildering as revelatory. It did not give us answers to the questions we came primed to ask. That was because, face to face with the pictures themselves, the questions turned out to be the wrong ones.

Go back to Lucien Pissarro's testimony. In common with almost everyone who cares about the subject, I had been saying for a quarter of a century in 2005 that we wouldn't understand what was truly at stake in the dialogue between Cézanne and Pissarro until we could look, for real, at the six or seven pairs of paintings they did of more or less the same motif, maybe painting side by side. Lucien, reminiscing, seems to confirm this assumption. And surely he can't be wrong: the pairs are a necessary point of reference. But when at last, in the MoMA show, we had the canvases hung next to one another, questions began to multiply; and, in my case, they brought on a loss of bearings. 'More or less the same motif', for a start – the phrase is mine, not Lucien's – came to seem a hugely inadequate description.

For example, the two painters' treatments of *The Garden of Maubuisson, Pontoise* (FIGS 12 & 21). Cézanne's and Pissarro's easels, if we take their view of the house on top of the hill at all seriously, could not have been planted more than a few yards apart.[14] And the Pissarro is fairly securely dated, to spring 1877: it seems to be the *Springtime, Plum Trees in Flower* shown two years later in Paris at the Fourth Impressionist Exhibition.

But then security peters out. It is not simply the apparent difference of season in the two paintings, and the different conditions of visibility the season brings with it, that begin to make the idea of 'pair' moot. What counts as much is the suspicion – I remember it growing upon me in 2005 – that Cézanne has chosen to return to Pissarro's spring subject here (and who knows how much later – six months? ten months? maybe even a full eighteen) as a way of engaging directly with the lessons of another Pissarro altogether, his *Landscape at L'Hermitage* now in Lugano (FIG. 22). That painting had been done two years before, in 1875. At MoMA it was hung in a separate room. But the longer I looked, the more *Landscape at L'Hermitage* seemed Cézanne's true point of reference.

The two pictures' questions are analogous – their aesthetic questions, that is. They have to do with orientation of ground plane and instinctive adjustment of ground plane to picture surface; with visibility through a broken screen of trees, which only affirms the presence, the vividness, of the solids the screen half-conceals (this is a basic Pissarro pictorial structure, which the full flowering of the fruit trees in the 1877 picture somewhat muffles); and with how to activate a palpable sky in a picture even when it is squeezed to the minimum by a high horizon full of distinct, brittle, silhouetted shapes. Cézanne was right to take the 1875 Pissarro, as opposed to the 1877 one, as providing answers in all three cases. (The sky

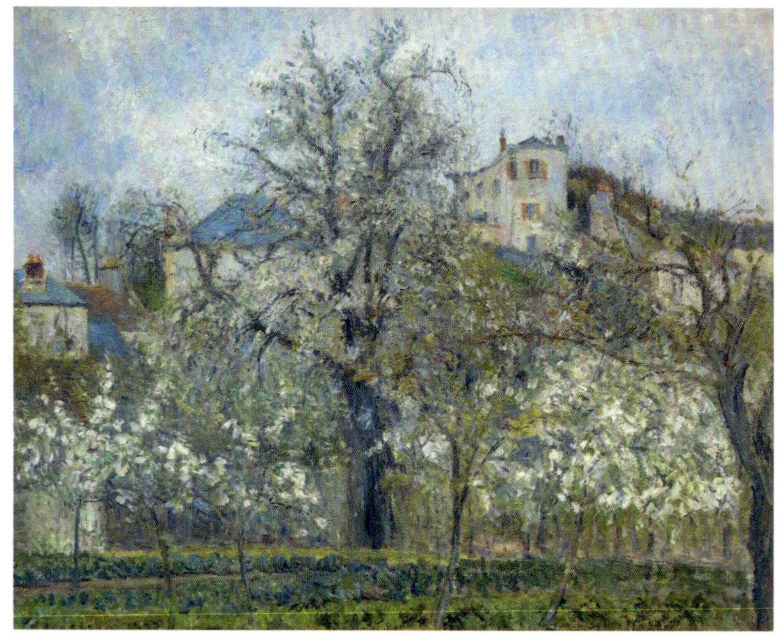

21. Camille Pissarro, *Springtime, Plum Trees in Flower*, 1877, 65.5 × 81 cm (25⅞ × 32 in.). Musée d'Orsay, Paris.

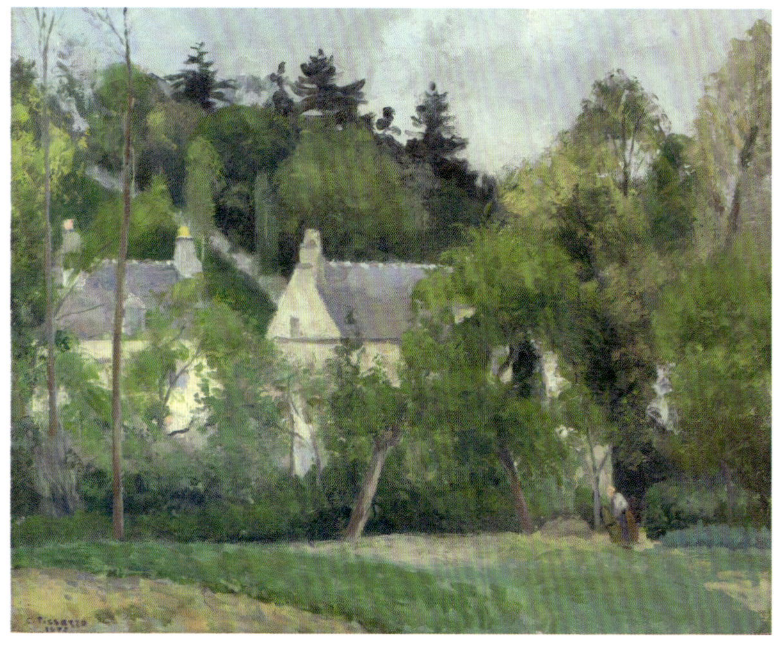

22. Camille Pissarro, *Landscape at L'Hermitage*, 1875, 54 × 65 cm (21⅜ × 25⅝ in.). Museo d'arte della Svizzera italiana, Lugano.

in *Springtime* is beautiful, but its relation to the land below and in front of it is essentially one of fusion not difference, blues and whites infiltrating everything. Compare the sky in *Cabbage Field* (FIG. 14), done the same year as *Landscape at L'Hermitage*.)

But all this still leaves me, as it did at MoMA, with the enigma of the three-way or three-term nature of the transaction – of what exactly Cézanne thought he stood to gain from engaging with the structure and texture of the one Pissarro, already a little more distant in time, by recapitulating the 'more or less the same motif' of another done more recently. I am tempted to say that unconsciously he may have sensed that this was how he could *best* the more recent Pissarro – by redoing the flowering orchard as Pissarro in 1875 would have done it. He would paint it in the same greens and off-whites (though robbing it of the earlier picture's evening gloom). In any case, he'd give it the same Île de France coldness. There may even have been a slight cruelty to the manoeuvre. I have a feeling that Cézanne, like any true admirer of Pissarro, secretly thought that Pissarro's great limitation as an artist was that he did not seem himself to know when he had produced a masterpiece – or, crucially, did not seem willing do the masterpiece again, to produce variations on it. (He was the anti-Monet in this.) Perhaps if he saw Cézanne producing one he would change his mind.

◆

I come back to the chapter's overall question. The reader between the lines so far will have gathered that, however much I think we underestimate Pissarro, I largely accept the banal comparative judgment as to Cézanne's and Pissarro's strengths. I agree with Pissarro, in other words. Cézanne was the greater artist – more tragic and outlandish, more relentless and single-minded – and therefore modernity's patron saint. Some critics were saying this about him as early as 1877, and by 1895 it was common wisdom with the few, confirmed by the laughter and contempt of the many. The verdict is banal, as I say. It is irrefutable.

But the hard question is this. What exactly follows from the comparative value judgment when we come to the dynamics of Cézanne's and Pissarro's dealings with one another? Does it follow that when Cézanne apprenticed himself to the older artist he apprenticed himself to something

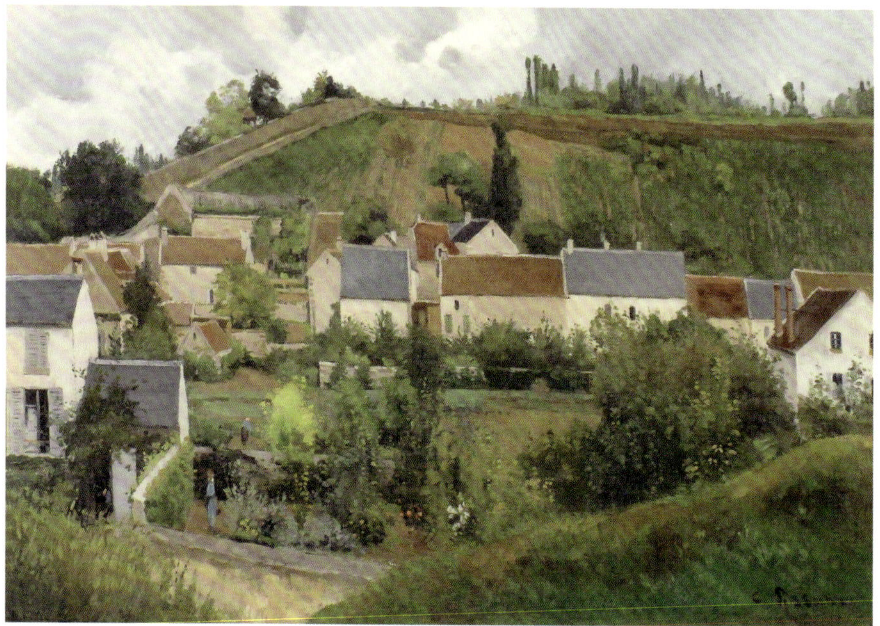

23. Camille Pissarro, *View of L'Hermitage*, 1867, 70 × 100 cm (27⅝ × 39⅜ in.).
Private Collection.

lesser than himself – to an artistic project that was essentially (too) simple, too sunny and unproblematic, for what turned out to be his deeper sense of life and art? This seems to be assumption that shapes most thinking on the subject.

Let us assume, on the contrary, that Cézanne went to work with Pissarro because he believed that in doing so he stood a chance of emulating something profound, something truly difficult – possessed of a kind of transparency comparable to Verlaine's, say, or a late song by Schubert, or even Blake's *Songs of Innocence*. Let us assume, further, that the something in question proved too difficult, in practice, for Cézanne to manage; although out of the 'too difficult' came in the end a set of artistic strategies, and means of apprehension, that were to carry painting to a level of dialectical energy – of anguish and fixity – that Pissarro would never attain. The evidence for the main proposal here – that Cézanne considered that in trying to imitate Pissarro he was trying to imitate something deep and enviable – is the whole corpus of Cézanne and Pissarro's work, the whole baffling interplay.

'Baffling' is the word – and again the chronology of Cézanne's dealings with the master speaks to the problem. One of the MoMA exhibition's most interesting arguments, for example, was the new conceptual shape it proposed for Cézanne's work in the opening years of the 1880s.[15] Certain of the key landscapes Cézanne did at this moment, as his mature manner crystallized – essentially *after* the day-by-day, month-by-month working with Pissarro had ended – made better sense, the show aimed to demonstrate, if they were seen as responses to the great Courbet-based Pissarros done fully fifteen years before. The juxtapositions were powerful. Next to the 1867 *Côte du Jallais* hung a Cézanne of the same hillside, seen from a spot a little further down the slope – undated, but painted no earlier than 1879; and next to the *View of L'Hermitage*, packed as it is with Cézanne-type solids, might be put the massive *Valley of the Oise*, done around 1881.

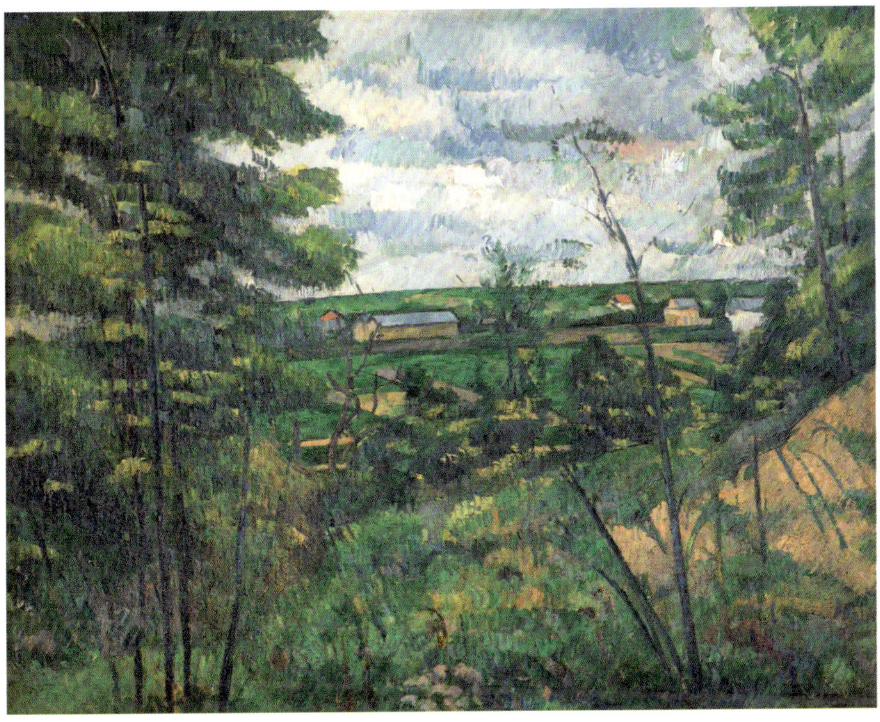

24. *Valley of the Oise (Plain of Saint-Ouen-L'Aumône)*, c. 1880–82, 72 × 91 cm (28⅜ × 35⅞ in.). Private Collection.

The show's basic thesis holds. The landscapes Cézanne painted in the early 1880s are a form of homage to the master, but also a final disentanglement from a still powerful set of examples. And from that fact we derive a corollary. A painter capable of seeing how formidable the Pissarro landscapes of 1867–68 really were, and of being haunted by them so many years later, must have seen Pissarro's initial move away from them towards the painting of 1870–71 as *prima facie* a deeply meditated change of heart – a difficult move, a productive negation. Unless he thought the move a mistake. But the evidence is all to the contrary.

Years later, talking about Pissarro to the young painter Louis Le Bail, Cézanne says specifically: 'If Pissarro had continued to paint the way he did in 1870, he would have been the strongest of us all.'[16] ('S'il avait continué à peindre comme il le faisait en 1870, il aurait été le plus fort de nous.') This is a precious fragment of talk, and it needs unpacking. First, I trust Le Bail's memory of the date. I think Cézanne was quite deliberately pointing to 1870 as opposed to 1874 or 1877, and meaning to distinguish the Pissarro of just before Impressionism from the one he worked with a few years later. And I would go one step further, though doing so is risky: I think that when Cézanne talks of 'the way Pissarro did in 1870' he is using shorthand – long after the event, remember – for 'how he did in 1867–70'. We happen to have lost, to the accident of war, most of the paintings Pissarro did specifically in 1870, and apparently there were many of them (it is among the great art losses of the century); but the one or two that survive make it clear that 1870 was still continuous, aesthetically, with 1867. There is a move towards brightness and lightness, partly provoked by Monet's example, but the massiveness – the solidity – of 1867 is still dominant. Courbet and Monet are held in balance. *Landscape at Louveciennes, Autumn* (FIG. 18), the larger of the two full-scale survivors from 1870, is, to repeat, a somewhat lesser thing than the greatest of Pissarro's 1867 productions – than the *View of L'Hermitage*, for example. But its ambition is vast. It wants the overcast bank in the foreground to be flooded with light. It wants the weight of the world and the levity of leaves in the sun.

There are paintings from around 1870 that manage the conjuring trick. Mostly they come from the following year – the work as a whole is shifting, but there are moments of wonderful retrospection. The Courtauld Gallery's *Lordship Lane Station*, done during Pissarro's exile in London – a triumph of format and understated asymmetry, as well as of English greyness – is one of them. So is the small canvas Pissarro did soon after his return to the Île de France, whose usual title is *Slopes of Le Vésinet*. We are looking back towards Paris down the Louveciennes slopes, the landscape modulating from orchard to arable – long narrow fields laid out on the flood plain. A grand chateau has survived the Prussians' bombardment. The picture is Pissarro's greeting to a terrain he thought he had lost; and, seemingly inevitably, he chooses a viewpoint and reverts to a palette that conjure up the solidities of four years before.

This is the moment in Pissarro's art to which Cézanne returns in the 1880s: he still feels its force field over a decade later. And the fact that he does so chimes in with his decision, in 1872, to apprentice himself to the master. For only a painter capable of understanding how great and potentially productive Pissarro's work had been in the late 1860s would have been able to understand Pissarro's extraordinary refusal of it from 1870 onwards – his move from massiveness to lightness, from sobriety

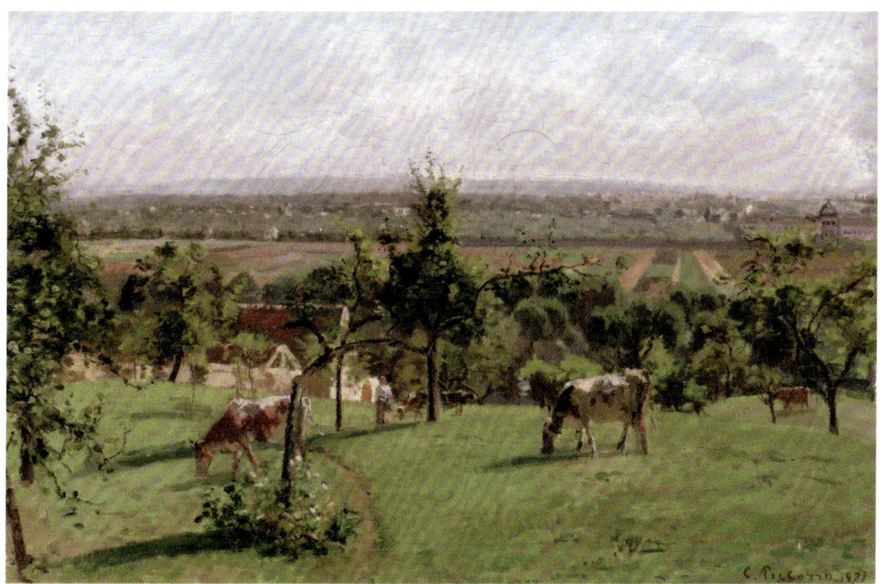

25. Camille Pissarro, *Slopes of Le Vésinet*, 1871, 43.5 × 65.5 cm (17¼ × 25⅞ in.). Musée d'Orsay, Paris.

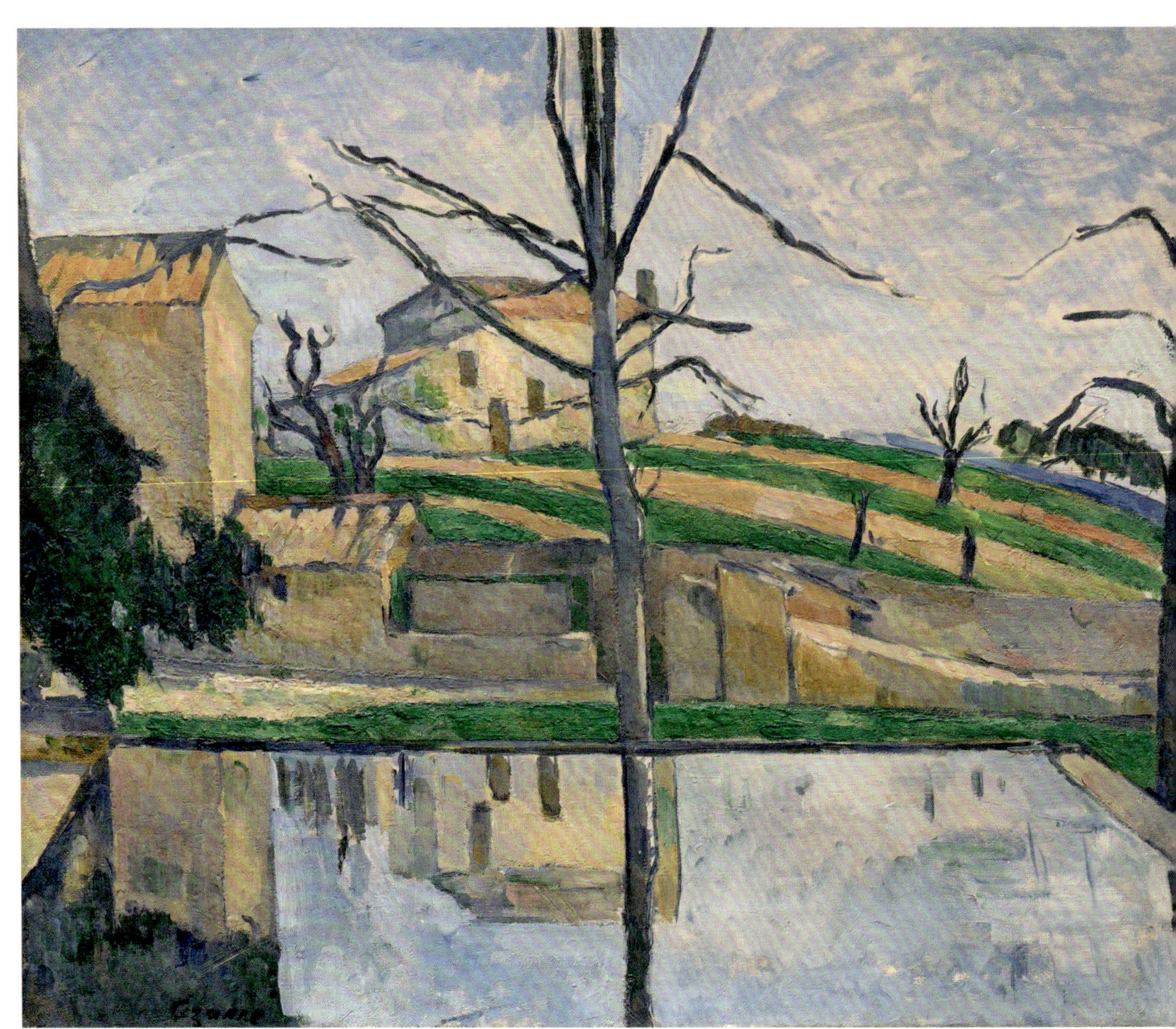

26. *Pool at Jas de Bouffan*, c. 1876–78, 47 × 56 cm (18½ × 22⅛ in.). Private Collection.

to scintillation – as the re-founding of painting it turned out to be. Only such a painter would be capable of asking: 'What is this lightness *for*?' 'What does it give painting that the previous strong synthesis did not?' 'Why would the painter of uncluttered, unemphasized, piece-by-piece weightiness – the perfect reconciler of Courbet and Corot – become the painter of coloured atmosphere?'

◆

This chapter's initial pairing was of Cézanne's *House and Tree, L'Hermitage* with Pissarro's *Bourgeois House at L'Hermitage* (FIGS 8 & 9). And the sheer strangeness of *House and Tree* does speak to something fundamental: you look at the picture's precipitous road and front lawn to the left, or the desperate staccato of its branches against the house front, window, hilltop, red chimney, and know you're in the presence already – impossibly – of the twentieth century. Picasso is looking at the picture over your shoulder. But *House and Tree* is an extreme point in Cézanne's progress (maybe Cézanne himself recoiled from it). Its weird electricity is part of the 1870s pattern – even the canvas's 'non-landscape' format speaks to the contrast between Cézanne's apprehension and Pissarro's – but far from typical. There was alongside it all through the apprentice years a humility, a hesitancy, a kind of inimitable *not-knowing* – which also led to the Cézanne Picasso took as his totem.

I turn to a quieter painting, therefore, though one perhaps just as uncanny; and finish by laying out – too briefly – the elements of the vision Cézanne happened upon in Pissarro's company. The painting in question is *Pool at Jas de Bouffan*. Again we struggle to fit it into a comprehensible sequence. John House thought it was done in 1876; others have put it a year or two later.[17] (You will notice that both *Jas de Bouffan* and *House and Tree* are signed. This, for Cézanne, is rare: it seems to have meant he considered the paintings finished enough for public exhibition.)

Surely the painter of *Jas de Bouffan* is trying to establish, over the pool in the foreground and in front of the wafer-thin tree, a specific kind of light – light in air. In this he remains Pissarro's disciple. So we understand the critic Roger Fry exclaiming, when first he saw the painting in 1906, that:

> the sky and the reflections in the pool are rendered as never before in landscape art, with an absolute illusion of the planes of illumination. The sky recedes miraculously behind the hillside, answered by the inverted concavity of lighted air in the pool. And this is effected without any chiaroscuro – merely by a perfect instinct for the expressive quality of tone values.[18]

Fry is not wrong (his hero-worship is touching) but somehow, if you look at the painting again, he seems to be ignoring the obvious. 'Absolute illusion'? Sky 'receding miraculously'? Lighted air in the pool 'answering' the sky above? Well, yes, possibly; but possibly not. Isn't what strikes home about the picture, straightaway but indelibly, precisely the fact that it seems to offer illusion one moment, and then, a moment later, illusion flattening and doubling back on itself? Miraculous recession, for sure, but, just as miraculous – naive *and* miraculous – clumsy adherence to two dimensions. Reality and reflection answering one another in many respects, confirming each other's geometry; but then the world in the pool floating free of the things above it, walls and windows taking on a second life, the sky spilling out from 'inverted concavity' and flapping in front of us like half-finished canvas. Just look at what happens to the farmhouse roof!

As so often with Cézanne the balance of oddity and accuracy in *Jas de Bouffan* is hard to hold onto in words. Fry's verdict on the picture never goes away. Cézanne has pinned down a particular kind of light here – sometimes I feel in the painting even a specific time of day, an early evening transparency answering back to *Cabbage Field*'s thickening and diffusion. Atmosphere remains one of Cézanne's great subjects. But the tree in *Jas de Bouffan* – the tree as it intersects with the water – shows the artist's attention going in a different direction. Space peels away from the totality of time, light and atmospherics, and starts to become a thing in itself. The building blocks of the wall in the mid-ground – is it a wall or a strange hacked-out escarpment? – are this new space's reality congealed. I say 'the space's reality', but surely in *Jas de Bouffan* the whole felt world, the spatial surrounding, ends up as *un*real – as uncanny – as it is real and matter-of-fact. Its solidity is ironized as soon as insisted on: the building

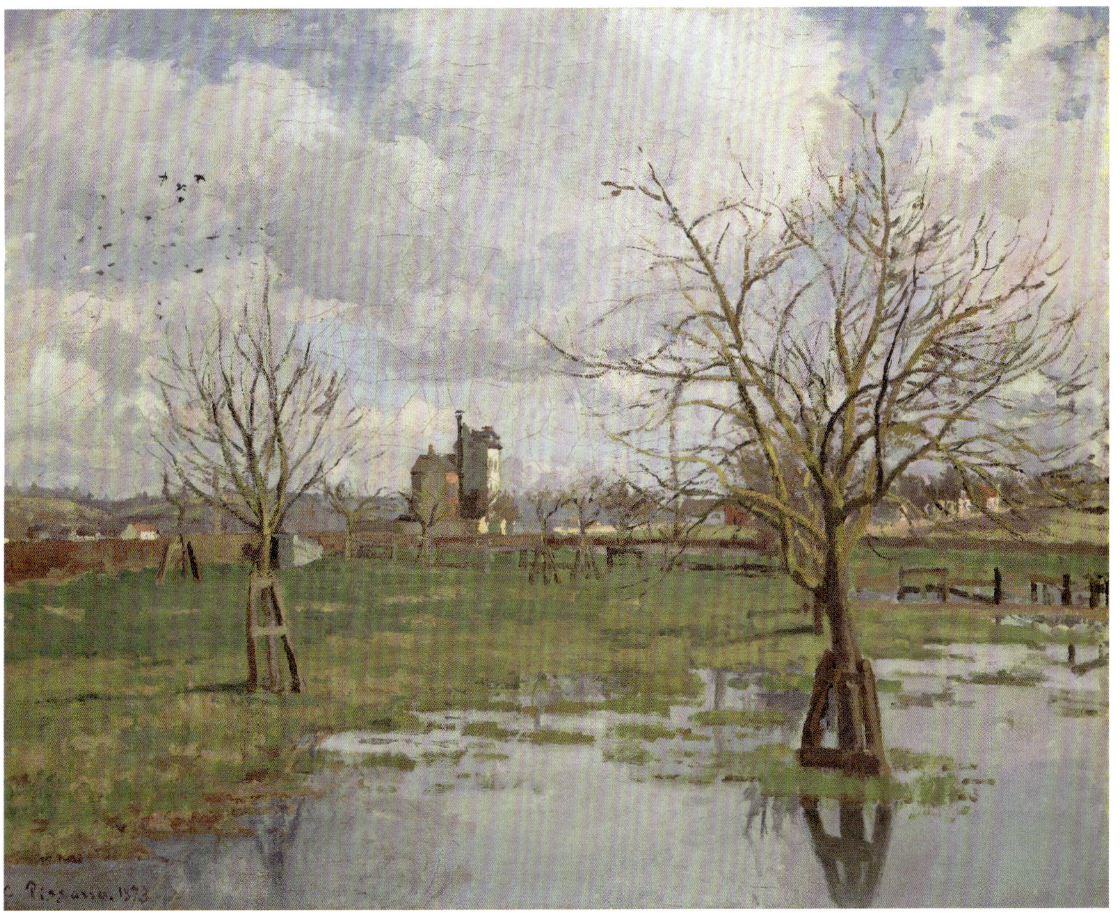

27. Camille Pissarro, *Flooded Fields at Saint-Ouen-L'Aumône*, 1873, 65 × 81 cm (25⅝ × 32 in.). Wadsworth Atheneum, Hartford, CT.

block wall, the reader will notice, vanishes in the pool's mirror. Space is becoming something palpable, yes, a separate entity; but therefore, it seems, a riddle. Colour is not so much the carrier of infinite gradation as the form *of* space. And therefore sensation itself – the moment of apprehension – is no longer felt, in the picture, as an opening onto a presence, a set of things ineluctably out there. There may indeed be a 'world' in *Jas de Bouffan*... but where has it come from? Where is our apprehension of it located? Even – though this question takes us beyond the terms Cézanne himself would have understood, or maybe tolerated – whose apprehension is it?

Not for nothing did Cézanne's later admirers talk about his art's impersonality. It is clear what they meant. But impersonality, in the face of a painting like this one, seems ultimately the wrong term: it sounds too assured, too aristocratic. Non-personality might capture things better. This seems to be time – the moment – as a non-person might intercept it. And space, in the pool – I look in particular at the pool's right lip and the wedge of reflection of a further tree going down to the corner – where a non-person could feel at home.

Modernity is loss of world. Cézanne is the painter who makes that cliché draw blood. And a very great deal of his painting's intensity derived, I think, from the fact of his coming across this new sense of things in the company of Pissarro. Put *Jas de Bouffan*, finally, next to Pissarro's *Flooded Fields at Saint-Ouen-L'Aumône* (FIG. 27). The latter is dated 1873. (Saint-Ouen was a few miles downstream from Auvers, a village just beginning to be a suburb.) Look at the stretch of land in *Saint-Ouen* leading off between the trees to the village... at the awkward pomposity of the house and chimney in the centre (pompous but somehow temporary)... the factory smokestack just visible through branches to the left... the birds battling the wind, the clouds still threatening rain... the reflection in the water of the fruit tree's supports. Humble and colossal. Every observation solid as a rock. A social world. The earth emerging after the flood. What must it have been like to have discovered, under such a painting's spell, that Pissarro's feeling for time and place – his anarchist confidence in history beginning again – could not be one's own?

2. Cézanne's Material

No one must touch me…

Cézanne to Bernard, 1904[1]

A few years ago, reviewing a show in London of Cézanne's *Card Players*, I began by saying: 'Cézanne, whose work was the touchstone for critical thinking and writing on art for more than a century, cannot be written about any more.' And went on:

> After a few minutes in the exhibition at the Courtauld, surrounded by *Card Players* and *Smokers*, one understands why. The mixture of seriousness and sensuousness in the paintings – I am tempted to say, in the best of them, of lugubriousness and euphoria – is remote from the temper of our times. And the quality of grim, eager pursuit of perfection within a deliberately narrow range – 'the only truly difficult thing is to prove what one believes. So I am continuing my studies' – is likewise deeply foreign. It has a nineteenth century flavour to it.[2]

The temper and pace of Cézanne's art are unthinkable, in other words, apart from the grave dogged optimism of a long-vanished moment. But that optimism was always perceived in his case to have taken a strange, maybe self-defeating, form. 'He dares', wrote a critic in 1895, at the time of Cézanne's first one-man show (the artist was in his mid-fifties and had been painting for three decades) 'to be harsh and as it were savage, letting himself be dragged to the limit, careless of everything, carried forward by the impulse that alone drives innovators, the wish to create a few new signs.'[3] Newness and savagery went together. Maybe perfectionism and loss of bearings.

Some of the things said above apply, I think, to the Getty Museum's *Still Life with Apples*, which is this chapter's main subject. 'Lugubrious' it is not. 'Savage' seems overpitched. But constrained or uncanny or in a state of high tension – keeping some kind of peculiar energy just under control – words like these do seem justified, or at least understandable. I look at the sugar bowl perched on its carpet, or the apples rolling off their plate, or the wall carved out of blocks of ice, and I know I am somewhere beautiful but dangerous. The most probable date for *Still Life* is the early 1890s, perhaps 1893 or 1894. We might recall that a few years earlier Camille Pissarro, writing to his son in December 1890, had reported the painter Armand Guillaumin as saying 'that Cézanne was in a madhouse… everyone then!… it's dreadful!'[4] (The 'tous donc!' is a reference to Van Gogh, whose suicide had taken place the previous July, and the mental collapse of Vincent's brother Theo.) The story turned out not to be true, but Pissarro and Guillaumin – both of whom had painted alongside Cézanne, admired him deeply, and regularly shaken their heads at his vulnerability and intransigence – found it plausible.

I have been mildly surprised since the review of the *Card Players* to find that its opening sentence, the idea that Cézanne cannot be written about any more, has gone on to be my most-cited remark. And among my most unpopular. Obviously I did not mean by the aphorism that writing about Cézanne would now, or even should now, literally come to a halt. There will doubtless be writing on Cézanne in the future. But the question for such writing (this is what I wanted to suggest) was how it now stood in relation to a previous century in which the very nature of modern art, and the nature of writing *about* art, ancient and modern, had seemed to turn on the Cézanne problem.

'Quel état faites-vous de Cézanne?': that had been one of five questions posed by Charles Morice in 1905 in his *Enquête sur les Tendances Actuelles des Arts Plastiques*.[5] It was an account – a reckoning – that for a hundred years went on being refashioned. And I think we could say that even the form of Morice's half-ironic interrogative was meant to mirror Cézanne's: that one of the things Cézanne stood for from the early 1890s till, say, 1977 (the date of a great valedictory Cézanne show at MoMA, which sticks in my mind as the end of an epoch) was precisely

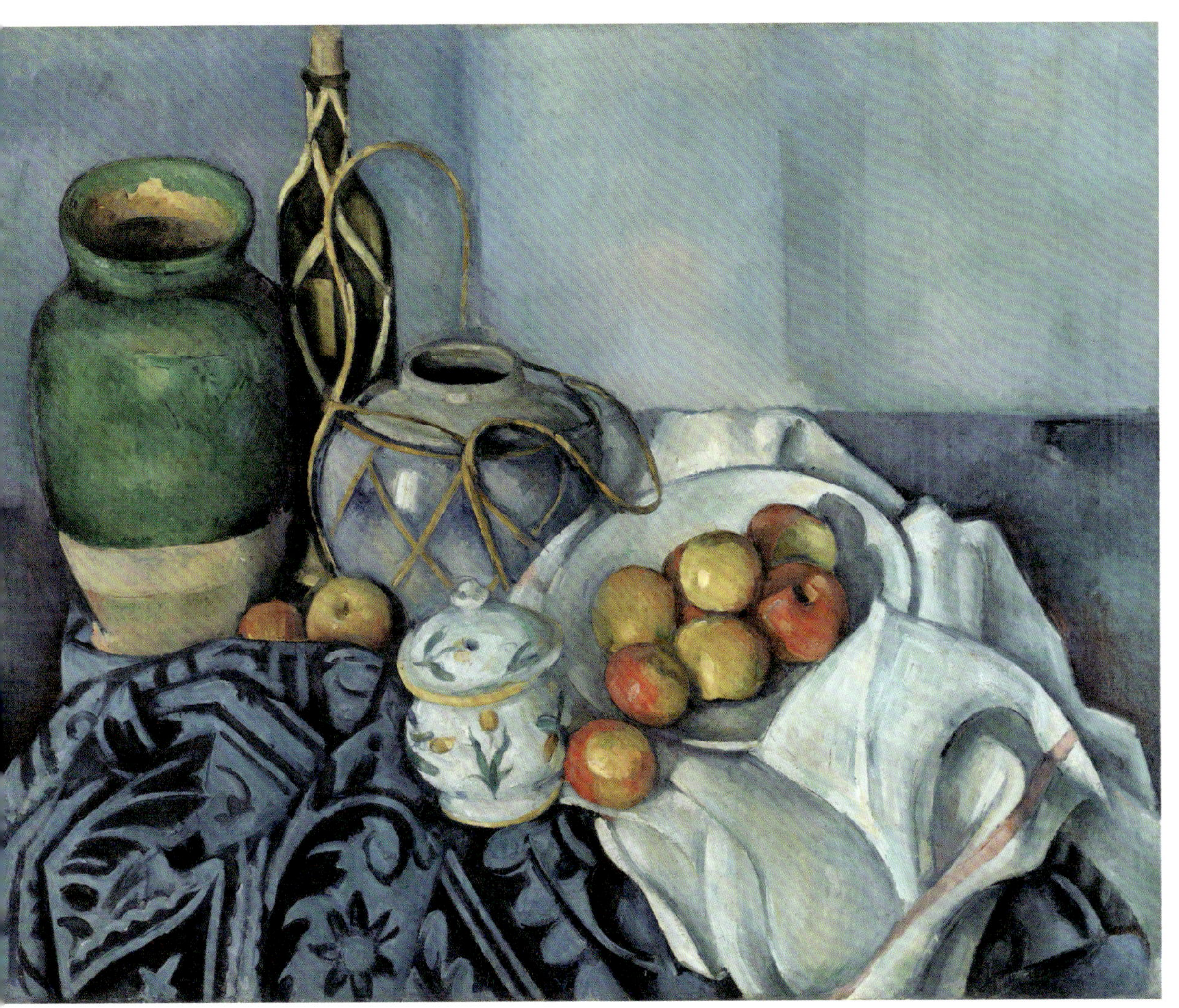

28. *Still Life with Apples*, c. 1893–95, 65.5 × 81.5 cm (25¾ × 32⅛ in.). The J. Paul Getty Museum, Los Angeles.

the idea of art, and therefore of criticism, as questioning, investigation, 'proving the difficult thing'. One respondent to the 1905 questionnaire said of Cézanne that 'he has taken, in face of nature, the attitude of a question mark' ('il a pris, en face de la nature, l'attitude d'un point d'interrogation').[6] This is clever and generous, and I think sums up one whole aspect of modern culture – or of French painting's special place within it. The image connects to a judgment which Kurt Badt, in a book on Cézanne from the 1950s, attributes to Nietzsche: that painting 'emerges as the last metaphysical activity within European nihilism'.[7] The phrase is put in quotation marks by Badt, though no source is given; and Badt seems to concede (his wording is not clear) that Nietzsche's verdict was originally meant as a characterization of art in general at the end of the nineteenth century, not of painting in particular. But apocryphal or not, the phrase points directly to the background assumption that made a kind of writing on Cézanne possible for a century, and that now, because the assumption is a thing of the past, puts writing on Cézanne in a strange, maybe fruitful, limbo.

We are no longer part of a world, that is, in which György Lukács could casually remark that Simmel was 'the Monet of philosophy; up to now there has been no Cézanne to succeed him' ('er war ein Monet der Philosophie, auf den bis jetzt noch kein Cézanne gefolgt ist').[8] (No prizes for guessing Lukács's candidate.) Or a world where Ernst Bloch, in his *Geist der Utopie* written in 1916, could let slip, as the first Battle of the Somme was in full swing, that Cézanne's apples were 'no longer fruit, nor fruit made over into paint; instead all imaginable life is in them, and if they should fall, a universal conflagration would ensue.'[9]

This world of writing – this world of belief – is remote from us. (I use the sentence from Bloch as the book's epigraph, but this does not mean I endorse it.) And it is not simply a matter of this world's having been, from our perspective, too often full of an overweening faith in Art, with high Hegelian rhetoric to match. For Cézanne could be admired just as much for his alleged matter-of-factness. Rainer Maria Rilke's letters on Cézanne, to the extent that I can glimpse their tone in German, seem largely free from Bloch-type exaltation. Cézanne is exemplary for Rilke above all in his restraint: his concentration, his empirical temper, his attention to the task.

In the English-language literature, the two great texts on Cézanne seem to me Roger Fry's and Meyer Schapiro's. (The latter has never entirely entered the canon of art history because, as I see it, the discipline remains uneasy with a book aimed first, in New York in 1952, at a broad American reading public. A volume in the Abrams 'Library of Great Painters' cannot quite belong on the shelf with *Die spätrömische Kunst-Industrie*. And even Roger Fry's book, with its whimsical Bloomsbury cover, and its origins in a catalogue essay for the Pellerin collection, floats somewhere between art world and academy. Art writing and art history, we could say, are always two separate entities – sometimes touching, mostly not quite.)

Both texts, Fry's and Schapiro's, are triumphs of plain style. Ernst Bloch is far away. But theirs is a plainness put firmly under the sign of Nietzsche's dictum. Painting *was*, Fry and Schapiro would have agreed, 'the last metaphysical activity within European nihilism'; meaning the last practice convinced of its eventual difficult access to Truth; and Cézanne's hostility to art with big ideas – his distaste for the Symbolists, his impatience with some of his admirers' philosophizing, his fierce anxious trust in what painting alone could tell him – was his (entirely nineteenth-century) contribution *to* the activity. In calling Pissarro 'humble and colossal' Cézanne described himself, and writing about his art has somehow to model or emulate that balance of qualities.

This is what I had in mind with my (admittedly too cheery) 'Cézanne cannot be written about any more'. The whole intricate structure of assumption that went with writing on Cézanne for a century, and which in some sense tried to ingest and keep alive the artist's own fragile metaphysic, is no longer available to us. Some will consider this a pity, some a relief. (Who in their right minds can now read Ernst Bloch without a shudder?) But whatever our judgment on the line of writing's ending, the end is surely a fact. And therefore certain questions present themselves, if writing about Cézanne – which for me *is* still writing about art 'in its highest vocation' – is not simply to reproduce the dead tropes and topoi of what was once a living language-game.

What would it be like (here is the question) *not* to have a view of Cézanne? Not to have a sense of his meaning for us, in other words, his lesson, his largeness – not to have his art 'fit' anywhere, least of all in a history of modern art? One of the great moments in the Cézanne century, I go on thinking, was May–June 1951, when the socialist journal *Partisan Review* carried an essay on the artist by the critic Clement Greenberg.[10] (The closeness in time and place to Schapiro's Abrams volume is part of the story: part of a battle of reckonings and lineages for the artist, in which always the wider nature of modern culture was in question.) Greenberg's title is touching: 'Cézanne and the Unity of Modern Art'. And of course the temptation, now the last five words of the title have such a period flavour, is to write a Cézanne premised on – organized around – a systematic reversal of all Greenberg's terms. There was no such unity as modern art, and insofar as there was a set of art practices roughly answering to the name, their common denominator was the pursuit of *dis*unity; and the most reckless pursuer – the madhouse always close – was Cézanne. But this too, I'm convinced, is too much of a view of Cézanne, too much of a totalization. I want, rather, a writing (which now may really be possible, in the ruins of a great coercive discourse) that finds ways to linger for a moment in the state induced, time and again, by a new Cézanne, or an old one encountered after long enough away: the feeling of everything else in the world (especially the world of art) being so *comprehensible* by comparison; the feeling of the world 'occurring' in this particular pattern of line and colour, and pushing both to behaviours that are more like conjuration than composition, more like...

◆

More like what? The kind of writing that I find best gets me not to have a 'view' of Cézanne, thus moving me closer to that first incomprehension, is a narrative of repeated looking. A lot of the chapter that follows was written in the gallery at the Getty Museum where Cézanne's *Still Life with Apples* is hung; and most of it – the notes I think are strongest – came in some sense unbidden, involuntarily, put down fast. When after a few weeks I began to be aware that I'd decided, without wanting to, what the questions were in *Still Life*, and wasn't any longer being trapped or intercepted by the insignificant – here a flower on a sugar bowl, there a label on a bottle of rum – I knew it was time to stop. I am an admirer of Paul Valéry's definition of the work of art as that object whose very character is that it goes on calling for, and rewarding, repeated viewing. But there is a difference between a viewing and a view. When all you are doing in front of a painting is confirming your view of it, it's time to take a rest.

In no sense, however, do I present these fragments of narrative as innocent or straightforward. A narrative always knows where it is going. Almost from the start the Cézanne 'issues' lay in wait. So be it. The issues are real. But if a narrative can come across them haltingly, elliptically, from an unexpected direction – if it can 'tarry with the negative', in Hegel's great phrase, for as long as possible – it will have served its turn. I was trapped by the flowers on the sugar bowl. I followed the curves of the straw holder on the rum bottle for minutes – hours – on end. Even now I don't know why.

And a notebook entry, by the way, is not necessarily – however immediate, however seemingly spontaneous – an exercise in Cézanne-type plainness. Cézanne *isn't* plain, or isn't only plain. He's plain and portentous. Roger Fry's affectless anti-metaphorical drawl is wonderful for him, but it will never quite displace Bloch's sense that 'if his apples should fall, a universal conflagration would ensue'. Plain style, unsurpassable as Fry's and Schapiro's and Greenberg's achievements with it may have been (Schapiro in 1952 was affected by the example of Greenberg's journalism in *The Nation*), is not enough. Plain style – Fry is the central example – was ultimately the voice of a modernist loftiness, a modernist closure against anything but Form. A narrative of looking may even offer me a way out of just that.

◆

The journal begins. On 12 January 2016 I get my first sight of *Still Life with Apples* after several years of living with it only in books.[11] The picture is slightly less heavy, less looming and substantial than I remembered; in reproduction it always looks cool and formal, the jars and bottles standing to attention, the white cloth folded to a knife-edge continuing the horizon line on the wall. In reality the set-up is more unruly, apples spilling off a plate, tablecloth twisting and billowing as if in a wind; and above all the scene is filled, unexpectedly, with atmosphere – suffused, almost subaqueous, the air thick with blue and green.

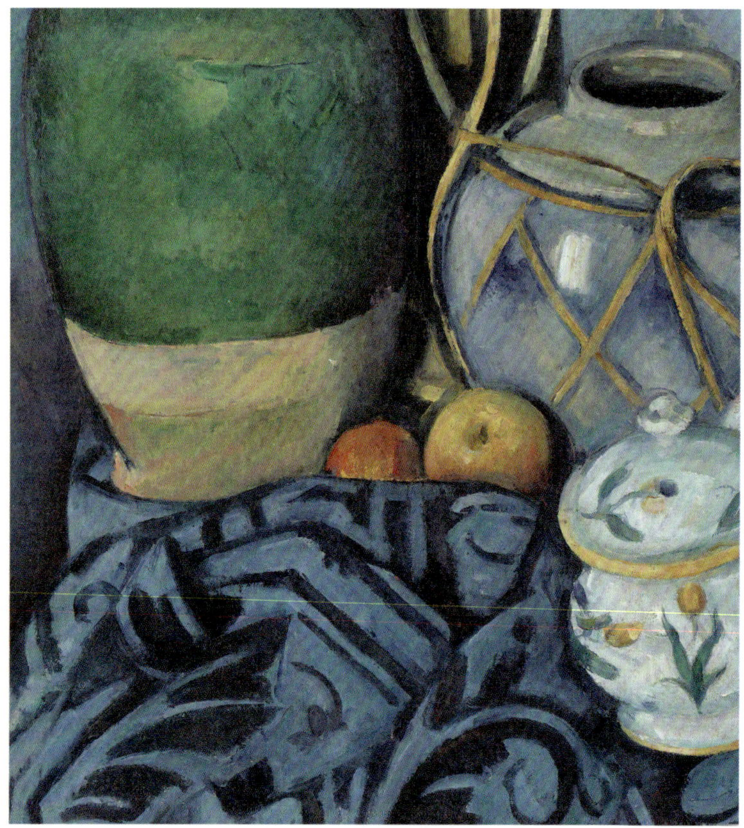

29. Detail from Fig. 28: *Still Life with Apples*, *c.* 1893–95. The J. Paul Getty Museum, Los Angeles.

Yet something else happens immediately in front of the painting, seemingly before I make these adjustments to memory and get a sense of the whole. I want to hold onto this occurrence for as long as I can. I think I see – I think I'm seized by – one particular cluster of events in the painting that strikes me as the fulcrum of its action. I say 'fulcrum' rather than 'punctum', the word we've inherited from Barthes on photography, because I don't think the cluster I find myself looking at – the point of stability – leaps out at me all at once and gives me, as the punctum is supposed to, the touch of the real. The incident in Cézanne is quieter: it is the triangle containing a couple of apples, over towards the left, wedged between the bases of the green pot and the grey-blue ginger jar. The apples nestle behind a fold of blue-and-black patterned cloth. And an extraordinary hard dark shadow falls – or better, unwinds like a coiled spring – from the larger apple's right edge. The blue-black of this shadow-line is intensified by traces of red. And once it starts on its way out of the apple's orbit, the shadow goes on slashing relentlessly – abstractly – downwards, becoming part of the pattern on the blue-and-black drape.

Let me leave the relation between the shadow-line and the blue material to one side for the moment. (I realize in retrospect, writing up these notes, that what is happening here – the passage from visual event to something whose status is more arbitrary, harder to put a name to – will turn out eventually to be central to the picture as I see it. But I don't at all see this on day one. I don't have a 'view' of the shadow.) What I see are the apples. And maybe they strike me as the picture's fulcrum because they and the edge of the blue material are so much an image – an epitome – of *containment*, of firm holding, two shapes nicely settled. Cézanne has worked hard at nesting the apples in place. He seems to have taken a bright yellow from the apple to the left – maybe it was meant first to establish a highlight – and put spot after spot along the top of the cloth, making the boundary between blue and yellow razor sharp.

This moment of safe settlement stands out. It's not exactly that the rest of the painting is *un*settled or altogether precarious (I'm not going straightaway for an uncanny Cézanne, ruled by turbulence and anxiety); but I do think that *Still Life*'s grand balances and felicities of arrangement look, from the start, like order imposed on insubordinate stuff. The apples rolling off the plate are the sign of that. And the perception of this quality in Cézanne – the valuing of the precariousness – goes right back to the beginning of the love of him. The fine anarchist critic Georges Lecomte, writing in the *Revue de l'Évolution Sociale* in 1892 – it is the *Ur*-text of the tradition of writing on Cézanne I've just been invoking – is already saying that 'In the heroic days of naturalism [he means the 1870s, when Cézanne acquired his first circle of admirers], people were pleased to celebrate the uncertain equilibrium of some of his studies from nature, their fortuitous *bizarrerie*, as if art could accommodate disproportion and imbalance.'[12]

But imbalance is perturbing. The two apples in their nest will surely put a stop to it. Is this why my eye goes to them? Perhaps Cézanne is quietly ironizing our wish (always) to be safely tucked up.

For a moment this morning I see the ghost of another much earlier Cézanne in *Still Life*, though what the ghost is doing I cannot yet grasp. But I do see it. The notebook reads: 'There seems to be something of *The Black Clock*'s wild red-lipped triton shell, lurking as unconscious residue in the strange whorls and openings of *Still Life*'s white tablecloth, especially as one moves in closer; and just look at the way the tablecloth finally opens onto the blue-and-black fabric, as if one were peering into an abyss, or a body's exposed interior.' (The *Black Clock* I'm remembering was painted probably in 1869 or 1870.)

Residues of the work Cézanne had been doing just before his apprenticeship to Pissarro crop up regularly in his work from twenty years later. The early 1890s are in general a time of memories. The famous letter Cézanne wrote to Émile Zola in 1886, responding to the author's gift of *L'Oeuvre*, had signed off, poignantly: 'Tout à toi sous l'impulsion des temps écoulés.' 'All yours under the impulse of times gone by.'[13] That impulse lived on. Cézanne's *Smoker*, now hung in the Hermitage (a painting that is almost certainly from the same moment as the one in the Getty), has another 1870 *Still Life* literally 'in the background', hung on a wall – a doom-laden lineup of *Pots, Bottle, Teacup and Fruit*, now in the Berlin Nationalgalerie. Recapitulation, overt or implicit, was part of the 1890s game. But I can't, on this first morning, make sense of the shadow presence of these things from the past: I don't have *Black Clock* vividly enough in mind.

◆

15 January, three days later: The object in *Still Life with Apples* I can't look away from today is the tall black bottle (Rilke thought it contained Curaçao, now we reckon it's just rum). And with the bottle come familiar Cézanne-type questions.

What is it to see an object, we want to know – the bottle and the two jars to each side of it, a regular solid, a definite cylinder, the brim and black interior of a jar – to see such objects 'in perspective'? What happens when we see an ellipse, knowing it to *be* a circle? There is a comparative anatomy of ellipses on offer here: the openings of the green vase and the ginger jar, the little sugar bowl's bright yellow rim, the interrupted edge

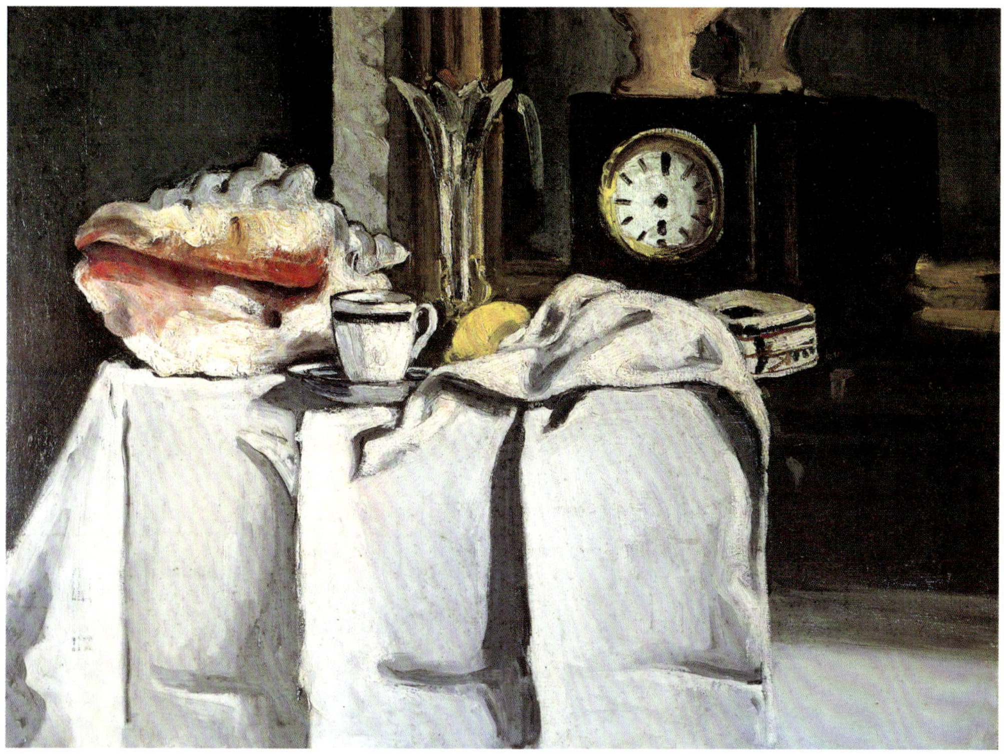

30. *The Black Clock*, c. 1869–70, 54 × 74 cm (21¼ × 29⅛ in.). Private Collection.

of the plate. The black bottle is the fifth term in the series. It does something to the other four elements. Again I am tempted to say it ironizes or destabilizes them; but it also helps them: its recessiveness is a foil for their solidity, their invitation to us to reach out and take hold. (Maybe the black bottle is a sotto voce reincarnation of the black clock.)

Let's concentrate on the bottle – the bottle and the peculiar play of line across its surface and in front of it. I take it that what we are looking at is some kind of straw sleeve on the bottle itself, and part of a label, and the handle of a bent-willow cradle and carrying handle belonging to the grey ginger jar. Could we say, borrowing a word from an already long-ago moment, that the bottle as we are offered it 'deconstructs' the notion we have of a cylinder, or even of a circle – of those as *properties* of a bottle as the eye takes hold of it? The term 'deconstruction' might really be technically appropriate for once, since what seems to be happening as

Cézanne paints the pattern of lines across the cylinder is just the kind of hovering between destruction and exposition Jacques Derrida was fond of. The network of shapes and sorts of circularity – tangents and repetitions and intersections of windings through space – does, partly, seem to open the simple reality of the bottle onto something like the discursive conditions of its being-for-us, its being-part-of-our-peculiar-intricate-*manufactured*-world-of-forms. A bottle – a form – is always trapped in some such de-realizing container. But to see that, or to set up the conditions for it to be seen, is not to tell us that the bottle is simply not there. And in any case – nothing could be clearer than in this example – in Cézanne, or in any deconstruction worth the name, what turns out to be transfixing is the way the set-up of lines seems to wander away from that first intention to *expose* circularity ('expose' in two senses) towards something more arbitrary, more contingent, more irresponsible. A 'play of form' we call it in English, never quite sure of tone of the word 'play'. Something has happened, we feel, that maybe wasn't really intended as the game got under way – something more arbitrary, as I say, more take-it-or-leave-it, more self-centred and *therefore* more absolute and unnerving.

The black bottle, to be clear, does not volatilize or simply fold into two dimensions. Its corked mouth is strongly marked, and part of its solid round base is set down, just sharply enough to be noticed, between the brown and grey of the two jars it stands between. What looks to be the bottom edge of the bottle's straw container is picked out there in yellow, almost as fiercely as the nestled apple right next to it. The yellow is emphatic – a painterly performance. The line of shadow (or whatever) that Cézanne has put along the bigger apple's left shoulder, to keep the base of the bottle and the apple distinct, is visible ten paces away.

A phrase from Lecomte's founding essay of 1892 that always crops up for me in front of Cézanne is his description of the strange *result* of Cézanne's commitment to the visual: that his paintings end by being 'exactes parfois jusqu'au désarroi' – 'exact sometimes to the point of disarray'.[14] The black bottle is a case in point. Or is it? Was it *exactitude* that led to the equivocation here – the instability? Is 'exactitude' the right word for whatever produced the play of straw and bent willow? Presumably there was an actual setting-up of things in space for the picture (we know from contemporary witnesses that Cézanne fretted and experimented with his still-life arrangements, wedging coins under plates and so on), and then a series of decisions, made as paint was put on – but again, is 'decision' the right word here? – that ended up having the bottle's label recede into shadow and the willow handle touch the straw precisely at its intersection. There is something wilful to this. Dogged attentiveness – exact to the point of disarray – doesn't seem to capture the mobility of mind involved.

We have, as it happens, a control. In the Metropolitan Museum's *Still Life with Aubergines* (FIG. 31), which surely was done at the same time as the Getty picture, using many of the same cast of characters, the black bottle and ginger jar are lined up, we could say, in 'unplayful' mode. The ginger jar's mouth is expository of the volume (the bottle) standing directly behind it. Its looping handle is moved to the side and reduced to a thin dark trace. The bottle's shoulder is not lopsided, or not in a way that attracts attention. Its label migrates to the edge, almost out of sight, disturbing and flattening nothing.

I shall come back and back in these notes to the question of disarray or destabilization in Cézanne; but here is a first stab at it. There *is* disquiet in a Cézanne – Picasso's word for it (for what he admired most in Cézanne's paintings) was 'inquiétude'.[15] Some of the disquiet seems to emerge from the actual strangeness of vision – the uncertainty of what it is to see – if and when a viewer focuses on the process honestly and refuses to take anything for granted. Certainly Cézanne did both. But obviously something else is in play when it comes to the look of the whole picture. The whole array – the *Still Life with Apples* – is disturbed and unstable (those spilling red spheres, that tipping plate, that earthquake landscape of blue and white cloth) yet composed and crystalline at the same time. And both the orderliness and the disturbance can strike us as features of seeing *and* features of manufacture – inventions, impositions, flashes of grim wit. Take the crisp fold at the top of the tablecloth, continuing the dark line of the dado. Or the whole brilliant hard decisiveness of the made pattern – made by machine and then by Cézanne the re-folder – on the blue-and-black drape. Or the anti-colour of the ice-block wall.

Maybe I was arrested first of all by the lines on the black bottle because they seemed to me the place in the picture where you actually *saw* obedience

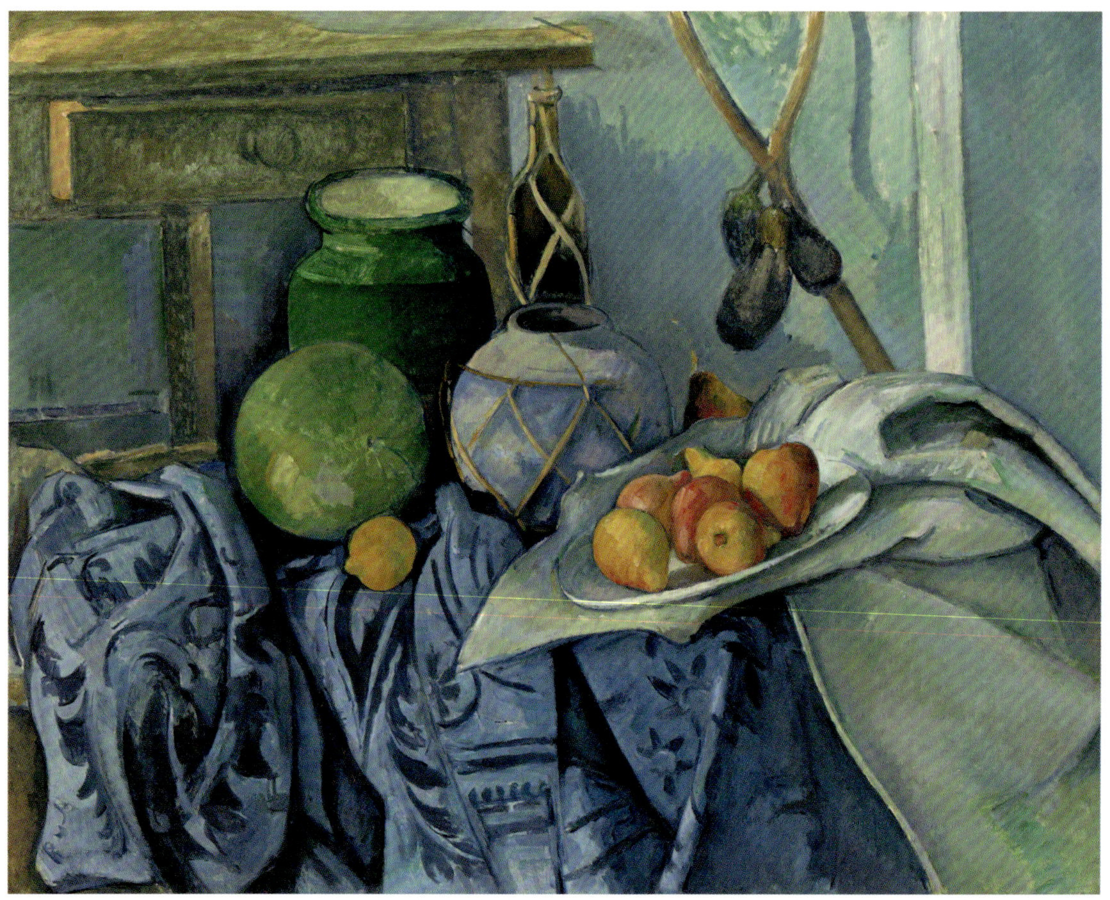

31. *Still Life with Aubergines*, *c.* 1893–95, 73 × 92 cm (28¾ × 36¼ in.).
Metropolitan Museum of Art, New York.

to vision – going along with vision's instabilities – transmuting into this other kind of wilfulness. But I don't think the wilfulness – the play of form – is autarkic. On the contrary: the balance of instability and monumentality in Cézanne – this inimitable formal language – is, I am sure, *directed to something beyond itself*, some distinct and important quality to late-nineteenth-century experience. But what quality? I can't yet say.

◆

I've brought in a reproduction of *The Black Clock*. I think I see why the painting cropped up in my viewing of *Still Life with Apples* the first time

I saw it, and I go on feeling that the two paintings are connected – that one is a kind of mirror image of the other. The hard straight folds in *Black Clock*'s white drapery – more like gashes than folds – and the way they pin the whole area of white to the picture edge: these are displaced (inverted) onto *Still Life*'s upper right quadrant. And that quadrant – the sheer 'unreality' of the ice-block wall – seems to me to have its origins in *Black Clock*'s strange movement through the looking glass. Look at the grey area top right in the earlier painting, where the clock without hands extends back and back into greyness.

Writers about *Black Clock* seem a little embarrassed by the wild sexual innuendo of the triton shell and its Delacroix lips. Obviously by 1890 Cézanne had long decided to do without this kind of machinery. But that was because he was now confident that the combination of deathliness and animation he had seen in things in 1870 – the co-presence of shell-lips smacking and clock stopped for eternity – could be restaged in a cooler, more earthbound register. The triton shell, by the way, makes a displaced reappearance in another still life done at the same time as the Getty's, a *Plaster Cupid* now in Stockholm (FIG. 32). Behind the plaster cast in the Stockholm painting, the blue-and-black fabric that figures so prominently in *Still Life* is twisted into a shape, an orifice, that is almost the triton reborn. Black clock becomes cast-iron fireplace. And the corner to the left of the triton shell, up top – in the earlier painting a positive hovering void – is done again as unreadable landscape, from which the dream curtain is drawn back. Pears fight for room on a crowded plate. The little Eros is no match for his animate surroundings.

The black bottle in *Still Life with Apples*, finally, is another revenant from 1870. It and the green vase were main players, in much the same position, in the Berlin *Pots, Bottle, Teacup and Fruit*.

◆

'Directed to something beyond itself.' I see now, looking back, that the occurrence of *Black Clock* and *Pots, Bottle, Teacup and Fruit* in connection with the Getty *Still Life* was already pointing me towards Marx. For *Black Clock*'s whole atmosphere is class-specific – over-starched, over-furnished, rigid with propriety, repressed, claustrophobic, in the triton shell even a touch hysterical. Never was a still life more bourgeois: it is an interior out of *Madame Bovary* or *The Turn of the Screw*. But the implications of all this did not dawn on me till later.

◆

17 January: *Still Life with Apples* (starting again) is special among Cézanne's still lives for having no established flat surface, however elliptically done, on which one or two things can rest. Maybe we think the bottle and the nested apples are placed on a table, but we are not shown the table itself. The green vase looks for a moment to be perched on the table corner, but then we see that it is standing in a fold (a curlicue) of the blue-and-black drape. The horizontal we are looking for is displaced to the folded line of the tablecloth at top centre and the line of blue going out from it – which itself blurs, snags, darkens. The surface below the line, which ought to be a wall (or even a tabletop), goes up in smoke. The Met's *Still Life with Aubergines* has a similar lack of table for anything to rest on. But towards the left in that painting we are allowed a brief glimpse. And of course in *Aubergines* the table that *must* be there but isn't is given a double – a kind of diagrammatic substitute – top left, straight-ruled, regular, cleared of detritus. But if that is the table and 'table-top level', what kind of arrangement can we be looking at closer to, and from where in the room are we looking?

Go back to *Still Life with Apples*. In comparison with *Aubergines*, where at least we seem to be facing things four-square, our eyes on a level with the most important objects, there is a feeling in the Getty picture that the basic landscape of the still life is tilted towards us. The apples rolling off the plate are the signature of that, but the whole fall of the blue fabric and tablecloth enacts the same strange movement. *Aubergines'* proximity is just as strange (only look at the apples on the plate in that picture, poised above empty space, or the final spike of the white tablecloth) but the Getty painting's treatment of the tipping and sliding of surfaces is, in the end, more unnerving – as if an entirely necessary, but utterly foreign, language for a new form of apprehension had come into being as the painting proceeded. *Aubergines'* space seems almost meant to be cryptic, so that it's possible to shrug off its unfamiliarity and enjoy it as a game; *Still Life with Apples* is 'exacte parfois jusqu'au désarroi'.

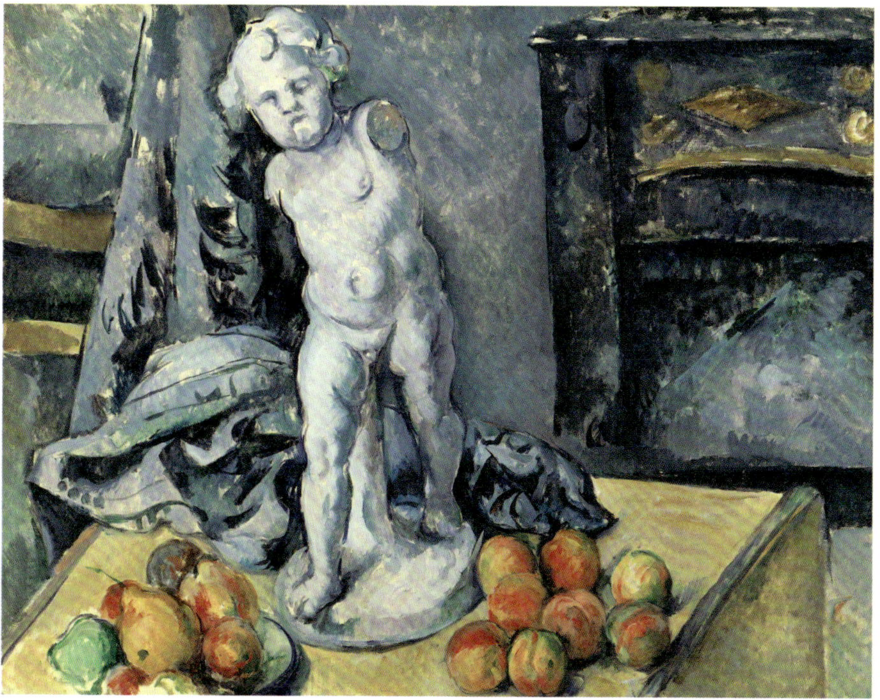

32. *Plaster Cupid*, *c.* 1894–95, 63 × 81 cm (24⅞ × 31⅞ in.). Nationalmuseum, Stockholm.

What is at stake here is a central feature of Cézanne's vision, which has often been talked about: his treatment of proximity and distance, and the part played in that treatment by objects' orientations – their inclination towards or away from us. Take *Apples, Napkin and Milk Jug*, now belonging to the Musée de l'Orangerie in Paris (FIG. 33). Whatever the tipping forward of the tabletop in *Apples and Milk Jug* may ultimately be 'about', surely the visual effect of it is not to move the objects arranged on the tabletop closer to us, putting them 'on the picture plane' or even 'on the picture surface'? This is what most twentieth-century criticism thought it did, or wanted it to do; but try as I may, I can't see the apples coming towards me. What the tipping table seems mainly to do in *Apples and Milk Jug* is make the emptiness of the painting's foreground – the un-crossable gap there between me and the object-world portrayed, the imagined hard transparency of the picture plane – emerge as a thing in itself. Not that this puts everything out of reach, exactly, or makes everything alien. There are no clocks without hands, no triton shells. The objects don't loom or grimace – they're all touchable, edible, ordinary. Yet the availability – even the Chardin-type knife on the table, its handle asking to be reached out to and held – *is* also a kind of remoteness. Look at the pewter milk jug – the quality of its blue colour, the perfection of its cylinder, the sharpness of its rim. Look at the disappearing (unholdable) stem of the wineglass.

The world is near in Cézanne, and it is vivid, but what that nearness and vividness truly are – what they are made from, what they amount to – remains a question. (We might want to say instead of 'near' and 'vivid' simply 'beautiful'. But the same question would apply.) Nearness and vividness are *on the other side of something* – this is the 'something' the painting's whole structure seeks to preserve, to make present for us – *that enacts a separation from us*. The tipping table in Cézanne, for instance, especially when the peculiar orientation is accompanied by a slight tilting from right to left (as in *Apples and Milk Jug*), is an estranging device – not an edging of everything into our space. It gives the world a ground level on which nothing, we come to feel, could finally take a stand; it makes a table we could never rest our elbows on or put our knees under. The higher Cézanne moves in relation to the tabletop, the more profound this loss of bearings. Look, for instance, at the 'world map' of a table spread out in *Still Life with Fruit Dish, Apples and Bread*, in the Oskar Reinhart Collection in Winterthur – where what we might hope would settle down finally into a straight bird's-eye view, a plotting of positions and solidities on the flat, turns out to be a territory in which each separate orientation seems to cancel (or at least ironize) the one next door (FIG. 34). Just look at the fruit bowl in relation to its base…

Even the triton shell – the fantastical in perception, the phantasmagoric – stands ready to reappear. The loaf of bread in the Reinhart *Still Life* has ears, eyes, mouth – a generally vicious look.

◆

Let's turn aside from the question of tipping and tilting in Cézanne for the moment and look at the question of folds. It is just as fundamental. The way man-made material, or even the continuous surfaces of the natural world – a screen of foliage, for instance, or the surface of the sea – the

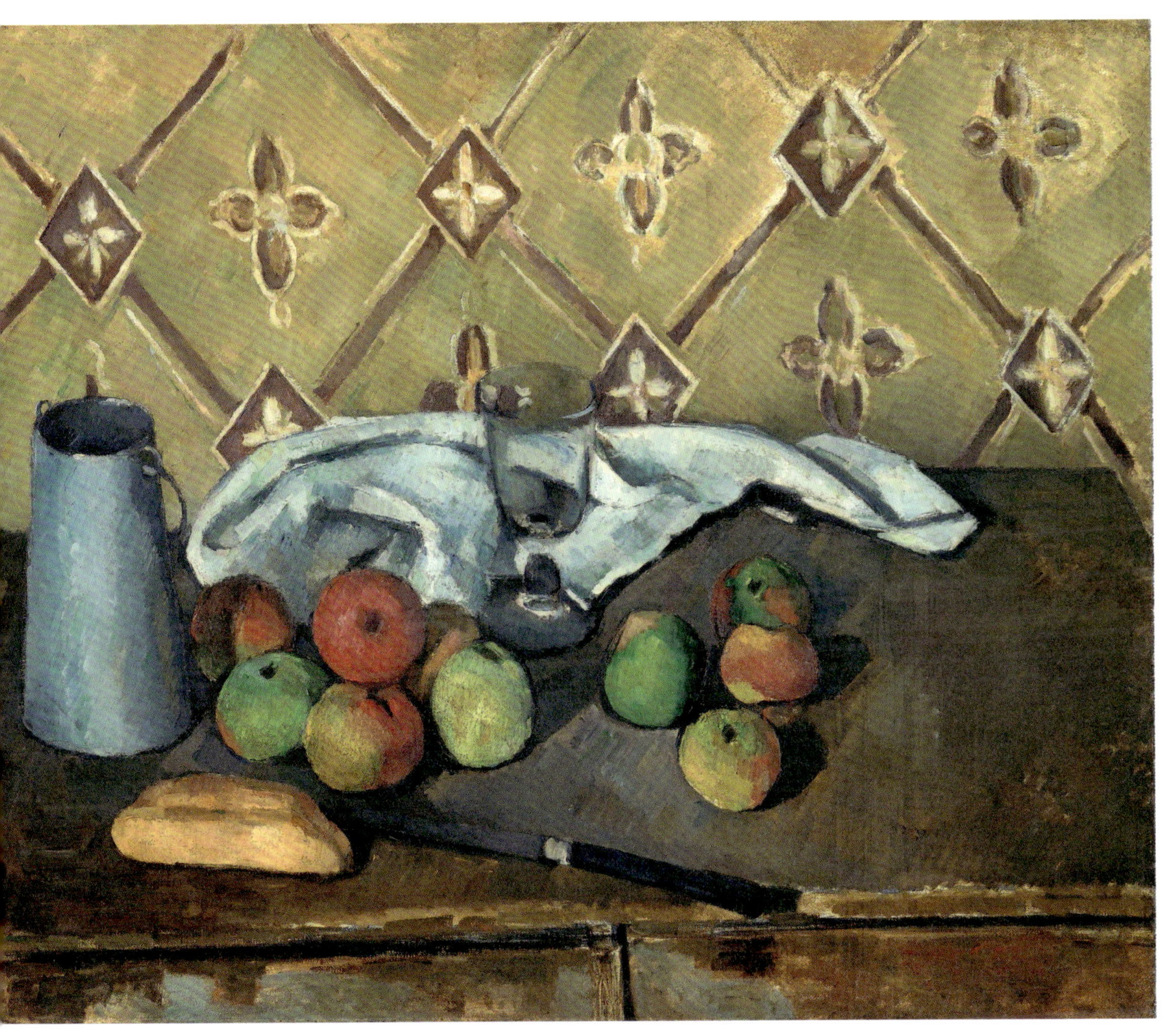

33. *Apples, Napkin and Milk Jug*, c. 1880–82, 60 × 73 cm (23⅝ × 28¾ in.). Musée de l'Orangerie, Paris, Jean-Walter and Paul Guillaume Collection.

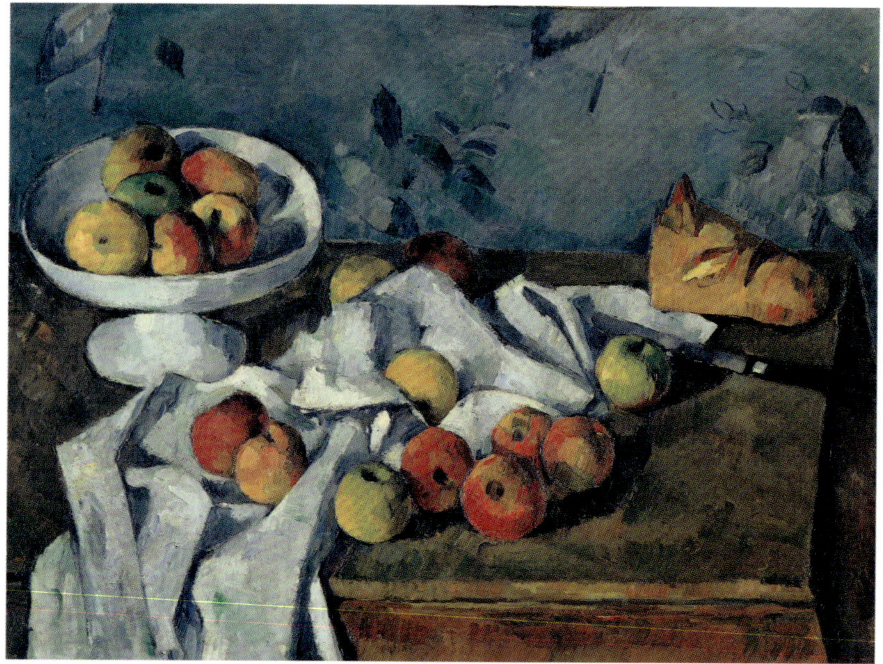

34. *Still Life with Fruit Dish, Apples and Bread*, c. 1880–82, 55 × 74.5 cm (21⅝ × 29⅜ in.). Sammlung Oskar Reinhart, 'Am Römerholz', Winterthur.

way such surfaces are folded and crinkled in order to catch the light: this is painting's life blood. I am fond of the moment in Dante when the poet, looking for a way to explain why his language has to admit defeat in the face of heaven's ineffabilities, reaches for a metaphor from painting. 'Because our speech, not to say our imagination, has no colours/ To match folds like these.'[16] Folds unfold colour, Dante is saying; but they also trap colour, or at least tie it down; they are, in painting, what makes colour adhere to – belong to – a world we can be part of. Yet there is always the possibility, Dante realizes, of an unfolding that leaves the object-world behind.

Ask the question of *Still Life with Apples*, then: What, when Cézanne takes the trouble to fold a compliant material into shapes and gradients that he thinks a painting can thrive on, does he do to the folds? Does he fold in order to flatten, to reduce three to two dimensions? Well, it depends. In the blue-and-black fabric here, perhaps that intention is uppermost. One might look for a moment at how the same fabric is treated in another picture from much the same time, *Curtain, Jug and Fruit Dish*, in a Chicago private collection, where the cloth's texture and softness and folding-in of darkness seem to be uppermost in Cézanne's mind (FIG. 35). The Getty's material looks impenetrable by comparison. What material *feels like* to the eye, and how its folding abets that feeling, can change radically from point to point in the same picture. Move from the Getty's blue fabric to the white tablecloth to the right. The folds and rolls of the tablecloth have almost a tough organic feeling to them, like the exposed surfaces of a polyp or viscera. If one saw the curving leg-of-lamb shape out of context – the one going up left from the red stripe, with a little more yellow in it than its neighbours – what would one take it to be? I'm not sure. It has the blubbery, rubbery resilience of a sea creature's limb.

And the hard straight crease on the cloth to the right in *Still Life*, ending in a spike? What on earth is it like? A hood… a helmet… a billowing spinnaker… The whole pattern of shapes deriving from the blubbery limb is bizarre.

Folds, in a word, are contrivances. No doubt in painting, as Dante believed, normally they do the work of disclosure, of exposition of solids and shading. But always they are liable to take on a life of their own. Or a non-life. The triton shell stands for that.

◆

18 January: Would it be possible to treat Cézanne's still lifes typologically? That is, to draw up a map of constant props in this kind of picture, of recurrences, types of preferred overall organization. Perhaps. If we had such a map, it might make us more sensitive to divergences from the norm – like the *Plaster Cupid* pictures in the Courtauld Gallery and Stockholm, for example (FIGS 41 & 32). Or the Barnes Foundation 'tombstone' *Ginger Jar*, which seems to me unique in its dark atmosphere, not to say its upright 'portrait' format (FIG. 36). (The grimness of the background here seems linked to the naivety – I'm tempted to say, the desperation – with which the picture, in the foreground, attempts to *break through* the picture-plane emptiness and have its apples be ours at last… close, closer, improbably magnified. Even the way the tablecloth is given space to hang down before us and come to a finish is uncharacteristic. Normally the tablecloth is there

to offer us a way into the illusion, which then we realize we cannot take. Here it's as if the offer and the refusal aren't needed – the object-world is *there* for us, its distance from us is just an ordinary fact of life. Or that's the picture's wish. I doubt it is granted.)

A typology of the still lifes, then, would have its uses. But the problems are obvious. There are too many bases on which such a typology could be constructed, even in terms of Cézanne's favourite props – 'ginger jar still lifes', 'green vase still lifes', chests of drawers, pink striped tablecloth, and so on. Which prop, when it recurs, produces a true group, a distinctive still-life 'world'? That is the question. I think the best candidate may be the blue-and-black fabric we see in *Still Life with Apples*. We have a dozen other paintings deploying the material – dating is, as always, speculative, but most of them seem to have been done in the first years of the 1890s. Is there something – some distinctive pictorial interest – the dozen pictures share?

I should say straightaway that an answer to that question emerged only slowly in my notebook, by fits and starts, over the course of several weeks. There was no eureka moment in the gallery. My thinking towards an answer is scattered through the notebook entries, and what I offer now is an attempt to pull the entries together and state my eventual sense of things. But I'd be misrepresenting what happened if I didn't register that, right from the start, I had an intuition about why the blue-and-black fabric was there in Cézanne, and what it did to the other actors on the scene. 'I think the blue and black carpet is the best candidate for the maker of a real connected world of objects,' I wrote already on 18 January, 'because it seems to stand in Cézanne's mind for the human urge to abstract from nature, to reduce, to simplify, to rhyme in form, to concoct decisive and somehow relentless (even cruel) alternatives to Nature's kinds of repetition and difference. The group of paintings with the blue carpet turns on – on but also against – that special human Will to Form. (In the two *Plaster Cupid* pictures, indeed, the war between organism and organization is made explicit.)'

This is still too cut and dried and categorical; but what follows in the rest of this chapter (as so often in writing about art) is essentially a working through of that January shot in the dark.

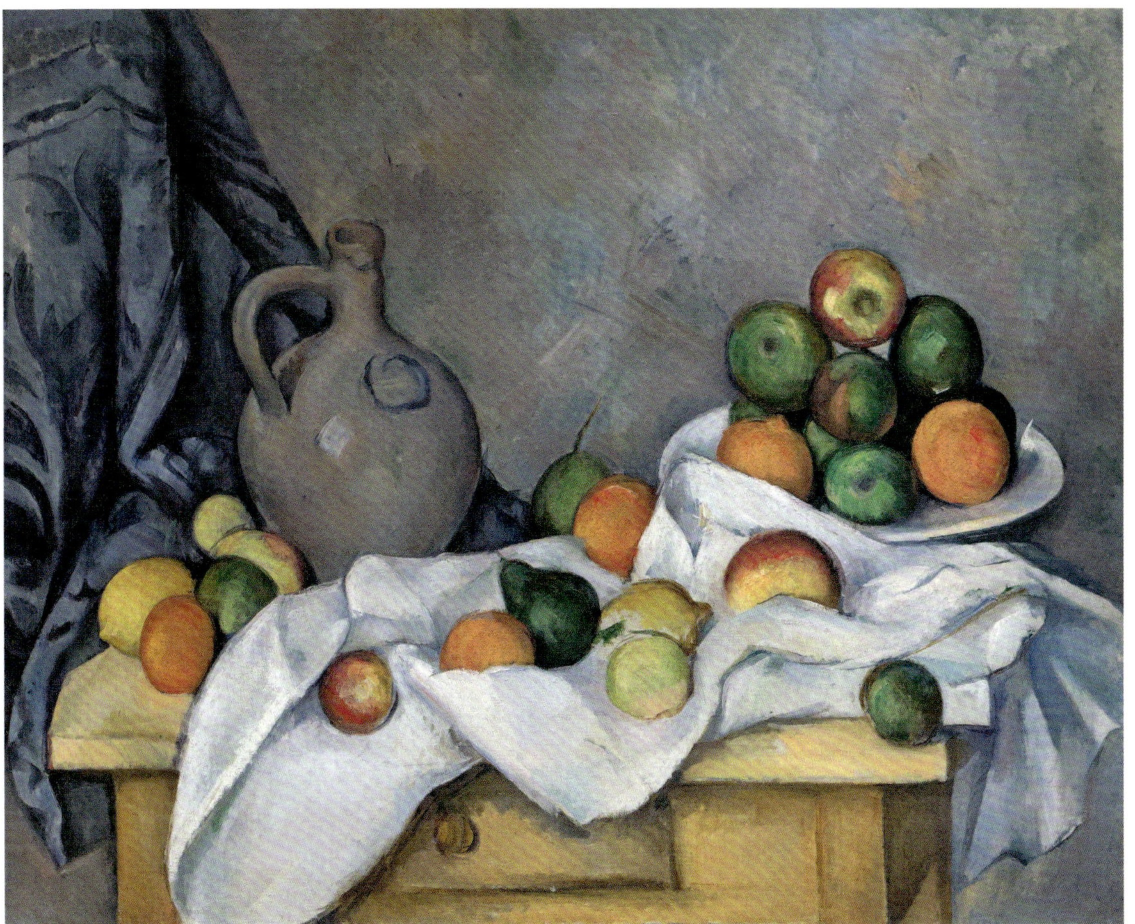

35. *Curtain, Jug and Fruit Dish*, c. 1893–95, 59 × 72 cm (23¼ × 28⅜ in.). Private Collection, Chicago.

◆

First of all, to state the obvious, the dozen paintings containing the blue material do not add up to a neat or consistent set. There are, for instance, half a dozen paintings where it seems that the proximity of things is the main fact of the case. It is an intercepted, seemingly arbitrary, proximity, if I can borrow a notion from Fritz Novotny's analyses of Cézanne's landscapes – a *too*-closeness, a slice of the real that does not seem to possess a centre or an understandable limit.[17] The closeness in these paintings seems accidental, and in one or two of them our very viewpoint colludes in the strangeness – seeming to come from an 'above' that offers the opposite of

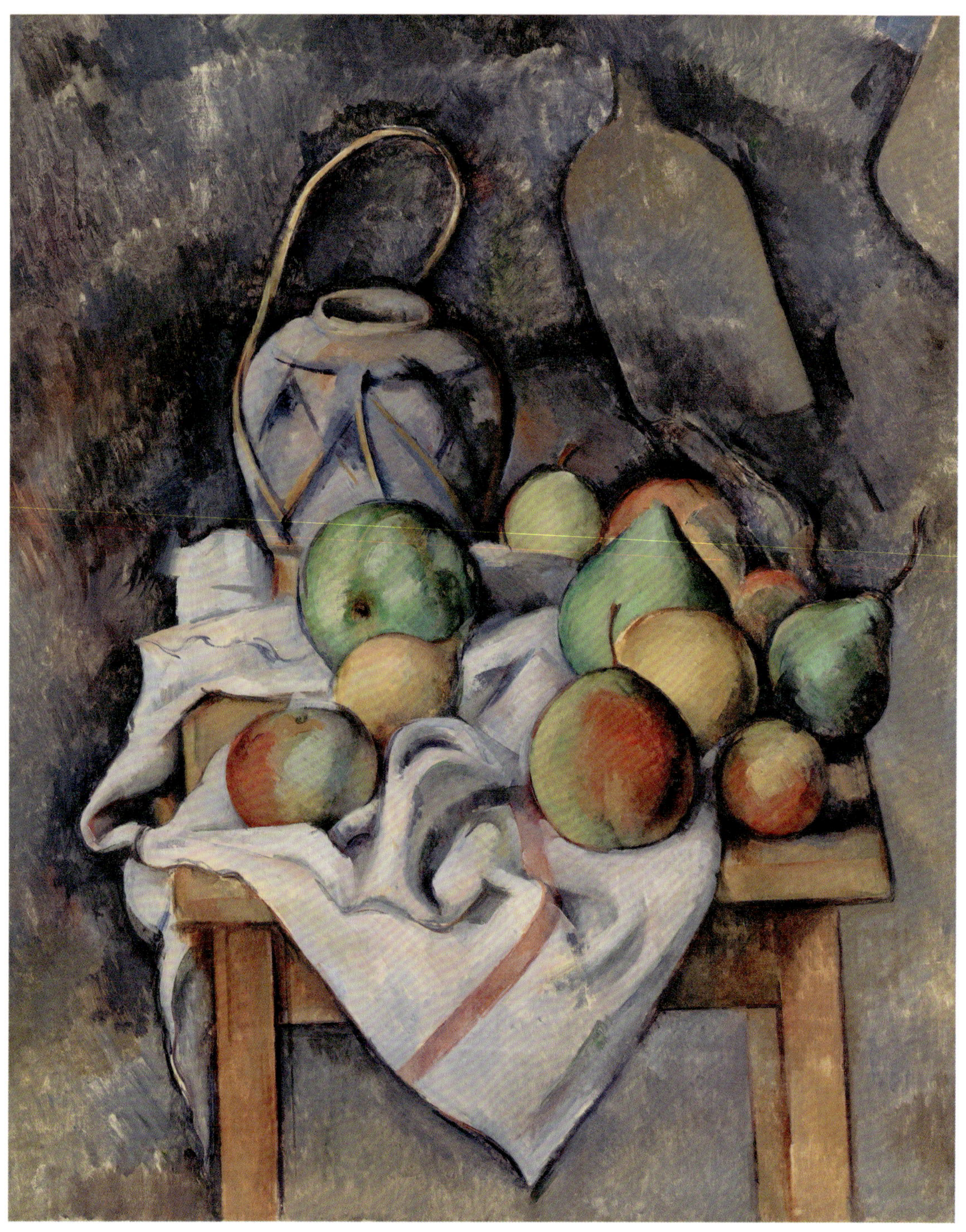

36. *Ginger Jar*, c. 1895, 73 × 60 cm (28¾ × 23⅝ in.). Barnes Foundation, Philadelphia.

comprehension and that is closed in claustrophobically by the blue drape or some other ungraspable backdrop. There is even a group of three or four paintings within the larger set – a *Pomegranate and Pears on a Plate* in a private collection, the *Dish of Peaches* belonging to the Reinhart Collection, a *Stoneware Jug* from the Beyeler Collection near Basel, perhaps the small *Fruit and Jug on a Table* now in Boston – that look to be almost parodies of proximity, intent on showing us how weird it would be to find ourselves finally in touch with things, fully 'in the world' (FIGS 37, 38 & 39).

(Compare *Pomegranate and Pears* with Cézanne's later *Pyramid of Skulls* [FIG. 55])

Equally, there are paintings using the drapery where the blue-and-black seems meant as a cool-coloured 'falling curtain' accompaniment to the spread of objects across a tabletop. I think it would be wrong to call this a specific subset: the lateral spread is an *interest* that seems active in various pictures, and that finally has its day in the highly unusual format – the stretched horizontal – of *Jug and Fruit on a Table* (FIG. 40).

Nonetheless, I think there is a genuine 'blue material' group, directly connected to the Getty canvas, within the larger dozen. *Still Life with Aubergines* (FIG. 31), we know, is immediately a sister painting. *Still Life with Peppermint Bottle* shares many features, and the blue material is even more dominant there – though cooler, more ethereal (FIG. 42). The two *Plaster Cupids* are part of the group, and we shall see in a moment that the Courtauld painting signals – plays with – its inherence in a 'blue material' transformation set (FIGS 32 & 41). The Beyeler painting and one that belongs to the Pola Corporation (FIG. 45) are in a sense outliers – the cast of object characters in both has shifted, and our viewpoint is specific and perplexing – but in both, the aliveness or deadness of the blue drape seems to be at issue, and the nature of the material's foldedness or flatness, as well as the way it collides with (or worms its way into) the world of living forms on the table. No doubt the Stockholm *Cupid* is the most florid example of this; but the fall of the Beyeler drapery is just as elaborate and almost as suggestive. These are the six paintings that strike me as the Getty *Still Life*'s companions.

◆

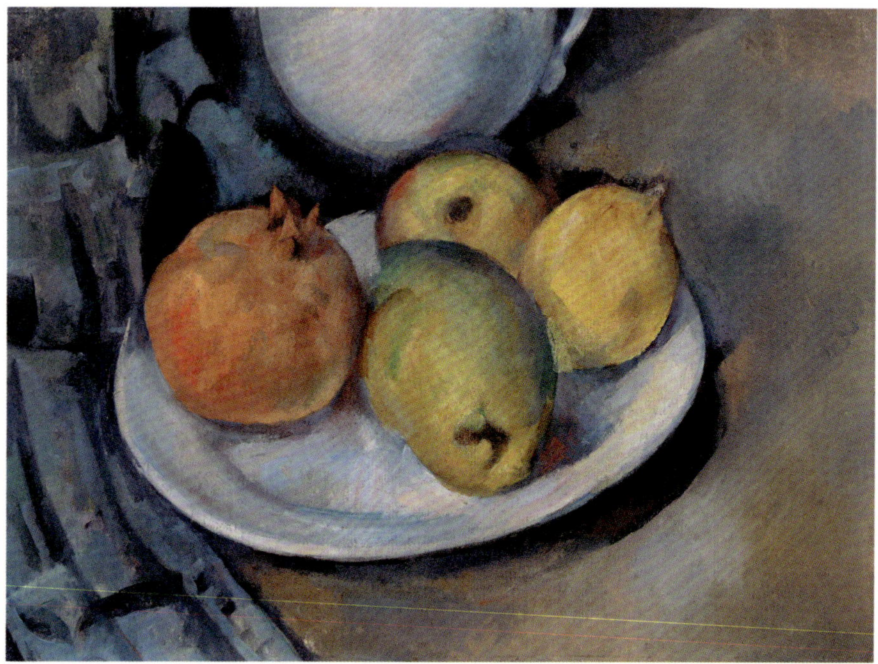

37. *Pomegranate and Pears on a Plate*, c. 1892–95, 27 × 36 cm (10⅝ × 14¼ in.). Private Collection.

What happens when we attend to the action of the blue material within this core set? I think that certain questions occur repeatedly, provoked by the way Cézanne has arranged things. How does the fabric stand in relation to the other objects on view, some of them folded into it, some standing apart? What is the balance here between *manufactured* pattern and the kind of rhymes and analogies we perceive in the world at large – between the lines on the fabric and the lines of the straw and willow holders, for example? And how does the fabric's pattern relate to the pattern 'on the flat' of the *painting*? Is the drape painting's representative? And (this question seems bound up with all the previous ones) where *is* the fabric? Where has Cézanne put it in space? What kinds of folds are in it, or (same question, really) what kinds of holding and enfolding are done by it? Maybe no kind at all…

Do we require specific evidence that these questions were on Cézanne's mind? Well, I hope not; but maybe we'd like to know how explicitly they cropped up, and how aware Cézanne was of their elusive, paradoxical nature – whether he recognized they were questions about the very nature of human contrivance, and therefore open to dialectical play. The London *Plaster Cupid* and the *Peppermint Bottle* are famous for giving us a clue. Look for a moment at the bottom left corner and lower left side of the *Plaster Cupid*. After a while – it is by no means obvious – you come to see that what's being shown is part of the *Peppermint Bottle* painting, which must have been propped against the wall in Cézanne's studio.

Let's leave aside what the picture has done to the parallel lines in *Peppermint Bottle*. Try simply to focus on the fruit and the drape as they reappear *as painted*. What kind of change takes place as they pass from one state to the other? The drape is simplified, but it is not clear to me that it is flattened, still less reduced to a stamped-out pattern. The drape in *Peppermint Bottle* looks harder and more mechanical. Everything there is lined up face front, obedient to the order of the picture plane: the blue drape is written across the transparency like a kind of script. But once the

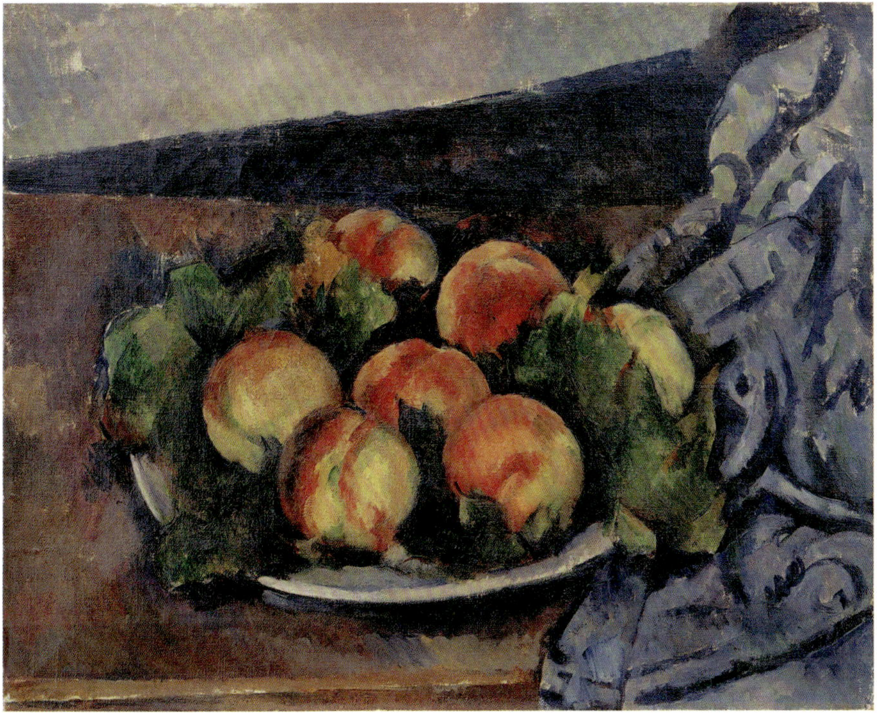

38. *Dish of Peaches*, c. 1892–95, 31 × 40 cm (12¼ × 15¾ in.). Sammlung Oskar Reinhart, 'Am Römerholz', Winterthur.

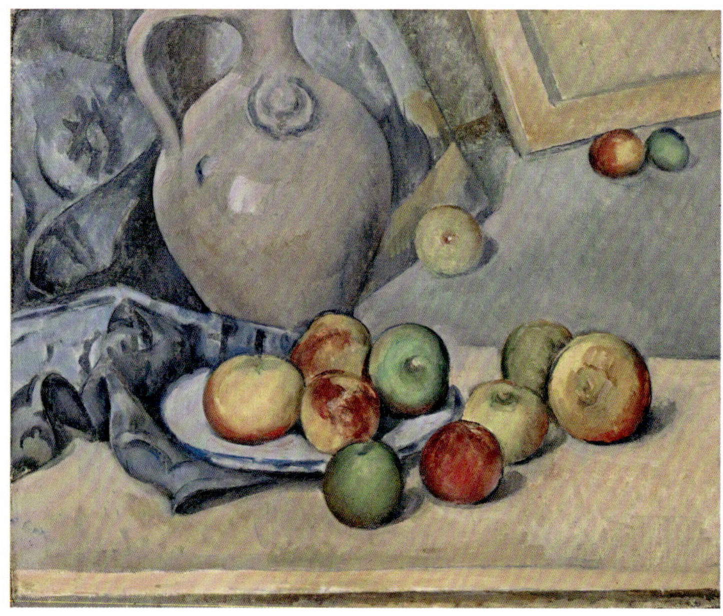

39. *Stoneware Jug*, c. 1893–95, 38 × 46 cm (15 × 18⅛ in.).
Beyeler Foundation, Riehen/Basel.

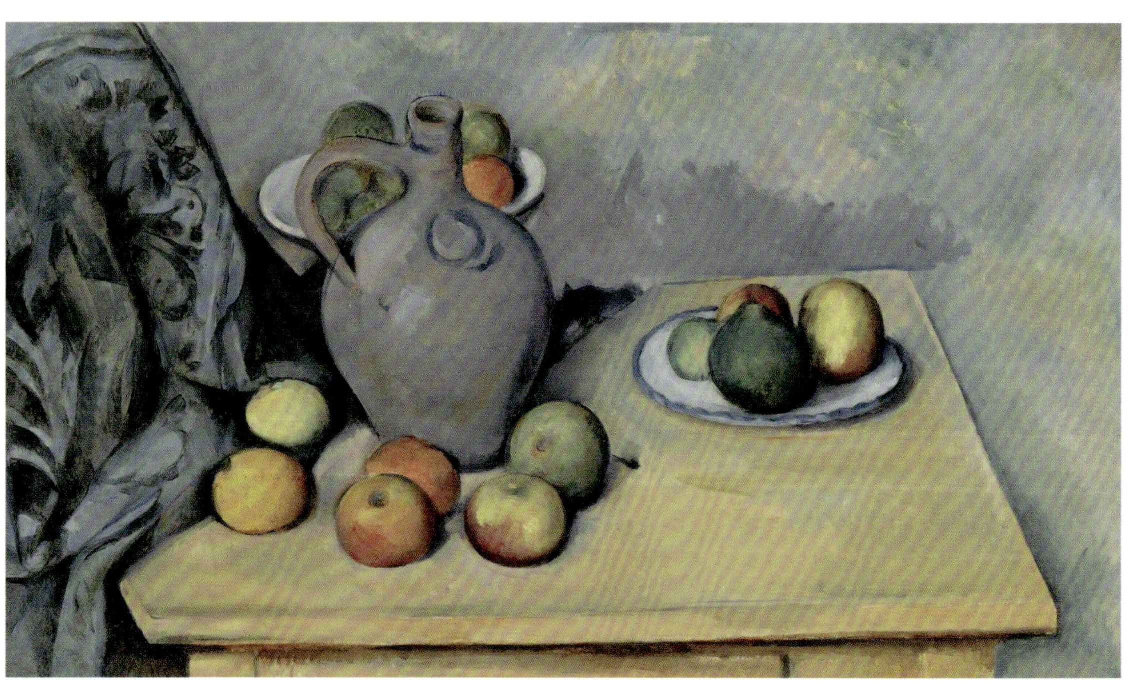

40. *Jug and Fruit on a Table*, c. 1893–95, 41 × 72 cm (16⅛ × 28⅜ in.). Private Collection.

canvas is turned back into space, as happens in *Plaster Cupid*, the whole equation changes. And then we notice the further dialectical move: for presumably at the start of things, bottom left in the *Plaster Cupid*, what we are looking at is the blue-and-black drape as it exists *in the studio* (laid out in a way analogous to the drape in the Beyeler picture), cradling the plate of apples. And then we follow the drape as it climbs in front of *Peppermint Bottle* leaning against the wall... And then – what? At what point does the painted fabric become the painted *painted* fabric in *Peppermint Bottle*?

◆

24 January: The blue-and-black fabric appears most often in these paintings as a drape or a curtain, hung usually at the left-hand side – almost like a curtain in Vermeer. In the Stockholm *Plaster Cupid* it looks as if it is pinned to the studio wall or looped over the top of a canvas on the studio floor.

So the Getty *Still Life*, and the Met's *Aubergines* and the Washington *Peppermint Bottle*, stand out from the group: they put the fabric in the foreground and give it a special distinctness. Its patterns are emphatic, savoured, monumental. Clearly the same material is being used, but from picture to picture there are remarkably few repeated motifs. The spiky flower-head crops up bottom centre in the Getty picture and towards the right in *Aubergines*, but the forms surrounding the flower-heads look different. The frond of leaves just to the left in the Getty painting seems to be there at right in *Peppermint Bottle*, but again its geometrical frame is new. The flower-head appears in the Beyeler picture and *Jug and Fruit on a Table* has a brilliant freehand version (maybe) of the bending frond. But the same thing happens: the motifs don't seem to be in the place they are given on the fabric when they are more crisply described.

The question of Form looms close. I imagine Mondrian looking at the non-fall of non-folds in *Peppermint Bottle* – or the non-space of the same picture's back wall – and taking them as gospel.

In the group as a whole, Cézanne's emphasis is constantly shifting. By and large, the blue drape is decor. It knows its place: it is a provider of chords, crescendos, dissonances. Our eyes are drawn first to the great organic *things* on the table and their massive or delicate containers. And yet

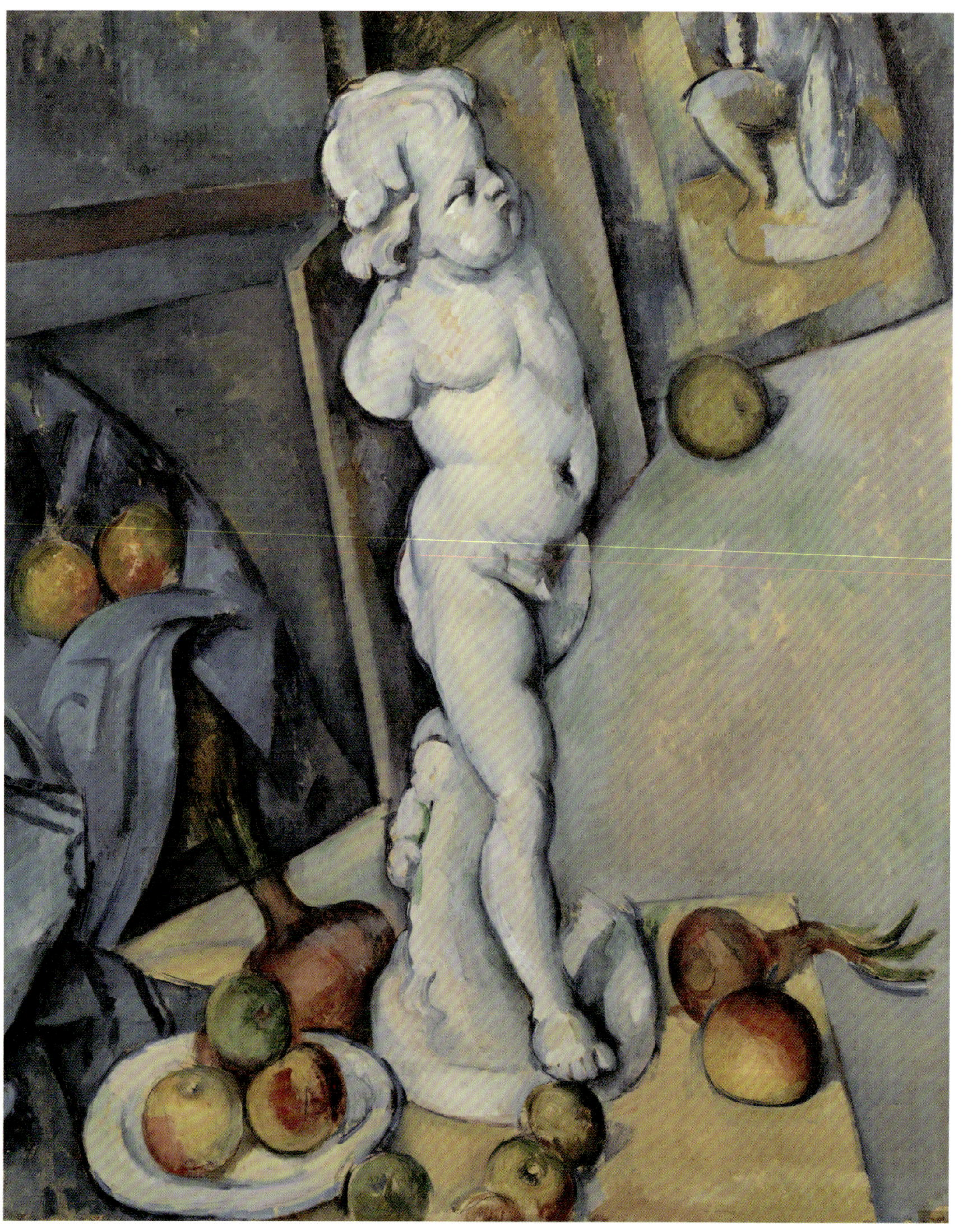

41. *Still Life with Plaster Cupid*, c. 1893–95, 70 × 57 cm (27⅝ × 22⅜ in.). Courtauld Gallery, London.

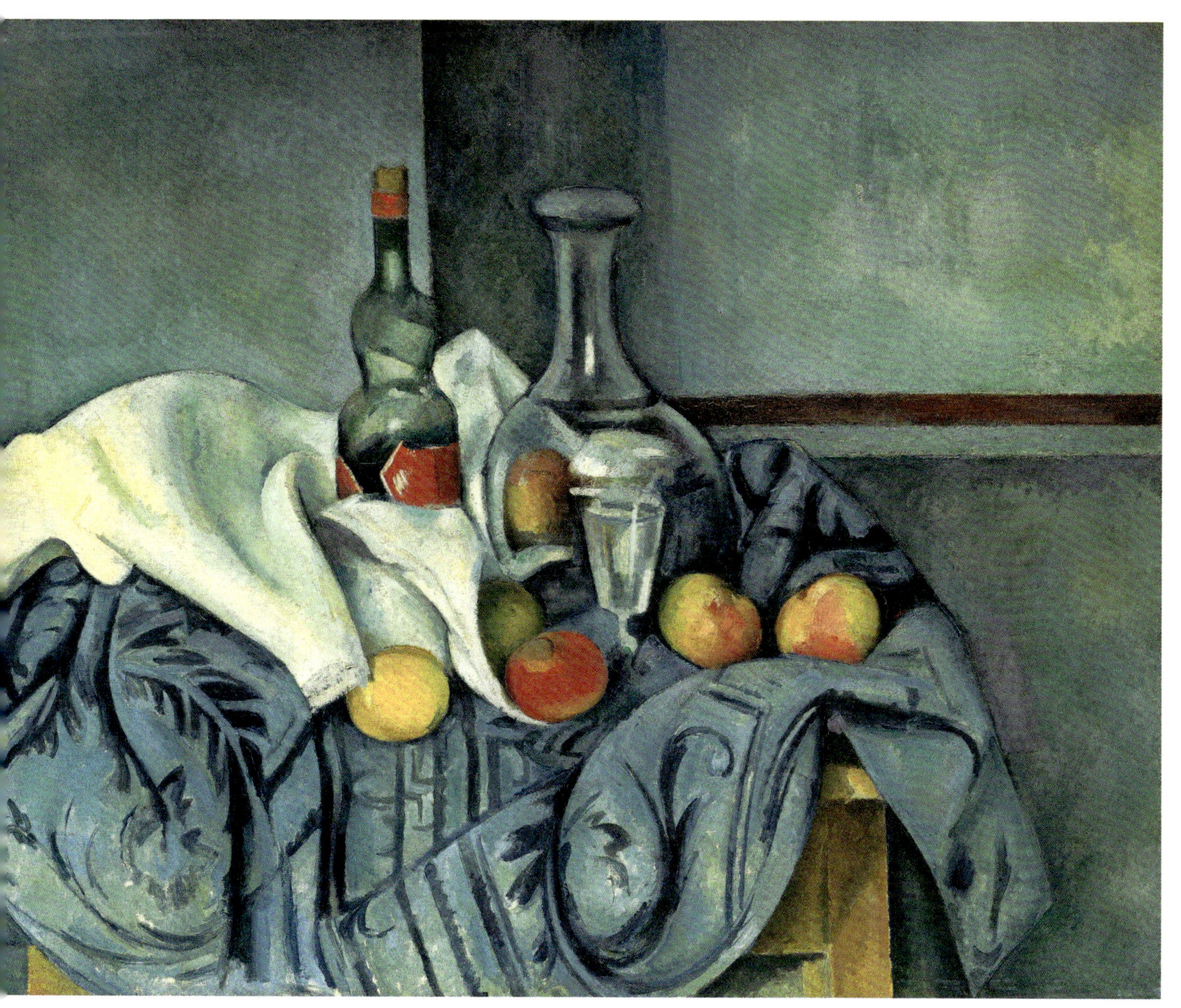

42. *Still Life with Peppermint Bottle*, c. 1893–95, 66 × 82 cm (25⅞ × 32⅜ in.).
National Gallery of Art, Washington, D.C.

the blue material's deference is double-edged. The muteness and steeliness of the 'decorative' in still life – always, but especially in Cézanne – possess their own power. Pattern can state or intimate an order, or a mode of understanding, that ends up containing – quietening – all the tipping and spilling, the insistence on 'being there', the 'coming to life'.

Calligraphy is too weak a word for the patterning as it occurs, for example, in *Peppermint Bottle* or *Still Life with Apples*: We aren't looking at the way something is written, we're trying to get hold of what the act of writing means. Cézanne is saying something about what Form is, humanly, epistemologically – about Form, maybe, as the species' best (though most chilling) work on the world.

◆

Turn back to the Getty *Still Life*. Where is the blue-and-black fabric put? What kinds of tangibility or intangibility does it possess? (Is it a carpet or a curtain? Does the painting expect us to care?) How is the fabric folded? In Dante's terms – in terms of European painting, which Dante's metaphor sums up so triumphantly – is it folded at all? Is it real? Is it 'material'? (I love, by the way, the fact that the English language uses the word 'material' to indicate, abstractly, a whole ontological state, but also, humbly and practically, a kind of textile. The blue-and-black drape is certainly material in the second sense; it's the weight we should give the first sense that remains in doubt.)

These questions, to repeat, were on my mind from almost the beginning; but after two weeks or so they began to crystallize. I have lost hold of the precise sequence of events here, but at some point in late January, thinking about the blue material's proximity and remoteness, a great nineteenth-century rumination on the subject came to the surface. It was from Marx, in Chapter 1 of *Capital*, where Marx is struggling to characterize the 'being-for-us' of the new world of mass-produced commodities and suddenly reaches for a spatial metaphor. Typically, this involves him reaching for Shakespeare. He remembers the lines in the bawdy house in *Henry IV, Part 1*, where Falstaff is jabbing obscenely at the woman who runs the house, Mistress Quickly, and says: 'Why, she's neither fish nor flesh; a man knows not where to have her.' And she replies: 'Thou art an unjust man in saying so: thou or any man knows where to have me.'

Marx, I noted (not quite accurately) on 25 January, says that 'the reality of the value of commodities differs in this respect from Dame Quickly, that we don't know "where to have it".' And I thought I remembered him also saying – this seemed relevant to the blue material's power but impalpability – that whatever the nature of the value a thing now had in our world of commodities, it had nothing to do with the facts of its *matter*. So I took down the sacred text from the shelves, and here was the famous passage:

> Commodities come into the world in the shape of use values, articles, or goods, such as iron, linen, corn, etc. [It is good that one of the items is a textile.] This is their plain, homely, bodily form... They manifest themselves... as commodities [however], or have the form of commodities, only in so far as they have two forms, a physical or natural form, and a value-form.
>
> The reality of the value of commodities differs in this respect from Dame Quickly, that we don't know 'where to have it'. The value of commodities is the very opposite of the coarse materiality of their substance, not an atom of matter enters into its composition. Turn and examine a single commodity, by itself, as we will, [Could we even say, 'Fold and examine it'?] yet in so far as it remains an object of value, it seems impossible to grasp it.[18]

I shall refrain from too much commentary. But two things, when I read the paragraphs in full, connected for me with Cézanne's vision – with Cézanne's sense of the new form of the object-world. First, the way Marx happens immediately on a spatial and sexual metaphor to describe it. And second, that Marx is certain that we have to do with the coming-into-being not just of a set of values or monetary labels attached to essentially the same world of things, but with these things taking on a new *reality* for us. The German is even more emphatic. It rings changes on 'Gegenstand' and 'Warenkörper' and 'Naturstoff' that Moore and Aveling's heroic translation cannot really manage. In the sentence following the ones just quoted Marx says of commodities that their value is 'a purely social reality, and… they acquire this reality only in so far as they are expressions or embodiments of one identical social substance, human labour.' Again the German can insist on the arrival of a true new identity, an ungraspable 'all-one-thingness', as the English cannot – 'Ausdrücke derselben gesellschaftlichen Einheit'.

I love the fact (which I stumbled on a day or so later) that when Rilke saw the Getty *Still Life* for the first time in Prague in 1907 he straightaway described it, in a letter on the train back to Breslau, as the one with a blue coverlet, coloured a 'bürgerlichen Baumwollblau': a 'bourgeois blue-cotton blue'.[19] Rilke registered immediately, that is to say – matter-of-factly – the belonging of Cézanne's material to a specific class world.

◆

Marx and Rilke were edging me towards a 'social' view of matter and space – of nearness and 'not knowing where to have it' – in Cézanne. But weren't they beckoning me in a too comfortable, too predictable, direction? Isn't there a side to Cézanne's materialism that *disdains* the social – that looks through the sugar bowl or the bourgeois-blue to something in our experience, some form of being, some 'thing in itself', that shrugs off the very idea of the human? Certain writers have thought so. In the same set of days that Marx and Rilke occurred, I remembered a phrase from letters Samuel Beckett had written in the 1930s to his friend Thomas McGreevy, under the shock of seeing Cézanne's *Montagne Sainte-Victoire* landscapes for the first time. I remembered him snarling at a previous tradition of landscape painting which it's clear that he saw, with all the Irishman's hatred of the great estate, as essentially sharing the attitudes of the landscape gardener – his phrase is 'the Reliability Joneses'. Landscape in Cézanne, he thought, had escaped at last from such lordly subjectivity. It had nothing to do with us: it was an 'unapproachably alien, unintelligible arrangement of atoms'.[20] I quote a letter from 1934:

> What a relief the Mont Sainte Victoire after all the anthropomorphized landscape… after all the landscape 'promoted' to the emotions of the hiker, postulated as *concerned* with the hiker (what an impertinence, worse than Aesop and the animals), alive

> the way a lap or a fist is alive… [Cézanne] seems to have been the first to see landscape and state it as material of a strictly peculiar order, incommensurable with all human expressions whatsoever. Atomistic landscape with no velleities of vitalism, landscape with personality, but personality in its own terms, not in Pelman's *landscapality*.[21]

Again, there is too much to comment on; but let me concentrate on the last sentence, and particularly the last two words. 'Pelman's *landscapality*' is a notion – a Beckett joke – that is probably lost on most readers, because it has to do with an early-twentieth-century regime of mind improvement, called after its main proponent Christopher Pelman. The regime promised to cure a range of mental problems, including forgetfulness, depression, phobia, procrastination and lack of system – in other words, everything in life that Beckett thought made life bearable. Pelman's method is a thing of the past, thank God; but it happens that I experienced its death throes as a child, in a parlour game of the 1950s called Pelmanism.

It was a game of still life. Objects were arranged secretly on a tray, then brought in and shown to competitors for a minute, no more. Then immediately players had to set down their recollection of as many items on the tray as they could. The key to success in the game, needless to say, was not to look at any one item on the tray *for itself* – to subsume it immediately into its mental category (a clock, a bottle, a pear, a skull), to arrange it in a pure transparency of the known, the recognized, the instance-of-a-concept. Beckett's contemptuous word 'landscapality' has, as I've suggested, the 'capability' of Capability Brown in the background; but it also means, à la Pelmanism, a set of things already – indelibly – composed, *knowable*, because 'seen under a description'.

Could we adapt Beckett's words to still life? Well, partly. A great Cézanne still life, like the one in the Getty, can look, at least momentarily – I shall adapt Beckett's terms – like an 'atomistic object world with no velleities of vitalism [lending it a specious animation], an object world that possesses personality, for certain, but personality entirely stated in its own incommensurable terms, having nothing to do with Pelman's *still-life-icality*'. *Still-life-icality*, we might say – trying to put into words the vision of still life

Cézanne's was out to annihilate – is the picture of an object-world entirely humble and familiar, but dignified by a kind of *im*personality which, alas, had become as much of a fine art cliché as 'sturdy commonplaceness' or 'peasant simplicity of form'. There had been a time, even Beckett would have recognized, when such a mixture of qualities had made still life great. I think of Chardin, as Cézanne did. But that time was long gone.

I am aware, of course – just as much as Beckett was – that for many of Cézanne's admirers it is just this mixture, of ordinariness and impersonality, that remains the key to these paintings' power. The humble and colossal. 'If these apples should fall…' But I am with Beckett in seeing something being done to the landscape or still-life objects in Cézanne – some displacement, some new kind of spatiality – that makes neither of the Pissarro adjectives apply.

◆

7 February: There is a further famous statement on landscape and subjectivity that I cannot help thinking of in connection with Beckett. It is something that the poet Joaquim Gasquet has Cézanne saying in one of their conversations (something I'm sure he did not say), and that was taken up in simplified form by the philosopher Merleau-Ponty. 'The landscape thinks itself in me.' 'Le paysage se pense en moi.'[22] I imagine Beckett coming across the quote in December 1945 in the little magazine *Fontaine* – this was where Merleau-Ponty's essay on Cézanne first saw the light of day – and choking on his gruel. 'The landscape thinks itself in me! Hiker's sentimentality! The landscape un-thinks me in *it*.'

◆

I believe, in a word, that any real account of Cézanne's still lifes ought to operate in the territory between Beckett's apprehension – his wild inhuman materialism, his sense of these things' ultimate remoteness from us and our wishes – and Marx's.

Return to the passage from *Capital*. Are we becoming (Pelman-like) too familiar with *Still Life with Apples'* unfamiliarity? Perhaps we should try to retrieve, with Marx's help, a sense – the Cézanne sense – of being stranded between some kind of simplicity and objectivity proper to the world of still life and something we can't get hold of and can't put a name to. Would it jolt things back towards the uncanny to put *Still Life with Apples* next to a painting that was clearly in some sense its prototype: the *Still Life with Commode* in Munich – done probably in the late 1880s (FIG. 43)? How would Marx have responded to the two? (It is, by the way, entirely regrettable that when the English language talks about the new form of the object-world, the word it uses is, or has become, technical: 'commodity'. The word Marx had at his disposal was more ordinary: 'Der Ware'. What a pity that the word 'ware', which has a good robust life in older English – 'Said the pie man to Simple Simon/Won't you taste my wares?' – did not seem quite alive enough in 1887 for Moore and Aveling to choose it! If we had been thinking about 'the fetishism of wares' for a century, and not the fetishism of commodities, I feel our thinking would have gone better.)

The world of objects in the nineteenth century, Marx proposes, and the new place we occupy in relation to them, has two essential characteristics. First, our objects have in some sense *become* our world: they seem imbued with a special power, a vitality, an animation, a humanness: they are more and more the forms of our desires, the way we think and feel our very being-with-others. (The Romantic feeling for landscape seems to have pioneered this new intensity, but the animism soon spread.) Beckett may have hated what happened to our picture of matter and selfhood as a result, but his was a voice crying in the wilderness. The second footnote in *Capital* is from a seventeenth-century English writer called Nicholas Barbon, a debating partner of John Locke, who states: 'Desire implies want, it is an appetite of the mind, and as natural as hunger to the body... The greatest number (of things) have their value from supplying the wants of the mind.'[23] This line of thought in Marx culminates in the great formula that anchors the end of *Capital* Chapter 1: '[In the world of commodities as we know it] it is a definite social relation between men that assumes, in their eyes, the fantastic form of a relation between things... [And as in religion] the productions of the human brain appear as independent beings, endowed with life, and entering into relation both with one another and the human race.'[24]

This is the first strand in Marx's phenomenology: a picture of the power, the seeming self-sufficiency, the false (or at least, paradoxical) autonomy of the wares we have invested with social 'life'. But the strand is entwined with another, which is just as insistent in *Capital*'s opening pages: the assertion that we live now in a world of objects – and we *know*, we sense that we do – whose reality for us, whose value and vividness, is fictive. It is a matter of representation, this new world, of purely symbolic exchange – not of use, not of touch, not of contact and manipulation. The power of our objects no longer depends on their here-and-now alteration of circumstance or satisfaction of need. And this is the enigma that shapes our looking and feeling: our objects have never been more ours, the essential, apparently living instruments of our purposes, but – here are the phrases again – we 'know not where to have them', 'they seem impossible to grasp', 'not an atom of matter enters into [the new things'] composition'.

No doubt the last phrase in particular, the 'not an atom of matter enters into their composition', must seem wrong – forced – as we move closer to the objects in Cézanne. The vividness and immediacy are *there*. But isn't what a Cézanne suggests to us most powerfully precisely the idea that vividness and immediacy may be one thing, but material existence – 'Naturstoff, Warenkörper' – another? Cézanne was convinced, and his paintings convince us, that colour and contour – the being of things in the eye – do offer us the best, the only real, picture of things-as-they-are. But is this because they give access to objects' *materiality*? Or to the objects' being-for-us *as representation* – as entities that are the more real for us *because* they 'seem impossible to grasp'?

I don't think that Marx believed such questions about the reality of the object-world arrived for the first time with industrial capitalism – remember the quote from Nicholas Barbon. But he thought that the paradoxes had been sharpened; he thought the kind of double identity of objects just outlined had come to define a 'world'. And with that came a special pathos, a dislocation – a nowhere-ness. It is this that Rilke and Lecomte sensed in Cézanne.

◆

9 February: If we wanted a painting to sum up the human world that accompanies Rilke's 'bürgerlichen Baumwollblau', then the best candidate seems to me *Woman in Blue* in the Hermitage in St Petersburg (FIG. 44).

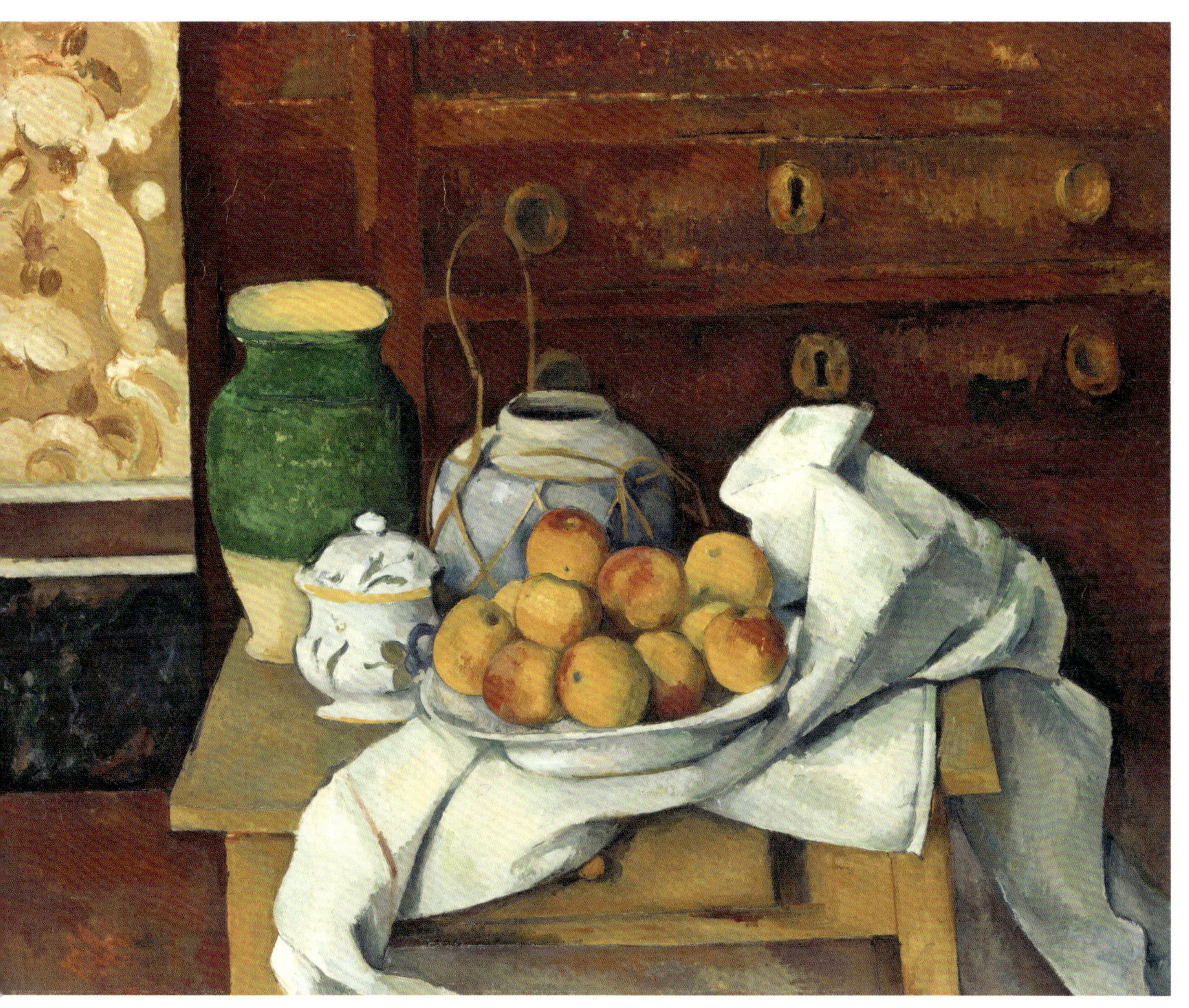

43. *Still Life with Commode*, c. 1886–88, 71.5 × 90 cm (28¾ × 36½ in.).
Bayerische Staatsgemäldesammlungen, Munich.

Once upon a time, writers on modern art spent pages expatiating on, and mostly disapproving of, the expressionlessness of portraits like this one – their lack of humanity. Perhaps it is our increasing (absolute) distance from bourgeois society that has changed things: anyway, these judgments now seem obtuse. *Woman in Blue*, as I stand in front of it, could hardly be fuller of affect, of social pain; and in it 'bürgerlich' blue is expounded as a social condition – blue as armour, as respectability, as stiffness and constraint, as inwardness… the whole sad heroism of modern life, of which Woman was the Don Quixote.

◆

Back to *Still Life with Apples*. What I have presented so far – the idea of there being a 'blue material' group of paintings, and the suggestion that Beckett's and Marx's thinking about proximity and remoteness in our relation to objects might help us get a handle on the group's concerns – is a framework for looking, not a key to the mysteries. It will have earned its keep if it suggests further, more detailed questions, aimed at the Getty painting's specific form. What kind of pattern, again, does Cézanne pursue, or devise, in the blue material? What sort of balance between animation and cold uniformity? And how does that balance shift from picture to picture in the wider group? Thinking again of the passage from *Paradiso*, I refocus the question at its heart: Does the material in *Still Life with Apples* have 'folds'? Does it open itself to light and darkness? Does light touch it? Or does it stand somehow in a different order of being – a different atmosphere – from the *lit* world of the ginger jar or the apples or even the crystalline back wall? How does Cézanne handle the contact between the blue-and-black material and his other props? I began, you remember, by noticing the two apples nestling in the carpet's folds. But I thought that the zone of contact between apples and fabric was, when one looked at it closely, peculiar. The way the shadow cast by one of the apples became a line in (or across) the fabric seized my attention. Is this kind of incident typical? How do we perceive, for instance, the resting – or is it floating? – of the little sugar bowl in the blue? How do we understand the being-in-space of the blue material when it appears finally – its facets as abstract as machine parts – bottom right?

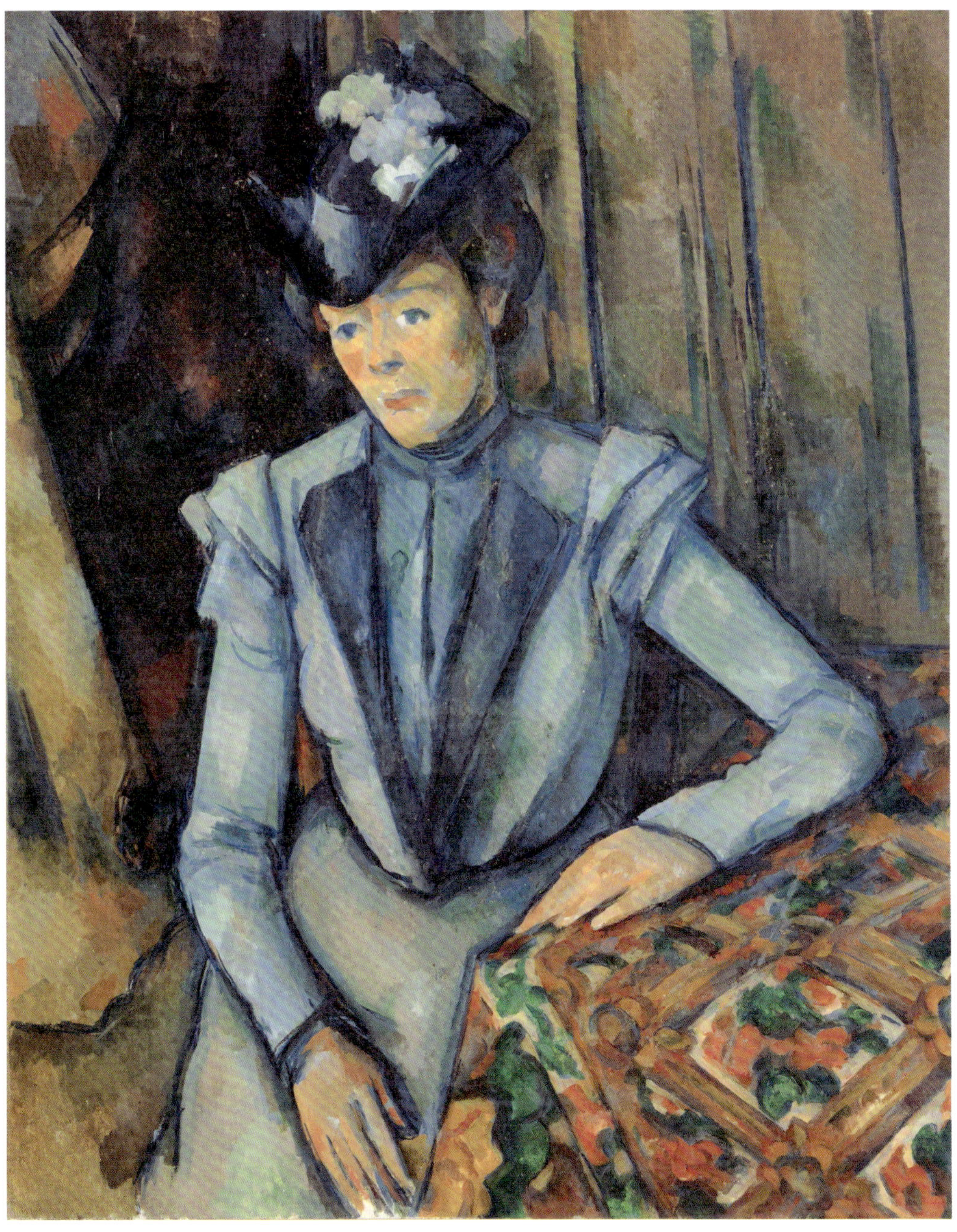

44. *Woman in Blue*, c. 1904, 88.5 × 72 cm (34⅞ × 28⅜ in.). Hermitage Museum, St Petersburg.

These are all questions, remembering Dante, about whether or not the blue material makes a 'world'. If so, and we even recognize ourselves in it, then a world of what kind?

Ask the same questions of the Pola Corporation *Sugar Bowl, Pears and Tablecloth* – it seems to me to push the logic of the Getty painting a few stops further. Obviously Cézanne values the objects he paints as familiars, solids that are part of a form of life he knows well, things imprinted with '*usages*' – this last is a term of value that crops up in his letters. But he is ruthless in disposing them – in the Pola *Sugar Bowl*, almost disposing *of* them – so that they end up no longer quite themselves. Already in the Getty picture the plate does not hold the apples, the green jar is eternally empty, the savour of ginger or sugar (or even rum!) is irrelevant to the shapes we are offered of their containers, and the apples are concentrations of colour and roundness, not taste – roundness on a roll, spheres tumbling through space. I would say that the Pola *Sugar Bowl* does no more than recognize – dramatize – this basic unfamiliarity. Look at the upright red pear closest to us in the painting, stretching and preening itself in front of the yellow. Or the two-dimensional lemon, bottom right, full stop. Or the uncanny 'non-pear non-apple' that forms the top right corner of the painting's blue drape, wedged far back in space, resting *where* on the table? – somewhere 'impossible to grasp'.

I am not for a moment denying that the beauty and lucidity of *Sugar Bowl*'s overall space puts such local paradoxes to sleep. But the lucidity is made out of the paradoxes. The table and wall are imprinted with nowhere-ness. The strange patch of dry brown hatchings just right of centre, forming a kind of hinge between wall and table, is nowhere-ness personified. It is the partner of the 'non-apple non-pear' to the left.

◆

We cannot solve the problem by declaring that *Sugar Bowl*'s strangeness makes it an outlier. Remember the foreground of the Courtauld *Plaster Cupid* (FIG. 41). Or look again at *Jug and Fruit on a Table* (FIG. 40). What happens to the back edge of the tabletop as it heads toward the grey pitcher? It is as if a carpenter had carefully sawed into it at forty-five degrees. Where does the blue drape go once it emerges on the pitcher's right side?

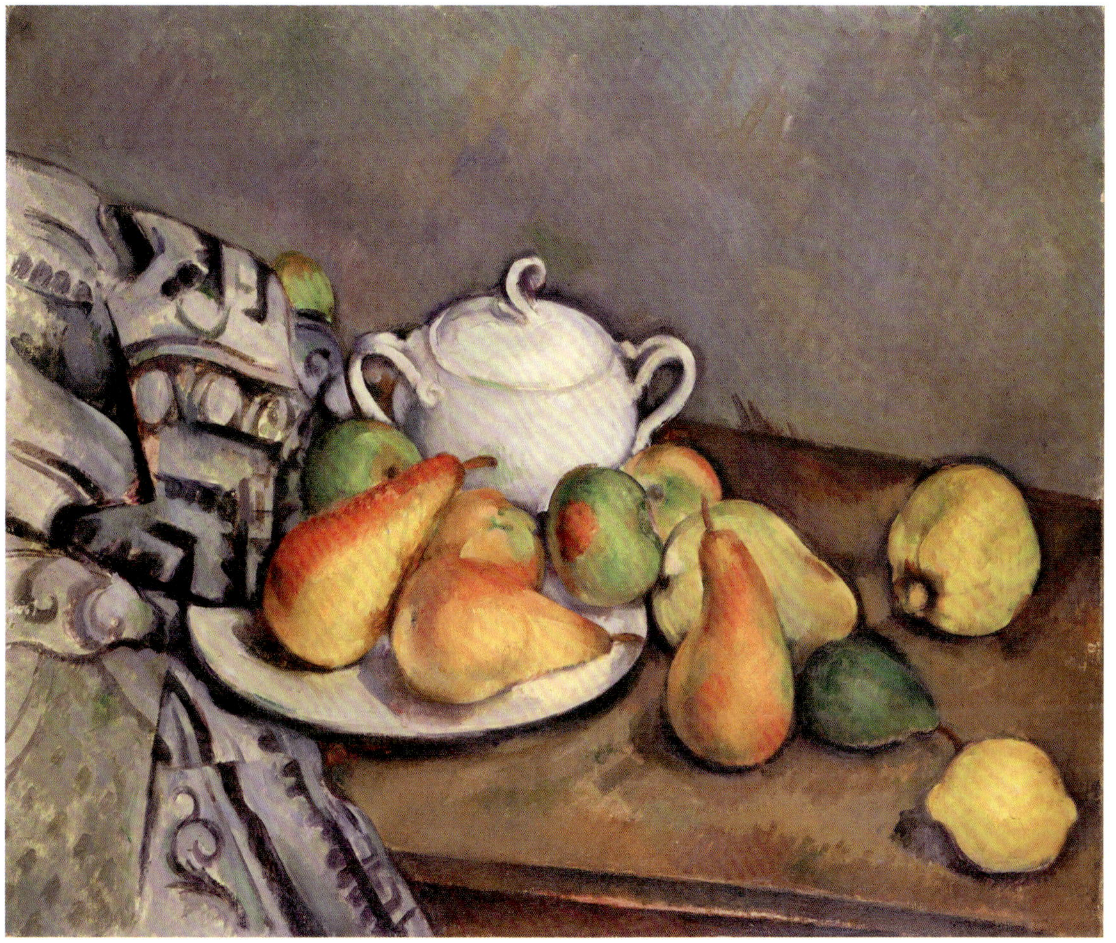

45. *Sugar Bowl, Pears and Tablecloth*, c. 1893–95, 51 × 62 cm (20⅛ × 24⅜ in.). Pola Museum of Art, Kanagawa, Japan.

It seems to twist and disappear into a void; and the void's top edge is again sharp-ruled as if by a T-square. The black of the void devours a lemon in its folds. Where on earth is the far plate of apples standing – the one behind the pitcher's neck and handle? The shape of the tabletop that the painting actually allows us – of course we know it must be rectangular, but knowledge is at war with perception – is a wonderful six-sided non sequitur.

Well, yes… vision is like this. Seeing is patchwork (*taches*) – in tension all the time with inattention and a priori. What is unique to Cézanne (here

I follow the lead of all his best critics) is the willingness to have space and solidity emerge *from* the patchwork – as they do even here, the pitcher shouldering the paradoxes aside.

Is it 'even here' or especially here? Is it 'the more flagrant the impossibilities, the firmer the whole reality'?

◆

16 February: Let me end by trying to counter an objection to the notebook's (the chapter's) whole means of approach – and indeed to the method of the book. Doesn't the Beckett-Marx-Rilke-*Black Clock*-'object-world' frame of reference I've been building simply operate at too high a level to capture what matters in Cézanne? Doesn't it leave too much out? Doesn't it look past the sheer doggedness and brilliance of Cézanne's *seeing*?

I don't think it needs to. Speaking generally about criticism for a moment, it seems to me that we have no choice, if we want truly to describe a complex object, but to move between two sorts of concern. Imagine we are talking of a poet of Cézanne's time – an Emily Dickinson, say, or a Stephane Mallarmé. The questions that crowd in immediately are obvious. What is the material this poet works with? What's her language, what's her diction? What is her attitude to rhyme, or verbal music, or assonance and dissonance, or difficult metres? What does she attend to at the level of making – of craft? But surely these questions cannot ever be disentangled from others just as immediate. What does Dickinson or Mallarmé *make* with the material? What world is it that emerges from the work done? What aspects of experience does this particular verbal music seem to be intending – discriminating, materializing? Does this poetic world have a character? Can we describe it overall? Can we relate the character to other accounts of the world which the poets may have been interested in, or simply had as a shared cultural inheritance? Dickinson in relation to a dying Christianity, or Mallarmé as embodying the fragile residual optimism of 'art for art's sake'.

Something like this is what I have been trying for in Cézanne's case. And always in the hope that framing a better answer to questions of the second type will not displace those of the first, which do in some sense have priority; but rather, will sharpen the questions, refocus them, letting the critic see the material (the verbal music, the handling of colour, the prominence of a kind of hatching) more precisely – because the intentionality of the material has become clearer.

◆

Early March: one last example. To the right of the little sugar bowl in *Still Life with Apples* (FRONTISPIECE) is a vivid, decisive green-grey mark, nearly vertical but tilted left to right, thickly painted and by the look of it put down very late in the day, as the picture neared the finish. The mark seals the right edge of the sugar bowl – that is especially the case when the mark is seen from a normal viewing distance. Notice that the green-grey is placed next to a parallel darker stroke of paint which is, we realize after a moment's hesitation, part of the sugar bowl's leaf-and-flower decoration. The green-grey mark, as I see it, is entirely necessary to the sugar bowl's three-dimensionality. But does it belong to the sugar bowl? Is it somehow a further glimpse of the bowl's white porcelain in shadow? In what sense is it 'material' at all? Where is it? What is it?

The same kind of questions occur everywhere. Look at the lid of the sugar bowl, for example – at what happens to its yellow rim.

Never, we may feel, looking at passages of this kind, has the presence of matter been registered with more vividness by a painter. But vividness is one thing, knowledge another. Cézanne's kind of vividness is inseparable from not-knowing – the vividness seems to be what *produces* the not-knowing. What *is* matter, the vividness asks, as the eye actually takes possession of it? Is it something tangible, or impalpable? Does matter as we see it – as we experience it in present circumstances – possess a location? Is it – could it be – our property? Or does the act of possession go in the opposite direction?

These are Cézanne-type questions. Right at the end of his life, writing to his son Paul, the old artist retreated in a letter to what looks like a final bedrock commitment. 'Les sensations faisant le fond de mon affaire, je crois être impénétrable.' 'Sensations forming the basis of my affair, I believe I'm impenetrable.'[25] It is a beautiful sentence. And when we ask in general what Cézanne thought sensations were, and what they were *of* – empirically, spatially, ontologically – 'impenetrable' seems right.

3. Cézanne and the Outside World

Nature, I wanted to copy it, I didn't get there.

Cézanne to Maurice Denis, 1906[1]

The word 'materialist' as applied to painting need not mean anything very deep. Painting has always prided itself on being, next to sculpture, the most object-oriented of the arts. A brushy surface is supposed to put the viewer directly in touch with things. Colour comes out of a tube into the eye. Most pictures seem happy with their gold frames. Even those painters (like Ingres or Mondrian) who wished to defeat the medium's dumb objectivity took it for granted that the quality was basic and stubborn, and could only very gradually be turned against itself. The gradualness – the slow cunning with surface and framing – is a large part of what makes their idealism interesting.

Cézanne is a special case. The words 'materialism' or even 'positivism' come up in connection with him – they came up from the beginning – but most often shadowed by a sense that his art exemplifies, perhaps even worsens, the slipperiness of both terms.

The question, put baldly, is this: Does the intensity of the *mark* in Cézanne – the special vividness of his colour, the salience and decisiveness of each touch of paint – derive from the mark's other-directedness, its search for the equivalent of something sensed, some message from the outside world, or from an altogether different (maybe contrary) logic, having to do with the brush mark's brute existence, its materiality, and its place in a process of manufacture? (Why do we think pictures are a different kind of thing from tools or necklaces or chiming clocks? Even 'touch' in the sentence before last may be smuggling in too much animation. Remember Beckett's 'incommensurable with all human expressions whatsoever'.)

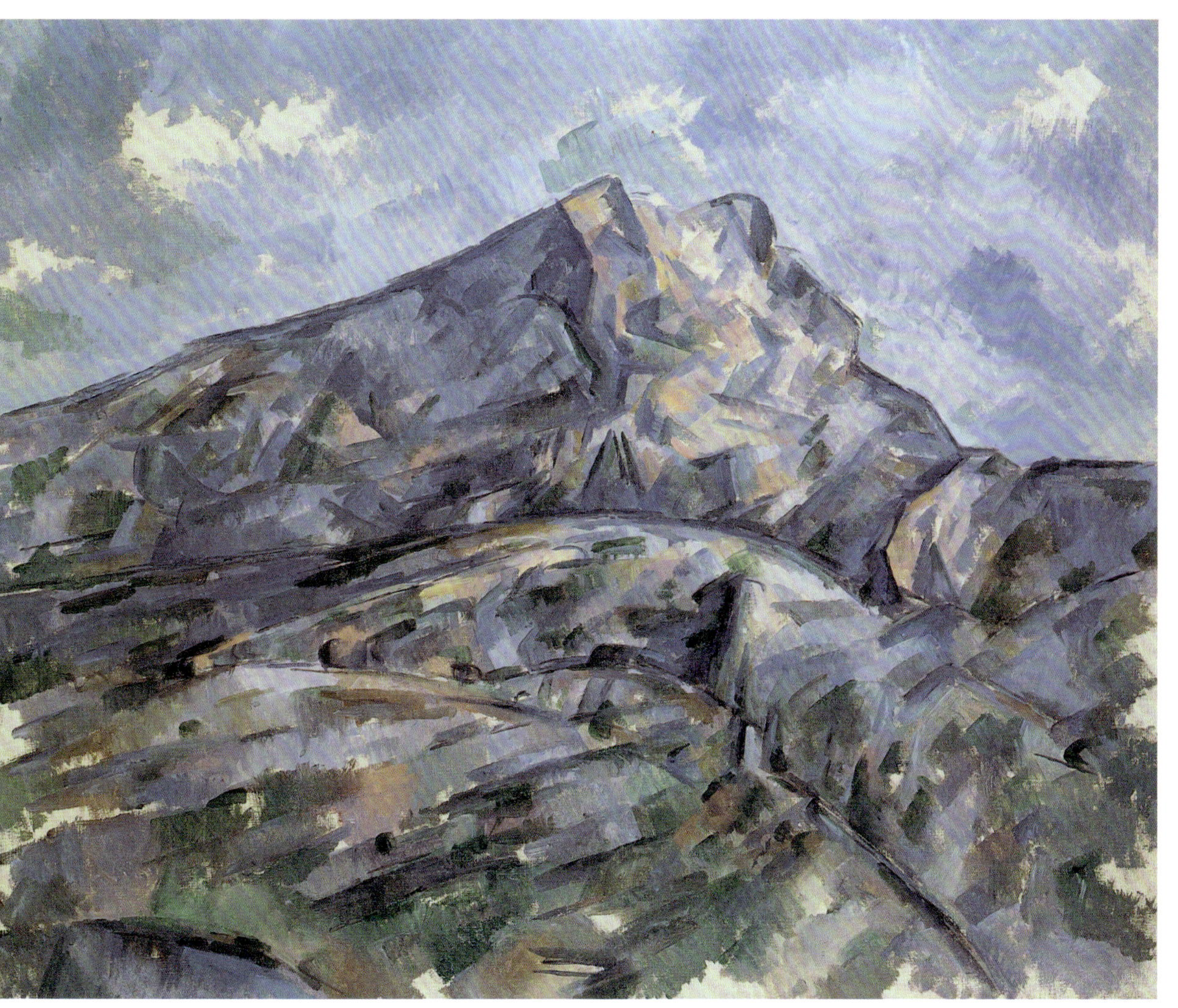

46. *Montagne Sainte-Victoire seen from Château Noir*, *c.* 1900–4, 65 × 80 cm (25⅝ × 31⅝ in.). Private Collection.

The normal answer to the first question just posed, whether asked of painting in general or Cézanne in particular, is to deny that the choice is either/or. The search for sensation and the mark's stubborn materiality aren't alternatives, we are told, but facets – moments – of one another. Well, perhaps they are. But perhaps not.[2] Perhaps Cézanne's art entertains the suspicion that they aren't; and therefore struggles against the recognition – almost, one might say, the temptation – of the mark's 'speaking to nothing' fundamentally... the mark as a cancellation of sense. It may be that Cézanne's unique vividness comes from the cancellation.

Behind this train of thought (and I believe it one provoked by Cézanne's painting, not imposed upon it) lies a more pervasive worry. For a point of view on the world to count as materialist, how ruthless is it obliged to be? In particular, how far down does it have to go in dismantling the idea – the assumption – of a knowing (experiencing) subject?

We have a sense of ourselves as implanted in a world – reaching out to it, orienting ourselves to it, having it come (or not come) to where we are. That seems indelible. The 'this-thereness' of things will never go away. But what is it, asks the materialist, that produces this picture of the world in the first place? Supposing (here is the sceptic's suggestion) that the 'this-thereness' were nothing but an effect of purely material processes, whose being – whose whole character – is deeply hidden from us, but which nonetheless *do 'take us over' at certain moments, displacing the self-evidence of the world*... whenever (rarely) we try to bring 'this-thereness' into the light, and paint (inscribe, dance, sing, give form to) the sheer fact of existence.

The multiplication of italics and quotation marks in the last few lines speaks to the fact that language is under strain when we go with the sceptic even a little way – that we are pressing towards a picture of experience that our language is unwilling to countenance. But that does not mean the picture is foreign *to* experience. Experience 'happens upon' the picture all the time – it bumps up against it. And the picture can possess a horrible vividness, however momentarily it flashes into life – however efficiently we repress it. *Cézanne* makes it vivid, some say.

◆

Let me concentrate on the canvas *Montagne Sainte-Victoire seen from Château Noir*, which for decades belonged to the Ford House Museum in Michigan (FIGS 46 & 48). The painting was probably done in Cézanne's old age – maybe as late as 1904. Most of the things I shall say about it are true only if lighting conditions are good. In most reproductions the picture's blues are too glossy, or else too greyed and sullen. But given steady north daylight (here I am guessing), or under a reasonably sympathetic mixture of tungsten and neon (which is how the picture was shown to me some years ago[3]), colour and texture, and colour and stroke-size, work on each other to aerate – almost levitate – the whole thing. The blues are translucent, floating into and over the answering parallelograms of green. The mountain looks crystalline, made of a substance not quite opaque, not quite diaphanous; natural, obviously, but having many of the characteristics – the crumpled look, the piecemeal unevenness – of an object put together by hand.

Colour is crucial to this effect, and deeply perplexing. There is a balance of greyed (though often semi-transparent) blues, strong greens, pinks, light opaque ochres. The stroke is a choppy, unlovely, inch-to-two-inch rhythm of wedges, hooks and scrubbed squares. It looks almost as if Cézanne were deliberately avoiding the smaller-scale dabs and curlicues of his classic pictures of Montagne Sainte-Victoire – the one in the Phillips collection, for example, or the Baltimore Museum quarry face with the mountain looming above (FIGS 47 & 54) – and trying for a crispness and angularity of touch carried over from certain aspects of his watercolours. Carried over but also broadened, flattened – I would almost say, brutalized.

Greens flood the foreground. The further away from the picture one stands the more the greens come into their own – because there the middle range of blues can be seen to rest and feed on them, drawing up patch after patch of the wind-blown, slightly unstable colour into its steel mesh. A lot of the greens were put on late, over the blues and greys, as if recoiling from their implacability.

Over the left peak of the mountain sits a small green 'cloud', with even a half-hidden scratching of red in the middle of it. What the cloud seems to do, visually, is pull the mountain back closer to the picture surface. If you screen it out, the green foreground and mid-ground loom suddenly too large and too close, and the final escarpment goes deep into distance. The cloud lightens the mountain and does not allow the dark left slope to predominate. Part of the reason most reproductions overdo the picture's sobriety is because they do not give the green cloud its due. In the flesh it's hard to keep your eyes off it.

Yet the picture's colour overall is inhuman: reproductions do not get it completely wrong. It is not the colour of rock or foliage, nor a blending of the two. It is crystalline, as I said – not resistant to light, not reflective or refractive. Light seems to go part the way through the blues and greens or get inertly trapped underneath them. The resulting texture is inorganic. The colour is at an infinite remove from appetite, foodstuff or flesh.

This only goes to make the bodily suggestions built into the landscape's mid-ground – in and around the foothills just before the final escarpment – all the more telling once they present themselves. And surely they do before long. The main edges and declivities of the landscape lend themselves irresistibly to physiognomic reading-in. There are limbs, buttocks, thighs, maybe breasts, a mons veneris with dark pubic hair. A languid body enjoying the sun, prone and glistening, under a plumped-up patterned coverlet. A body of cut glass or faceted flint. An aged face, eyes screwed up against the dazzle.

The philosopher Richard Wollheim was fond of pointing out that often in Cézanne access to a landscape is partly halted, or at least slowed down, by an empty strip in the foreground, echoing and strengthening the picture's bottom edge.[4] A good example would be the road in *Hillside in Provence* (FIG. 3). Wollheim, characteristically, wanted us to understand this stopping place as an invitation to moderate our eager appropriation of the world: to build a measure of distance and inaccessibility into our dealings with it, and therefore psychological poise; in the end to know it more deeply. Maybe so. But of course the point in making the comparison here (and something of a Wollheim kind could be said of the Phillips and Baltimore versions of *Montagne Sainte-Victoire*, with their incomplete foreground trees) is to have the *lack* of barrier or entry-plane in the Ford House picture register as the great fact – the loss of bearings or limits – I think it is. The segment of blue holding the picture's bottom left corner strikes me as a vestige or parody of a structure Cézanne has

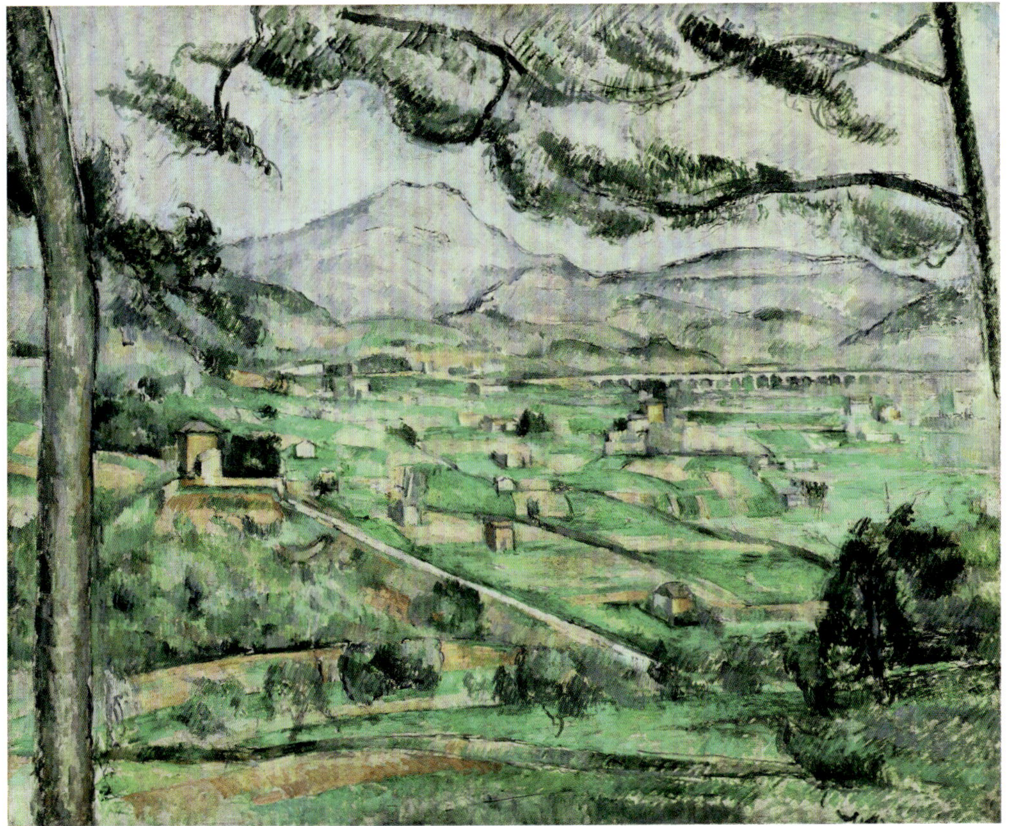

47. *Montagne Sainte-Victoire with Large Pine*, c. 1885–87, 60 × 72.5 cm (23½ × 28½ in.). Phillips Collection, Washington, D.C.

deliberately denied himself. No poise or slowness here. We go straight to the middle-ground.

That is, straight to the impossible object: the non-human, physiognomically teeming surface 'out there', not remote but not nearby. Somewhere a viewer cannot quite place. The painting is naive (but also humane and understanding) about our wish to have that middle distance be *our* world, invested with shapes we half-recognize. Everything is metaphor in it. Mountains are excuses for bodies. But equally, the picture is certain that painting can put a stop to fantasy (to the Unconscious's endless reading-in and gobbling up and multiplication of part-objects) by the sheer singularity of its colour and texture. They will make the mountain a mountain again – put it at a determinate distance. Make it an object whose whole

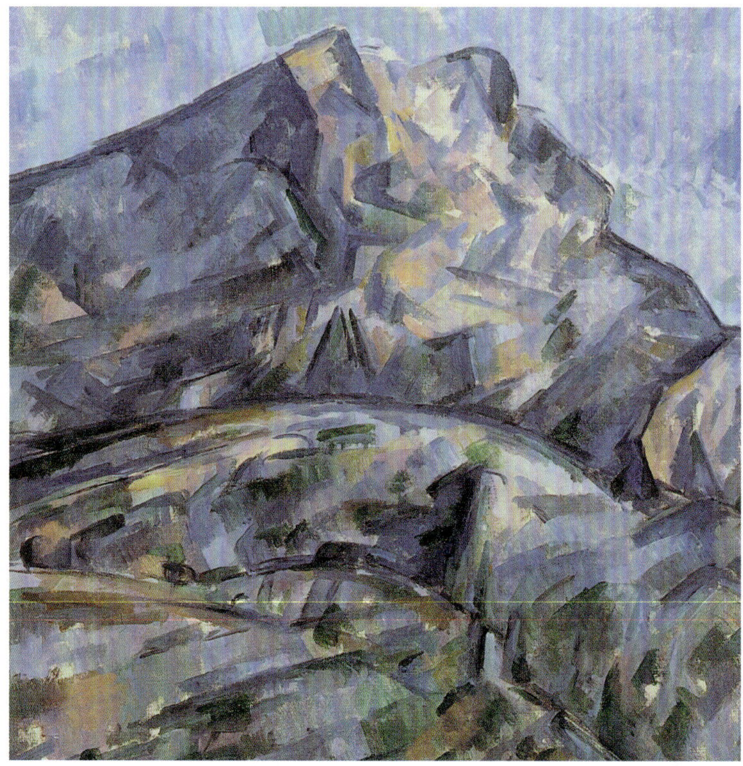

48. Detail from Fig. 46: *Montagne Sainte-Victoire seen from Château Noir*, c. 1900–4. Private Collection.

structure and materiality, as opposed to mere accidents of surface, will have nothing to do with us and our script.

This is quintessential Cézanne, I believe: no doubt harder and fiercer than usual in the Ford House picture, but with a ferocity and hardness that are always waiting in the wings of the graver, more elaborate structures in other paintings, ready to transfigure them. (The trees in front of the Baltimore quarry face, for instance, do not ultimately put up much of a fight against the attractions of the rock wall beyond them: in terms of touch and substance, they are sucked into the general firestorm of yellows.) We are treated in the Ford House picture to the spectacle of two kinds of understanding of the material world confronting each other nakedly, with no other mediation than the painter's will.

What makes this particular *Montagne Sainte-Victoire* a touchstone, then, is the way its vision of nature is both among the most openly, naively physiognomic Cézanne ever did, and at the same time the most remote and indifferent to human wishes. The least habitable, the most anthropomorphized. The most like a body, the least like an organism. Dreamlike and machinelike. The two contrary qualities depend on one another, I think: there could not have been such a free flow of desire and analogy if it had not taken place in such an artificial, unplaceable medium – if the landscape body had not looked as though it were made from folded cardboard or hammered tinfoil.

Hence the picture's strange wedges and right angles and jostling quadrilaterals. Even to call them 'handling' is to miss Cézanne's point: they seem to issue from a pattern book, or a slightly clumsy programme or mechanism. No doubt at a distance they are taken up into the rustling, ascending turbulence of the mountainside and are roughly translatable into rocks and trees; but even as they do, they never stop marking that ascension as a contrivance, assembled from disparate parts. A landscape is not an organism, the marks say: the way our mind and eyesight put together the pieces of a mineral and vegetable world, and make a scene of them, is not, or need not be, analogous to the way a particular organism's parts are arranged and counterpoised – even if (and this too the painting is full of) landscape painting usually thrives on the idea that it is.

I do not mean to suggest, finally, that the painting's non-human texture and colour are utterly forbidding, or even uncanny. Those qualities would be a comfort, interpretatively speaking: they would put the mountain back into a familiar dialectic of remoteness and sublimity. But that is not where Cézanne has placed it. The non-sublime (but also non-intimate) character of his landscapes is what makes them truly unsettling. Colour in the Ford House picture, for example, has too much lightness and definiteness for it to usher in the notion of infinity. The object-world is uninhabited as opposed to infinite: no more nor less elusive to the mind, we may feel, than the blue-and-black textile in *Still Life with Apples* (FIGS 28 & 29). The rock face's colours are not even cold: they are warmed just enough by pinks and ochres. Non-human is not the same as hostile and refusing. The mountain may be a machine, but it isn't made of metal or synthetics. We try out the 'hammered tinfoil' analogy, but in the end greens and blues defeat it. Crystalline does not mean *dead*.

The further I go in describing the two vectors of Cézanne's dealing with the material world, you gather, the less sure I am about how they align with one side or the other of my original 'ourselves in a world'/'mere material processes' distinction. Certainly the mountain has a non-human, implacable, mechanical aspect to it; but that character seems to me the key to its being established by Cézanne as truly a fact *out there* – another reality, looking back at us. It doesn't reduce the mountain to a set of marks just 'here', simply something we've made or made up.

There is a kind of stand-off in the picture, to put it more strongly, between mark-making as mechanism (following paths and discovering rhythms thrown up by pure procedure) and mark-making as a kind of ineradicable anthropomorphism. Making marks 'stand for' *anything* is impossible (says the picture) unless we conceive the thing we're trying to depict as somehow human – unless we make metaphors of the mountain's features and give it a 'face'. The world (says the picture) must at root be all one substance, made out of the same stuff as ourselves. Otherwise, how could we begin to represent it? And yet there is always a counter-movement to this in the act of representation – a counter-intuition. The Ford painting is almost a lesson in, a demonstration of, the turn. For the very moment (says the picture) at which a depiction reaches out most irresistibly to the thing out there *is* that at which it mobilizes the accidents and duplicities of mark-making most flagrantly, most outlandishly – no doubt in the service of pointing through them, and somehow *with* them, to that other body which is their guarantor. No wonder we can never be sure where mere materiality ends and 'world' begins. Each thrives interminably on the other's images and procedures. An account of matter will never be rigorous enough, or vivid enough, to seal itself against the other's metaphorical pull.

◆

Right-thinking art-lovers have been taught for several decades now to hold the category 'aesthetic' in suspicion. The word is elitist. It is held to usher in a world of universals, at the opposite end of the spectrum from the concepts we need if our aim is to grasp the work of art's particularity – concepts like 'history', 'ideology' and 'production'. I understand what brought on the right-thinking suspicions in the first place, and in terms of sheer class gut-feeling I still largely share them. The word 'Bloomsbury' is my least favourite in the language. But as an approach to the problem of the aesthetic dimension or impulse in human affairs I don't think high-minded disapproval gets us very far. In particular, not far with pictures.

I need, therefore, to say briefly what is meant by the word 'aesthetic' when I use it, and why I think I have to. Let me distinguish between the aesthetic impulse and the aesthetic illusion. The former is simply the urge people feel to make the *form* of their statements and descriptions embody, immediately and aptly, the truth-claims, or content, or meaning, of the statements and descriptions in question. This impulse seems to me ineradicable and ordinary. In every production of a sentence (including even the stodgy ones I am producing now) formal elements of various kinds – intonation, assonance and dissonance, syntactical symmetries or redundancies, rhythm, timbre, pacing – play against the constative or performative sense, enforcing it, staging it, ironizing it and so on. This is a priori. It has to do with the inherence of thinking and communicating in actual, peculiar stuff, and with that stuff providing irresistible opportunities for persuasion. Form is a great persuader, we think.

In this sense, then, the aesthetic is part of life. We should give up feeling it belongs to Clive Bell. All the same, I want to keep a place for some suspicion of the category, partly because I think Cézanne may have shared it. There is such a thing as aesthetic illusion. By that I mean the belief, or working assumption, that the aim of the aesthetic impulse can be fulfilled, at least locally, once and for all: that there are moments when form embodies truth in a way unassailable to further challenges, and independent of the mere 'positionality' of speakers, describers and receivers. Philosophy has had many names for this moment, and often staked a great deal (maybe everything) on its existence. 'The sensuous [or sensory] appearance of the Idea' was Hegel's formulation. The moment of passage, in other words – of stable or stabilizable relation – between Idea and object-world, or thinking and sensory appearance.

This brings me back to the questions the chapter began with. Consider the nature of the brush mark in Cézanne. What kind of existence does it have for us (what kind did it have for Cézanne)? If it has vividness, even 'life', where or what do they derive from?

◆

We surely will never escape from the common-sense belief that signs of any sort, painted or otherwise, are part of a world we know primarily *through the senses* – a world which is always already 'experienced', made up of perceptions, intuitions, acts of consciousness; onto which the sign opens and from which it derives its ultimate substance, its actuality as visual (or audible or gestural) stuff. This whole language – this vocabulary of matter and sense – was threaded through my summary of the aesthetic case. Of course it was. For built into our very idea of the aesthetic moment is the notion of the aesthetic rescuing us from abstraction, or from mere material production of persuasions, and putting the sign back in touch with reality. The aesthetic is that moment (this is the claim) at which the materiality of the sign is grasped again and grandly played with, but precisely *as* 'phenomenal substance', as part of a world of stuffs and perceptions. It is this tourniquet of the world's substance and the sign's substance – or better still, of the texture and structure of a set of brush marks, say, and the very texture and structure of being – it is this twisting together and analogizing of *procedures* and *intuitions* that the aesthetic brings up to the surface of signifying, and lets us revel in once again.

What would it be like for art *not* to do this? Not like Cézanne, by the look of it; and maybe not like any artwork we would count as such. Nonetheless in practice the very twisting and grasping can lead artworks, on occasion, to come to suspect – and to voice or envisage the suspicion – that maybe what they are doing is not analogizing or 'realizing' at all. This suspicion is not anti-aesthetic, precisely. But it is a kind of horror, and elation, at what the work of form might be about. I sense that horror and elation in Cézanne.

No doubt the only way I can make that sentence seem less bald and ominous is by showing what I mean by it in relation to particular paintings – even particular sequences of brush marks. But before I do that, let me state again what questions seem to me worth asking of paintings in general with the category 'aesthetic' in mind. From the cluster of problems touched on, I take two. First, the notion of the aesthetic as a moment of adequacy of form to content, in which form is revealed as the necessary clothing of an intuition. And second (another way of putting the same

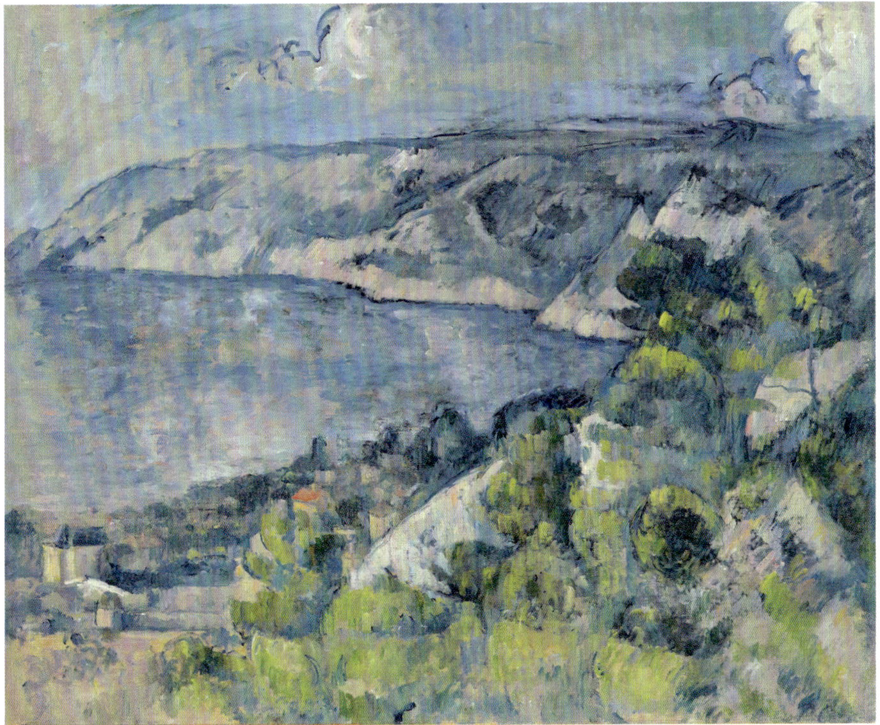

49. *The Bay of L'Estaque*, c. 1880–82, 60 × 73 cm (23½ × 28¾ in.). Philadelphia Museum of Art.

point, essentially), the notion of the aesthetic as a moment or dimension of representation in which the true sensuous *reality* of the sign is retrieved. The aesthetic – I quote a commentator on Kant's *Critique of Judgement* – 'is always based on an adequacy of the mind to its physical object, based on what is referred to... as the concrete representation of ideas – *Darstellung der Ideen*.'[5] The relation of form to content, in other words, is rooted in a relation of mind to world. The one relation analogizes the other. And the world, I've been saying, is unthinkable save as a texture and structure of phenomena, of sensate experiences.

These givens, to repeat, are built deep into the category 'aesthetic' as it comes down to us. And Cézanne's achievement has been taken to epitomize them. 'In a picture like "L'Estaque"' – here is Roger Fry in 1910, discussing a painting now in the Philadelphia Museum of Art – 'it is difficult to know whether one admires more the imaginative grasp which has built so clearly for the answering mind the splendid structure of the bay, or the intellectualized sensual power which has given to the shimmering atmosphere so definite a value.'[6] I retain from this sentence the phrases 'built so clearly for the answering mind' and 'intellectualized sensual power'. They are the aesthetic in a nutshell; and no doubt Fry meant us to catch the echo of Hegel above all in the latter.

The assumption of adequacy and totality, then, and the assumption of sensuousness, of 'imaginative grasp' – the concept 'aesthetic' is built around just these terms. Now in the case of Cézanne the first assumption has always been challengeable. Obviously there is a side to Cézanne's art that lends itself to a discourse of unfinish, disparity and inadequacy of sorts. His pictures are 'exactes parfois jusqu'au désarroi' – I quote Georges Lecomte again.[7] But the point is that excitement or bewilderment over Cézanne's 'disequilibrium' (another word that crops up in the early responses) has coexisted entirely peacefully with the structure of assumptions about the aesthetic I have outlined so far, and with our taking Cézanne to exemplify them. Disarray and inconclusiveness either function as a kind of brilliant *descant* to totality in the pictures – 'the splendid structure of the bay' and so forth – or they are taken as the form totality assumes in this modern instance. Modern experience just *is* this evenness and disequilibrium in high tension. It looks as though the notion of the aesthetic in Cézanne is only going to be open to radical reworking, then, if the second assumption is put in doubt. That is, if we start again from the (obviously uncongenial) supposition that the individual brush marks in Cézanne do *not* analogize or open onto 'sensations' or phenomena: that they posit a lack or failure of any such opening or analogy; and that they do so precisely in their material individuality as marks – their atomized facticity, their separateness.

I know these are counter-intuitive suggestions. ('Counter-intuitive' about sums it up.) And I do not want to revel in their disagreeableness. They are disagreeable, and on the face of it preposterous, because they seem to go against the qualities that critics and philosophers have always valued in Cézanne – what look like vividness and openness in his art to the least incident of seeing. Of course vividness and openness are the right terms. But I want to ask: Out of what circuit of intentions and assumptions, and intentions and assumptions defeated in practice, or altered beyond recognition (including the painter's) – out of what circuit does the vividness come? I am not saying, again to state the obvious, that Cézanne's project did not exist under the auspices of nineteenth-century positivism. Of course it did. But the question is: What did 'existing under the auspices' actually give rise to? A doubting, anxious not-quite-confirmation of positivism – of the belief that all knowledge is derived from sense-data, from experience of natural phenomena – or its doing to death in particular passages of paint?

◆

I shall ask these questions mainly of *Trees and Houses*, a painting in the Walter–Guillaume collection in the Musée de l'Orangerie in Paris, done probably in the mid-to-late 1880s (FIGS 50 & 51). It is a typical Cézanne from the period; and one main characteristic of the painting – one that Cézanne's admirers have fed on through the decades – is the appearance of steadiness and consistency of attention across the whole field. The canvas is covered by a skin of even, equal touches, as if individual sense data have been registered, punctually, patiently, one by one and assembled slowly into a scene.

Certain parts of the picture seem to want to signal, almost dramatize, this drawing-together of singular perceptions. Look at the low front wall of the houses, for example, and the odd space – half light, half dark – between the two. It is made out of upright small bricks of brown and mauve, the edges of each brick blurring into one next door, as if to suggest a dusting of undergrowth. The same upright stroke is in evidence, tilted to left and right of vertical, in the mid-ground fields or along the light brown path that cuts through them, and at place after place in the trees – sometimes believably as moss or foliage, sometimes as free-floating notation. I've no wish to deny that these kinds of marks (art historians call them 'the constructive stroke') contribute to the painting's evenness and delicacy; nor that evenness of attention is the picture's most touching quality.[8] But the regular brush marks are always on the verge – and sometimes over it – of not 'applying' to anything in particular. And they coexist with other sorts of painterly activity, which make their placid atomism look not so much tentative as flimsy.

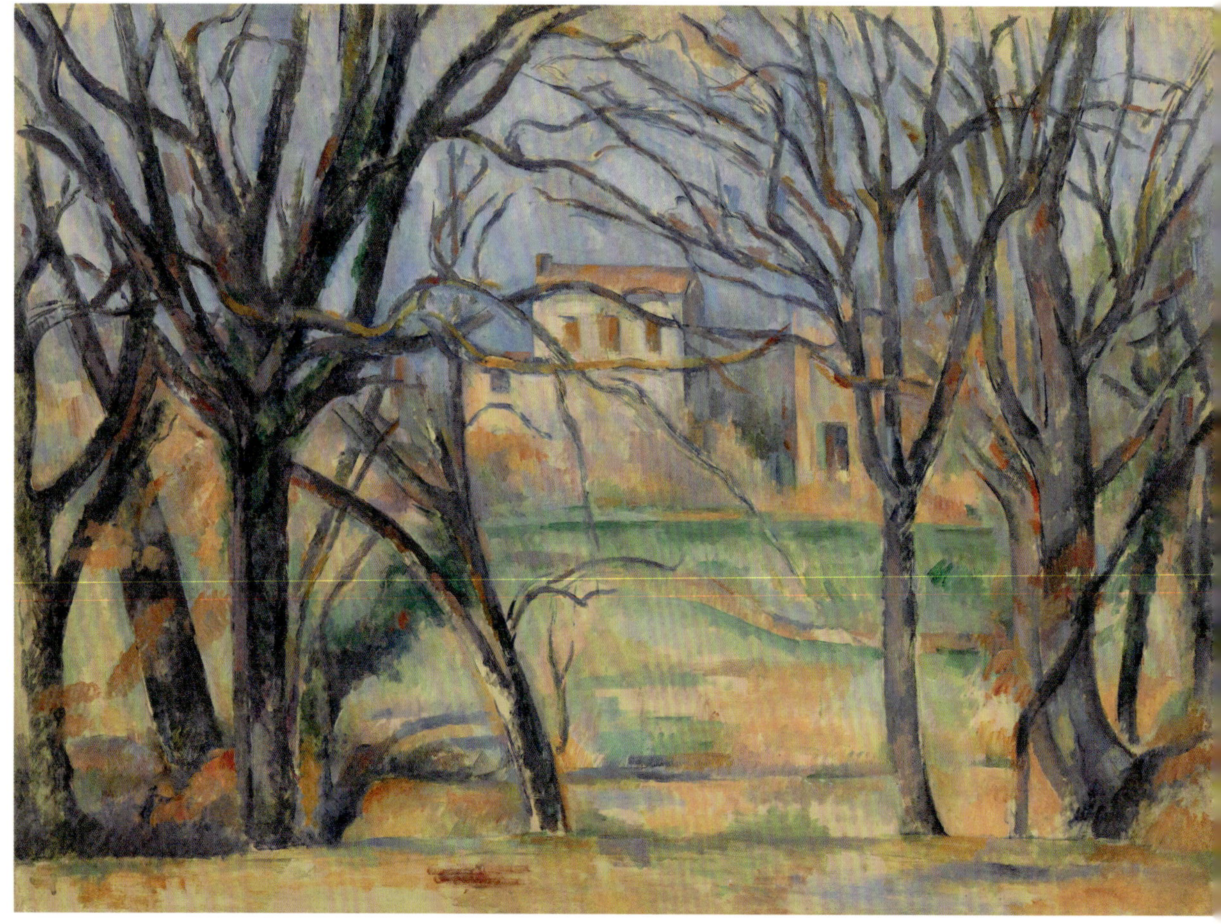

50. *Trees and Houses*, c. 1885–86, 54 × 73 cm (21¼ × 28¾ in.). Musée de l'Orangerie, Paris, Jean-Walter and Paul Guillaume Collection.

Look at the tall central house, for example, the one with the red roof. Look in particular at the marks of the brush that are meant to put together, into a single sequence on the flat, the line of the house's red eaves, the faint shadow the eaves cast and the gentle curve of a branch half-concealing them – the last seemingly in a plane parallel to the house front but much nearer to us. Then, focusing on the right-hand side of this already small area, look at the triangle of sunlit wall between the eaves and the branch, and a second branch, maybe sprouting from the other, which seems as though it must be twisting toward us and down, crossing in front of the branch it sprouts from. We have only just started. In the angle of the two branches there is an area of muted blue; it consists, when we look closer, of two broad smears of grey-blue and off-white paint, the first overlapping the thicker branch and the second apparently painted over a line of blue-violet just above it – the line we are invited to take as the twisting branch beginning. The off-white, as I say, seems to override the twisting branch; but the branch fights back. There is a final thin trace of paint – purplish, more cursive and transparent – painted in turn on top of the blue shadow. And then on the underside of the thicker branch there is another kind of paint-mark, pale orange-brown picked up from the top of the roof and applied more lightly and dryly, putting the thick branch in silhouette. And an oilier brown on the shuttered window just to the right, which half invades the blue-purple of the branch that hides its top edge. And all of this – trying now to move back from the local adjustments and see what they do to the wider pattern of branches and shutters and plaster and tile – all this ferocious involution of mark-making around the intersecting branches is constantly altering their relation to the open, more insubstantial, floating 'flats' of the other two windows at the left, and to the lighter, more discontinuous brown of the branch bisecting the house below.

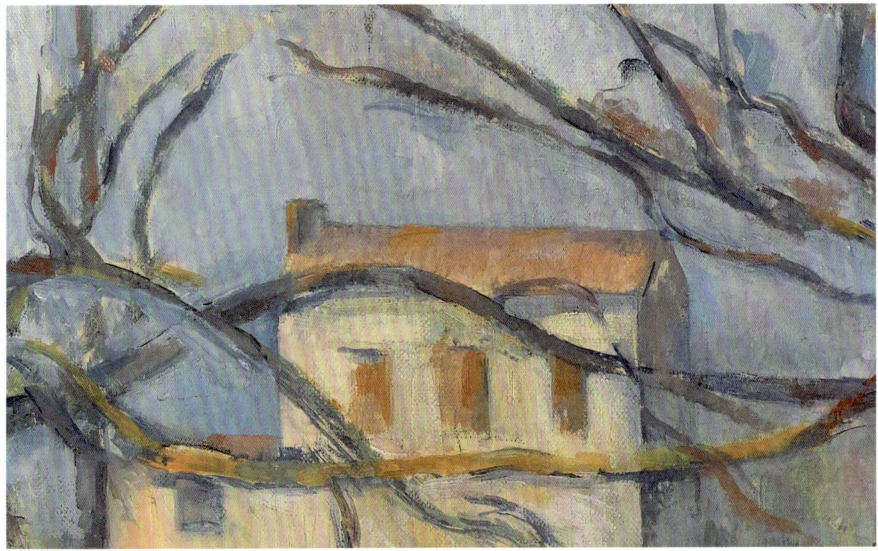

51. Detail from Fig. 50: *Trees and Houses*, *c.* 1885–86. Musée de l'Orangerie, Paris, Jean-Walter and Paul Guillaume Collection.

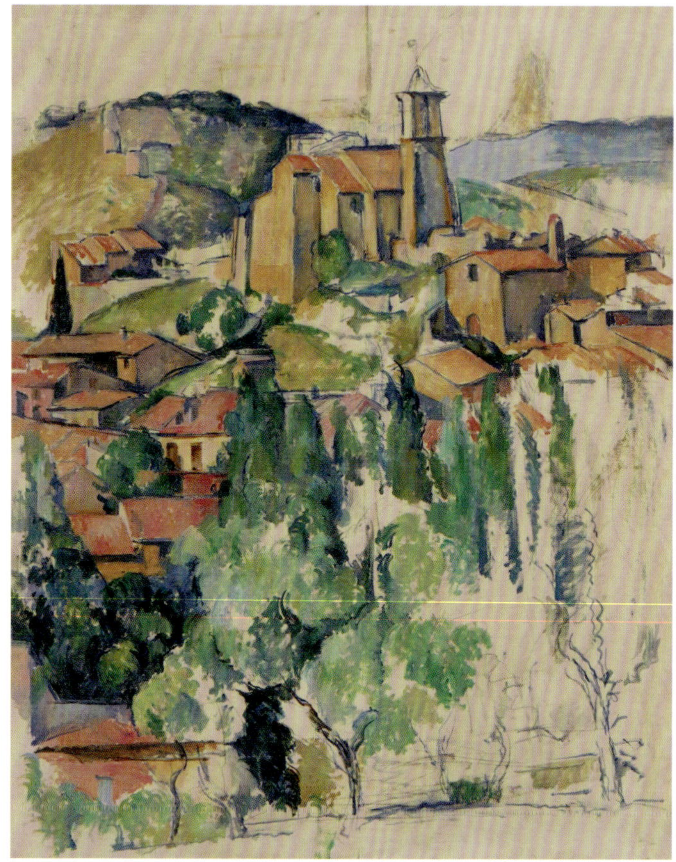

52. *Village of Gardanne*, c. 1886, 92 × 73 cm (36¼ × 28¾ in.).
Brooklyn Museum of Art.

I choose to focus on this area of *Trees and Houses* partly because, long ago, it seized my attention in the Orangerie and once seen was endlessly absorbing. And also because it strikes me as typical of many other such organizing incidents in Cézanne's work – places where foreground and background come into active, difficult touch. These are the pictures' seams, as it were, and have to be tightly stitched; whereas a lot of the pictures' broader visual material – the approximations of grass and undergrowth, or the signs of foliage – can be left flapping comparatively loose (the looseness also being part of Cézanne's proposal). *Edges* are difficult. Foreground and background are potentially crutches for the mind, which painting should put in question. There are plenty of paintings – the *Village of Gardanne* in the Brooklyn Museum, for example – where the spatial seams of the subject have been left mostly empty, as if the painter had deferred them to a time of totalization that never arrived.

The question I promised to ask of the *Trees and Houses* sequence, remember, is what pattern of intention drove it and how the intention may have shifted, as the sequence went on, between a piece-by-piece *analogizing* of paint and vision (paint and sense data) and an intimation, visible in the very brush marks, of the marks coming to obey a different logic – not a logic of analogy at all. I am not looking for an iconoclastic answer to the question of what Cézanne 'thought he was doing', in which we discover that Fry and Schapiro and Georges Lecomte got the painter all wrong. On the contrary, I want to go with them as far as possible. Here, for instance, is Roger Fry:

> Cézanne, inheriting from the Impressionists the general notion of accepting the purely visual patchwork of appearance, concentrated his imagination so intensely upon certain oppositions of tone and colour that he became able to build up and, as it were, re-create form from within; and at the same time that he re-created form he re-created it clothed with colour, light, and atmosphere all at once. It is this astonishing synthetic power that amazes me in his work.[9]

I believe that what we are looking at in the marks describing branch and roof is a fair example of such concentration and synthesis. And partly – partly – the passage answers to Fry's line of thought.

Take the violent forward movement of the smaller branch. I interpret the to-and-fro of brushstrokes around this movement – the evidence of fine-tuning and improvisation going on right up to the last minute, and maybe in a sense never having been brought to a stop – as Cézanne's trying to see if a play of *directions* in space, and one the eye seems not to be able to lay hold of completely, could be made as much part of an uninterrupted paint surface as the front of the house just below. I guess Fry's 'purely visual patchwork' is helpful here. ('Je vois. Par taches.') Putting aspects of the world into the same surface is, for Cézanne, putting them into the eye. But the twisted branch as Cézanne sees it isn't simply an optical phenomenon, at least as the term 'optical' is commonly understood. The branch's being in the eye *is*, as I understand Cézanne's metaphysic, its being over there in space, its being 'outside' not 'in' – its taking place at a distance, staying separate and self-sufficient. This is the Cézanne effect. The world has to be pictured as possessed by the eye, indeed 'totalized' by it; but always on the basis of exploding or garbled or utterly intractable data – data which speak to the impossibility of synthesis even as they seem to provide the sensuous material for it. The branch flickers between possible positions, possible identities. 'We know not where to have it.' 'It seems impossible to grasp.' But it's there all the same.

Now I make my iconoclastic move. Because in the end I wonder whether these *are* the terms in which the sequence of marks we have been looking at makes sense. Do the marks follow, or go on following, a logic of visual sensation? Are 'synthesis' and 're-creation' the right words for the force that drives them? Or is the logic they come to pursue generated out of a different set of opportunities and constraints, which sounds in the telling a bit less exalted? Let us call them 'formal tactics' as opposed to 'imaginative grasp'; material accidents as opposed to perceptual complexity; ironic, automatic facility, not 'intellectualized sensual power'. Fanatic display and technical imperiousness, I'd even say; in any case, not Fry's 'supreme spontaneity, as though he had almost made himself the passive, half-conscious instrument of some directing power'.[10] In the realm of the aesthetic, spontaneity is always presented as a ventriloquism of the world, a giving over of will to intuition. But why? Why should the will not be in unflinching charge – a will that is ultimately happy to settle for a world made up of separate and incommensurable realms, each one of sheer procedure? Are not the marks we have been concentrating on *procedural* with a vengeance? Are not they more like a Nietzsche aphorism than a paragraph of Proust? Fierce, declarative and self-cancelling, not edging toward the truth of consciousness step by qualified step.

◆

These are rhetorical questions. And as usual the answer to them is yes and no. Let me give the answer first in general terms and then see how it applies to the *Trees and Houses* brushstrokes.

Cézanne's is the most radical project of nineteenth-century positivism.[11] It stakes everything on the possibility of recreating the structure of experience out of that experience's units. I am sure Fry was right in this basic hypothesis. But the very radicality of the project delivers it. Because this painting stakes everything on the notion of the unitary, the immediate, the bare minimum of sensation, the momentary-and-material 'ping'; because it goes on and on searching for ways to insist that here, in this dab, is the elementary particle out of which seeing is made; because it fetishizes the singular, it discovers the singular as exactly *not* the form of 'experience'. It shows us a way of world-making in which the very idea of a world – the very idea of totality or synthesis or Fry's three-times-repeated word 'power' – is not drawn from some prior texture of unit-sensations 'out there', and therefore (potentially) 'in here'. It follows that notions as seemingly basic as foreground and background may no longer apply. (Look back at the sequence of marks in *Trees and Houses* and see if they do.) Maybe not even inside and outside. Nor experience and representation. Nor 'now' and 'then'.

Of course, what we get of this other way of world-making in Cézanne is no more than a glimpse. But 'glimpse' in Cézanne exactly does not mean that the other possibility appears momentarily or just round the edges of things. The glimpse is everywhere (in Cézanne's last two decades). The non-identity of mark and marked is foundational. I call it a glimpse only because non-identity of this sort cannot be thematized: it cannot once and for all replace the world made of sense data that it shadows. It *shadows* that picture of seeing and knowing; it disperses and thins it out; it reveals the logic of the singular and re-creative to have nothing to do with the subject of sensation. If the reader then wants to know what phrase I would put in place of 'subject of sensation' – and any one phrase is bound to be over-stressed, or over-neat – the one I would opt for is 'object of the exercise'. The logic of the singular and constructive in Cézanne has nothing to do with the subject of sensation but everything to do with the object of the exercise.

That formulation will do, as long as we do not allow 'object' and 'exercise' to collapse back into yet another version of the same old story of aesthetic rediscovery (this one beloved of a certain kind of modernist critic) – the sensuous reality of things being rediscovered 'here', on the surface, where the picture is made.[12] But there is no 'here' in painting. Picturing is not a physical matter. Least of all in Cézanne, in the nine or ten (typical) marks we are looking at. The exercise called picturing is a deep, notional, physically irretrievable *dimension* – a dimension of social practice. And the 'object of the exercise' in Cézanne is the object posited by that strange line of thought, or anti-thought, we call eighteenth- and nineteenth-century materialism – by that project pushed and stressed (as it very often was) to its utopian limits. Materialism in this guise is unthinkable – *the* unthinkable. It is the unknown that the sensorium keeps at bay. The world of objects reached after in Cézanne, and laid before us in all its manifoldness, overtness and pungency, could hardly signal its counter-factual status more clearly. It is a horizon of meaning, an *alternative* to experience, a contentment with non-identity. Nobody is saying, least of all me, that such contentment could be lived in more than fitfully.

The thing to recognize about the *Trees and Houses* sequence, then, is that there is no one point within it at which the phenomenal is displaced by the material or formal. The displacement is there and not there from the start – in the very first brush mark of the sequence, supposing the terms 'first' and 'sequence' could ever be stabilized, which they cannot. *There* and *not there* all the way through: from (not-) first to (not-) last. This is the Cézanne effect. Always, at every point, there appears to be reference to the nth degree, fierce and immediate, punctual, acute; but always the reference is haunted by the fact of its precisely being (only) to the nth degree: that is, a touch or a point or a patch in a merely numerical, repetitive, indeed 'formal' sequence, of degrees to the nth quantity, with *this* one only *implying* the nth – meaning the final, infinite place in the series, the non-numerical, non-repetitive, unpredictable moment at which reference is secured. This is the anxiety, and also the utopian horizon, that drives the fanatic process on. The next mark might (somehow) not be a mere sign in a sequence but a true figure of things seen – a figure that cancels the marks preceding or raises them to a different power.

Interminability and hesitation in Cézanne are thus not rooted in an epistemology of addition – though of course some such naive positivism is operative, at the level of ideological framing and self-understanding – but in an (equally naive) Hegelian prevarication, a waiting and hoping for the moment at which the addition of units turns quantity into quality. What goes on in practice is not so much addition as erasure: that is what the logic of our nine or ten brush marks suggests. Or maybe 'erasure' is over-stressed. Call it 'interference', then: a radical (at times a positively melodramatic) interference of each unit with those it is put next to – the hope being, I think, that erasure and interference might save the mere sequence from itself and make its unities into a world. Cézanne is looking for a mark that would not be a further 'one' in a series, but a kind of 'zero', with the power to replace the dab after dab of addition by a sudden connectedness and unity – by a truly magical multiplier effect. There is no such mark, of course. Effects like this are beyond painting's grasp. But the fact that they are is precisely what generates vividness in the sequence of marks that concerns us. The sequence is required to show that no feat of painterly energy, no moment of 'supreme spontaneity', no demonstration of 'intellectualized sensual power' can ever perform the aesthetic conjuring trick. Vividness, then, is the vividness of defeat. The vividness of procedure. *Even this*, says the painting, cannot secure the 'Darstellung der Ideen'. You see why the 'even this' had to be so monstrously good.

◆

Therefore consistency of touch and colour, the guarantor of sensuous reality in Cézanne, is always in his painting the other face of disequilibrium or dispersal of energy. Evenness in his work has a forced, or counter-factual, quality. It is a device, not a condition. Put a Cézanne next to a Corot and that is immediately clear (FIG. 53).

Writers about Cézanne have often felt called on to answer the question: What, do we think, was going on in the painter's mind during the famous endless minutes he sometimes spent between brush strokes – the minutes his portrait sitters recall so ruefully? Any answer is going to be figurative. I imagine Cézanne looking round, as it were, for a *rule to follow* for the next mark, and hesitating because he wished not to recognize that no such rule existed. He did not want to know that any next mark he might make would be accurate and inaccurate at once; and accurate

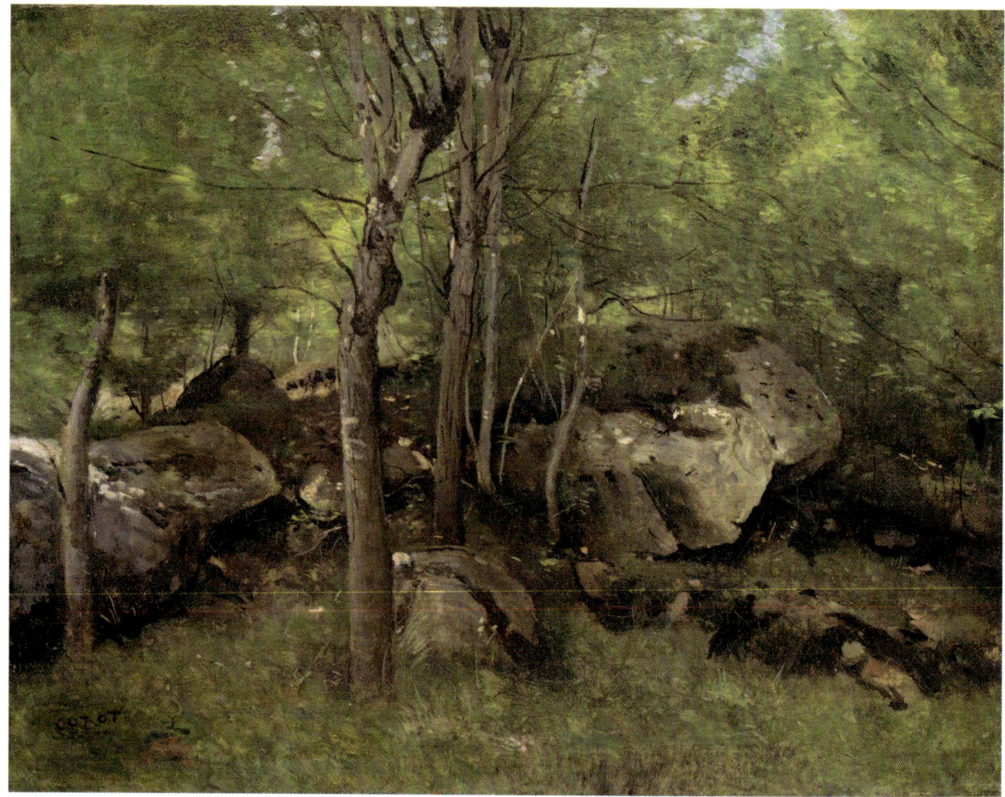

53. Jean-Baptiste-Camille Corot, *Rocks in the Forest of Fontainebleau*, c. 1860–65, 46 × 59 cm (18⅛ × 23¼ in.). National Gallery of Art, Washington, D.C.

above all by reason of what he would do to it – the force he would apply to it more than the sight of it in relation to whatever it was of. Marks respond to each other as rhymes, or beats. But it was exactly this being always inside a metric or a rhyme-scheme that Cézanne would not accept.

Look at the way any sequence of marks, even one that strikes out for the detail of optical experience as unflinchingly as that in *Trees and Houses*, is overtaken by a logic of contrivance not perception. Look at the way something so basic and constitutive of painting as 'calling on the accidents of process' – which no one in their right mind (certainly not Cézanne) objects to – sets off an unstoppable automatism whereby accidents become what the process is directed *to* as well as *by*. The words we need to describe the process are contingency, performance and will; not necessity, imagination and 'half-conscious instrumentality'.

Again, there's a sentence of Roger Fry's which seems to me to sum matters up. I admire it greatly, and find myself disagreeing with it more or less phrase by phrase:

> [Cézanne's] composition at first sight looks accidental, as though he had sat down before any odd corner of nature and portrayed it; and yet the longer one looks the more satisfactory are the correspondences one discovers, the more certainly felt, beneath its subtlety, is the architectural plan; the more absolute, in spite of their astounding novelty, do we find the colour harmonies.[13]

Felt certainty, satisfactory correspondence, architecture, absolute harmony: whatever the noise on the aesthetic message, Fry is saying, its essential character remains the same. The Cézanne I am proposing is one where none of these terms of value applies, and the list of implied contingent negatives – I am precisely not going to name them, I want them to go on unappeasedly haunting Fry's positives – is what gives this painting its strength.

◆

I said I did not want to end the chapter with an iconoclastic answer to the Cézanne problem, but inevitably my rhetoric has drifted that way. 'Forced' and 'automatism' are hard words. I should try to amend their tone. I realize that in putting accident, performance and will in place of necessity, imagination and openness I look to be preaching a heartless creed. But what if I settled for the words 'practice, exercise and object' rather than 'spontaneity, experience and subject'? At least then the ethical balance becomes less clear. We know what violence has been done (and still is) in the name of the latter triad's brand of naturalism. In any case, ultimately I refuse to go along with the notion that an aesthetic of performance and will is, by its nature, less humane and empathetic than one of totality and phenomenon. I do not think it need lead us in Nietzsche's direction. Part of Cézanne's importance to me is that in him it does not.

What other direction, then? Answering this question without falling into bathos involves me saying what I think Cézanne's art is 'about' – beyond

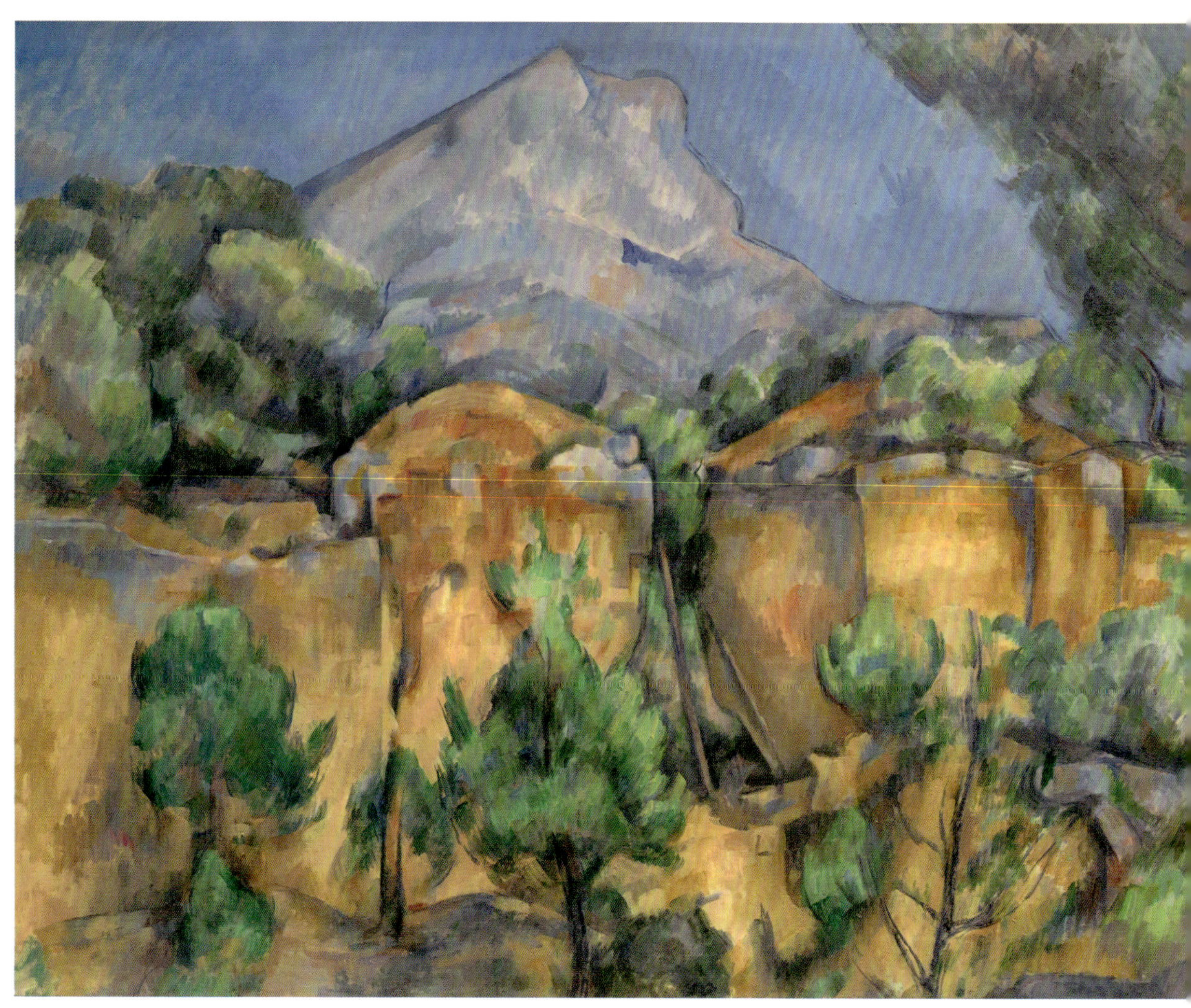

54. *Montagne Sainte-Victoire seen from Bibémus Quarry*, c. 1895–1900, 65 × 81 cm (25⅝ × 32 in.). Baltimore Museum of Art.

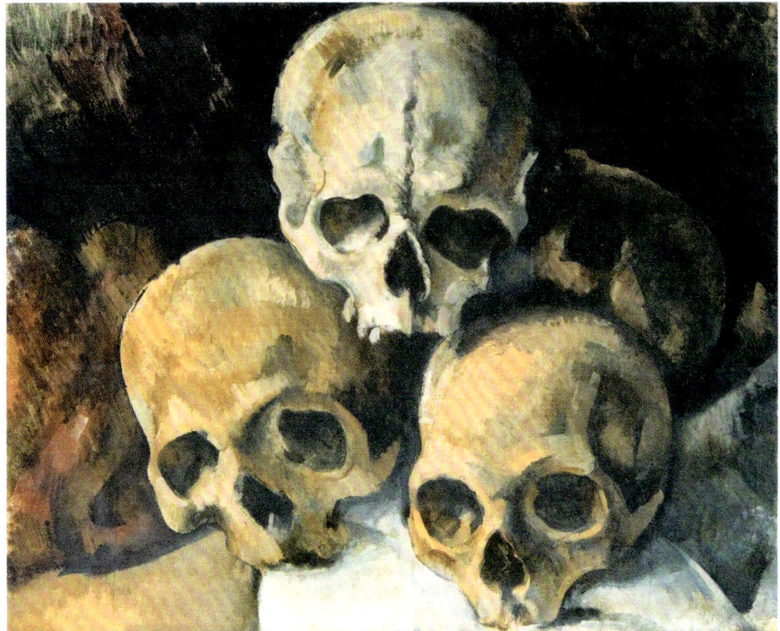

55. *Pyramid of Skulls, c.* 1898–1900, 39 × 46.5 cm (15⅜ × 18⅜ in.). Private Collection.

the trying and failing to stay true to the facts of vision, which is certainly a main part of it. I flinch from doing this, or doing so more explicitly than in my description of the Ford *Montagne Sainte-Victoire* (FIGS 46 & 48), because of course the proposals about the world and our knowledge of it – and I am sure Cézanne's art contains such proposals – are deeply embedded in technique. That is part of the pictures' argument. Yet if I do not at least sketch an answer, I shall have colluded in what seems to me the dreariest remainder of the early-twentieth-century myth of Cézanne: the myth of his paintings' utter ineffability. Because a picture is not a proposition does not mean it cannot be translated into one or more. 'Technical' and 'ineffable' are not cognates.

Put side by side the Baltimore Museum of Art's *Montagne Sainte-Victoire seen from Bibémus Quarry* and the painting, probably done around the same time, now called *Pyramid of Skulls*. I know the pairing is tendentious, and that *Pyramid of Skulls* is exceptional in Cézanne work; and equally, when I suggest that we read the one (more typical) painting in light of the other, I am not meaning to elicit some idiot detection of a hidden iconography. The two central rocks in the quarry are not disguised skulls, and Montagne Sainte-Victoire is neither a skull nor a pyramid. Yet I do want to say that the view from Bibémus is at one level a view from the tomb. And that the skulls intend, by the simple act of pyramiding, to give form to death and therefore survive it. (The pyramid is the first and last form of the aesthetic illusion.)

You see the problem. Because the embedded propositions in Cézanne are so simple and primordial, and so entirely dependent on ironic feats of matter – of paint – to breathe life and death back into them, putting them into words is exactly betraying 'what they have to say' about material existence.[14] And about where the recognition of the human world as one of accident, device, persuasion and will might actually lead us. Not necessarily, it seems, into a realm of deep nihilism or contingent power. But certainly into some kind of graveyard or charnel house.

I died for Beauty – but was scarce
Adjusted in the Tomb
When One who died for Truth, was lain
In an adjoining Room –

He questioned softly 'Why I failed'?
'For Beauty', I replied –
'And I – for Truth – Themself are One –
We Brethren, are', He said –

And so, as Kinsmen, met a Night –
We talked between the Rooms –
Until the Moss had reached our lips –
And covered up – our names –[15]

We should not need Cézanne's painting *Boy with a Skull* to know that death is this artist's deep subject. Any of the later portraits would convince us of that. In all of them costume and posture are rigid, and ineffectual, against the surrounding pressure of the void. Nature, in the landscapes, is Emily Dickinson's Moss. It goes on 'deathwards progressing to no death',

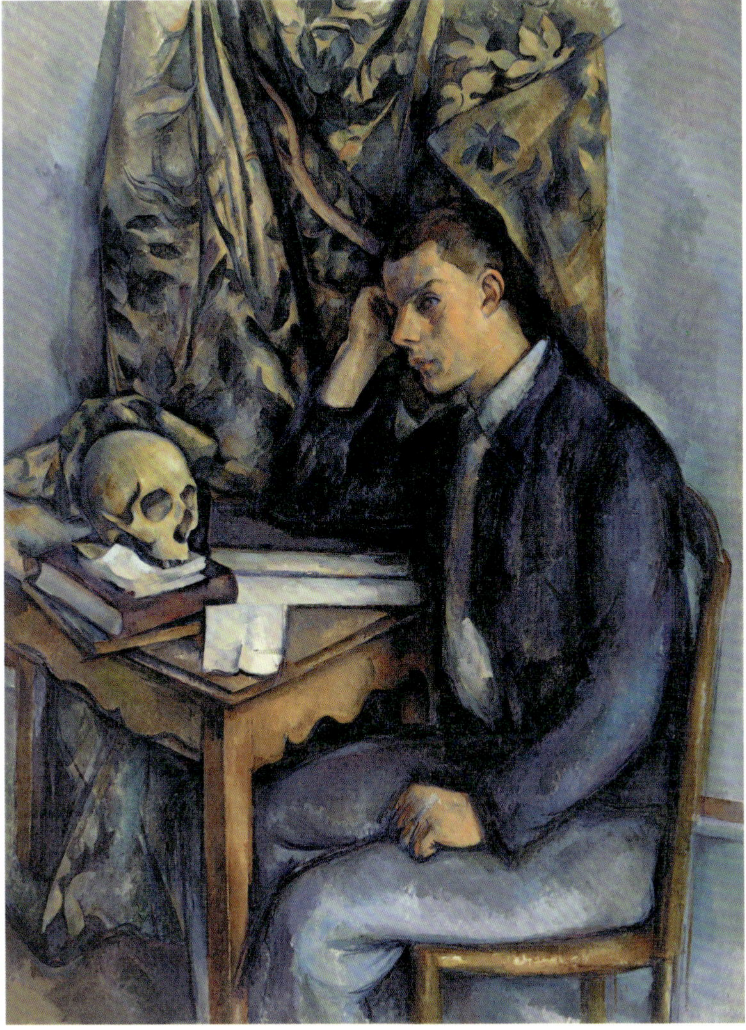

56. *Boy with a Skull*, c. 1896–98, 127 × 94.5 cm (50 × 37⅜ in.).
Barnes Foundation, Philadelphia.

'forever decaying, never to be decayed'.[16] Its presence in the folds of *Boy with a Skull*'s stiff tapestry, or on the tablecloth of *Woman in Blue* (FIG. 44), is no doubt quietly accurate about its normal place in Cézanne's bourgeois world. Most people are in no danger of dying for Beauty. Out there, on the other hand, is the mountain above the quarry. Nature reaching our lips. Whether its deathly animation is consoling or enraging is something, I believe, Cézanne's pictures never stop trying to decide.

4. Peasants

If I succeed with this bloke, the theory will be true.

Cézanne on one of his portraits, 1905[1]

This chapter tries to find words for the five paintings Cézanne did, probably in the early 1890s, of peasants playing cards. Writing about the paintings is scarce.[2] There seems to be a feeling in the literature, half admitted, half suppressed, that the canvases do not quite fit with other great things from the same period – a series of massive still lifes, in particular, typified by the one in the Getty Museum; some touching portraits of Hortense Fiquet; a big square-format *Under the Trees* apparently made with Cézanne's one-man show of 1895 in mind; and a sequence of *Bathers* that looks to be moving up gradually, year by year, towards Old Master size. At the time, it was the *Bathers* that captured his fellow Impressionists' imagination: Pissarro did a swap of an old landscape of Louveciennes, no less, for 'several admirable small *Bathers*' from the 1895 show, and the *Bathers* I illustrate here – barely two feet wide, but massive and electric – found its way into Monet's collection.[3] The early exhibition history of the *Card Players* is hard to reconstruct. Vollard included *Les joueurs de cartes* in a show at his gallery in 1899; but the show's catalogue no longer exists and the sketchy reviews in the press do not help in identifying which picture it was. Paul Cassirer showed a *Card Players* (the one eventually bought by Samuel Courtauld) in Berlin in 1904. From 1907 onwards, pictures from the group start to figure in Cézanne exhibitions and criticism – even then a little tentatively.[4]

No one knows for sure the order in which the *Card Players* were painted, and even our placing them roughly between 1891 and 1895 rests on no good documentary evidence: we have a letter from the poet Paul Alexis, dated February 1891, which mentions that 'During the day, he [Cézanne]

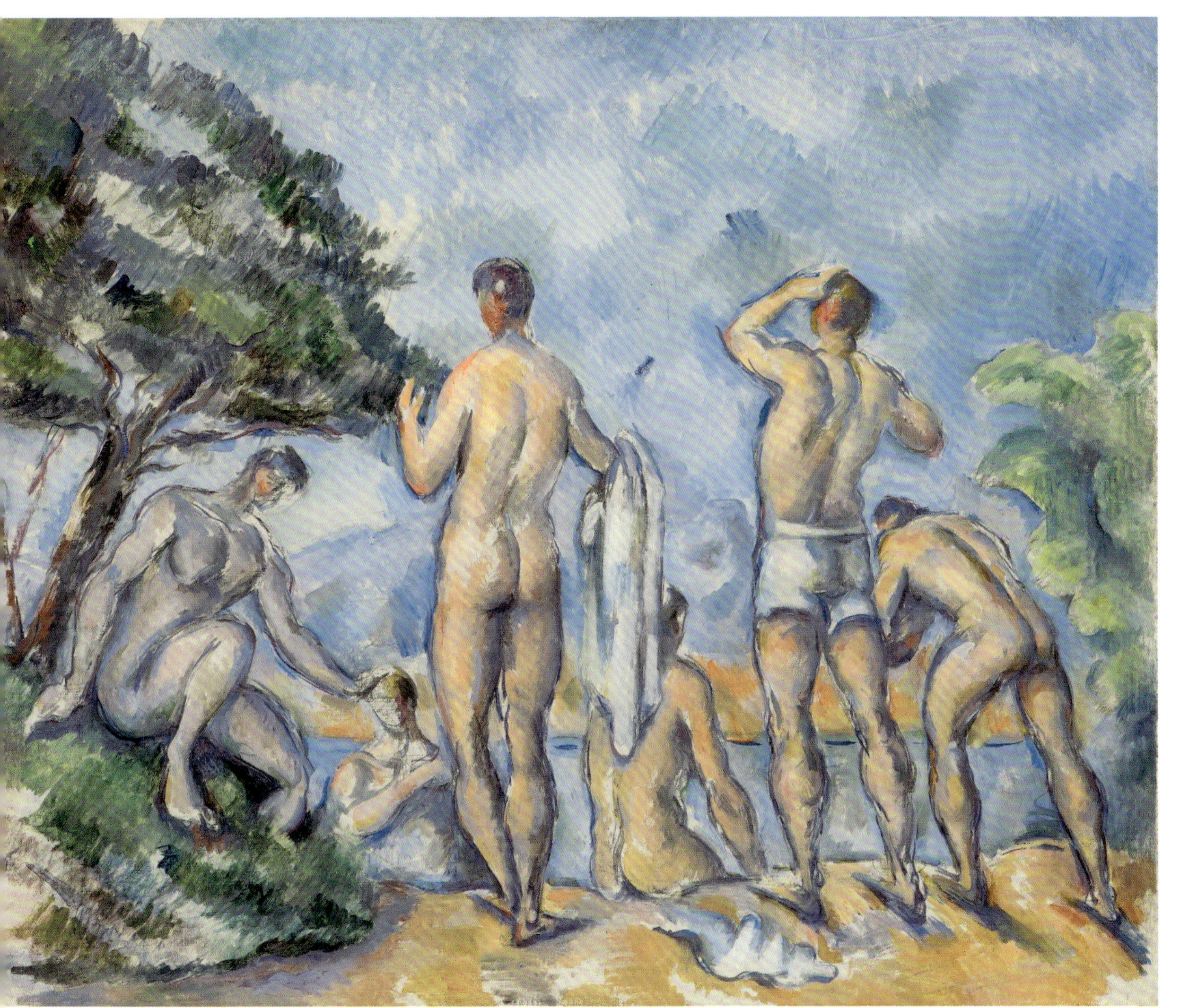

57. *Bathers*, *c.* 1890–92, 53 × 64 cm (20⅞ × 25¼ in.). Saint Louis Art Museum.

paints at the Jas de Bouffan where a worker serves as model, and one of these days I'll go and see what he's doing.'[5] But 'ouvrier', you notice, is in the singular, and anyway Alexis is reporting what he has been told rather than seen for himself. If we try to tie a picture to the piece of hearsay, the best candidate seems to be *The Smoker* now in the Kunsthalle Mannheim (FIG. 59). Signac, much later, said that Alexis owned *The Smoker* for a while;[6] here too the recollection has nothing in the record to back it up, but it would be nice if it were true; especially because, as will become clear, I am inclined to see Alexis's traces in the *Card Players* themselves.

My sense of the sequence of the five canvases is as follows. (The order is hypothetical, and the reasons for my reconstruction, which diverges from those of the experts at several points, will be largely implicit in the descriptions I give.[7]) The first completed, I think, was the midsize painting in the Metropolitan Museum, measuring 26 by 32 inches (FIG. 58). It looks to be preparatory to the largest of the series, now in the Barnes

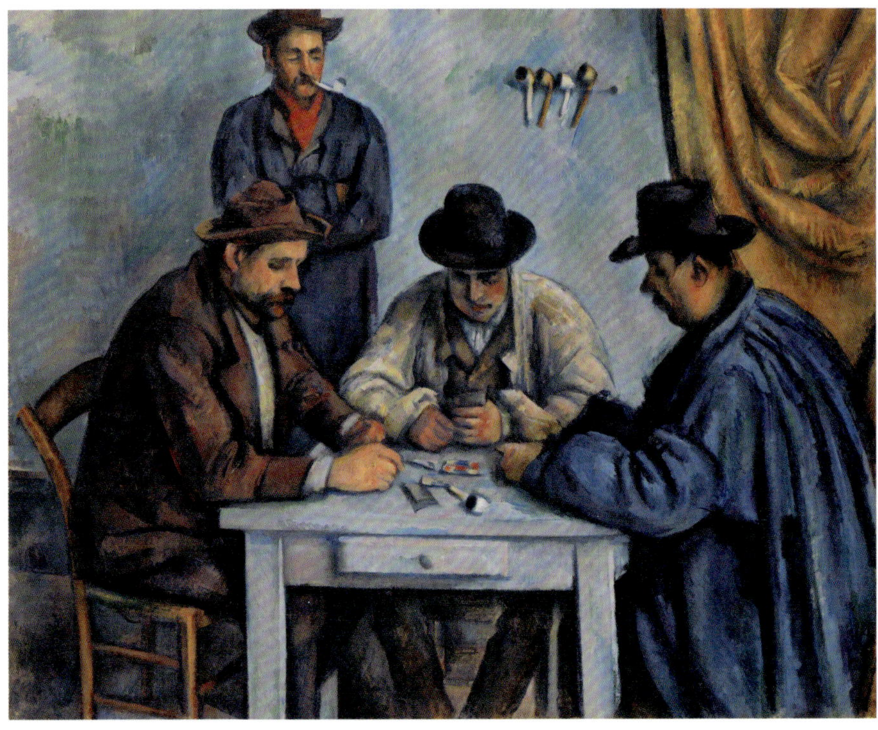

58. *The Card Players*, c. 1890–92, 65 × 81 cm (25¾ × 32¼ in.).
Metropolitan Museum of Art, New York.

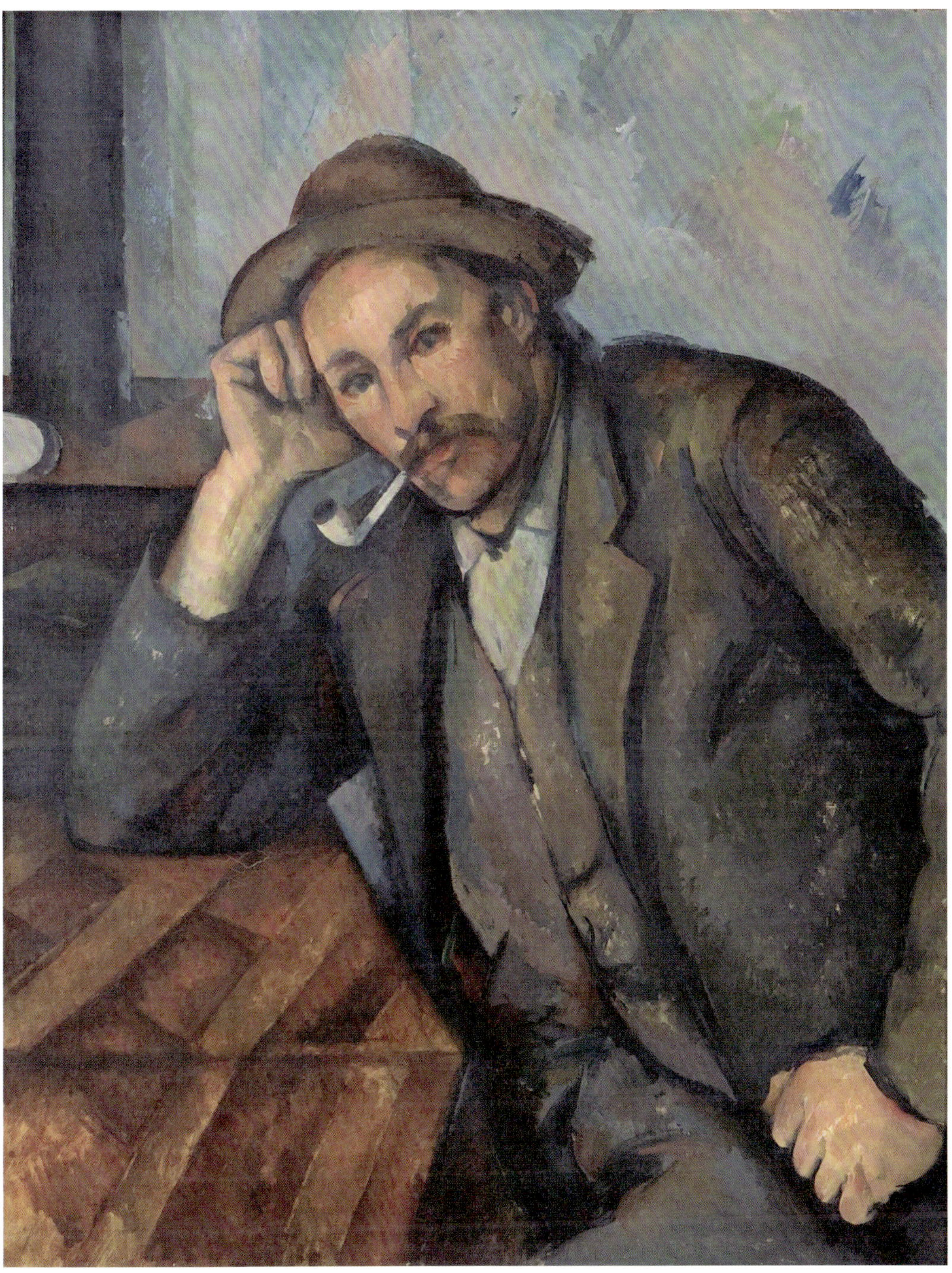

59. *The Smoker*, *c.* 1891, 92 × 73 cm (36¼ × 28¾ in.). Kunsthalle, Mannheim.

Foundation in Philadelphia, which is slightly over 4 feet 5 inches high and six feet wide (FIG. 60). This last was an exhibition picture – its scale and subject matter would not have been out of place at the Salons – but it seems never to have been shown in Cézanne's lifetime, nor at the great retrospective at the Salon d'Automne just after his death. Reproductions exaggerate the Barnes painting's blueness and heaviness. Of course, the picture is solid – solid as a rock. But recently restorers have stripped it of a greying varnish, and the thinness and speed of application of Cézanne's paint have leapt back to life. Depth and solidity in Cézanne are not, even in a heavily curtained interior, purchased at the price of loss of immediacy (or not when things go well): they come out of the flutter of sensation: that's the central claim. When later on I face the question of actual massiveness and obstruction in the *Card Players*, particularly in the fabric across the wall at right, the balance of qualities in Cézanne's brushwork – the decisiveness, the brevity, the raciness however grave the colour – will make everything hard to describe, even approximately. (Is the curtain in the Barnes velvety or homespun?)

After the Barnes canvas comes a group of three paintings with just two peasants at the table. I think the canvas that once belonged to Auguste Pellerin (who also owned the multi-figure picture for a while, before selling it to Barnes) may be the first of the three (FIG. 61). It is the largest: 38 by 51 inches. This is only two-thirds the size of Barnes's picture, but still one of the biggest paintings Cézanne ever did. The massiveness of the two figures is unmistakable. Then there are two small-to-midsize oils, now in the Musée d'Orsay and the Courtauld Gallery (FIGS 62 & 63). The Orsay painting is slightly smaller: just over 18 by 22 inches. The Courtauld's measures 23 inches by almost 29. I use the words 'small-to-midsize' a bit uneasily, because one of the several kinds of uncanniness associated with the last two paintings is that the scale of both – I mean the effect of the scale, or how that scale is experienced by a viewer, and above all the scale's purpose – is so difficult to pin down and make sense of; even, or maybe in particular, when the two are hung side by side. Meyer Schapiro called the Orsay *Card Players* small but monumental. It was the monumentality, by the look of things, which made him think the painting 'undoubtedly the best'.[8] I see what Schapiro was reacting to, but one result of being able

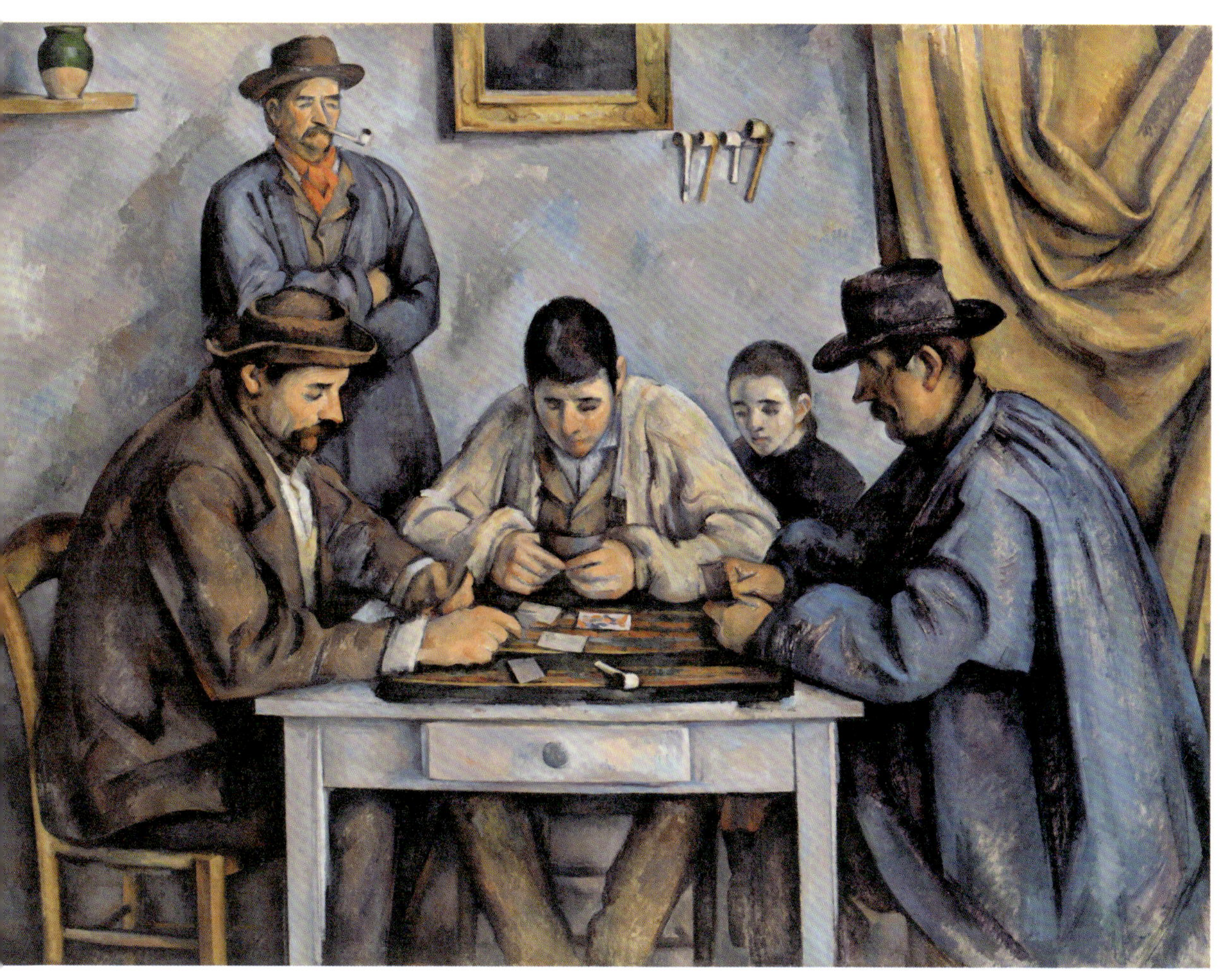

60. *The Card Players*, c. 1890–92, 135 × 181.5 cm (53¼ × 71⅝ in.). Barnes Foundation, Philadelphia.

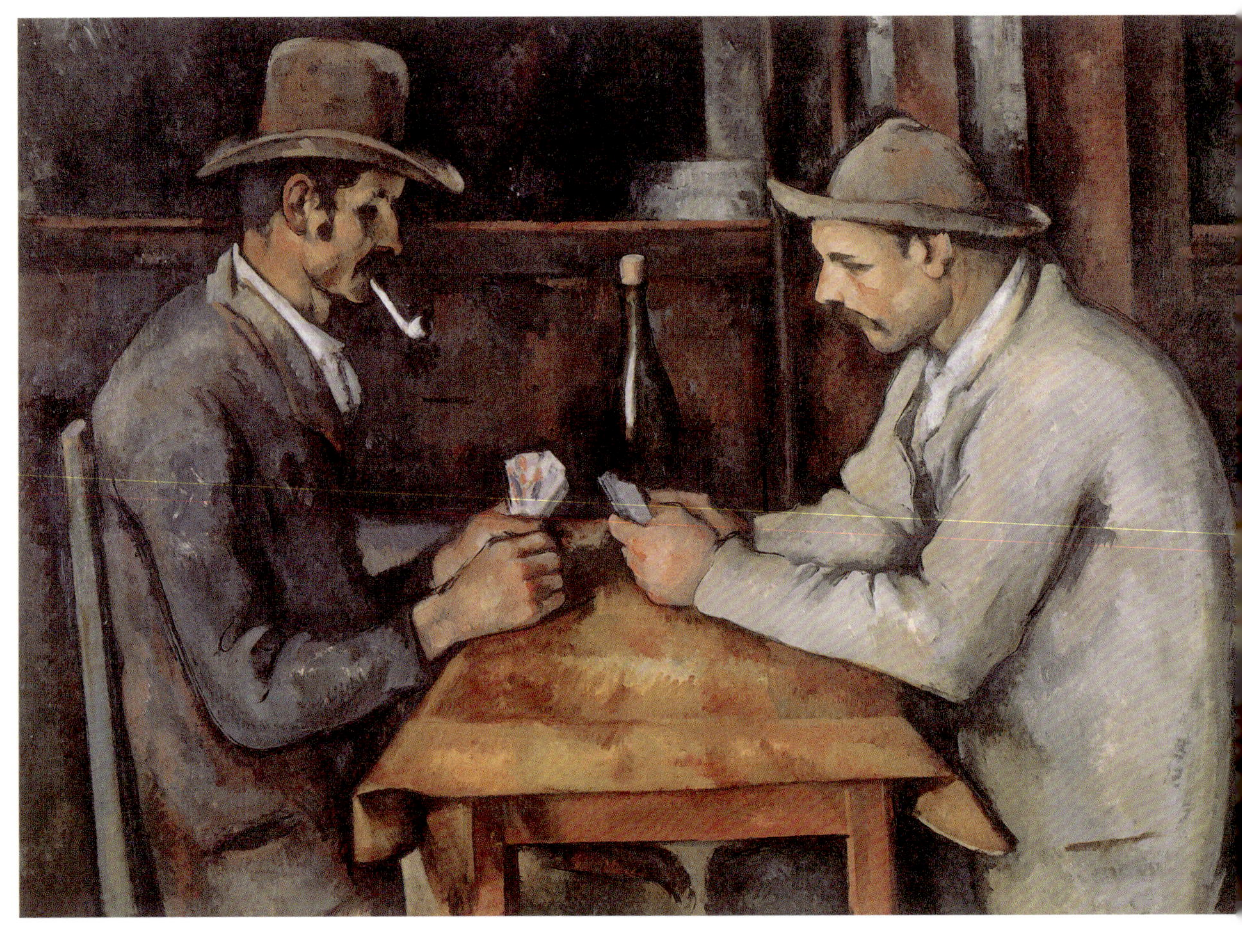

61. *The Card Players*, *c.* 1892–94, 97 × 130 cm (38¼ × 51¼ in.). Private Collection.

to size up the Orsay canvas next door to its double – this happened at the Courtauld in 2010 – is, for me, to make the characterization 'monumental' seem less than the truth. The smallness of the Orsay picture is altogether a stranger thing when your eye moves to-and-fro in reality (as presumably Cézanne's did) between it and its slightly bigger companion.

The Orsay picture looks compressed. Of all five *Card Players* it is the one, I think, in which the whole of the image comes closest to obeying the logic of the forms to be seen underneath the table, knees wedged together in contrasting trousers, which throughout the sequence is spellbinding and surely meant as an image – a tremendous synecdoche – of pictorial compactness and horror vacui. I shall argue in the end that the play of forms under the table does *not* govern or epitomize the spatial logic of the *Card Players* overall: that the little underworld is there, so to speak, to present the viewer with a model, almost a memento, of the kind of space that, in Cézanne's view, a true picture of a room now had to dispense with. But dispensing with it was hard, and in a sense regrettable. A picture of people close to us in an interior surely carried with it a promise of containment – an easy emphatic packing-together of forms, with the picture rectangle (itself drifting instinctively towards the square) somehow *being* the room, offering the room's four walls. This was the natural bias of the subject: Cézanne had memories of Dutch painting in mind. I think, to repeat, that the achievement but also the difficulty of the five *Card Players* has to do with their acting against that bias; relegating the bias, even with a touch of irony, to the too-small square beneath the tabletop. (Compare the Getty apples nested in their cloth [FIGS 28 & 29]). But it must maintain its power, that bias. It must, to any painter wanting completeness, still be appealing. The Orsay painting is most under its spell.

It is striking, when the Courtauld and Orsay versions are hung together, how decisively the Courtauld *Card Players* seems to move to counteract the Orsay table's tremendous four-squareness, and how little, in comparison with Orsay, the forms under the Courtauld's table attach to, and provide a key for, the peasants on top. I understand Schapiro's admiration for the dialectical to-and-fro between the players in Paris, with their opposites of colour and drawing and even character; and I too love their solidity and naive anchorage to the picture's sides; but I find myself more deeply

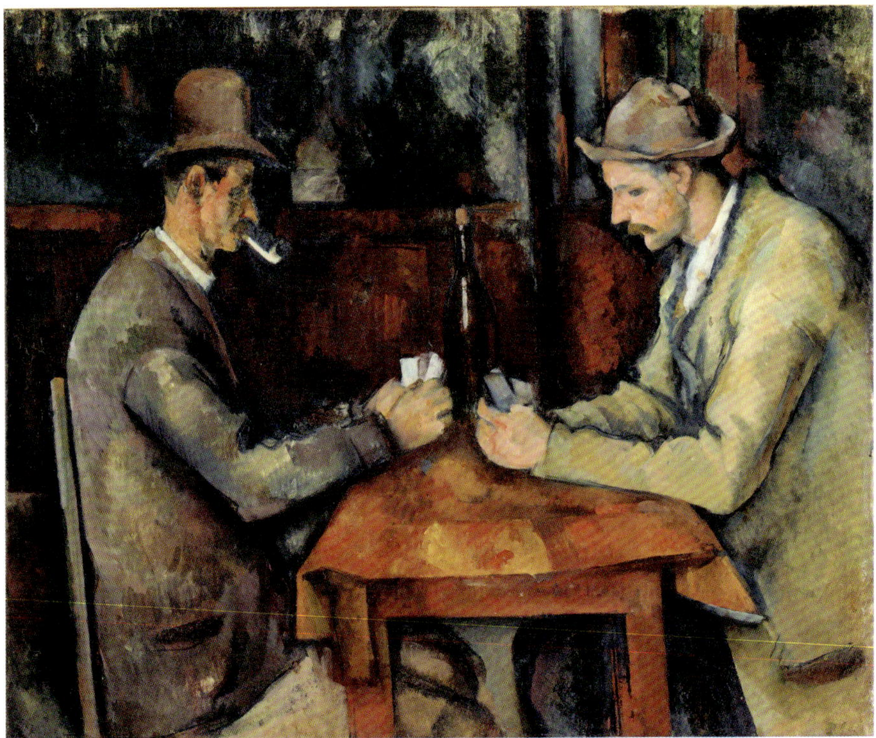

62. *The Card Players*, c. 1892–94, 47 × 56.5 cm (18½ × 22¼ in.). Musée d'Orsay, Paris.

drawn in the end to the Courtauld's miniaturization and marooning of its figures – the way it moves them back a little, the way the right-hand player is tipped and swivelled just enough for symmetry to be broken. I find the strange slightly stretched rectangle of the Courtauld painting – the actual shape of the canvas, especially compared to the Orsay's – a stroke of genius. Without the least braying of modernist trumpets, contingency – a slight unmooring – has entered the room. The two peasants strike me as more fully *makers* of the world they are in. The picture rectangle is less a priori, less idealized. The weird pulling and smoothing of the table back and back into depth, and the flattening and stretching and separating of the players' hands, and the fading of the bottle barrier and the nestling of the right-hand man's sleeve further and further into the hard but unresisting tablecloth – all these play a part.

In the Orsay picture the front face of the table and the tablecloth half covering it have the finality of a sign-language, balanced and hieratic,

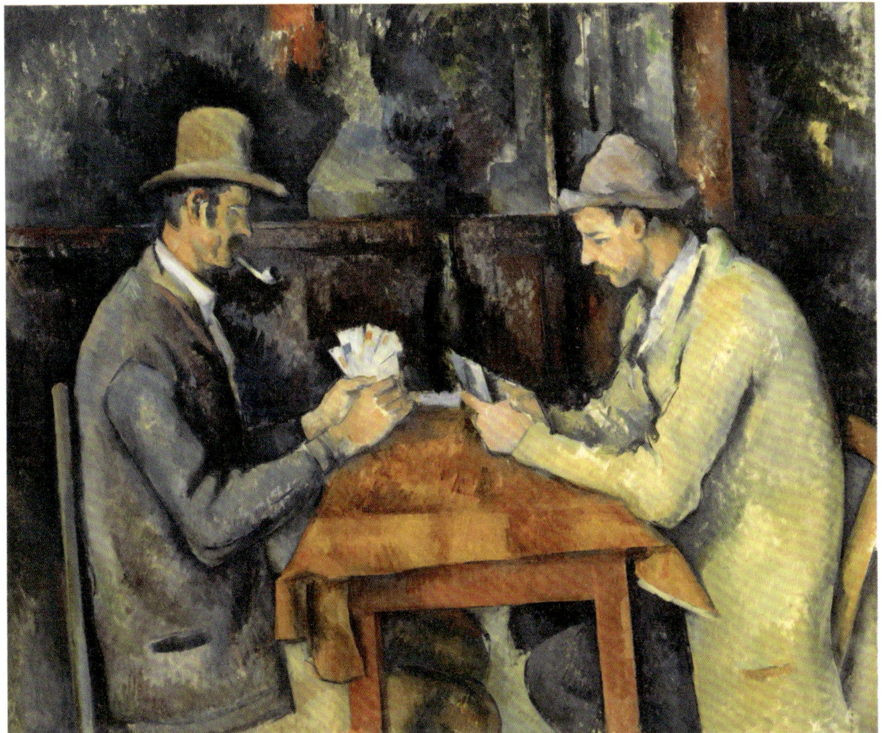

63. *The Card Players*, c. 1892–94, 60 × 73 cm (23⅝ × 28¾ in.). Courtauld Gallery, London.

with the cloth arranged as if to disclose the table's perfection – a curtain pulled back from a mystery. None of this survives in the Courtauld painting: everything is tipped a little off kilter. And it is a sacrifice, this loss of solidity. I regret it, until I see again the fierce cutting edge of the tablecloth at right in the Courtauld, and the space carved out around it. The Courtauld's right card player is, to borrow a phrase from Keats, still 'feeling about for his couch of space'. The table seems too small for him. His knees are no longer solidly aligned. His chair might almost be pushed back on two legs. This is a card game, not a sacred rite.

◆

I had intended this chapter to begin systematically with questions of chronology and size, and already I am far off track, disagreeing with Schapiro about the most elusive – disputable – things. But how could it be otherwise? My subject is the *Card Players*, and I am trying to tune into their form and semantics. At the risk of bullying, let me say that this seems to me equivalent in difficulty to following the harmonic logic of Beethoven's last quartets, or the movement from paragraph to paragraph in Kant's First Critique. I think that art history's slight embarrassment at this kind of analogy – the feeling that an art historian making it runs the danger of moving painting into some cultic or trans-historical space – has come to be the discipline's cross. In practice it functions as an alibi (which for some reason the discipline seems constantly to need) for not exposing oneself to what painting is capable of, and not pushing language to follow in painting's wake. I envy the musicologist's certainty that Beethoven's use of music's resources makes most of his listeners, including the professional one, scrabble to hear adequately and think hard enough.

I scrabble with these five Cézannes. My attempt to get on terms with them will therefore, somewhat nervously, go in three directions, or out along three rough lines. I hope in the end they connect. I shall first try to ask – or at least establish as an overriding matrix for the questions that come next – what Cézanne may have thought followed from his choice of subject, working men at play; and what his canvases suggest he felt was now involved, this being the late nineteenth century, in making a picture of peasants intimate (intimate as opposed to argue or assert) that embedded in the game the men have chosen – implicit in the circumstance of meeting and sitting together and following familiar rules – something wider and deeper, which the men were happy to share, was reiterated. Or maybe we should say it was externalized – indeed, monumentalized (that word again). Something I want to call, following a famous line in Wittgenstein, the men's form of life.

How does *painting* portray such a subject – such simple yet powerful formality, such confidence in common? That is the question. Let me give a preliminary answer. I think it does so above all by discovering the scene's distinctive space. Which is to say, it tries to lay hold of the way the particular set of class actors occupy their surroundings, in this case the space of a room. Or should we say, the way they *make* that space by occupying it and playing the old game within it? So that Cézanne's subject, it follows, is the space of a room *as it comes into being in the game*, in the moment of waiting and concentrating – the force of the game's rules for participants, the players' mild suspense, the gravity of those looking on. 'The life of their separateness' is Schapiro's great phrase. (In the Barnes picture the onlookers are specifically figured, you notice, and they are a strange duo: a pale slight child with a widow's peak, maybe a little homeless and ghostly; and an upright smoker, not convincingly planted on any floor, infinitely removed from the table yet superintending it. He is full of the blue of the room's back wall. The shadow he casts is phantasmagorical. The Metropolitan's painting has the smoker more engaged with the game, but I'm inclined to make that a reason for the Barnes canvas being Cézanne's second and better thought. Remoteness, in the case of both Barnes onlookers, seems to be all. And eventually, in the Orsay and Courtauld pictures, remoteness of viewing is made fully structural, in a typical Cézanne way. It belongs to us viewers in front of the scene: it inheres in the impenetrable picture plane.)

So this is my first question: the nature of room-space and occupants. But answering it leads immediately to a second wider one, which has haunted most writing about Cézanne (weaving in and out of the chapters so far): namely, what was Cézanne's habitual, characteristic sense of space in painting; and in the light of that habit, what was the special challenge he faced when he chose to paint an interior – a space hemmed in by four walls? I think, as I said before, that those who have written about Cézanne have instinctively felt that the *Card Players* do not quite fit. A room and a game – an easy or even a stiff reciprocity – do not tally, they seem to have reckoned, with Cézanne's whole sense of life. What makes him the late nineteenth century's great portraitist, for example (I think of *Woman in Blue* and *Boy with a Skull* [FIGS 44 & 56]), is his willingness to show reciprocity lost. Self-enclosure – absorption, apartness – is the condition he seems most drawn to. The homelessness of the sitter is echoed in the perplexity of the play between two and three dimensions. Maybe so. But the question ought to be, then, whether the alienness of the subject matter in the *Card Players* – the foreignness of its space and mode of habitation to Cézanne's basic intuition – in the end provoked some of his best thought.

This is too abstract. Let me interrupt the putting of questions and remind the reader simply of Cézanne's unique way of being (pictorially) in the world. This new apprehension arrived early and was discovered above all in landscape. It is already there in the painting from 1871 called *The Railway Cutting*. (Like the *Bathers* Monet bought [FIG. 57], the picture is small but all-encompassing.) Putting *Railway Cutting*'s sense of space and identity into words is not easy, and in any case I do not want to claim that the landscapes of the following thirty-five years all follow the early painting's line. But Fritz Novotny was right to say that what is unprecedented in Cézanne's landscape vision – here is *Railway Cutting*'s representativeness – is the feeling that real, 'felt' closeness or remoteness have disappeared and that everything has retreated into a strange middle distance.[9] The things shown are vivid, certainly, but somehow untouchable: laid out like toys on the floor of a nursery, their intensity imagined more than experienced; emphatically *there* in paint, but with nothing in the picture leading towards them, inviting identification or contact; eternally (and the language of eternity does somehow seem to be called for) out of reach.

As a description of Cézanne's art more generally, 'imagined more than experienced' may seem wrong. But let me again defend it. Of course, everything for Cézanne is staked on seeing – on striking through to a physical, phenomenal event in the eye. But in practice, I've been arguing, this event in Cézanne takes on a kind of immediacy and intensity that *severs* it from the ordinary (multiple, pragmatic) world of the senses. (The colour of the men's flesh in the *Bathers* Monet owned is a good example.) Eyesight is raised to a higher power: the world it offers is too good – too distinct, too immediate – to be true. Maybe it matters that the first perfect realization of this vision came in a picture of a railway driving its 'abstract' economical furrow through a hill. And how – here is my question, ultimately – can the space of a *room* be reconciled with this structure of apprehension? Are not room-space and cutting – room-space and space cut out arbitrarily from an endless continuum – sheer opposites? What have four walls and furniture to do with Cézanne?

Well, they coexist only very uneasily. Turn, for instance, to a painting from much the same moment as *Railway Cutting*, the poet *Paul Alexis Reading to Émile Zola* (FIG. 65). The date the painting is most often assigned in the literature is 1869–70, but I'm inclined to push it a year or so later. (Note

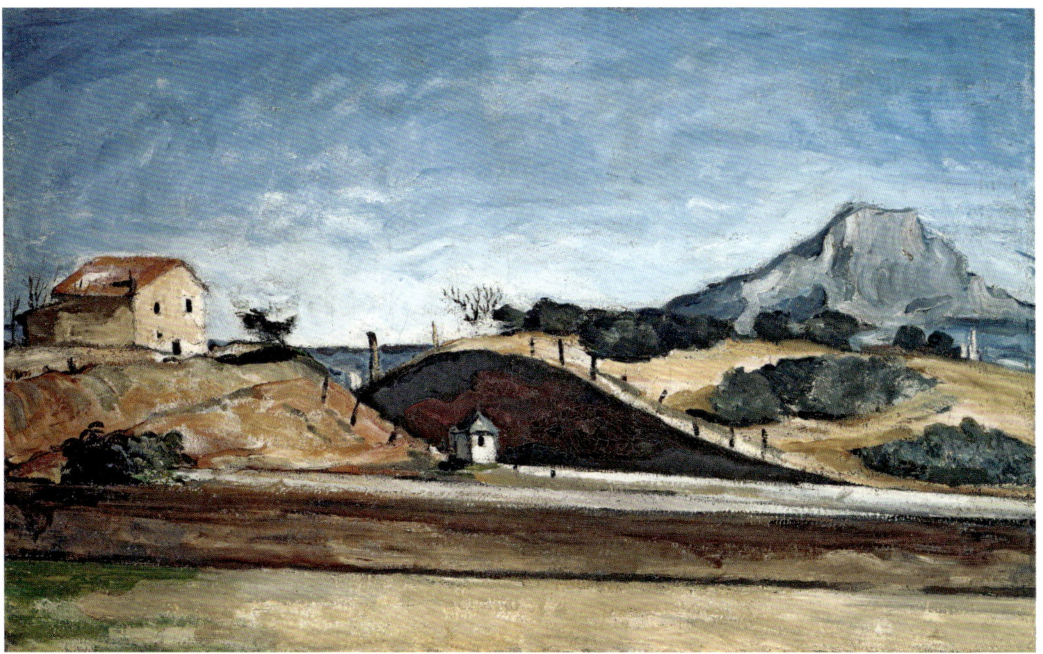

64. *The Railway Cutting*, c. 1870–71, 80 × 129 cm (31⅝ × 50⅞ in.). Bayerische Staatsgemäldesammlungen, Munich.

the landscape painting on the wall, which looks like a relative of *Railway Cutting*.) I enter *Alexis and Zola* into the story of the *Card Players* for several reasons. I am surprised that it has not been thought of before in connection with them.[10] It seems to me the *Ur*-form of the *Card Players*; which is not to say that Cézanne had the early painting consciously in mind those many years later. But a very great deal, for him, had been at stake in the picture of his two friends. It was his deepest dream of an interior in common. If we think of the Barnes painting as in some sense a return to the Alexis territory – an effort to make the dream real again – it seems fated that so many of the earlier motifs resurface: the curtain migrating from left to right, the painting on the wall in much the same position, Zola's carnal, boyish red smock losing its mobility and changing to crystalline blue. But I am not making out the Barnes painting to be a poetry reading in disguise. All I suggest is that *Alexis and Zola* 'lay behind' the *Card Players* – and that it is not surprising it did. The picture was latent in Cézanne's mind, as his most intense first effort at picturing room and sociability.

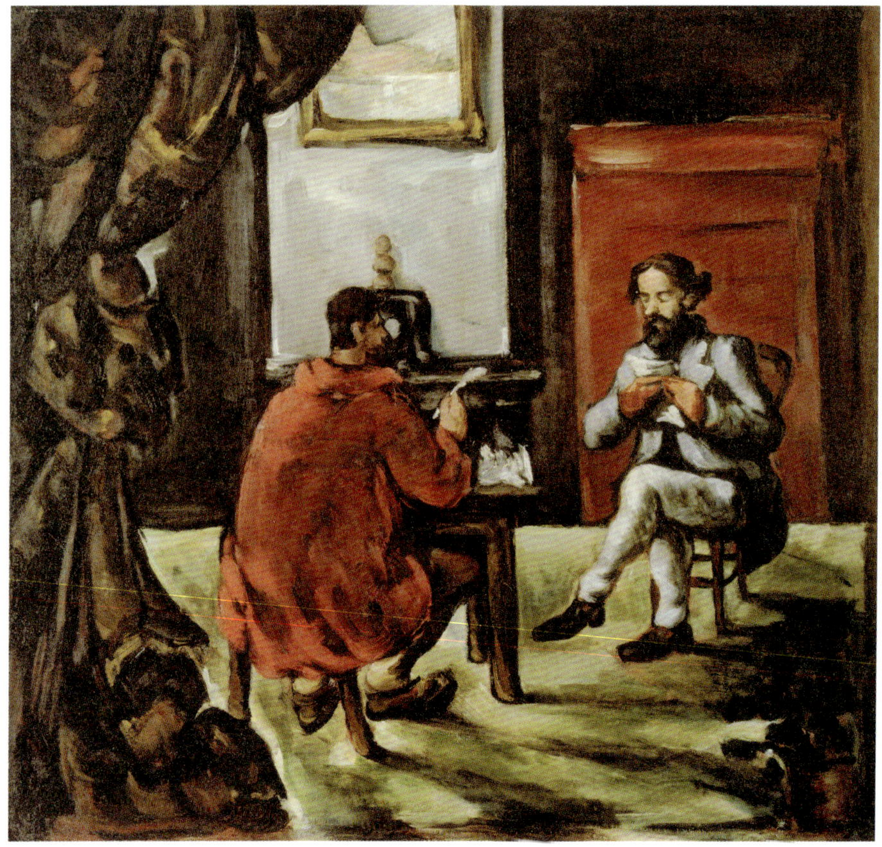

65. *Paul Alexis Reading to Émile Zola*, c. 1870–71, 52 × 56 cm (20½ × 22 in.). Private Collection.

The space depicted in the more famous, slightly earlier version of *Alexis and Zola* is, by contrast, not room-space at all (FIG. 66). It shows how foreign to Cézanne's natural imagining an interior really was. 'Room' here gives way to dream-veranda, 'wall' is replaced by shutter and void. (There are presentiments of the folding doors and sliding panels that make up the café background in the Pellerin *Card Players* (FIG. 61). It is only the second *Alexis and Zola* that tries to imagine the whole room. And how fraught that imagining is! The great curtain struggles to anchor the motility of the floor. Light glances across it, ebbing and flowing like shallow water in sunshine, and shadow consumes the flowerpot at bottom right. The back wall is massive and multipartite, perhaps meaning to speak to overdone bourgeois solidity (which of course the young writers shrug off), and yet the wall is mined and overtaken by a black that is funereal, impalpable, fantastic. It is the black of *Black Clock*, done at much the same moment (FIG. 30) – the clock, or something like it, even reappears next to Zola's pinhead.

Alexis perches on his chair – his pose, by the way, is shadowed by one struck earlier, in another painting, by Cézanne's father – as if sitting down were the most temporary and delicate thing a human being had ever been called on to perform. With due reservations, I do think his precariousness

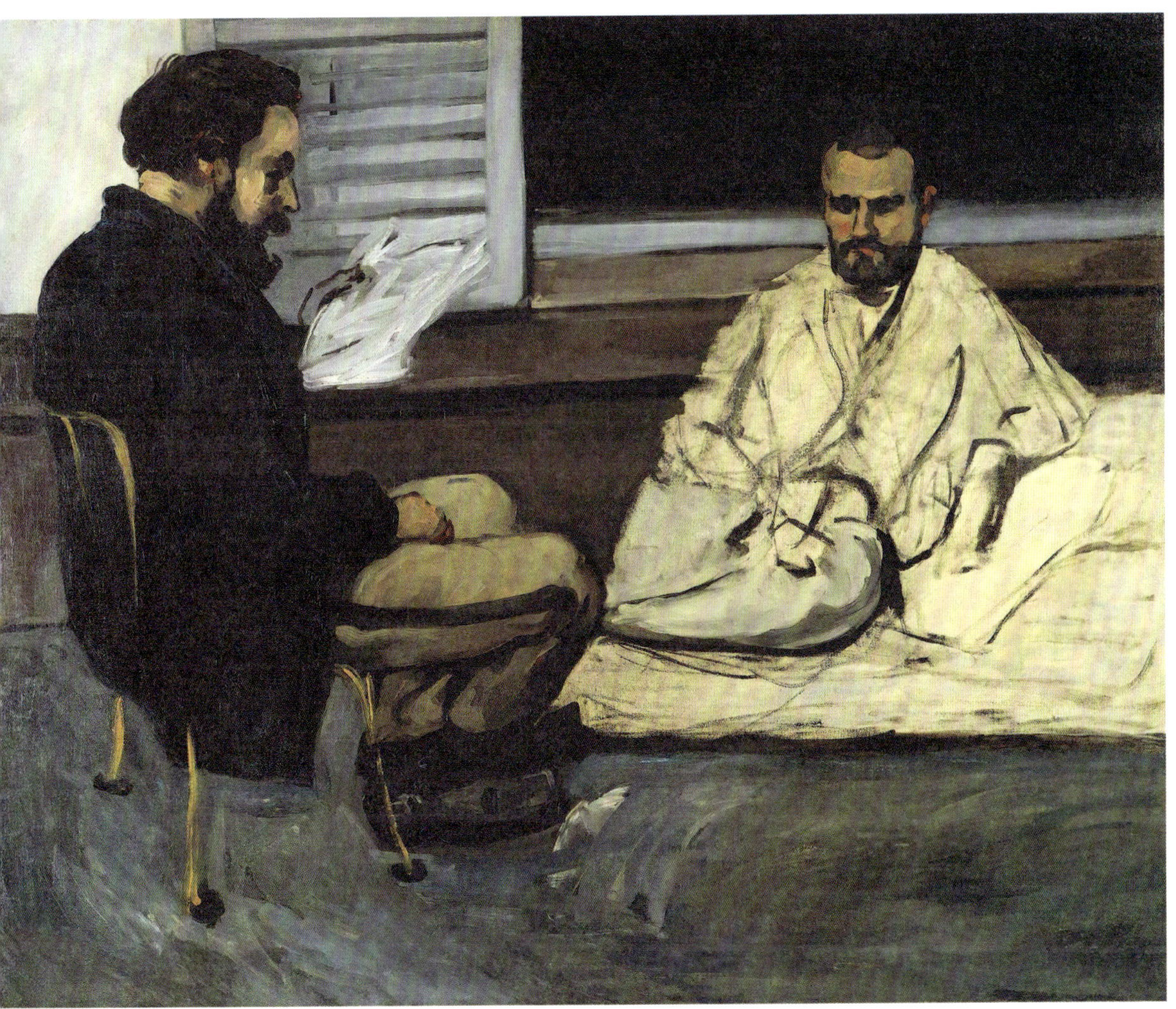

66. *Paul Alexis Reading to Émile Zola*, c. 1869–70, 130 × 160 cm (51¼ × 63 in.). Museu de Arte de São Paulo.

points forward to the player at right in the Courtauld (FIGS 63 & 73). And the whole back wall in *Alexis and Zola* seems to me to anticipate the way Cézanne treats surfaces of this kind in his later work. Of course, back walls are a vital part of most still-life set-ups, and of many great portraits; but the wall in Cézanne is repeatedly – often brilliantly and bafflingly – an interrupted, unstable, perforated, half-concealed boundary, opening onto heaven knows what.

Questions one and two, then, have to do with space: room-space in the five *Card Players*, and the tension between a normal room's proximity and finiteness and the way the world most often took on form, in still life or landscape, in Cézanne. Question three homes in on the room's rear wall.

I want to take seriously the fact that in painting the *Card Players* Cézanne allowed himself, or was bound to acknowledge, a massive end-stop to the illusion, a thus-far-and-no-further. This, to repeat, was against his habits. (The creased sheer face of Montagne Sainte-Victoire, which might have functioned as an outdoor equivalent to the Barnes wall and curtain, in practice was most often made to suspend the very ideas of distance and boundedness, and be the place where the in-betweenness of the world was clinched.) And it seems that as the *Card Players* series developed Cézanne did look even here, instinctively, for ways to make the wall something else. But not straightaway. Again, the anomalousness might turn out to be an opportunity.

At the start of the series, once the solid back wall had presented itself, its all-too-obvious repetition of the picture's surface – a reality that Cézanne was a master at acknowledging, but always dialectically, not in the form of a flat repeat – was allowed to bring on a set of positively florid metaphors of painting itself, the concrete activity, taking place across the wall, or maybe even *as* the wall. In the Barnes painting, how enormous and naive the metaphors are (FIGS 63 & 73)! The enormous bland curtain twists and hardens into the right-hand peasant's smock, as if bodies in pictures essentially materialized out of coloured folds – and then only partly, the inanimate becoming animate against the odds; and the dark painting (or is it a mirror?) hung on the wall in the centre stands sentinel, clamped in its frame, casting a shadow, offering (internally) either blankness or infinite depth; and in answer the pipes and vase, on their string and shelf, hover in front of the wall's surface, the vase hardly belonging to pictorial space at all, as if (again the hint at ontology) a painting were always most deeply an arbitrary rectangle into which – or out of which – the things of the world occasionally float, familiar but transfigured, taking on momentary life. The dark painting is high and central, but empty and incomplete. *Railway Cutting* is not far off.

◆

These are my lines of enquiry. I dream of the three lines edging closer, so that in the end the full density of the matrix from which the *Card Players* emerged will be clear. But I did say 'dream'.

Let me start with the metaphors on the wall in Barnes – maybe the curtain in particular. I want to hold in the mind's eye the great drape in *Alexis and Zola*, and the one in *A Modern Olympia* (FIG. 6: done at much the same moment as *Alexis and Zola*), and see them as variations on the pulled-back curtains common to Cézanne's heroes, Rubens and Veronese. We should recall the hangings swept unstably aside in many a great Cézanne portrait and still life. If we want further evidence of how much the motif of the curtain seems to have mattered to Cézanne, then we could enter in the astonishing 'drapery study' from just before the time of the *Card Players*, in which curtain and wall and shadow – curtain and picture surface – become the picture as a whole (FIG. 67). (The canvas measures 3 feet by 29 inches: quite large by Cézanne's standards. It looks to be related to the shifting backdrop in a portrait of Hortense Fiquet.[11]) And then finally, intimidatingly, there are the curtains in the strangest of all Cézanne's big figure paintings, the *Mardi Gras* (FIG. 68).

Previously I called the painting of *Alexis and Zola* the *Ur*-form of the *Card Players*, but *Mardi Gras* is the more obvious foil: closer in time – it was done probably two or three years before the peasant pictures – and grander, more contrary. It embodies and monumentalizes the mining of room-space from within that one would *expect* from Cézanne. Maybe this is why Cézanne's enthusiasts go on averting their eyes from it. It is too thoroughgoing, too programmatic. And Cézanne himself, one senses, could not continue living on this tilting floor, this curtain drawn back on utter dissolution and obliqueness. Who could? The whole thing has a stifling,

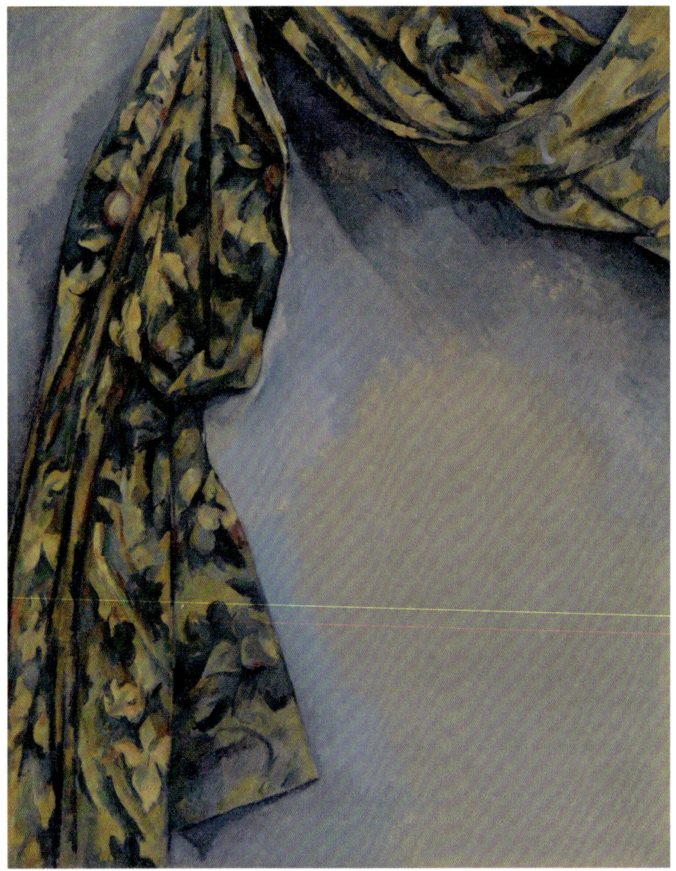

67. *The Curtain*, c. 1888–90, 92 × 73 cm (36¼ × 28¾ in.).
Abegg-Stiftung, Riggisberg, Switzerland.

perverse, unconvincing proximity, as if the two figures flashed up before us in a peepshow. Surely one job the Barnes painting was intended to do was exorcize the *Mardi Gras* ghost.

But curtains – let me concentrate on them. The trope goes back, as Cézanne knew well, to the beginnings of Renaissance illusionism: at least to the fabulous gold hangings wrenched back across the wall of Mantegna's *Camera degli Sposi*, revealing the scene on the other side. It is there, of course, magnificently in Vermeer; and sometimes I think I see traces of *The Geographer*, say – an engraving of Vermeer's painting was published by the *Gazette des Beaux-Arts* in 1866 – in the *Alexis and Zola*.[12] But it is Veronese whom Cézanne would have thought about most deeply:

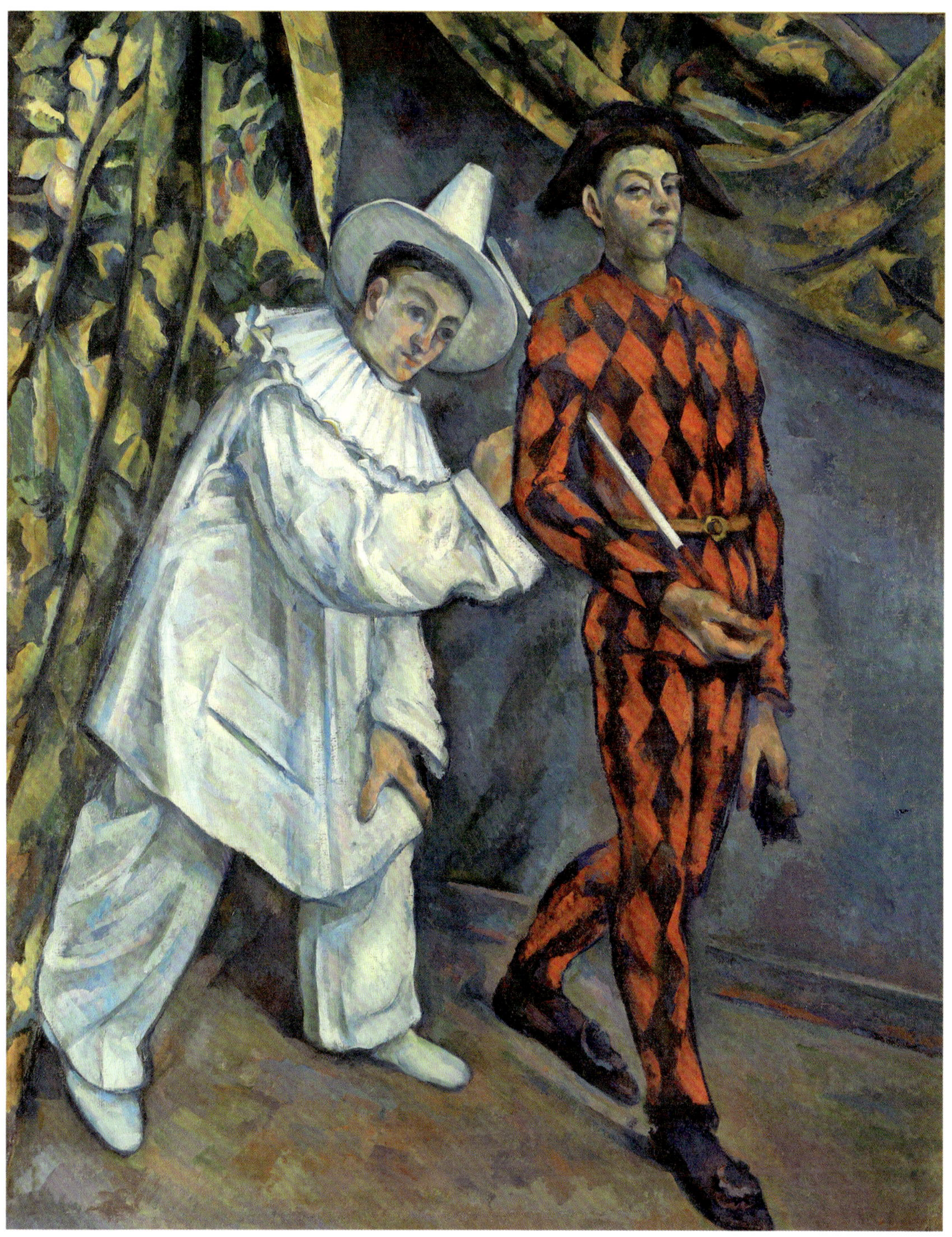

68. *Mardi Gras*, 1888, 102 × 81 cm (40¼ × 31⅞ in.). Pushkin Museum, Moscow.

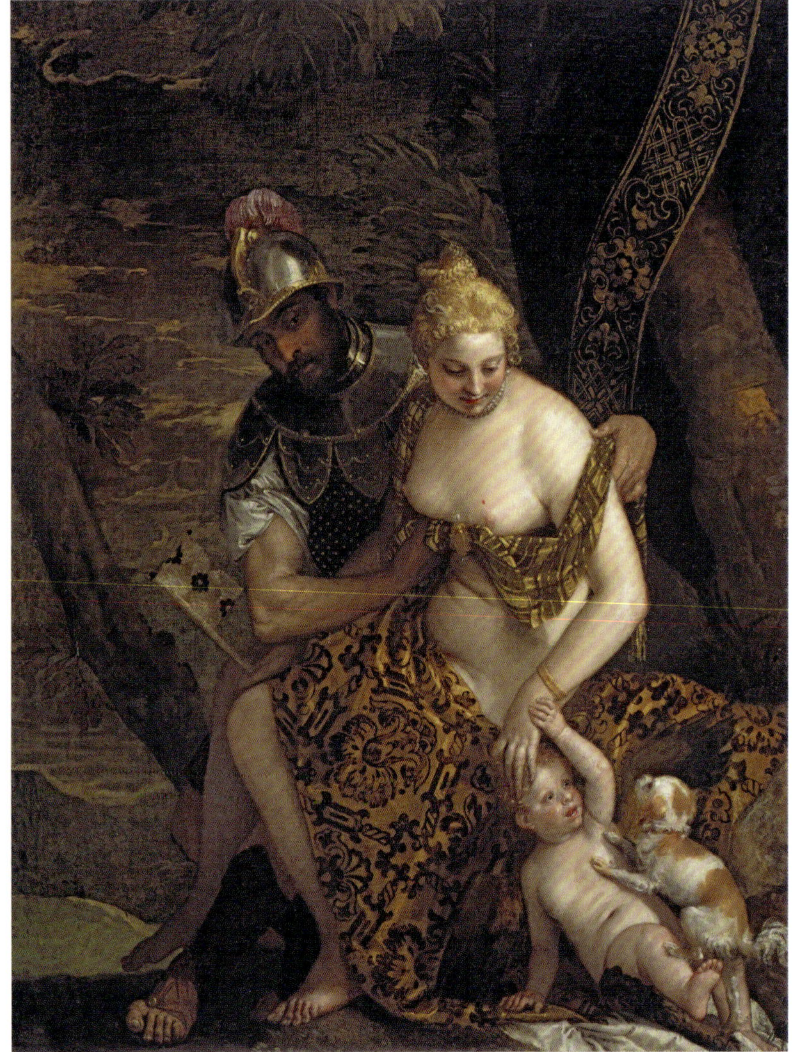

69. Paolo Veronese, *Venus, Cupid and Mars*, *c.* 1580, 163 × 125 cm (64¼ × 49¼ in.). National Galleries of Scotland, Edinburgh.

dreaming forwards, for instance, from the grand cascade of twisted bed-canopy and clear red toga on the right side of Veronese's *Raising of Jairus's Daughter* in the Louvre. Dreaming forwards… building into his own world of drapery a sense of the immense, inimitable weight of clothes and curtains as they occur in so many paintings of Veronese's maturity… or even in the prints after the master Cézanne could have studied, like Desplaces's great rendering of *Respect*.[13] So that in the end I choose as the Barnes *Card Players'* full companion – companion, not influence – the astounding meta-picture by Veronese, *Venus, Cupid and Mars*, in which the billowing curtain holds the whole foreground illusion in its folds. (Cézanne could have seen a workshop version of the painting in Chantilly, but the team of assistants there have given up – understandably – on the main point of the original: gone is the torque of the tapestry backdrop into and round the figures, and gone the ungraspable fading and sliding of Venus's room-space into a half-real, half-fantastic landscape.[14])

Put *Venus, Cupid and Mars* side by side with the Barnes *Card Players*, but hold *Alexis and Zola* in memory. The curtains in all three pictures, I'm proposing, stand for the 'outside' of representation – the heaviness, the materiality, that has to be pulled back for the optical to be got to. The curtains are the weight of the world: things in their ordinary enfolded confusion, their tactile value.

And even this does not quite capture Cézanne's and Veronese's point. Yes, the drapery is everything in the world that a picture has to draw back – push to one side, declare not its province – in order for the world to *be* pictorial. But the stuff and its weight are still there in the picture; and in the Cézanne they morph outrageously into a figure (the seated peasant in blue), or rather, into a set of mountainous folds that seem to intimate, as I said before, that 'figure' is always secondary to encasing, extrapolating *material*. Figures come out of folds. Folds are what figures are. Again Dante's metaphor comes to mind.[15] The same thought seems alive in *The Smoker* now in the Pushkin State Museum in Moscow, another picture from the mid-1890s, where sleeve and curtain are explicitly continuous, and the curtain is rhymed with the curling edge of an oil painting on the wall (FIG. 70).

And yet materialism of this kind, strong and strange as it is in Cézanne, is never the painter's last word. In the Pushkin canvas it is counteracted by the multiple, incomprehensible transparency of the space-world under the table – illusionism moving off (in a way analogous to Veronese's *Venus, Cupid and Mars*) into multi-dimensional dream. And in the Barnes painting the curtain is answered, maybe balanced out, by various kinds of pictorial incident – as if by weights and counters moved along the fulcrum of the painting's top edge. By the framed picture, central but incomplete. By the pipes' naive leaping into life. By the smoker's head with its halo of pale blue. And above all by the vase at top left. I put my stress previously on the unreachability – the fundamental homelessness – of things in Cézanne. The vase is an epitome – a brilliant, witty miniaturization – of that. Between it and the symmetry under the table there is total war.

One cannot imagine – look again at the shelf and the play of shadow top left – Cézanne's world with *corners*, even corners ironized or destabilized. His walls go on forever. (In this respect the contrast with Picasso, for whom the power of the corner is completely a given, could not be stronger.)

◆

The Barnes painting is a masterpiece. The only reservation I would have about it – but is it a reservation so much as a way of getting its structure clearer in the mind? – is that, in contrast to the later *Card Players*, the *action* in Barnes, which is to say also the spatiality, does seem to divide in two. The space of the wall and the watchers is one thing – at once immobile and restless, massive but elusive, its great metaphors held in suspense – and the space of the table and players another. I think the background in the end does enough to animate, and even interrupt, the great placidity in the foreground; but my sense of Cézanne's way forward from Barnes is that he sensed the possibility – which surely he always wanted in painting – of background and foreground being more at one. Of composure and contingency being interleaved.

Focus on the young man behind the table in the Barnes, his smock, shirt and waistcoat assembled as if from a set of interlocking separate pieces, and his cards the colour of steel; and then move to the strange small figure at his shoulder (FIG. 72). The little girl is an intruder, a visitor from nowhere: it could hardly be clearer that outside the circle of the three men at table things and persons loom up in isolation, as from a great beyond: the dark painting on the wall is quietly dominant; the girl's black-and-white deathliness does enormous work. Maybe too much. I think Cézanne went on instinctively *fearing* (rightly) his own power of pictorial estrangement – the way 'middle distance' in his work could so

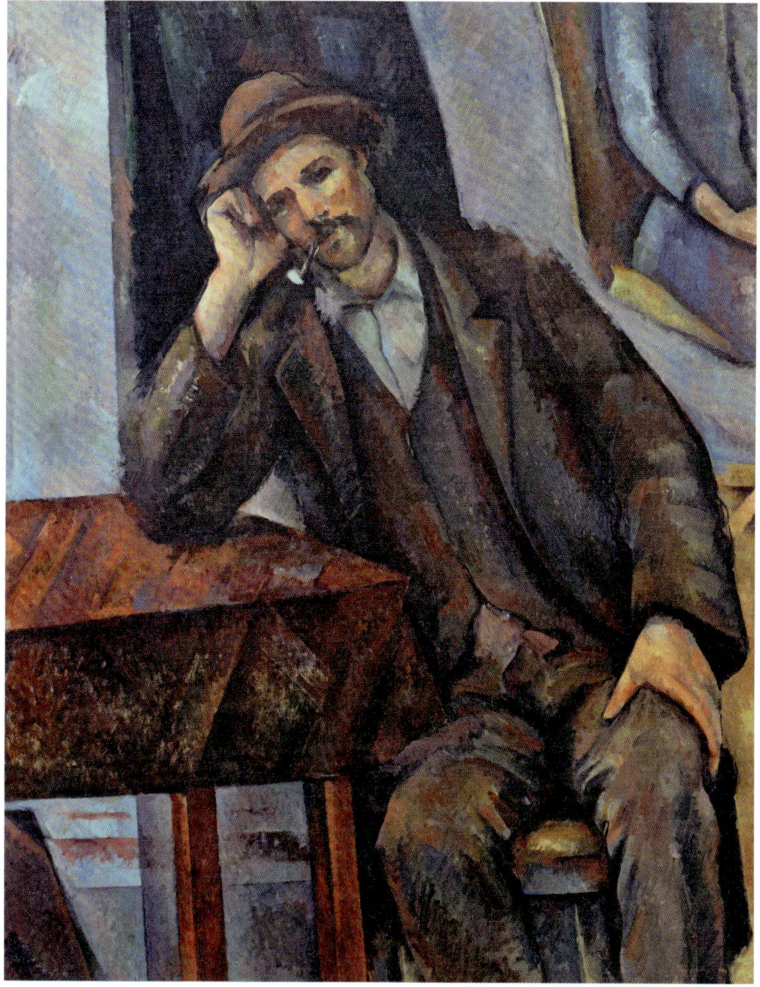

70. *The Smoker*, c. 1893–96, 92 × 73 cm (36¼ × 28¾ in.). Pushkin Museum, Moscow.

easily take on an uncanny, almost sinister force. One thing that happens in the last three *Card Players* is that dream theatre gives way to slice of life.

The phrases that just came up with reference to the girl in the Barnes – 'deathliness', 'dream theatre' and so on – need further justification. They are partly a response to the oddity of the spectator as we are given it – is it a girl or a boy? would be one question – and partly to what we know of the figure's prehistory. The immediate source of the onlooker seems to have been a painting Cézanne saw regularly in his local museum at Aix, a *Card Players* by the Le Nain brothers.[16] The girl in that painting, looming out of the darkness, is a touching invention. A child looks wide-eyed at the doings of her elders. How much she understands is not clear. And this idea seems to have lodged in Cézanne's imagination from very early on, in truly dreamlike – nightmare – fashion.

I called the 1870 *Alexis and Zola* the *Ur*-form of the *Card Players*. But in the 1950s the art historian Kurt Badt pointed to a much more ancient and infantile image source,[17] which crops up in a letter Cézanne sent to Zola in January 1859 – a full decade earlier than the painting celebrating the young men's freedom at Medan (FIG. 71). The drawing in the letter was done two days before Cézanne's twentieth birthday. Zola was just three months younger. What is happening in the drawing hardly needs spelling out: it is a scene of ceremonious cannibalism, with a skull set down on the table between two vaguely eighteenth-century figures and three more small individuals, by the look of them children, standing ready to partake. The verses below give the main players' names. The two men in the doorway are Dante and Virgil, and the figure at the right of the table is the Father – inviting his children and grandchild ('l'ainé, le cadet, le petit-fils') to make a hearty meal. Badt was struck by the similarities between the cannibal feast and the Barnes *Card Players* – the same rigid symmetry of father and son, plus mirror-image legs underneath the table; the same transfixed children; even the same picture on the wall. He believed that Dante and Virgil at the door were the first forms of the weird couple in *Mardi Gras*. Nowadays, when psychoanalytic readings are out of fashion, Badt's is passed over in silence in the literature.[18] And what Badt does with the drawing – his determination to map out an Oedipal drama in it which the Barnes *Card Players* essentially repeats – *is* predictable and excessive, in a period sort of way. But I think the basic link he makes between the Barnes picture and the drawing – back to the nineteen-year-old's revenge fantasy – is persuasive. One does not have to be a Freudian to sense that making the Father the master of the feast, as Cézanne's poem does, is essentially a displacement of the wish to make him the object of it. Cézanne and Zola play all the parts: they are Dante and Virgil, recoiling in horror; they are pseudo-Father and son on either side of the table; and they are, touchingly, with the honesty

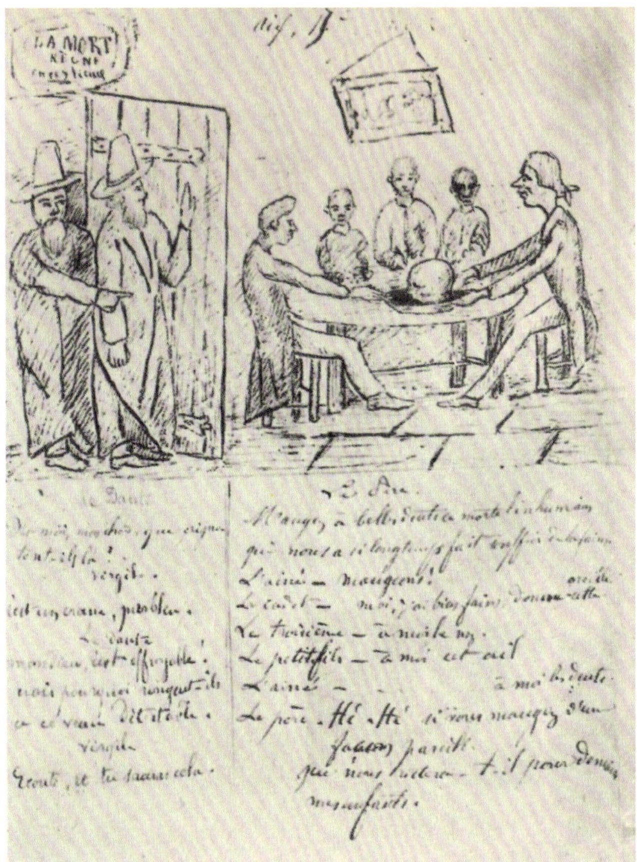

71. *Symbolic Drawing, 'La Mort règne en ces lieux'*, pen and ink, 1859, dimensions unknown. Private Collection.

of the unconscious, still the disbelieving, uncomprehending children, astonished at their own adolescent rage.

Kurt Badt called the fantasy of 1859 'the Ugolino drawing', remembering a gruesome episode in the *Inferno*. I am not sure this is helpful. I'd prefer to give the crude sketch a more general title: something that would do no more than establish that deep down, for Cézanne, people gathered for a game or ceremony round a table are always playing with the weight of the world on their shoulders – playing a game with death. The little girl in the Barnes picture, come straight from the scene's buried starting point, knows this. Between her and the dark profile of the right-hand player, entombed in his armour of blue, there is a tense sad parity.

◆

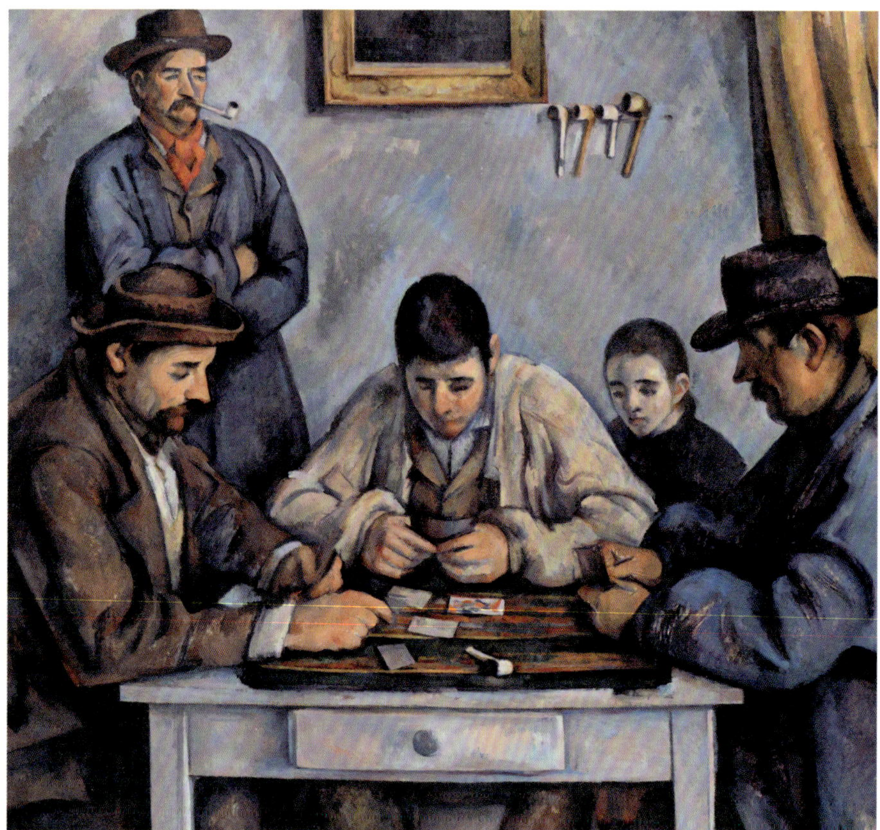

72. Detail from Fig. 60: *The Card Players*, c. 1890–92. Barnes Foundation, Philadelphia.

I turn to the Pellerin, Orsay and Courtauld pictures (FIGS 61, 62 & 63). What the three final pictures are trying for, especially if Pellerin's was the first of them, is clear enough in general. They move towards a *moment* of sociability, as opposed to Barnes's forever-ness. They attempt to secure a spot of time in which the solidity of a form of life is still evident, but where one senses the age-old and the temporary – almost the age-old and the makeshift – in balance. (Hats worn indoors speak to the former; the café backdrop maybe to the latter.) The famous quote from towards the end of Cézanne's life – 'I love above everything the aspect of people who have grown old without doing violence to old habits' ('J'aime sur toutes choses l'aspect des gens qui ont vieilli sans faire violence aux usages')[19] – rather suffers from being extracted. It is led up to by a typical piece of self-deprecating irony. 'These days in reality everything is changing, but not for me, I live in the town of my childhood, and it's in the look of people of my own age that I see the past again.' ('Aujourd'hui tout change en réalité, mais non pour moi, je vis dans la ville de mon enfance, et c'est dans le regard des gens de mon age que je revois le passé.') He knows the fragility of the illusion. And even the much-quoted sentence that comes next ends equivocally. The people who have grown old without doing violence to custom are essentially passive, he says, 'letting themselves follow time's laws' ('en se laissant aller aux lois du temps'). And then he says, 'je haïs l'effort de ces lois.' This is difficult. Michael Doran seems to me to have wrenched the sense when he translated the phrase as 'I hate people's efforts to escape these laws.' It surely just means that Cézanne hates the effort – the force – of time's laws. As we all do. But he is not saying the force is escapable. 'Aujourd'hui tout change en réalité.' In Cézanne's art the 'everything changing' is everywhere. That is what the early twentieth century got right about him.

Of the three last *Card Players*, the Pellerin version seems the most static. It looks in reproduction – but real life may utterly refute this – as if the composure of the canvas, with its curious intermediate scale, was bought at the cost of greyness. It is hard to think of a Cézanne from the 1890s that looks less animated in terms of colour: the right-hand grey coat seems almost a true cool monochrome and the smoker's face is carved out of wood. If this is true and not a trick of photography, then surely Cézanne would have been dissatisfied. Colour either animated a world for him or deserted it. The Pellerin picture has an airless, compartmentalized look. Something about its very shape, and the fit of the figures to the shape, is sepulchral. The Courtauld picture is *reckless* in its attempt to disinter the scene – to destabilize and reanimate it, and flood it with a greyness that would not be that of a tomb. It could well be, as presumably Schapiro thought, that the Orsay painting was a *rappel à l'ordre*.

Compare the Orsay and Courtauld pictures again. The Courtauld's is a wider world, seen from a slightly (decisively) greater distance, with the table more tilted. The two peasants, as I said before, are pushed back a little from the table, occupying and stabilizing it less. Focus for a moment on the table's inner frame and the balance of knees within it: the contrast is touching. The space of the game – I am repeating myself – is more firmly established in the Orsay picture: the relation of bodies to the picture edge is a pictorial enactment of that, but so is the warmth and solidity of the two players' colour – the fierce reds, for example, florid and supercharged on face and hand, the purples on the left-hand player's shoulder and hat, the greens all over the dun coat. Everything that speaks to the peasants' game's *happenstance* quality – its café surroundings signifying a true change of world from the Barnes painting's throne room[20] – is there in the Orsay version, but just subordinate, just (still) background. In the Courtauld the background has entered the game, and started to ruffle the peasants' implacability (FIG. 73). Just look at the right-hand player's sleeves! Or the effect of the patches of primer showing through both players' clothes. There are things in the Orsay picture that are astonishing and definitive in ways the Courtauld cannot match: the touch of light on the front face of the tablecloth, for instance, or the fountain of blacks in the window. But they are more than made up for by the Courtauld players' levitating pockets, or the geometry of the right-hand peasant's cards and two fists. Don't the hands on the table in the Orsay look a bit inert in comparison?

Let me go back finally to the table, and the question of the table's proximity to us. This is always a crucial parameter of Cézanne's pictorial thinking. What happens at the so-called front of a painting – of course, it is so-called because paintings do not *have* fronts and backs – is the fulcrum of the Cézanne effect. It is what Cézanne habitually does to our assumption of nearness – of entry across a painting's threshold at its bottom edge – that is the key to that 'out-of-reachness' Fritz Novotny described. What I go on to say now applies to the whole sequence of *Card Players*: the Barnes painting should again be central.

I think that the change in the nature of the room's – the picture's – background is paralleled, as the series goes on, by a change in the way its nearest objects relate to the picture plane. The picture plane is a *notion*, remember. Certainly it has specific effects in (on) painting: painters imagine it as they work, and adjust what they are doing (the particular forms and objects they want to materialize) to the impalpable 'picture plane' idea. It is the impalpability – the virtuality – that is spellbinding. Let us suppose, says a painter like Vermeer or Veronese, that in front of the pictured

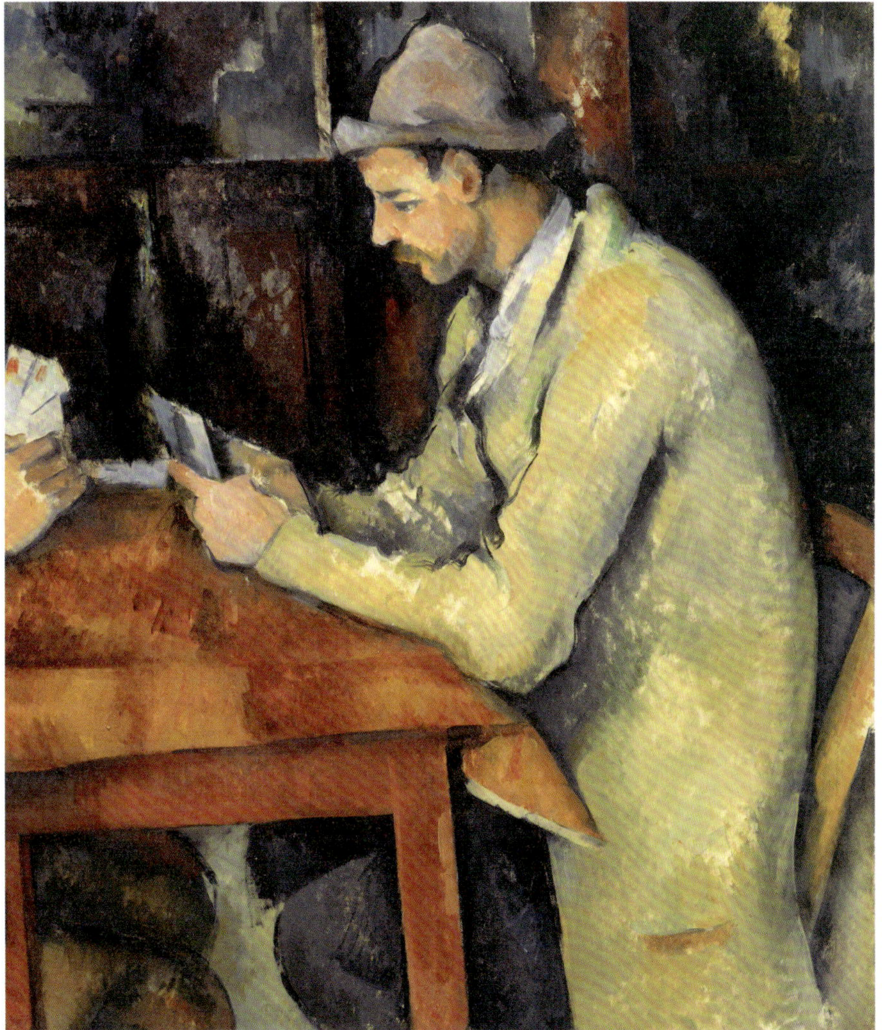

73. Detail from Fig. 63: *The Card Players*, *c.* 1892–94.
Courtauld Gallery, London.

scene is stretched, from edge to edge of the rectangle, an imaginary hard flat transparency – transparent but ineluctably *there* – which spells out the nearest nearness possible, in opposition to the back wall's thus-far-and-no-further. This is what the curtain is drawn aside to reveal. It is the threshold of the visible world – the threshold made present.

It would be too easy to say that Cézanne came to disbelieve all this and simply filled in the emptiness. (Clement Greenberg comes close to making that kind of argument.) He did not – he was too completely part of the Rubens and Veronese tradition. And therefore he went on feeling the pull of the invisible window. He went on (as painters do) signalling it, introjecting it. The table in the Barnes painting, as I said, is an epitome – a measure, a miniature, a projection – of the picture rectangle. In all kinds of ways, but certainly including frontality and transparency. (It does not matter that the transparency is played with and contradicted, as it is under the table towards the left, where table leg and player's trouser swap places interminably. For transparency is a fiction. It can reassert itself against any amount of pictorial wit.) The table is the *front* of things visible, we might say, and its hollowness only makes the solidity of the Barnes back wall more palpable. Even the void in the little picture there, repeating and reversing the emptiness under the table, does not disturb the thus-far-and-no-further.

In the last three paintings this balance shifts. In the Courtauld picture especially it is the table's less and less graspable relation to the picture plane – its lack of a felt four-squareness or even proximity – that seems in turn to mobilize the wall and window, if that is what they are, behind the two men. Non-wall and non-window, they end up being. Non-background. (Only look at the contrast with Pellerin and Orsay. The Pellerin painting still struggles to assemble a room-space, but the room might as well be a mausoleum. Orsay pushes the back wall up close to the figures, and has it end as a grid into which the figures are fitted – almost clamped. The bottle slots into the structure with a faint click. It is only in the Courtauld that the back wall – longer, more tilted, more muted, the bottle disappearing into it – fully attains its own makeshift spatiality.)

A last way of putting it would be this. It is the Courtauld painting, I feel, that most fully deserves to live in the same space as the greatest of Cézanne's still lives – the Munich *Still Life with Commode* (FIG. 43), for example, from a few years before. I bring it on again as my touchstone.

In neither picture do instability and strangeness rule. The peasants are sitting comfortably. The café is not painted by Degas. In *Still Life with Commode* the solid cupboard, the immoveable table, the familiar cast of pots – they do indeed stand for endurance, for known value. They too, just as much as the card players, sum up a form of life. The vase has come down from its far Barnes corner; the cloth twists towards us invitingly; we may still be able to touch. But Picasso was right, alas. The most fully pondered and realized Cézannes – in this, *Still Life with Commode* is typical – put the idea of 'reaching out to touch' in question. Vividness is one thing, availability – humanness, use-value – another. The still life on the table in Munich is *somewhere else*, as far from us as a tray of offerings in an Egyptian relief. These things belong to the past. Maybe the implacability of space in Cézanne is always, most deeply, a sign of this severing of time – this discontinuity. Do not do violence to 'usages', the pictures say, but be aware you observe them from an outside, an afterwards.

◆

The 'everything changing' has entered the room. Yet the players resist it; they occupy the world of the table and the space of the game with a composure that is unique in art – a finality, a perseverance. To call it stubborn would be condescending. We are as close in these pictures as Cézanne ever came – for all his difference from Pissarro – to the world of experience Pissarro spent a lifetime exploring. It is worth recalling that in 1891–92, at just the moment the *Card Players* series was taking its first steps, Pissarro had done a large double portrait of peasants – two women workers resting in an orchard, talking – as centrepiece to a retrospective of his career (FIG. 74).[21]

Hovering on the edge of *Card Players*, in other words, is the reality of class. Maybe in the Pellerin painting that dimension of things is even 'noted', with almost a novelist's smile. There is something about the left-hand player's tilt of hat and crisp sideburns and pinched cheeks that pulls him into the orbit of a story – a comic tale, sure to end badly – by Maupassant or Daudet. The Courtauld and Orsay paintings (this is their splendour) step back from this kind of concreteness.

Class was a *question* in Cézanne's Provence: that was the trouble. Cézanne himself, who by the 1890s had acquired his own circle of Provençal-nationalist admirers, knew at first hand the play of refusals and idealizations surrounding the notion.[22] If 'France' was to be resisted, said the Midi intellectuals – the enveloping nation-state understood by them, as so often in the past two centuries, as the engine of an all-consuming

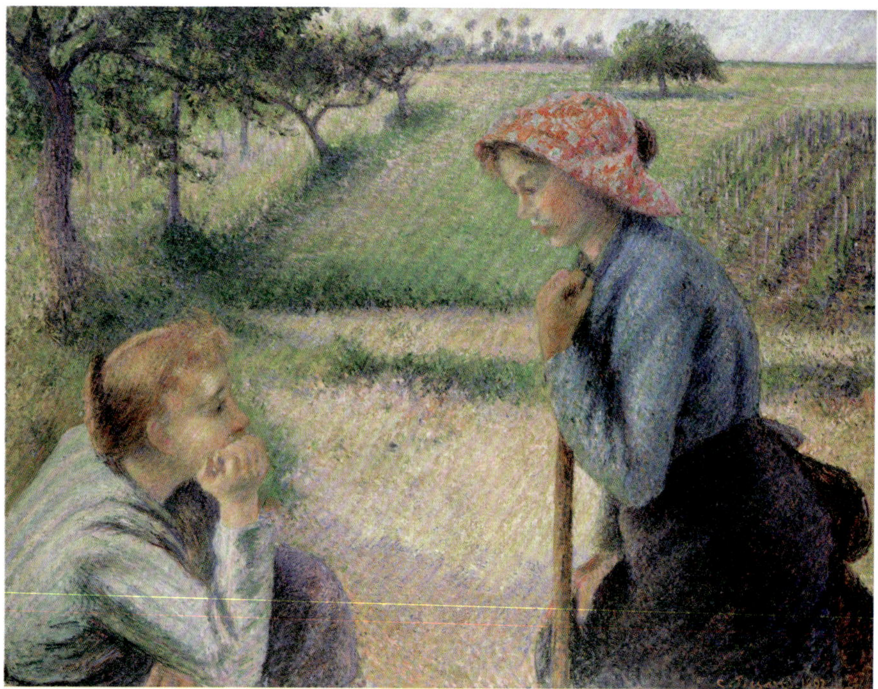

74. Camille Pissarro, *Two Young Peasant Women*, 1892, 89 × 165 cm (35⅛ × 65 in.). Metropolitan Museum of Art, New York.

modernity – it would be the peasant who held the line. There was no other sufficient force. And in the peasant's very fatalism, conservatism and autarky might lie the germs, so these intellectuals hoped, of a new-old society. Smaller, no doubt; more tight-knit, narrow-minded and slow-paced; rooted in language and shared memory; mythic and materialist; back in touch with the eternity of the earth.

The men in *Card Players*, I want to say finally, have no such future in their bones. No *Angelus* sounds for them from the fields outside, no tragedy of *La Terre* is in the making. The great symbolic battles of the Third Republic are over. The immense work of aesthetic concentration that went into making the *Card Players*, whose overall logic I've been trying to follow – the work done on space, proximity, balance and imbalance, reciprocity, animation, massiveness, confinement and loss of boundaries – was above all an effort to free picturing from those battles and cancel their deadly *mise en scène*. Cézanne's peasants, in a word, are moderns like us.

5. Matisse in the Garden

It's frightening, life.

Cézanne to Émile Bernard, 1904[1]

This chapter is mainly devoted to a painting by Matisse, *The Garden at Issy*, done most probably in the last half of 1917 (FIG. 75). Cézanne, I shall end by arguing, is *Garden at Issy*'s presiding deity: I think of the canvas as a darker cousin, almost a negative, of his strange *Red Rock* (FIG. 4). But Cézanne keeps company in the Matisse with other inevitable masters of French painting in the late nineteenth century – with Monet and Renoir in particular. Looking at *Garden at Issy*, then, leads to the question of Cézanne's place in the wider line of art called 'modernist', which Matisse was so determined to continue. It seems a good question for the book to end with.

Matisse's *Garden at Issy*, on the face of it, is all form, all shape and colour, all deliberate surface. But there is also something desolate about it, something unnerving. *Red Rock* looks buoyant in comparison. So the question arises, as often with modernism: What kind of balance of attention – what kind of movement from surface to depth – is the viewer expected to maintain in front of a painting of this kind? And that question is inseparable from another having to do with the painting's circumstances. *Garden at Issy* was painted at a terrible moment in French – and European – history. Nineteen seventeen was the third year of World War, with no end in sight. It was a year of discouragement and disaffection, marked by mutiny (in France) and revolution (in Russia). As Matisse sat at his window in the Paris suburbs he would have been able occasionally to hear the sound of guns from the front. The following year two German shells fell on his garden studio. In summer 1917 his elder son Jean, aged eighteen, received his mobilization papers, which the family had been dreading, and went off to a camp near Dijon to train as an aeroplane mechanic. Matisse went to visit him later. 'They live like pigs,' he wrote to his wife in December.[2]

The questions this chapter revolves around are basic, not to say naive and primordial, and it feels strange to be posing them again so explicitly. 'How does a painting of this kind demand to be treated?' 'What kind of language is appropriate to it?' 'How much can be said about it – at all persuasively, that is – beyond a specifying of its features and a list of its painterly debts?' Modernist art, just because it was so often a search for a wholly new relation between form and content (having lost faith in the old ones), makes questions of this sort unavoidable – part of the act of seeing. Explicitness and modernism go together. A picture is nothing if it does not state up front the terms on which it is to be understood. But in *Garden at Issy*'s case, to repeat, the terms – the formal language, the look of things – are shadowed by something implicit, something undeclared. Is the date 1917 (which Matisse chose not to inscribe in the picture) relevant to the thing we are looking at? In any case, 1917 or not, how does a moment in history *appear* in a painting? Does it ever? Isn't a painting – a good painting – one that has freed itself from circumstance, from temporality? These are questions concerning art and occasion in general, and could as well be asked of Velázquez's *Surrender of Breda* or David's *Tennis Court Oath*; but they are sharpened and made more difficult, I think, by the particular nature of Matisse's aesthetic – Matisse's very view of existence.

Matisse was a hedonist. He spent his life staking everything on pleasure. Painting for him was part of the good life, alongside food, sunshine, female beauty, amiable views out the window. And in this he was representative of a central strand in the art we call 'modern' – the Monet and Renoir strand, we might call it, the Bonnard strand, the *Lavender Mist* and *Door to the River* strand. Matisse's is a strong example of a deliberately hedonistic art: art dedicated to the proposition that the only hope, in a corrupt and invasive culture, is to put one's trust in the realm of the senses, and expose oneself utterly – naively, almost idiotically – to the play of light and the pleasure of the natural world.[3] I give as example his *Open Window at Collioure*, done in summer 1910 (FIG. 76).

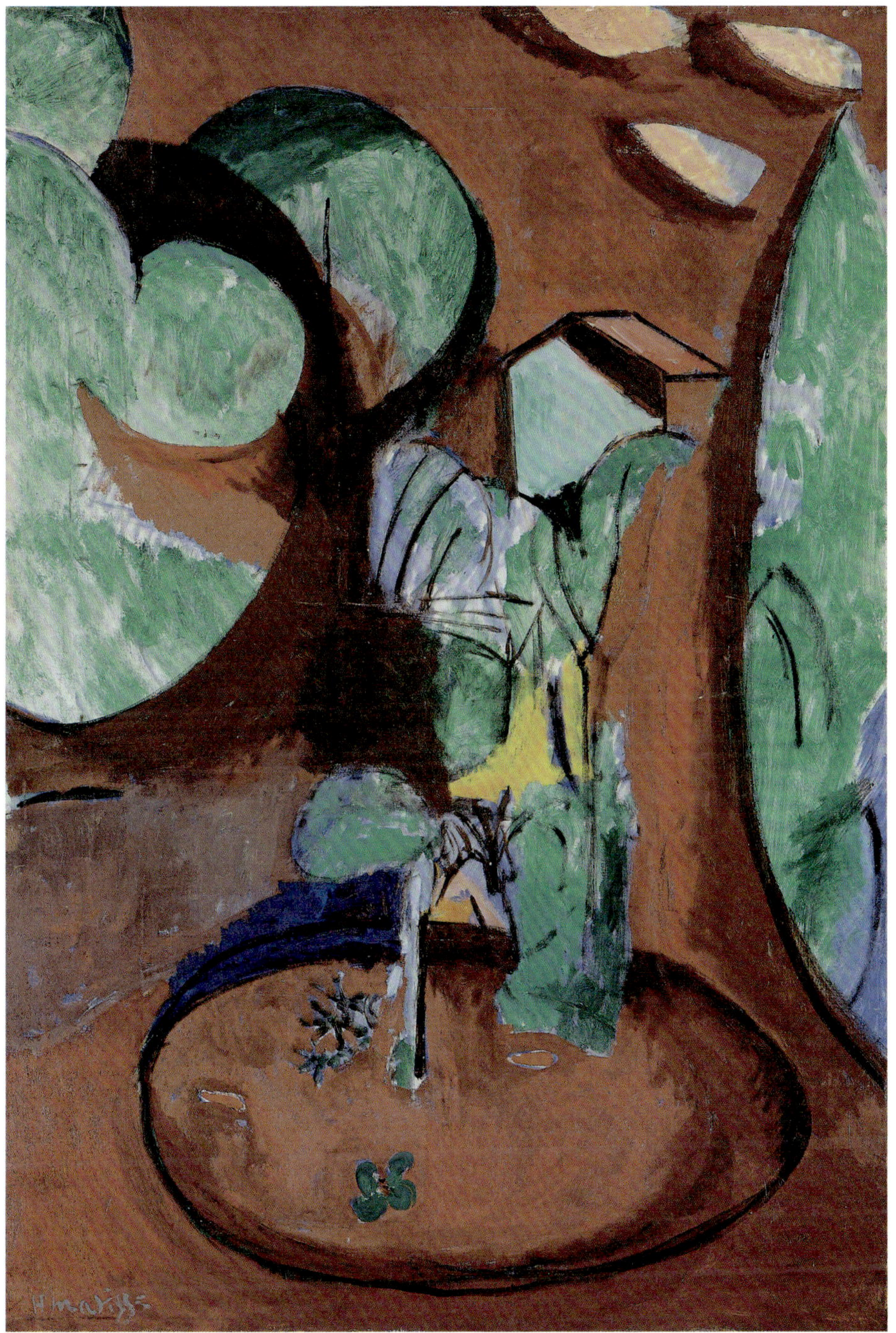

75. Henri Matisse, *The Garden at Issy (The Studio in Clamart)*, *c.* 1917, 130 × 89 cm (51¼ × 35⅛ in.). Beyeler Foundation, Riehen/Basel.

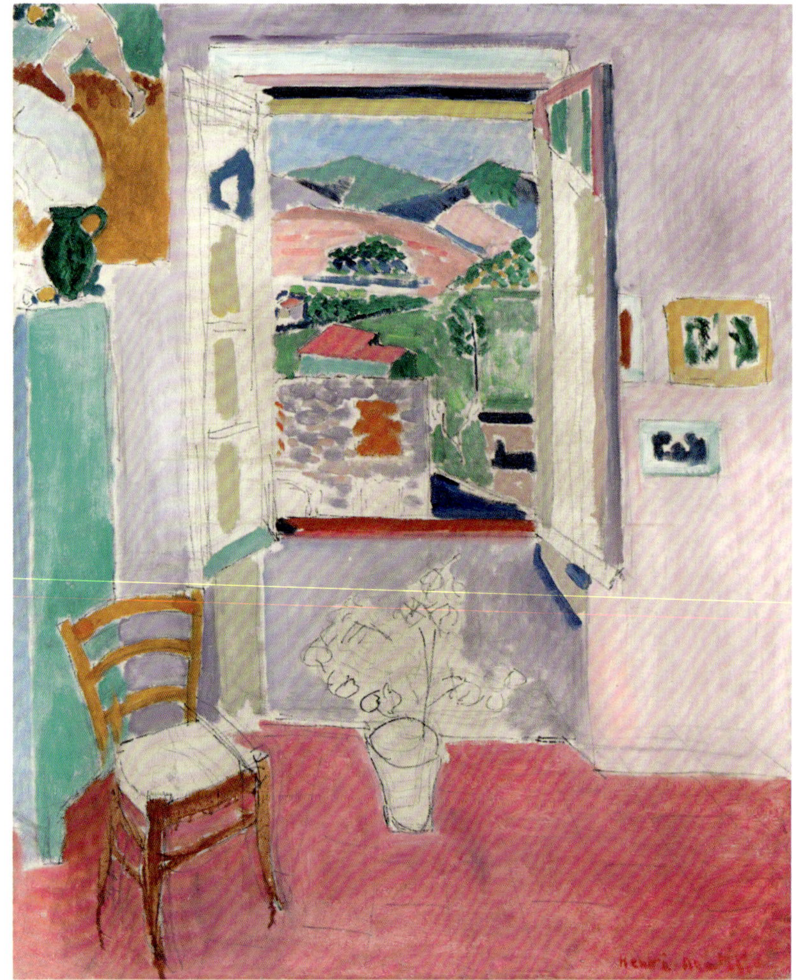

76. Henri Matisse, *Open Window at Collioure*, 1910, 73 × 60 cm (28⅝ × 23¾ in.). Private Collection.

Obviously this view of art is open to challenge. (Maybe in the age of Extinction Rebellion it seems a little less unreasonable than it once did.) Certainly the view was, for much of the nineteenth and twentieth centuries, often held to be a counsel of despair, or a gospel of flimsy solipsism – all the more vehemently because those who denounced it realized that, whatever they said, more and more of the artists who mattered had come to believe in it. Painting itself, art's very survival, seemed to depend on the Renoirs and Matisses of the world. But why?

'You ask me for some verses for your little collection, some verses about *Nature*, is that it?' – this is the poet Baudelaire writing to a friend in 1853.

> Verses with woods and great oak trees in them, and greenery and insects – no doubt the sun? But you know full well that I am incapable of tenderness toward vegetables, and my spirit rebels against this *shocking* new Religion… I shall never believe that *the soul of the Gods lives in plants*, and even if it did live there it would not interest me in the slightest, and I'd go on considering my own soul a thing of far higher price than that of a set of sanctified vegetables. Indeed, I've always thought that there was in Nature, always flowering and renewing itself, something oppressive, grim, cruel – something on the edge of impudence.[4]

These words are aimed at Corot, Courbet, Rousseau, Barbizon – that is, at everything that had already made French art great. And would continue to do so. (Poor Baudelaire had only glimpsed what sun-worship would make of French painting. Monet and Seurat lay in the future. But you can imagine the poet snorting at Matisse's view out the window if he had lived to see it.)

There is, however, one aspect of Matisse's painting that Baudelaire might have warmed to; though for many of his viewers – maybe most of us in the present – it is part of the problem. A hedonistic art, says Matisse, ought not to pretend it is anything other than a luxury. Painting is a luxury item. Pleasure is something you pay for, and the vast majority of men and women can't afford it. Up on the wall to the left in *Open Window*, to make the point, is part of a painting Matisse had done three years earlier, and which he seems to have wanted to preside over his time down south in 1910. Its title is simple and unashamed: *Le Luxe 1* (FIG. 77). And I suppose that for us its nomination of naked women as the number one luxury item – better even than sunshine and sanctified vegetables, it seems, and certainly inevitably part of the package – only makes things worse. It may be possible to approve, or excuse, hedonism as an attitude in the abstract. But in the concrete doesn't it always end up glamourizing Women belonging to Men?

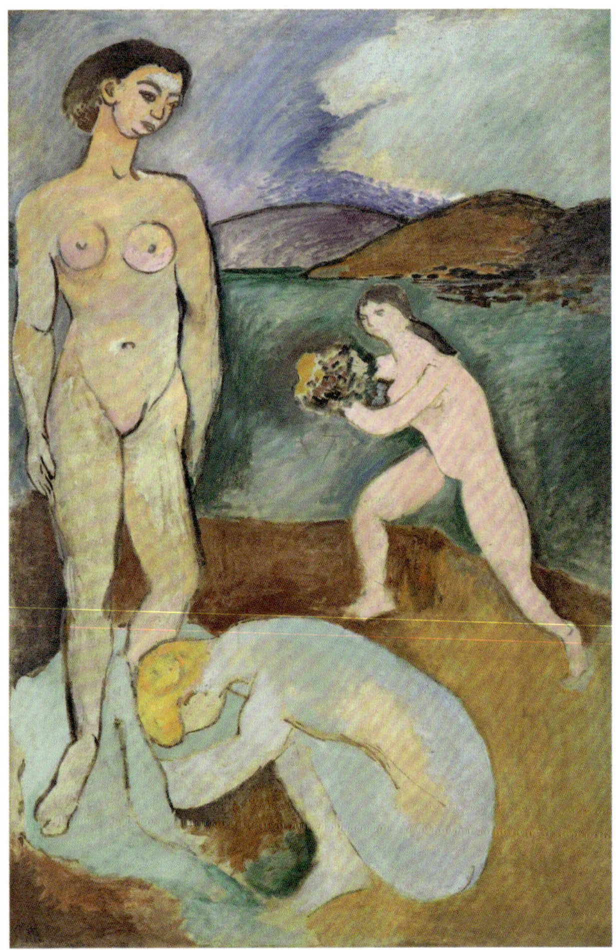

77. Henri Matisse, *Le Luxe 1*, 1907, 210 × 138 cm (82¾ × 54⅜ in.). Centre Pompidou, Paris.

Matisse must have known (this is another way of putting it) that *Le Luxe 1* on the wall put him squarely in the territory of Renoir. We could compare the painting to Renoir's *Bathers with a Crab*, done around 1897 – in particular the sequence of figures at the Renoir's left-hand side. And what on earth did Matisse think he was doing with such an invocation? Didn't he know that Renoir – Renoir-type eroticism – was a liability?

Sometime in 1918 Matisse went to visit the aging master. Arthritis had crippled the old man's hands and he was sitting at his easel, painting with a brush tied to his fingers. 'The pain passes, Matisse,' he said, 'but the beauty remains.'[5] I find the remark very moving. I confess to preferring it to most other modern art war cries. But I too, like all right-thinking art-lovers, am embarrassed by the remark's proximity to what has become Renoir's most famous boast, or confession: 'I paint with my penis.'[6] (Can the reader make out that the nude centre stage in *Bathers with a Crab* is threatening the one on the ground to the right with a crab? Oh Lord… Is the crab a penis or a vagina?)

Renoir embarrasses us. Hedonism in art shouldn't be like this. But doesn't Renoir reveal what hedonism actually is, stripped of its grand bland words like 'pleasure', 'the senses', 'delight', 'sensation'? Isn't *hedonism* embarrassing? Isn't it always a scandal to admit what you desire? But then how on earth did an art like Matisse's, or Cézanne's, *or* Renoir's at his best, come out of the scandal?

◆

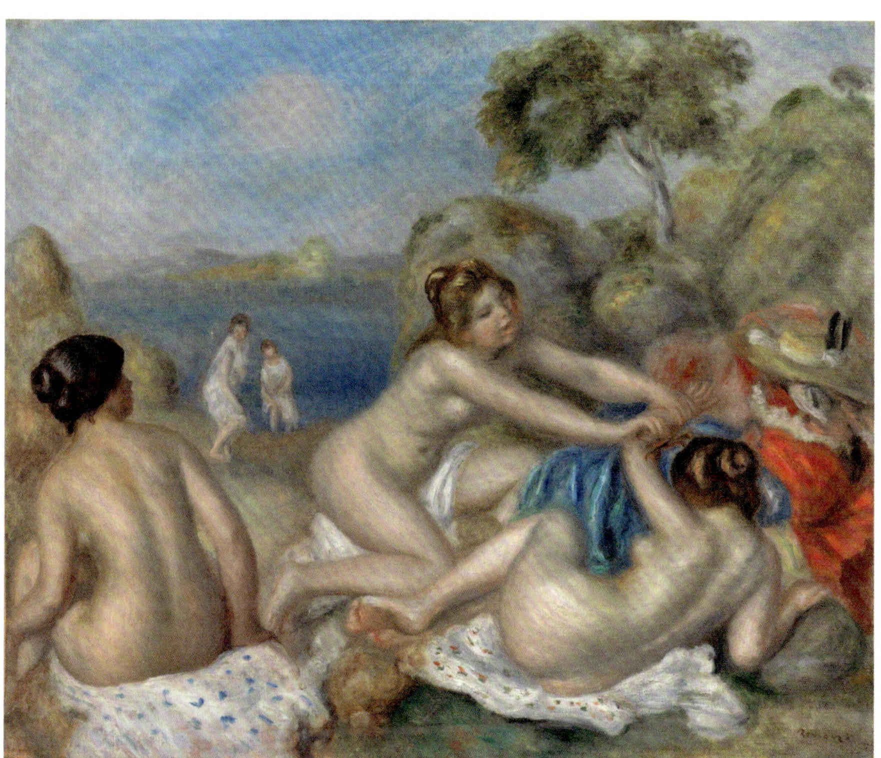

78. Pierre-Auguste Renoir, *Bathers with a Crab, c.* 1897, 55 × 66 cm (21½ × 25⅞ in.). Cleveland Museum of Art.

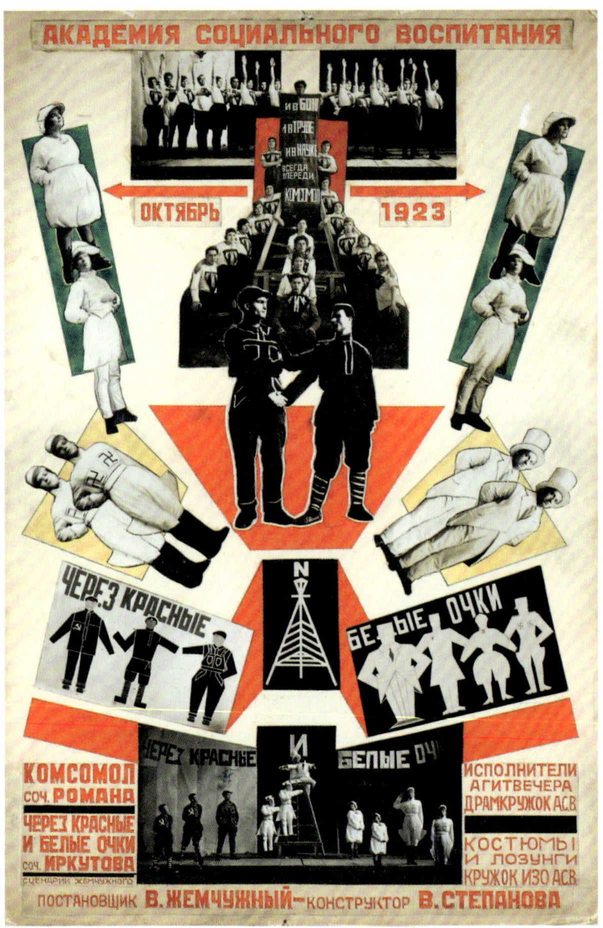

79. Varvara Stepanova, *Through Red and White Glasses*, poster, 1924, original dimensions not known.

I start again. Let us move – at the risk of utter cognitive dissonance – a handful of years into the future, and put alongside *Le Luxe 1* and *Bathers with a Crab* a poster designed in 1924 by Varvara Stepanova, immortalizing a piece of agitprop she had just staged at the Academy of Social Education.[7] *Through Red and White Glasses* is the title. The performance's subject (among other things) had been the emergence of Soviet woman.

Modern art in the twentieth century was to have many strands, and some of them exposed art nakedly – maybe brutally – to the political and social realities of the age. Stepanova's women do not look to be anyone's erotic property. Their clothes are certainly not luxury items (only the dead White males on the right still go in for frippery like top hats and spats). And in any case these are details: what matters to Stepanova – what speaks to a new subjectivity and collectivity in the making – is the whole jagged un-beautiful show.

Some modern artists – and they were very far from being a lunatic fringe – thought the only way that strange thing called the 'artwork' might preserve some of its visionary and critical force in the new age was by ceasing to *be* Art and allying itself with – fusing with – the practices of craft or design, or of built space, or of public (overtly political) persuasion. What came out of the pattern of practices that resulted often came close to realizing the dream. Stepanova is a case in point. But it was precisely characteristic of the new art situation that this imperative – call it the 'Art is Dead' imperative – was answered from within modernism by an equally powerful countercurrent. I look back *Through Red and White Glasses* at Matisse's *Studio, Quai Saint-Michel*, done in the dark months of March and April 1917 (FIG. 80).[8]

We might call this kind of answer to Stepanova the 'Art is All That is Alive' proposal; or at least, the proposal that art was now all that was worth *living for*; and that art was a form of life that, if it was to be preserved at all in the face of its various counterfeits, now had to be lived in – lived for – with a terrible heedless intransigence. I take Matisse to be a strong case of that heedlessness, that enclosure in the notion of Art-as-a-way-of-life – the conviction that one's practice, one's medium, could somehow substitute itself for the imperatives and instructions on offer from the culture at large.

But the doubts here are indelible. Surely it makes sense to assert that a stance towards life like that exemplified in *Studio, Quai Saint-Michel* is a form of escapism, and to decry it as such. Matisse as a man is wide open to the charge. Some of us are haunted by the memory of his wife and daughter's decision, during the darkest days of the Second World War, to protect the artist from knowing that the two of them were involved with the Resistance, lest it disturb him in his work. A modernist is rarely a hero. But modernism's defenders say this in reply. Who are we to question Madame Matisse's sense of priorities? Art is one thing, she seems to have thought, and Resistance another. Are the things that art can do – that maybe only art can do – to be sacrificed to the demands of dark times, of barbarism? Isn't that to concede the field *to* barbarism?

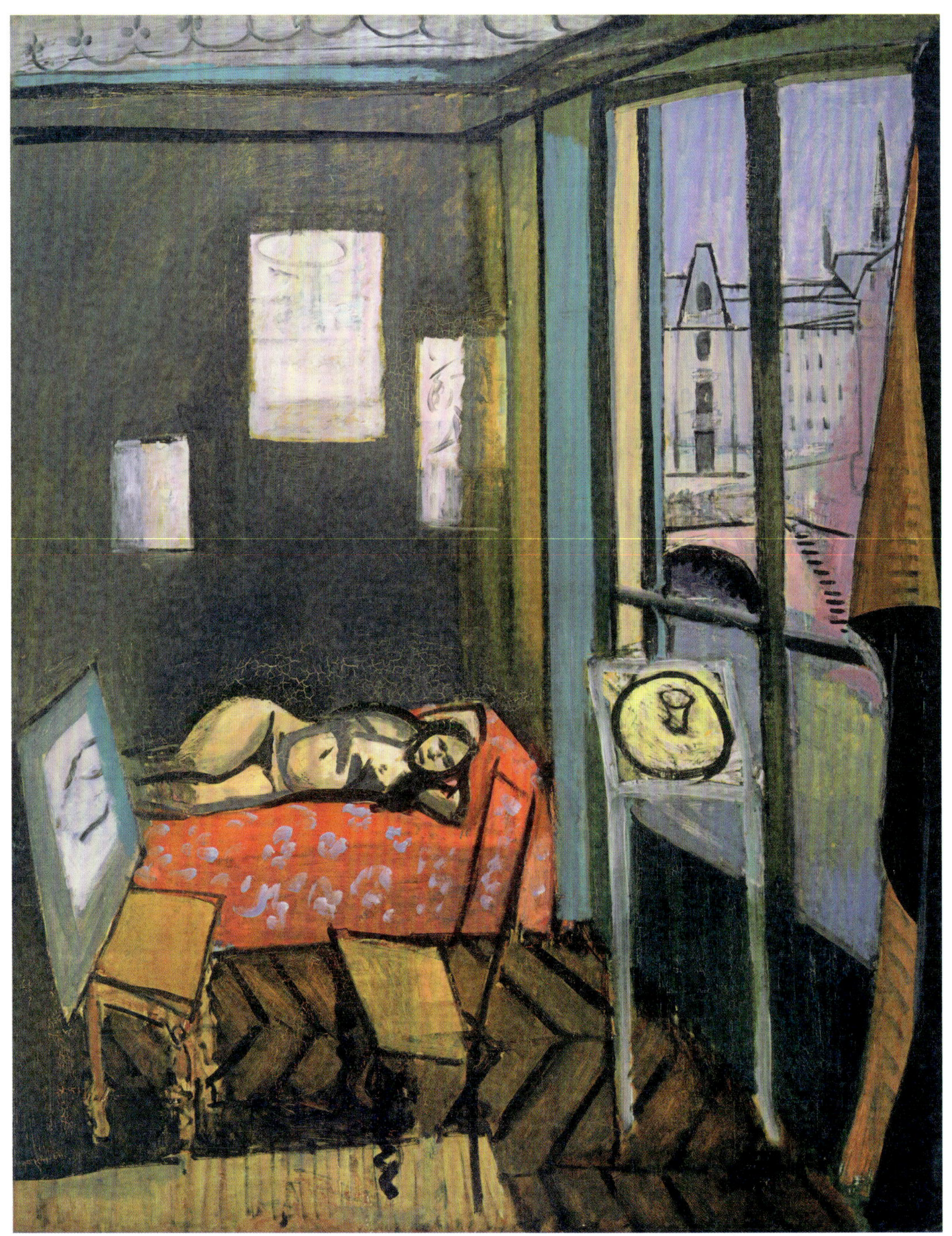

80. Henri Matisse, *Studio, Quai Saint-Michel*, 1917, 148 × 117 cm (58¼ × 46 in.). Phillips Collection, Washington, D.C.

Matisse's art – maybe art in general, at such a moment of disintegration and untruth – *depended* on enclosure in a realm of pleasure… on a fierce, naive aestheticism. Humanly, this may have been questionable. But historically, shouldn't we applaud Madame's decision to preserve it? For isn't the Matisse challenge, the Matisse paradox, ultimately this: that it is *Matisse* who leaves us the deepest account we have of the nature, the structure, of experience in the very circumstances to which mother and daughter were responding? That is: Who gives us the better account of 'life' in the twentieth century, Matisse or Stepanova? Or come to that: Matisse or Léger, Matisse or John Heartfield, Matisse or Siqueiros, Matisse or Immendorff (FIG. 81), Matisse or Andy Warhol?[9] Did any of Matisse's strong contraries come up with a better, more dreadful, picture of privacy and vulnerability in the new age – of the little space of pleasure invaded by an all-dissolving darkness – than that provided by *Studio, Quai Saint-Michel*?

The choice, however, is a false one. For it seems to be the very nature of the twentieth century that it invites, in a sense prescribes, entirely opposite and contradictory art tactics in face of its enormities. Hedonism – ruthless aesthetic concentration – is one of them. And its

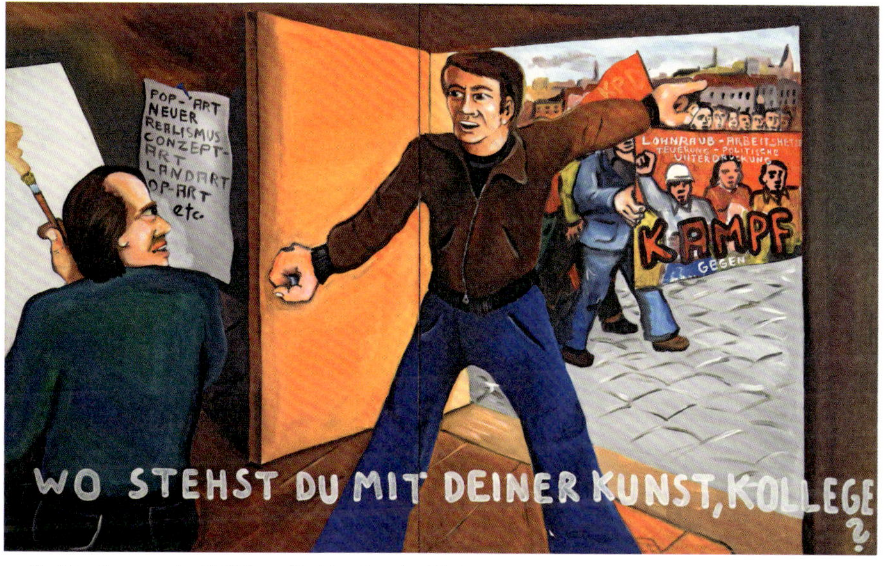

81. Jörg Immendorff, *Where Do You Stand with Your Art, Comrade?*, acrylic on canvas, 1973, 130 × 210 cm (51¼ × 82¾ in.). Musée d'art moderne de Paris.

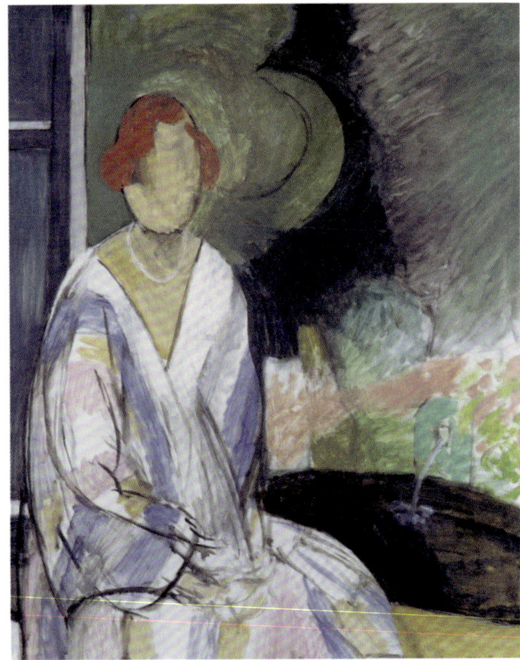

82. Henri Matisse, *Woman at the Fountain*, 1917, 81 × 65 cm (32 × 25⅝ in.). Private Collection.

seeming sealing of art off from 'the world' may well turn out to be the way – one way – of having 'the world' *enter* the picture and find form there, declaring its most unwelcome hidden truth. To put the question baldly, then: Is the aestheticism and hedonism of a painting like *Garden at Issy* – begun about two months after *Studio, Quai Saint-Michel* was finished – a force that severs it from its surrounding circumstances; or does it on the contrary have those circumstances not be 'surroundings' at all, but inherences, *in* the work, in the form of the work not its content, completely materialized in a medium?

So *Garden at Issy* it is – I hope now with Stepanova's anti-pastoral as its shadow.

◆

No one can be sure when Matisse painted the canvas now owned by the Beyeler Foundation, but for various good reasons John Elderfield believes it was finished between June and October 1917.[10] It is a formidable piece

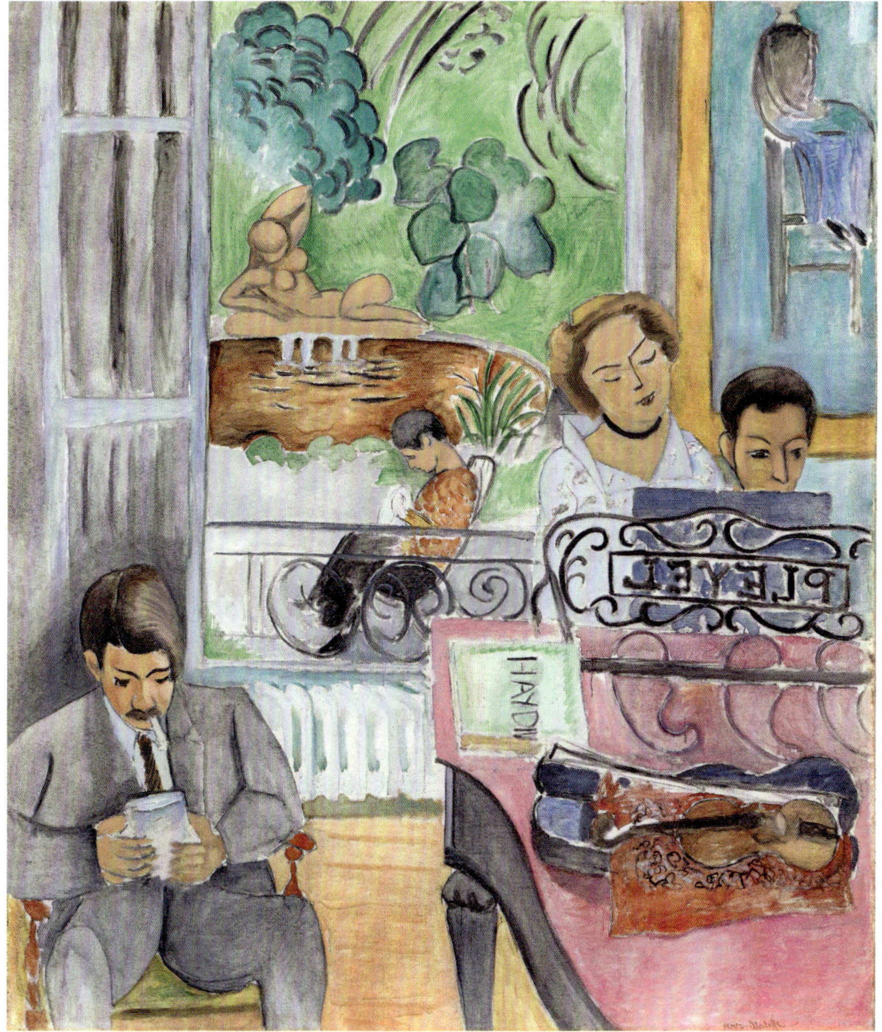

83. Henri Matisse, *The Music Lesson*, 1917, 245 × 210 cm (96½ × 83 in.). Barnes Foundation, Philadelphia.

of work: just over four feet high and almost three feet wide – by some way the largest in the group of landscape paintings Matisse did that summer. The motif is essentially the same as that in the background of Matisse's *Woman at the Fountain*, presumably also from 1917, or the view through the window in a much better painting, *The Music Lesson*, which we know Matisse turned to during the same summer months. You will notice that these other treatments of the view both have the garden prospect ending in greenery, with no glimpse of the sky. There may be sky in *Garden at Issy*: an earthen sky, with peculiar bright arrowhead clouds floating in it, casting unlikely shadows, sharp as knives. Apparitions. There is certainly a house of sorts in the garden, also sharp-edged and bleakly lit; so that in many respects the closest previous rendering of the subject by Matisse is the exquisite pencil-on-paper glimpse he gives us in a drawing from 1916 (FIG. 84), presumably a study for the great painting *The Piano Lesson* (FIG. 96) (where in the end all detail in the world through the window is cancelled out). The 1916 drawing does include, very laconically, the eaves of a small house. Maybe it shows the sky. Reaching further back in Matisse's career, the small house is certainly there outside *The Blue Window* of 1913; and perhaps – the actual geography of the garden does not help much, in fact – the house is Matisse's garden studio. A title that the Beyeler Foundation offers as an alternative to *Garden at Issy* is *The Studio at Clamart* – Clamart being the name the Matisse family favoured, a bit wilfully, for their neighbourhood in west-of-Paris suburbia.

You will see that I've begun my account of the Matisse simply by bringing on a surrounding of other pictures, to which *Garden at Issy* looks as if it must belong. This approach to understanding an artwork – let's call it the 'art in artistic context' approach – is surely necessary to any genuine understanding. It's not an approach one opts for, exactly: it is what understanding consists of. The flurry of pictures I just deployed, for instance, just *happened*, or so I believe, as part of seeing this difficult object and struggling for a first orientation to it. They were a precondition of seeing, or seeing of any adequacy. This seems to me true of art in general, but a fortiori true of an art like Matisse's, which has deliberately – defiantly – chosen the world of pictures *as* its world.

But immediately this needs to be qualified. The 'art in artistic context' approach seems very often to think that presenting the preconditions for seeing a picture – having it take its place in a family of connected representations – *is* seeing the picture, or saying all that need be said about the seeing. This is obviously wrong. Or perhaps we should say: it is obviously wrong for strong strange pictures like *Garden at Issy*. It is wrong, paradoxically, for those pictures – the key pictures, most often, in modernism – where deep inward concentration on means, fierce enclosure in

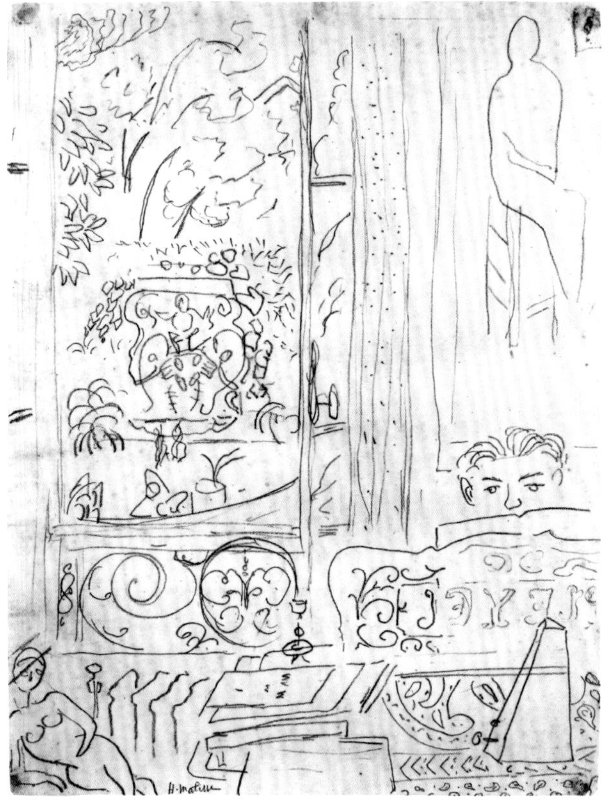

84. Henri Matisse, *The Piano Lesson*, pencil on paper, 1916, 62 × 47 cm (24½ × 18½ in.). Private Collection.

a pictorial world, results in a strength that is not like any kind of pictorial strength we have seen before. Ordinary modern pictures – like Matisse's *Woman at the Fountain*, for example – do 'take their place' in a mere array of approximate versions of themselves. Art in context interpretation is what they call for: it represents their un-thought belonging to a set. But *Garden at Issy* – this is my first and abiding intuition in front of it – is as ferociously *thought* a picture as can be imagined. It seems to be pushing towards a conclusion that puts it at odds with everything it half-quotes or half-remembers. And it half-quotes and half-remembers enormously (recklessly) too much – far, far more than the obvious points of reference that have come up so far. Hedonism doesn't mean 'not thinking', then. It doesn't mean fooling yourself that your eye is, or ever can be, innocent.

Paintings crowd in on you as you paint. A studio is full of ghosts. I would say that the deepest reason for *Garden at Issy*'s austerity and simplification, which are extreme even for Matisse, is the degree – almost, the naivety – of its exposure to so many other remembered prime objects.

Further interpretation, it follows, will again be a matter of identifying those objects. We have to stick with the first order of debts and quotes. This may seem a touch disappointing. Why don't I get on and tell you what the half-quotations mean? But here's my first proposal about how to proceed. (I think the proposal applies to art in general, but certainly it applies to Matisse.) The deeper the thinking involved in an artwork's way with its sources, the more imperative it is that interpretation stay on the surface – that is, resist the call, which all strong pictures do invite, to put the point of the half-quotations into words. Of course, the quotations invite it – you know from the beginning of looking at *Garden at Issy* that something else is being depicted than a back yard in the suburbs – but they resist it at the same time. *Garden at Issy* resists with a vengeance, and surely in the first place resisted its maker. For when I said it was as ferociously *thought* a picture as could possibly be imagined, I certainly did not mean 'thought consciously or verbally'. The more ferocious a thought in painting, I reckon, the more unavailable is that thought to the painter's interpreting second-order mind.

Hedonism in art, in other words, may well be just the term we have for an art that won't be 'thoughtful', won't be *smart* – because it thinks that intelligence is useless in circumstances like those of 1917. A response to catastrophe can only really happen at the level of instinct, intuition, unconsciousness. It only happens when idiot pleasure is allowed to reveal the pain at its heart.

The shapes in the garden – those cusps and shards and hand-axe points – are Matisse's way of thinking. They come from levels of his mind I doubt he was aware of, or wanted to be. One or two of the more superficial levels I think I can identify.

Take the green circles and flanges top left in *Garden*, for example, brushed thinly enough to suggest some kind of interior modelling, but then silhouetted so harshly in black that they seem like cutout flat discs. Do they not issue direct from the foreground of Matisse's *The Moroccans*

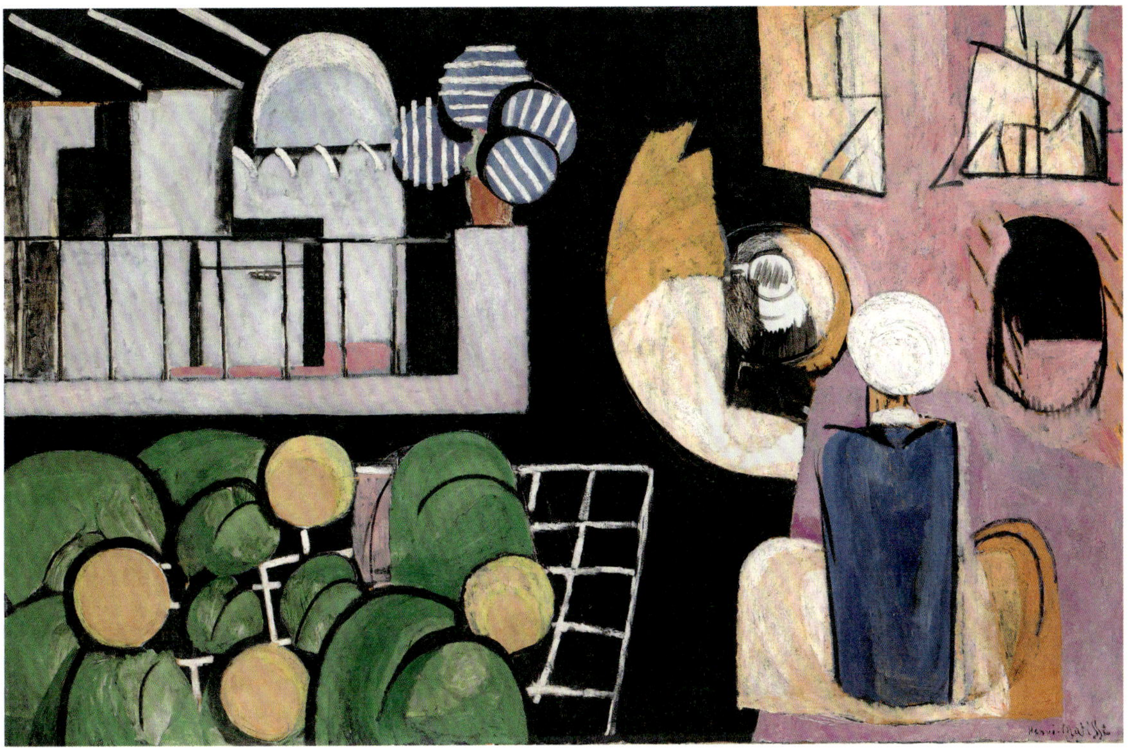

85. Henri Matisse, *The Moroccans*, 1915–16, 181 × 279 cm (71⅜ × 109⅞ in.). Museum of Modern Art, New York.

painted (or finished) the year before? The shapes in *Moroccans* seem to have been triggered by a traveller's memory of melons and leaves on a tile floor, but this memory secreted in parallel – maybe dangerously – the suggestion of Arabs all huddled and prostrate in prayer.

Staying with the area top left in *Garden at Issy*, and moving downwards, the curving deep black that overflows from its initial outlining function at the edges of the green flanges, spreading in a stop-and-start patchwork all across the picture centre, is an episode that turns up repeatedly in Matisse's painting around this time – again I remind you of the grim wartime date. The effect of the black on the picture's surface and depth, and in particular the effect of its escape (its leakage and overflow) from any one figure, is most often perplexing: it surely is in *Garden at Issy*. The shadow that occurs in *Portrait of Auguste Pellerin II*, which Matisse had worked on through the opening months of 1917, strikes me as the

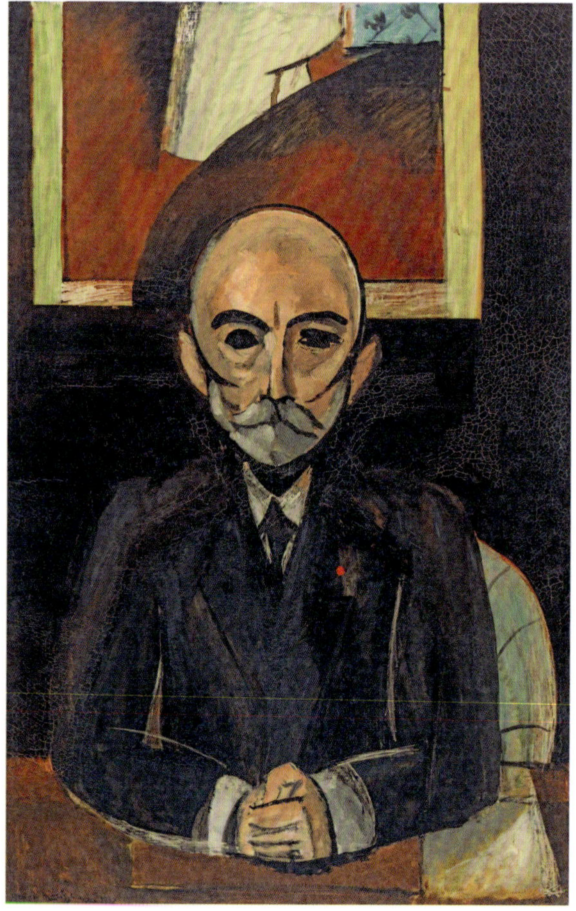

86. Henri Matisse, *Portrait of Auguste Pellerin II*, 1917, 150 × 96 cm (59⅛ × 37⅞ in.). Centre Pompidou, Paris.

closest – and weirdest – comparison (FIG. 86). (I should mention in passing, for reasons that will emerge later on, that the picture on the wall in the portrait of Pellerin, which the shadow half-obliterates, happens to be by Renoir: his *Portrait of Rapha Maître* from 1871.)

It is striking that in both these reiterations of himself in *Garden at Issy* – the Moroccan non-melons and the Pellerin shadow-path – Matisse is going back to moments in his recent work where a focused shape or a kind of pictorial motion (a sweep of the brush or the hardness of a circle silhouetted in black) seems to generate an order that once happened upon seems entirely 'right', but that nothing else in the painting prepares the way for. Compare *Shaft of Sunlight, Woods at Trivaux*, done this same summer of 1917 – another picture with *Garden at Issy* latent in it, especially in its use of black and brown (FIG. 88). Matisse remembered Pissarro once telling him that in Cézanne there was never any real sunshine, only a constant overcast.[11] Few pictures are as fundamentally sunless as *Garden at Issy*. But *Shaft of Sunlight*, in spite of its title, more than prepares the way. (Matisse's woodland, we may think, does to the landscape trope of 'light in the clearing' what Cézanne's *Pool at Jas de Bouffan* [FIG. 26] had done previously to 'mirror image in the water'.)

Oh, and I should register the most obvious thing of all about *Garden* – so obvious, indeed, that it seems almost a deliberate art-historical marker offered by Matisse, to himself and others, as palliative to the rest of the

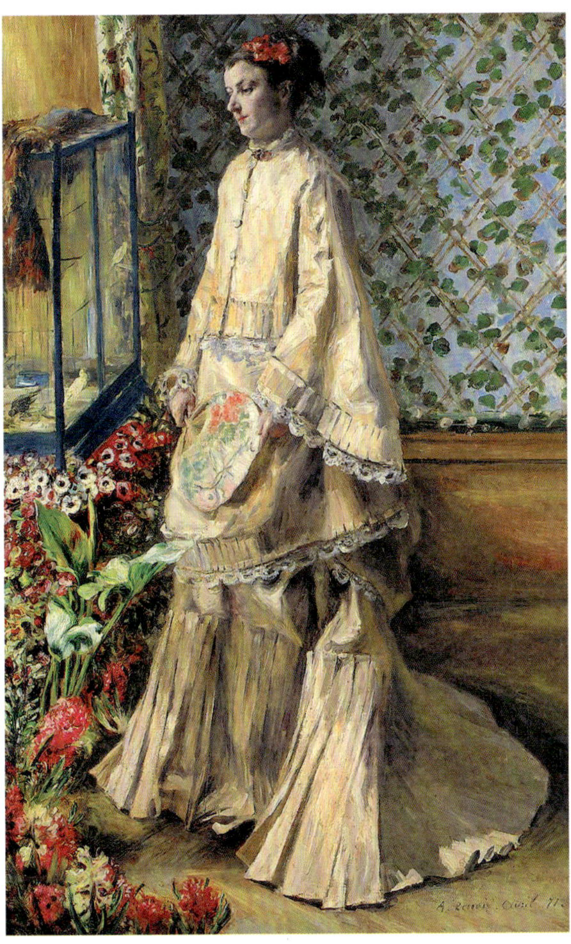

87. Pierre-Auguste Renoir, *Portrait of Rapha Maître*, 1871, 130 × 83 cm (51¼ × 32¾ in.). Private Collection.

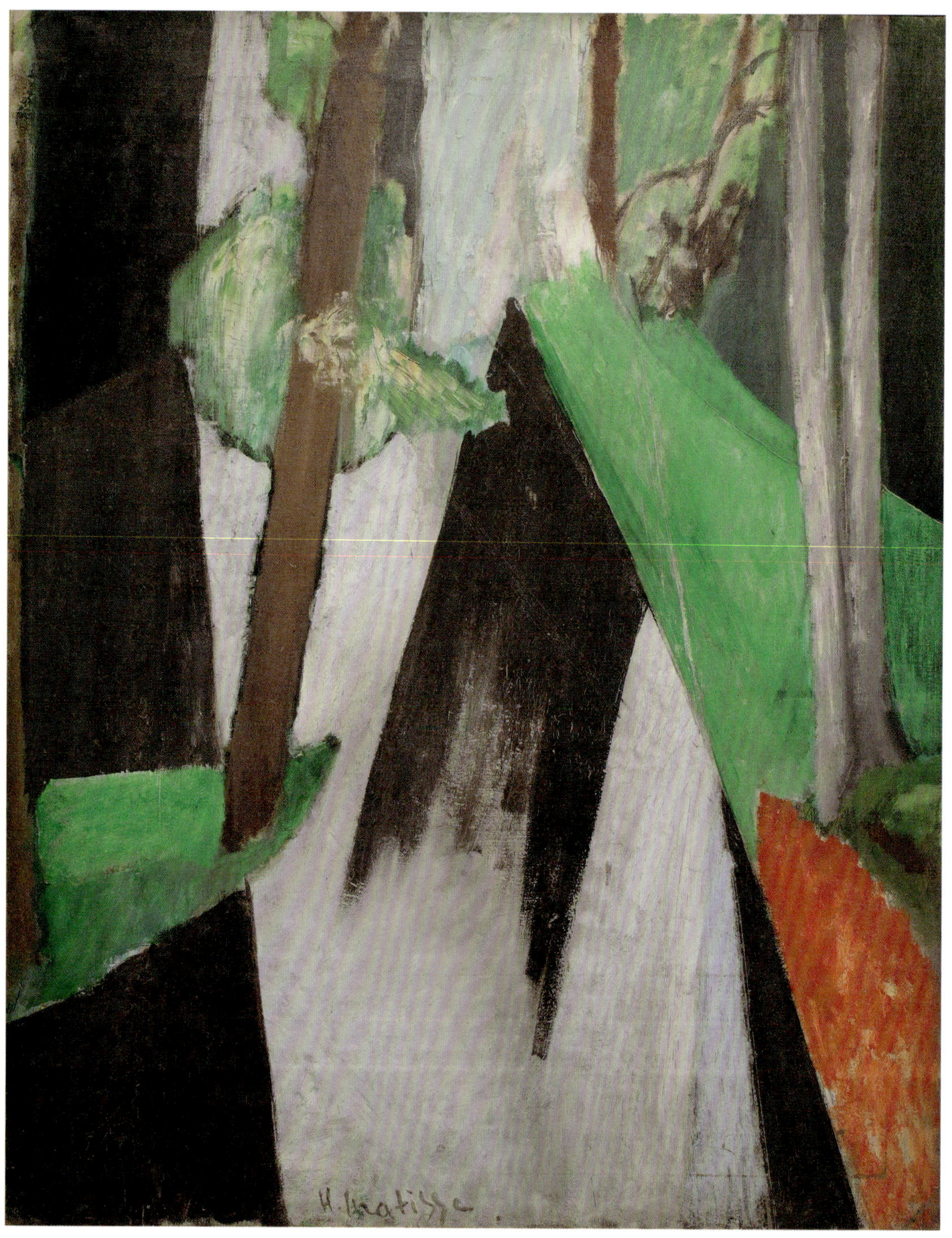

88. Henri Matisse, *Shaft of Sunlight, Woods at Trivaux*, 1917,
91 × 74 cm (36 × 29⅛ in.). Private Collection.

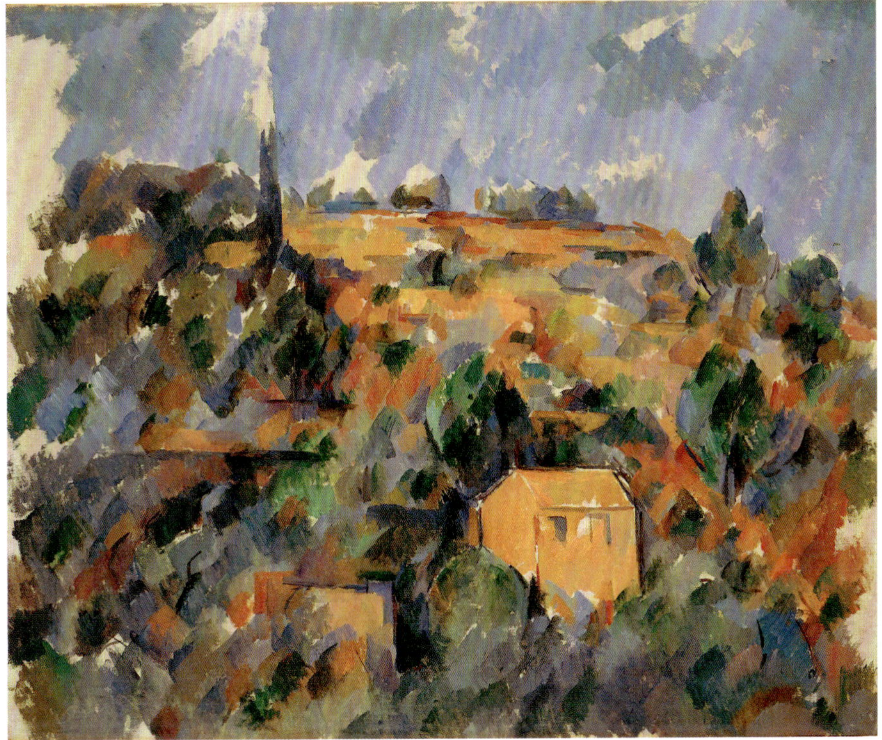

89. *Houses on the Hill*, c. 1902–5, 66 × 81 cm (26 × 31⅞ in.). White House Collection, Washington, D.C.

picture's vertigo – that the little house in the garden *is* Cézanne. That is to say, a typical Cézanne moment – compare *Houses on the Hill*, for example, from the early 1900s – in which the neat geometry of the man-made floats up out of the endlessness of sensation, and tries, unsuccessfully, to pin it down.

◆

So far, what I have offered is a weak interpretation of Matisse's *Garden*. This has been deliberate. I have wanted above all, or in the first place, to enact in my response to the picture the weakness, in terms of self-knowing discursive consciousness, of Matisse's own understanding of the tokens and references he was deploying. I think that painting such a picture (and in this the picture is typical of the line of modernism from which it emerges) involves a suspension of understanding, so as not to allow the tokens and references to 'mean' prematurely. This is basic to modern art's hedonism. Don't *know* what you mean, says the hedonist. For the world of knowing is what truly impinges on human freedom, and it is irremediably corrupt; if you 'know what you mean' you will end up meaning only what the world already knows, and that isn't worth knowing – it isn't true. Know only what you are doing – what you are painting. (Be like Cézanne, dealing with the phantasm 'Peasant'.)

The word 'prematurely' just cropped up. I was suggesting that a painter like Matisse is concerned first of all to find a way – a way of painting – in which the tokens and references he's obliged to work with are not allowed to mean prematurely. But 'prematurely' here is a strange word. What, in French painting from Monet to Matisse, is meaning *maturely*? This is French painting's essential question. Maturity, meaning the strange deep thing we call 'meaningfulness' – of the sort Matisse found, we know, in Giotto in the Arena Chapel in Padua – is just beyond us… it is beyond the resources of the culture we belong to. 'I've found three reproductions of Giotto in Padua,' Matisse writes to Bonnard in 1946, 'and am sending them to you. Giotto is for me the summit of my desires, but the road that leads toward an equivalent, in our epoch, is too long, too formidable [his word is 'importante'] for a single lifetime.'[12] It is a letter from one old ill man to another – Matisse was seventy-six as he wrote it, Bonnard seventy-eight with only months left to live. I shall do no more than state here, declaratively, under its spell, that having begun thinking about *Garden at Issy* at roughly the same time I was starting a sequence of work on Giotto, I've found that I cannot escape from the feeling that somewhere in the background of *Garden at Issy* lies the barrenness of the desert in Giotto's *Dream of Joachim* – the barrenness, but also the sharp-edged angel in the sky.

'Somewhere in the background.' You see that I have leapt, more or less without warning, from weak interpretation to the strongest of the strong. And this too (here's my other proposal about method) is seemingly a necessary feature of any interpretation worth the name. Not only will it finally present itself as *over*-interpretation – as leaping from surface resemblances to the heart of the matter – but it will not even pretend that the leap is validated, or provided for, by the empirical evidence first adduced. All this, to repeat a previous point, is true in general, but

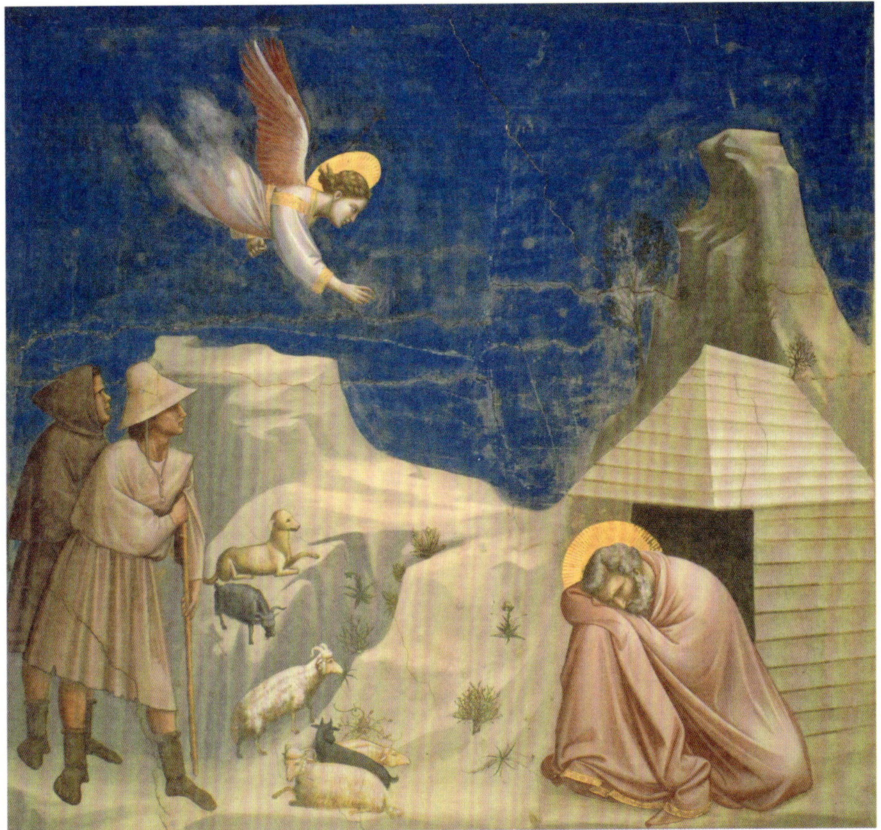

90. Giotto Bondone, *Dream of Joachim*, fresco, *c.* 1303–5, 200 × 185 cm (78¾ × 72⅞ in.). Arena Chapel, Padua.

true a fortiori of modernism. For Matisse's half-quotations and quasi-repetitions are deployed, I think, to keep the heart of the matter hidden. The heart of the matter, in a modernist artwork, is to be held in abeyance by *form*, by procedure. Form is the way towards it, of course; but always at the same time what keeps it in abeyance – prevents it from crystallizing prematurely (meaning 'ever') to the proposition-seeking mind. And so the war-cry of the art historian Caroline Arscott – 'over-reading a painting is a methodological principle with me' – seems entirely justified.[13] Over-interpretation is just the name we give to the moment when criticism admits – gives a gasp at – the gap between form and content. And without the gasp, what on earth will we find to say about a painting like *Garden at Issy*?

◆

Yet Giotto alone cannot be the key to the mystery. Our subject is a garden, not a sheepfold in the hills. Therefore I turn to other gardens – in their way just as distant from Matisse's as the *Dream of Joachim*, but which seem to me the matrix from which his *Garden* is trying to escape. To be literal for a moment: we are looking in *Garden at Issy* out towards a little space of pools and fountains and lily pads and herbaceous borders. Gertrude Stein recalled the artist talking with a light irony about his 'petit Luxembourg' in the suburbs.[14] And in French painting, for an artist in 1917, a garden in the suburbs can mean only one thing. It must be Monet's garden we are looking at, the one that first materialized in 1866 – massive, inviolate, shaded and sun-drenched, its lawn specked with daisies, women gliding across it, the eternal *hortus conclusus* that Monet was to make his own.

We know already that during the years of wartime Renoir was on Matisse's mind. He paid visits to the master in Cagnes-sur-Mer in 1917 and 1918 – maybe the first coincided with a journey south to see his conscripted son. 'The pain passes, Matisse' seems to have been said on one of these occasions. And Renoir is unmistakably Monet's companion in Matisse's practice at this time: his gardens too are *Issy*'s antetypes. Take the *Garden in the rue Cortot, Montmartre*, for example – its spiralling space and midsummer colour, its touch after touch of sunlight, its far thicket of blue, its image of sociability over the fence.

'The beauty passes, Renoir, the pain remains': that is *Garden at Issy*'s response. For are not all gardens – here is the thought that *Garden* keeps at bay, and yet happens upon darkly, in a year of trench browns and camouflage yellows – are not all gardens paradises, but also places of confinement? (It is perfect that Rapha Maître, in the painting on the back wall of the portrait of Pellerin, looks off frame, in the month of the Commune – we are told that Renoir painted with the sound of guns never stopping outside – into a golden cage for budgerigars.[15])

No doubt if we look at *Garden* with Renoir and Monet in mind, the edge of irony and annihilation to Matisse's picture is unmistakable. The miniatures of lily pads on the pool surface tell the story. Gardens are factitious, they say – fictions, reservations, Luxembourgs.[16] The real Jardin du Luxembourg in 1917 was filled with artillery emplacements.

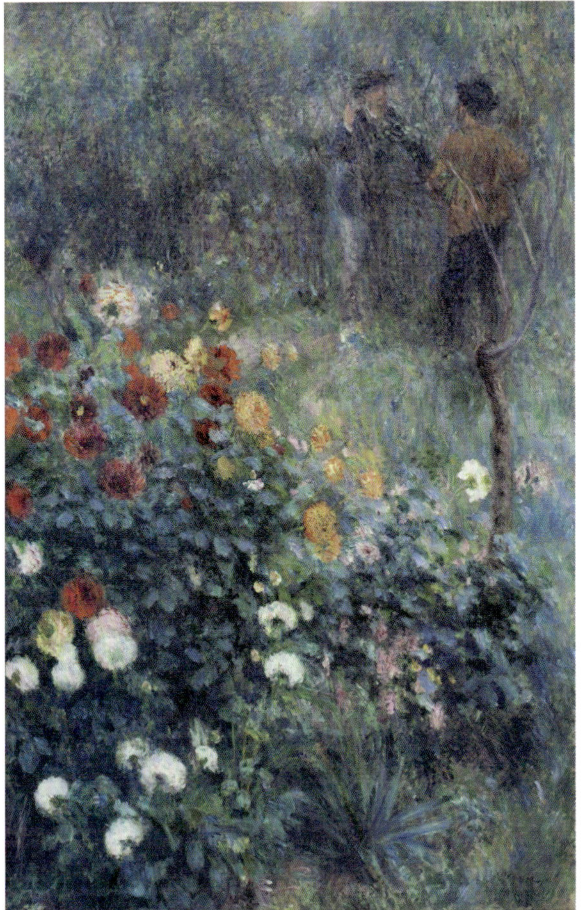

91. Pierre-Auguste Renoir, *Garden in the rue Cortot, Montmartre*, 1876, 154 × 89 cm (60¾ × 35 in.). Carnegie Museum of Art, Pittsburgh.

But oh, the completeness of the garden dream! The solace, the safety... Monet was a scandal for the serious-minded, then as now, but his was the vision that had *made* modern painting, and which modern painting abandoned at its peril. For in him hedonism had taken on a true monumentality.

I have been pointing to darkness in Matisse's *Garden*; but darkness is, dialectically, only a moment here in a stronger and stranger totality. The earth colour of ground and pool and trees and sky is on the edge of negativity, yes: it will not relinquish the look of deadness, of sterility. But Matisse is never simply a Naysayer. If the anti-Monet conjuring-trick works – this seems to me Matisse's wager – the world will be earthen and atmospheric at the same time. Modern art is obliged to be anti-Monet, the picture concedes, but it will be less than nothing without the hedonism

Monet stands for. So the kernel of the *Garden* – here is my next-to-last interpretative throw – may be the wonderful moment high up in Monet's 1873 *Luncheon* where his young wife's bonnet is hung on an overhanging branch. Impossible *ownership* of nature, this. Look back at the green and black circles in the Matisse, it follows, and see underneath *The Moroccans* the straw hat and black bow in the trees.

◆

Monet's hedonism, then, is one pole of attraction in *Garden at Issy*; but the other is Giotto's deep feeling for 'nature in its barrenness'. For in the end I do return to the *Dream of Joachim*: I cannot put aside the conviction that

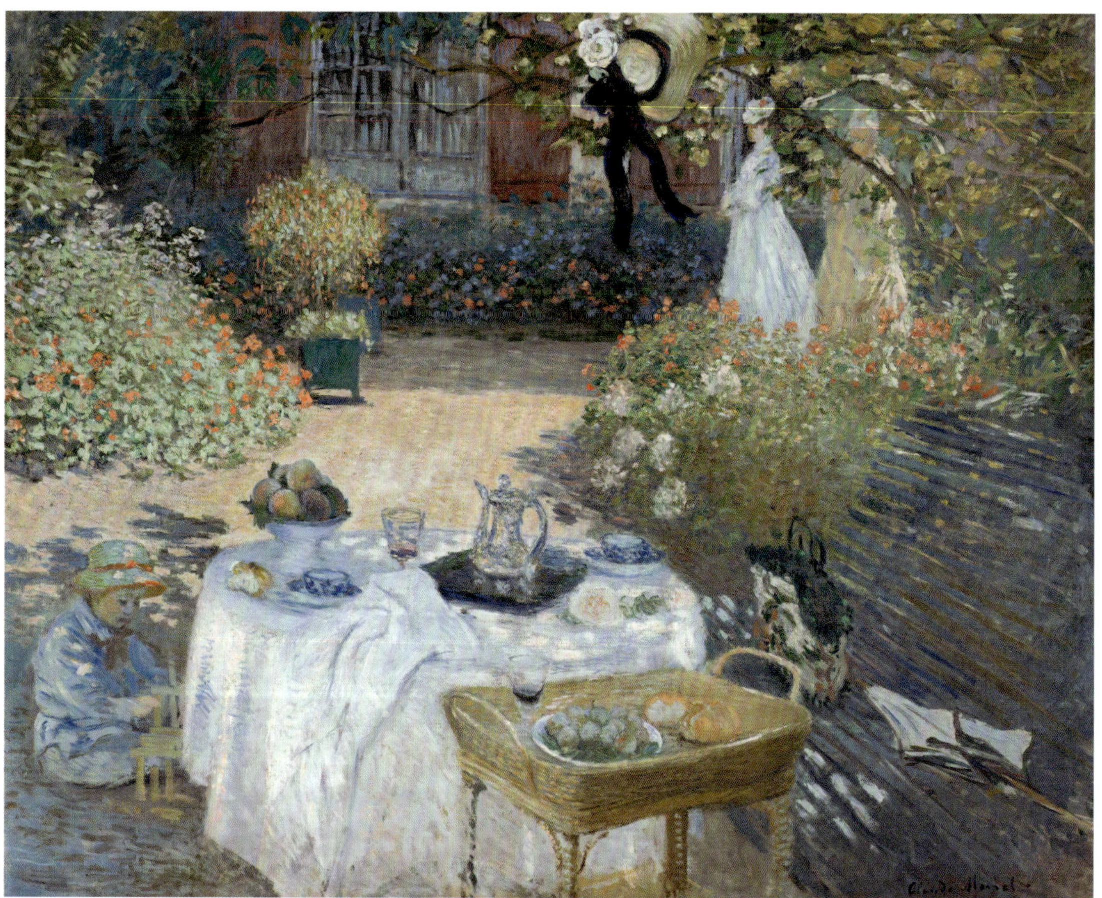

92. Claude Monet, *The Luncheon*, 1873, 160 × 201 cm (63 × 79¼ in.). Musée d'Orsay, Paris.

the scene in the Arena Chapel is *Garden at Issy*'s true inspiration – down even to the Cézanne-type house, since for me Joachim's dark mountain hut finally trumps the more obvious source.

The story of Joachim, to tell it briefly, is one of barrenness and miraculous rebirth. The old man is childless. His offering in the Temple has been refused. So he takes his shameful sterility into the desert, to share the fate of his shepherds; and then in his sleep an angel comes to him out of the blue, announcing that his wife Anna is with child. This particular Giotto, of all the great sequence in the chapel, is the starkest and simplest: it depends on equal and opposite great shapes of grey and blue in balance within the rectangle. Perhaps we could say that Matisse's ambition in *Garden* was to replace Giotto's contrast by continuity. He would take the blue of *Dream of Joachim*'s sky – the blue that had meant so much to him, and on which he had rung such reverent changes, above all in the years round 1917 – and make the sky the colour of earth. Water and air and earth would be all one thing. Barrenness – the cold of a Paris winter – would be part of the picture, but not its deciding note. The grey of Giotto's desert, with sheep scrabbling for foodstuff among the thorns, would give way to just enough of brownness, redness, resonant black. The pink wedges in the sky at Issy are, so to speak, the angel's garment crystallized; an angel's garment but also a rain of Léger-type artillery shells. The answering pileup of half-circles at top left are anti-haloes. The sky in the garden is sullen, but also electric. New life may be stirring. Even the yellow and blue of Giotto's halo and air are allowed, one notices, to put in a vestigial appearance, displaced downwards on the far side of the pool.[17] Is even the great sweep of black to the left ultimately a dark version of Giotto's little desert ravine – the one the goats are looking down into?

Giotto is mobilized in 1917, I think, above all as a means to escape Monet's force field. Monet's vision – this surely was Matisse's ultimate quarrel with it – had been glorious but ungrounded. Taking pleasure in Nature was, so Monet believed, always ultimately dreaming, floating, losing one's footing, writing one's name on water. The *Nymphéas* are the poem of that. And we know that Matisse went to Giverny in May 1917, just weeks before *Garden at Issy* was begun, specifically to see what Monet was up to in his 'Grandes Décorations'.[18] What he saw was stupendous.

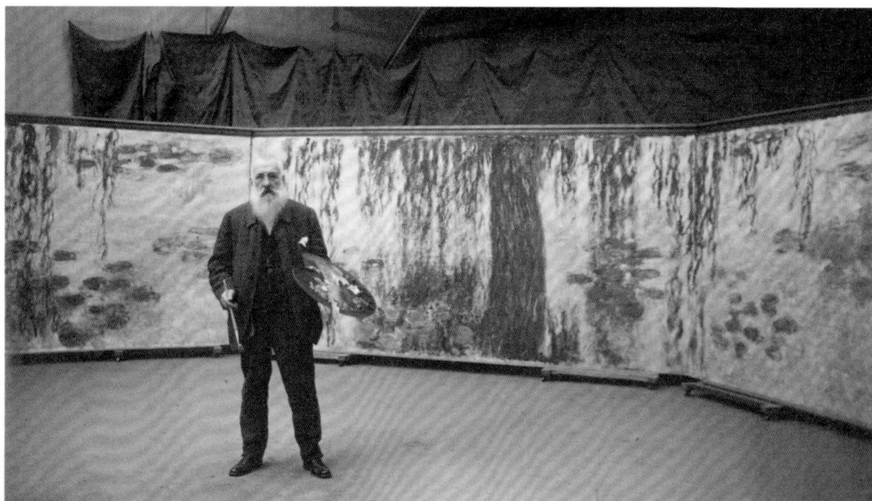

93. Unknown photographer, *Monet's Studio, November 1917*, photograph. Durand-Ruel Archive.

No one was better equipped to grasp its metaphysics. Was *Garden at Issy* Matisse's immediate response? I believe so. And the painting was homage and refutation – above all in terms of format and colour. The nearby world as Matisse experienced it would be *upright*: domestic, pictorial, pressing forwards to meet us – a view out the window, not a great unreeling ambience. It would be green and brown, not blue and yellow. The viewer in front of it would feel the world's strangeness, for sure, but also its plainness, its ordinariness. Its earthen quality. How the visit to Monet must have clarified things.

◆

Let me try to sum up, returning specifically to the question this chapter began with: the nature of Matisse's hedonism. Let me put the question crudely, moralistically – for surely the ethical question has been hovering in the background through the previous pages. How can *this* be the painting 1917 demanded? Take away the question's hectoring tone and ask it matter-of-factly – of Matisse, and of modernism as a whole.

Is it the case, in a word, that the hedonism and obsession with medium of one main strand of modernism, the one claiming Matisse as its standard-bearer, *closed* that strand against the world of experience – the catastrophe – all round it, or was it on the contrary the only means art had at its disposal to truly expose itself to that catastrophe? Exposure here meaning not 'referring' to the world, assembling and chronicling its appearances, but having the stuff (the structure) of experience enter and shape the work from within.

The very way I am staging the question, of course, suggests what my answer is going to be. I do think *Garden at Issy* is 'of its time', in ways that are all the more chilling, more ominous, for being literally indescribable. But again, dialectically, the danger here is that answer seems too obvious, too easily reached. For it is precisely part of Matisse's wager, I think, that it should *not* be – that the charge of escapism, of emptiness, of mere aesthetic exercise, should never go away. I think that precisely this is the quality to modern experience that Matisse never stops returning to – that is, if you like, his subject. This razor's edge between an emptiness of feeling, an evacuation, a weightlessness, a world in which Art has declined to a moving of formal counters on a groundless brown ground – between this and a recognition of what that emptiness *feels like*… its terrifying character (under the blandness), its darkness, its hardness and cruelty. It *is* – it has to be – a razor's edge. For the coexistence of hedonism and anxiety, or blandness and blackness, is the thing to be painted.

And this may be what lies behind the overall character of the reading of *Garden* I have given you: its evident restlessness, that is to say; and in the end its recklessness, when I bring on, as my token of barrenness and 'bare life', a fresco from six centuries previously.

Restlessness first. I think the barrage of too many possible pictures, too many quotes or half-quotes from Monet and Cézanne and Renoir and Matisse himself, to which I've subjected you over the past twenty or thirty pages, is true to Matisse's method. But true in two senses. Matisse exists fully – obsessively – in this world of other paintings. Fully, but *also* restlessly, as if he is never quite satisfied that he has found the point in another painter's past, or his own past, from which the tone of the present moment might begin to be built. He's never sure if he's invoking Cézanne or parodying him; doing a *Nymphéas* of his own or doing dirt on the whole *Nymphéas* idea; hanging on to the memory of Giotto's miracle in the desert or finally expunging miracle – transcendence – from the wilderness we are in.

◆

Put *Garden at Issy* next to Cézanne's *House near Gardanne*. It is strange that *Garden* immediately looks warmer and above all closer. The house and mountain in the Cézanne seem more remote – more alien to us, more closed off, settled in their impenetrable places. The Matisse is a *garden*, after all – its space ought to belong to us, it ought to offer us a place of safety. But does it?

Maybe the first impression, seeing Matisse's picture with Cézanne's as foil, is one of warmth; but warmth in *Garden* doesn't seem to be associated with comfort or familiarity. Everything in *Garden* is unmoored, hard-edged, not planted on any ground. Nothing has a bottom edge that attaches it to the earth. The *scale* of everything in Matisse – even compared with Cézanne, whose way with scale can be baffling – is an outrage. Look at the smallness of the lily pond, the fountain, the blurt of foliage growing up from the pool, the preposterous lily pads. Take that, Monet!

Keep the ridiculous pool in sight, but widen the focus to include the looming hand-axe of green to the right, floating in a void, silhouetted by an anti-shadow. Even *Red Rock* appears natural in comparison (FIG. 4). The longer you look, the more everything in Matisse's garden becomes a weapon or an artillery shell. And yet the world – focus on *House near Gardanne* again – is not simply alien to us. We can't stand back from it and contemplate it as an aesthetic phenomenon. We'll never get *used* to its not being ours. What is it that one of Matisse's friends said of him in 1904? – 'The anxious, the madly anxious Matisse.'[19] Or again, on Matisse in 1907: 'so vehement… so tormented.'[20] But that torment, in 1917, cannot be stated… dramatized… brought on as a condition to be 'expressed'. No force we can put a name to is making the world look the way it looks here. And in any case, we might be scaring ourselves with spectres where there are none. This might be just a little lily pond in the suburbs.

◆

I said at the start of this chapter that Cézanne was *Garden at Issy*'s presiding deity, and I need finally to say how. Compare *Garden at Issy* to *The House with Cracked Walls*, a painting Cézanne did in the early 1890s (FIG. 95). The formats of *Garden* and *House with Cracked Walls* are comparable, and

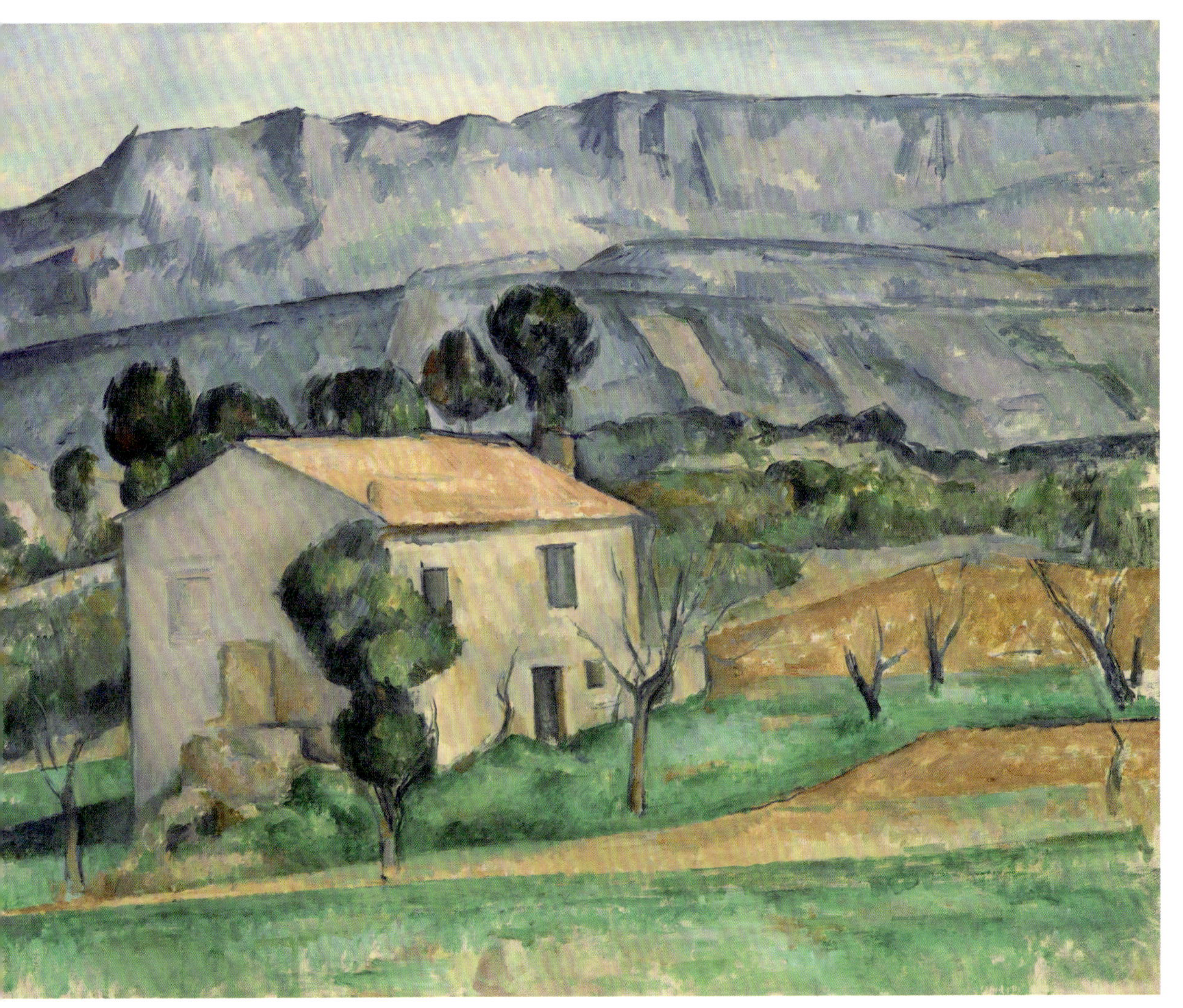

94. *House near Gardanne*, c. 1886–90, 65.5 × 81 cm (25⅞ × 32 in.). Indianapolis Museum of Art.

special for both artists: Cézanne uses an upright rectangle of this kind very rarely for a landscape painting done in the open, as opposed to under trees; and the shape seems to be associated here with an effort to sew the human (the habitation) *into* the landscape and have it participate – maybe a touch melodramatically – in the ground plane's pitching and rolling.[21] We look up at the ruin as if from the bottom of a ravine. In *House near Gardanne* the farmhouse had borrowed some of the far mountain's massiveness as well as its impenetrability; in *House with Cracked Walls* it is reduced to a shattered façade, pushing the earth's fault lines skyward. (Fault lines, but also what look to be leftover edges of terracing, choked with brush – past efforts at cultivation as ephemeral as the one-time right angles of the house.)

Is Cézanne *Garden at Issy*'s presiding deity? I think so; but the moment one looks at *Garden* in relation to any particular Cézanne, the counter-arguments (counter-intuitions) start. In the twenty years between *House with Cracked Walls* and *Garden*, for example, doesn't there seem to have taken place – leaving its traces in every touch of colour – some kind of pervasive loss of faith in painting, some shift in ontology, some final dis-illusion? 'Modern art' has arrived. Matisse is admitting and resisting the fact. No artist in the early twentieth century had worked harder to keep alive the attitude to art (the attitude to the world) that Cézanne exemplified – worked harder to admit into the bones of his painting an awareness of loss and distance, and yet have painting preserve the 'sensation' nonetheless... even if, increasingly, it was the sensation of loss. This is what *House with Cracked Walls* stands for, in Matisse's view – this is the dialectic he goes to Cézanne's painting to learn.[22] He sees in Cézanne a world still *animated* by its ruin. Painting remains a thing of the senses, an encroachment, an actuality – even if, more and more, the 'this-thereness' it cherishes is built from dislocation, marginality, sardonic apartness and merciless isolation. ('Je fais abstraction de mon individualité,' as Cézanne once put it.[23])

Do any of the above descriptions apply to *Garden at Issy*? I doubt it. Even the extremity of the nouns and adjectives just brought on – prompted by *House with Cracked Walls*' strange motif and viewpoint, its high-key colour, its tortuous drawing – seems wrong in the face of Matisse's browns

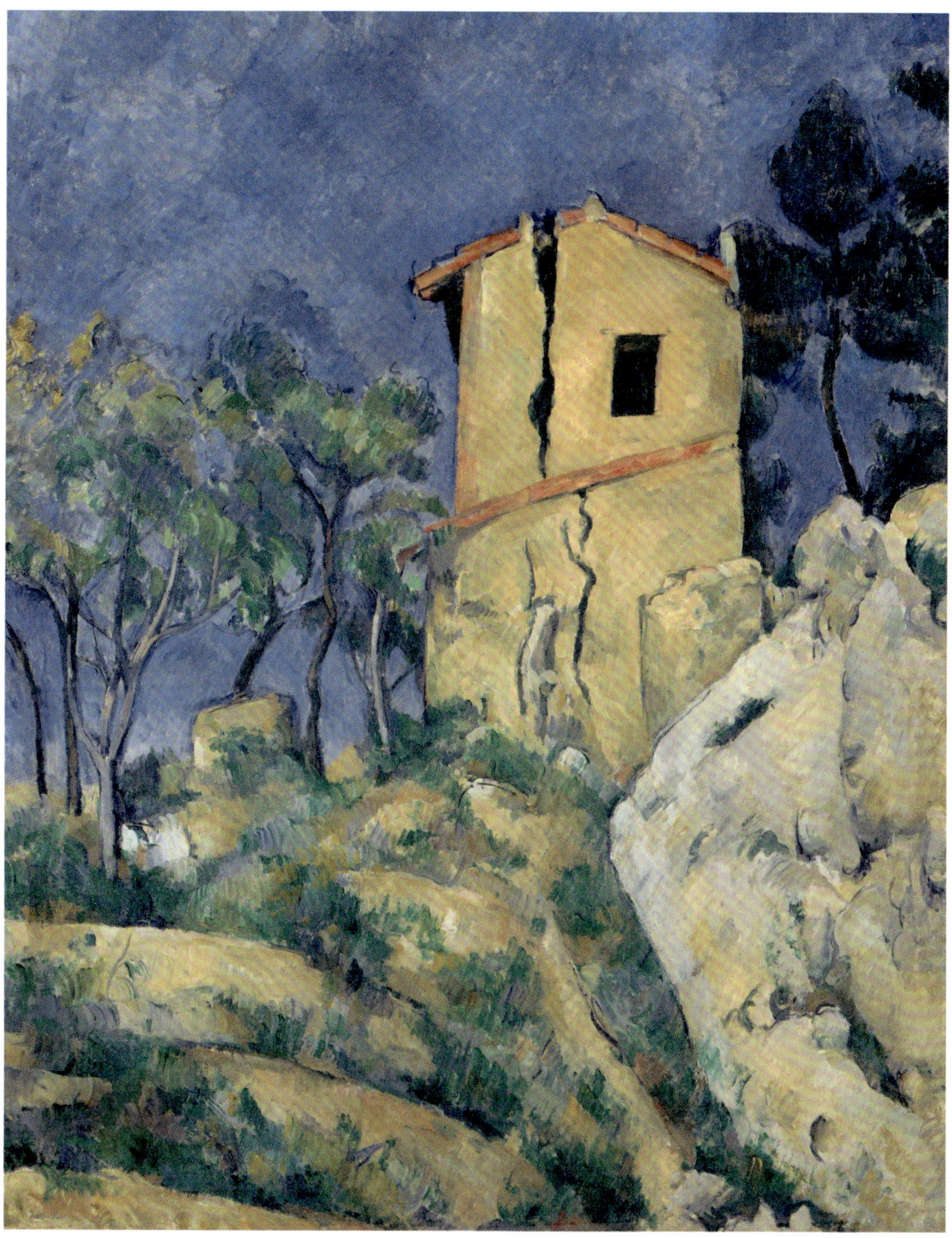

95. *The House with Cracked Walls*, c. 1892–95, 80 × 60 cm (31½ × 23⅝ in.).
Metropolitan Museum of Art, New York.

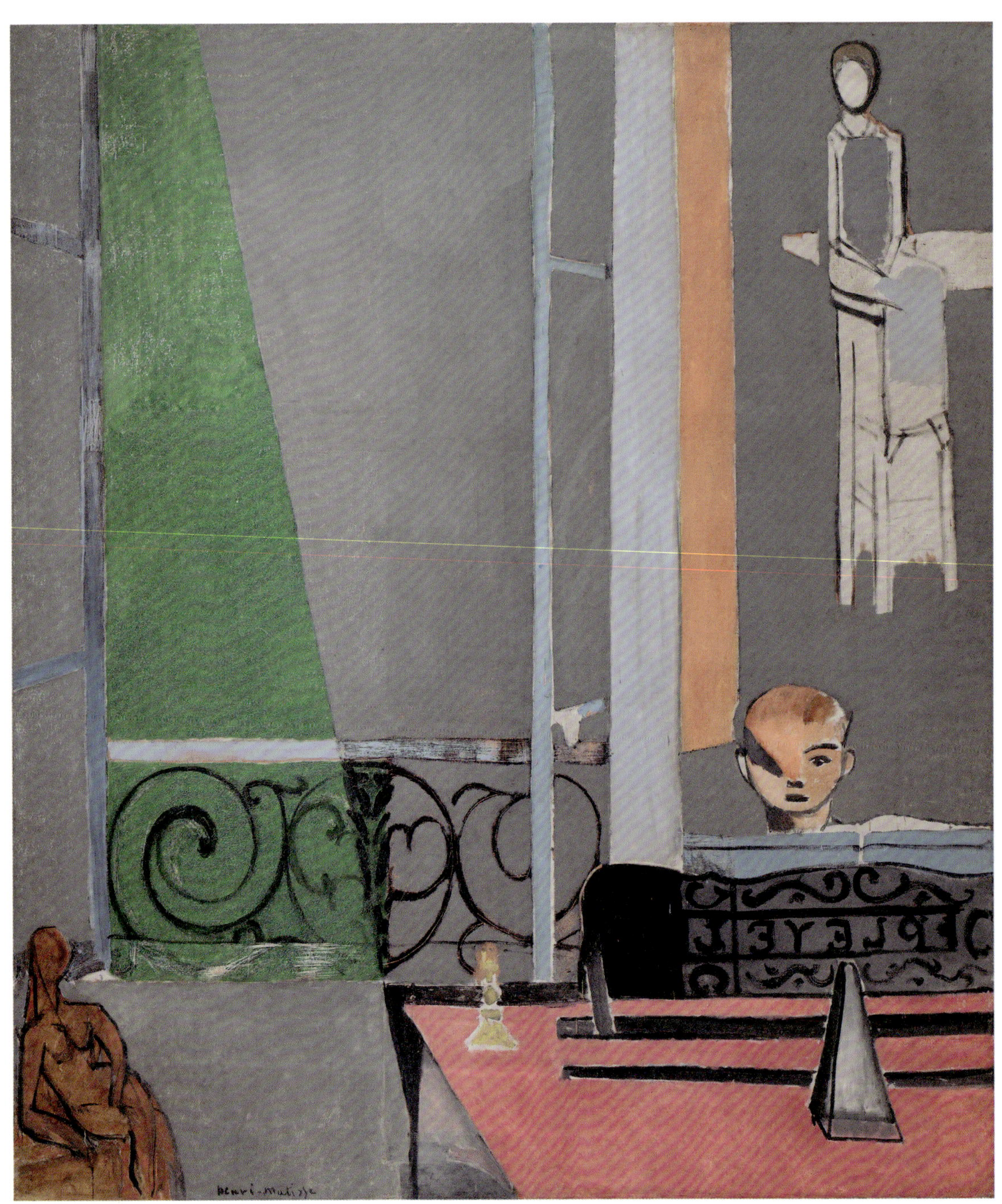

96. Henri Matisse, *The Piano Lesson*, 1916, 245 × 213 cm (96½ × 83⅞ in.). Museum of Modern Art, New York.

and greens. The greens especially – never has the colour been moved further away from the animate, the organic. (One admirer of the painting told me she had always seen it as the colour of arsenic.[24]) And yet the world in Matisse hasn't simply entered the realm of non-life, of mechanism. His *Garden* is a burying place for natural forms, not a cold alternative to them. Its blacks and browns – particularly the shifting, particulate, not quite luminous brown – are still overtaking the earth and trees, filling the lily pond with silt, making an anti-sky; they cannot *escape* from the dismal work of cancellation and arrive, at last – irrevocably, triumphantly – in the new world of the unlived.

◆

We should be grateful for the animation left us. The paintings Matisse did in 1916 and 1917 seem to me to carry on a conversation in and around just this topic. *Studio, Quai Saint-Michel* puts the question in agony (FIG. 80). Art is all there is, it proposes: the beauty of the body is something to be clung to, naively, idiotically, even if the half-effaced trace the body leaves on a sheet of paper speaks unmistakably to its vanishing… even if the thick black paint intended to halo its contours and fix its splendour cracks and bites into its insides like the last stages of a cancer… even if the non-pictures floating on the non-back-wall are so many X-rays announcing the worst. No artist, least of all Matisse, could go on living in such a state of total exposure. Already his great *Piano Lesson* had put the contrary case. Art *is* enough, that picture said. Art can (must) draw a curtain – an impenetrable transparency – on the outside world. It will turn its back on *Studio, Quai Saint-Michel*'s canting floorboards and absurd tipping table, and move the hopeless vulnerability of *Studio*'s ceiling out of sight. It will paint grey on grey. It will fix its eyes on the fugue on the music stand and lay out its colour chords to the tick of the metronome. *Garden*? What garden? War? What war?

Garden at Issy is the view out of *Piano Lesson*'s window. Missiles are in the sky. Sappers have trampled the flowerbeds. Trench browns are everywhere. But the sun – or is it a shower of incendiaries? – still shines.

Conclusion

And anyway,' he added, tapping his forehead, 'painting… it's inside here!'
Cézanne to François Jourdain, 1904[1]

I return to *House near Gardanne* (FIGS 94 & 97). It is a characteristic mid-period Cézanne, done most probably around 1885, and I believe it concentrates – epitomizes – many of the qualities this book has been trying to come to terms with. Seeing the painting in the Indianapolis Museum of Art, hung a few feet away from Seurat's dazzling *Channel at Gravelines*, is an experience that doesn't fade. The whole enigma and splendour of French painting is on display.

Cézanne's painting (like Seurat's) is not particularly large – *House near Gardanne* is 26 inches tall and 32 inches across – but the stretch of country it shows has a formidable implied scale. Nothing really indicates how high the mountain range in the background is, but colour establishes it as stern and remote.[2] Yet the scene as a whole is not wild. The house and fields in the foreground, and the stunted remains of an orchard, are ordinary and modest – part of a world any lover of landscape will feel at home in. Words like 'plainness' or 'ordinariness' come to hand, but in the end don't seem adequate; because the ordinariness of the house and surroundings is accompanied by a kind of distance, an apartness. The house in particular is shuttered and impenetrable. We have been here before.

Apartness, yes, but not Giotto's bare mountain. Nor are we anywhere near the wilderness – the emotional register – of *House with Cracked Walls* (FIG. 95). The quality pervading *House near Gardanne*, and it is characteristic of Cézanne at his strongest, is, rather, one of familiarity and unfamiliarity, nearness and apartness, coexisting.

Look at the picture's bottom six inches. In the foreground, hard against the picture plane, is a characteristic passage of thinly painted greens,

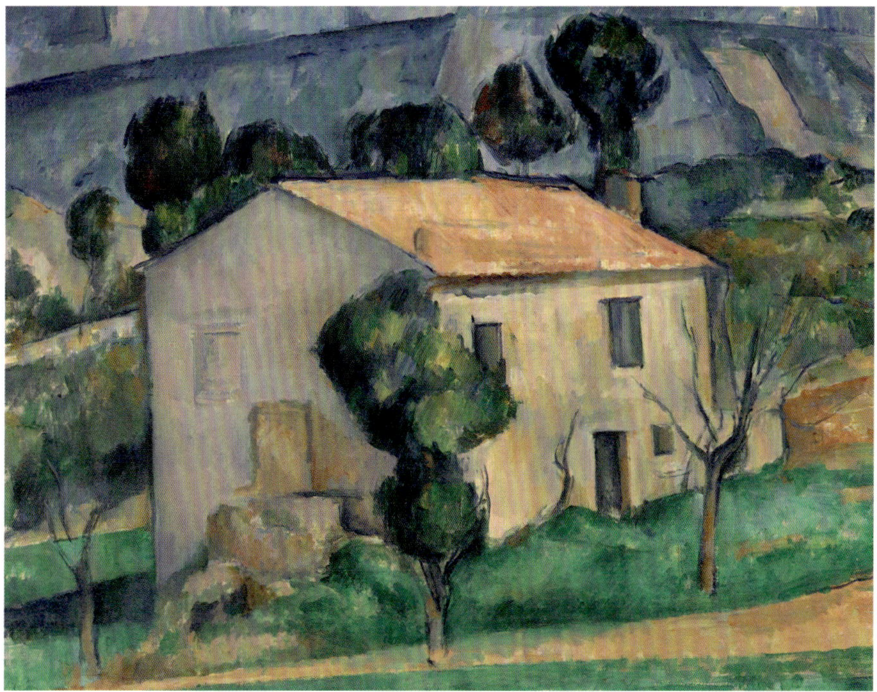

97. Detail from Fig. 94: *House near Gardanne*, *c.* 1886–90.
Indianapolis Museum of Art.

yellows, a touch or two of pink. The grass is singing. And then, further back, there's an earthen path. Does it climb a small slope by the house? Does it disappear for a moment behind a tree? Further to the right, the path seems to flatten out and lose its edges. Maybe the general lay of the land hereabouts – what look to be two brown tilled fields and an orchard between them – is pulling already uphill. Maybe not. The hummocks of green next to the house are elusive and the hard diagonal of the more distant field is like a parody of perspective, promising and not delivering. One's eye switches back to the other side of the house, over to the left, and picks up the answering line – the false continuation – of the field's diagonal in the weird green line cutting through the branches of a tree. (As if the tree had been sliced thin and put under a microscope.) The longer one looks at the larger shapes of brown and green back to the right – looks at them as a sequence of fields and cleared earth – the more one loses a sense of the fields' orientation. The wisps of trees only make things worse.

None of this – this characteristic Cézanne play of invitation and impossibility – ends up simply robbing us of 'world' and putting 'painting' in its place. The field still shimmers in the light; the path's warm dryness is *there* in the touches of brown. The reality made up of such things (such appearances, such sensations) is what any painter must return to if painting is to have a point: it is where we are, what we want to see again, we never doubt it. But our place in that reality – our entry into it, our sense of its proximity, its offering us a ground or a 'way' – these are unstable. And the instabilities are not marginal or outlandish in relation to our occupation of the world (our humanity); they are ordinary; they go with the plainness and sobriety.

Focus on the house in *House near Gardanne*. No doubt a viewer soon begins to notice the local oddities and dazzlements disturbing its plain four walls – the floating black windows, the trees interfering, a staircase of hay (is it?) climbing one side. But step back from the oddities for the moment and look at the house as a whole; look at it in relation to the fields and hills and mountain; look at the house's *place*. Does it have one? Is it part of the landscape? 'How far Cézanne had moved from the snapshot puerilities of Manet et Cie' – this is Samuel Beckett again – 'when he could understand the dynamic intrusion [in the scene] to be himself, and so landscape to be something unapproachably alien, unintelligible arrangement of atoms, not so much as ruffled by the kind attention of the Reliability Joneses.'[3]

I wish, once more, to resist Beckett's extremism. 'Unapproachably alien' can't be right. But the self – the house – as intrusion: that speaks to something. The basic choice Cézanne makes in *House near Gardanne* to move the building off slightly to one side of the picture rectangle need not, of course, have disturbed its centrality one jot. But everything in the painting ends up abetting – intensifying – the asymmetry. The house isn't central, and in some sense it isn't *anywhere*. It 'fits' in the landscape snugly – but like a piece in a jigsaw, not a thing on the earth. Even a building like *House with Cracked Walls* seems more a part of some felt reality.

◆

I shall try to approach the homeless quality of the house, homelessness being a quality fundamental to Cézanne's achievement, by focusing on

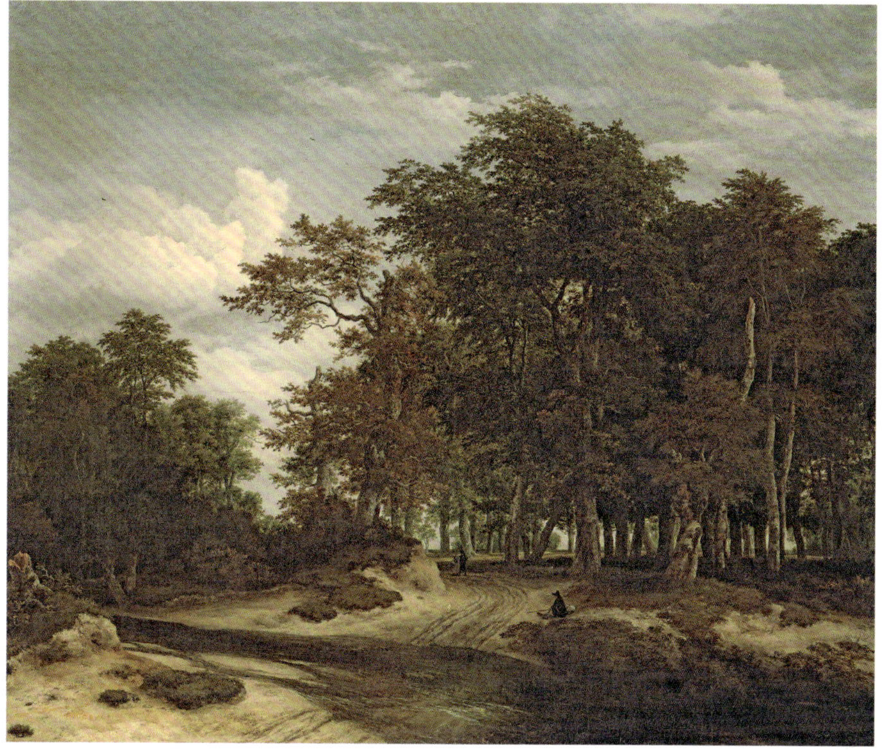

98. Jacob van Ruysdael, *The Great Forest*, c. 1655–60, 139 × 180 cm (54¾ × 70¾ in.). Kunsthistorisches Museum, Vienna.

the notion of 'way' in landscape – the way landscape painting usually arranges a scene so that an onlooker can move through it, imaginatively; and in particular, how the viewer is granted entry to the illusion in the first place and placed on a ground. Always with a view to understanding what *House near Gardanne* – its bottom six inches or so especially – does instead.

At this point I need an enormously strong and considered example of a path in landscape doing its proper work, and the one I choose is Ruysdael's *The Great Forest*, from around 1660, now hung in the Kunsthistorisches Museum in Vienna. Cézanne never saw the painting, but he saw many like it; and I believe it was this strand in the landscape tradition – the Dutch strand, and the nineteenth-century French and English moments deriving from it – that he thought embodied what the genre was truly capable of, and what, therefore, his own landscapes must ingest and leave behind.

◆

The reader will see immediately that *Great Forest* offers its viewer – remember that the painting is enormous in comparison with Cézanne's, four-and-a-half feet high and close on six feet wide – a clear way into the scene it brings to life. There is a track leading into the forest, and wayfarers. 'Stopping by woods,' to use Robert Frost's shopworn phrase, is a recurrent landscape figure. The track in Ruysdael is wonderfully materialized, and the cart ruts speak to its being incorporated into a world of commerce and production. Maybe even of recreation – the far couple on the path, coming towards us round the bend, seem to have time to kill. But the way is not crassly complaisant to human needs. The road is carved through sand, or soil that looks not much use to a farmer, and the access to the scene it offers – especially in relation to the picture's bottom edge – is off-centre, oblique. And of course it immediately goes under water. The water is not deep, and the path soon resurfaces. A ford is not a threat. The view of the path under the water is beautiful – the painting turns on it. But this cuts both ways. We gain entry into the painting's world, but we have a moment of looking down at the entry – the joining of place to place – through the clear fast stream, whose flood banks are duly noted.

Ruysdael, then, may be Cézanne's opposite, but his opposition is shot through with a consciousness of – an extraordinary invention of signs for – what is involved in making the material world available. (He is not a Reliability Jones.) The exact balance of light and shade in *Great Forest* – of uncertainty in the weather and of shadow not quite becoming gloom – is, as so often with the Dutch, a further carrier of thought. We might say, returning to space and ground specifically, that Cézanne does no more than bring Ruysdael's pervasive 'out-of-the-wayness' up to the surface. If Ruysdael's sense of nature's separateness and elusiveness – of grounds shifting and paths petering out – had not been there in the landscape tradition, Cézanne's art would have been more captious and paradoxical than it is. For again, 'out-of-the-wayness' is not a dominant in *House near Gardanne*: we are not put down in a wilderness or no man's land. Less so, on the face of things, than in *Great Forest*.

The landscape tradition is capacious, in other words: it is subtle, it is intense (as well as being often bland and obtuse). Inevitably it works with repeated figures of human occupation – the rest by the wood, the cottage in the clearing, the edge of the city in sight – but the lynchpin paintings of the tradition are always conscious of these stories and structures as invented and contingent, 'one way of looking at things'. Ruysdael's painting is shot through with such consciousness; and this has partly to do, I think, with its belonging to a surrounding world of landscape painting in which stories and structures were constantly being pushed, stretched, tested, sometimes almost to breaking point. There is a to-and-fro between Ruysdael and Rembrandt, for instance, on just such matters – or so I believe. Compare Ruysdael's extraordinary *View of Naarden*, done in 1647 – Naarden lies a few miles southeast of Amsterdam, on the Zuider Zee – with a famous etching by Rembrandt dated 1651 (FIGS 99 & 100).

The Rembrandt's traditional title is *The Goldweigher's Field*. (It is somehow fitting that the fields in the picture foreground turn out never to have belonged to the big state dignitary whose name later got attached to it, but to one of Rembrandt's very ordinary creditors.) The view in the etching, such as it is, is of Haarlem on the far left horizon; Saxenburg next, even less of an interruption; a church tower, presumably that of Bloemendaal; and three long strip fields in the mid-distance with labourers bleaching linen.[4] The comparison with *View of Naarden* could go in many directions, but let's stick to the matter of ways and ways in. There *is* a point of entry in the Rembrandt: the repeated dark strokes of the needle centre left, and the strong shadow cast by a bit of earthen kerb, establish one. There is a roadway; but almost nothing in the etching – no wayfarer of Ruysdael's kind, no movement from dark to light to dark – gives the road any depth or narrative authority. It swerves off left and disappears. The land breaks up into roughly equal but non-equivalent segments: fields, polders, dune-land, a low wood, an arm of the sea. 'Touch', above all, in the etching – the deliberate blur of the needle; touch colluding with format, long empty spaces everywhere – seems to conjure the world away, for all the firmness of our first ten or twenty strides into it. Or maybe 'conjure the world away' is forcing the note; because again, as in *House near Gardanne*, it is not that nature becomes suddenly excessive or formidable. Ruysdael's *Naarden*, when we look back at it, seems more dramatic. It's just that the very lack of incident in the Rembrandt, its stretch of country's

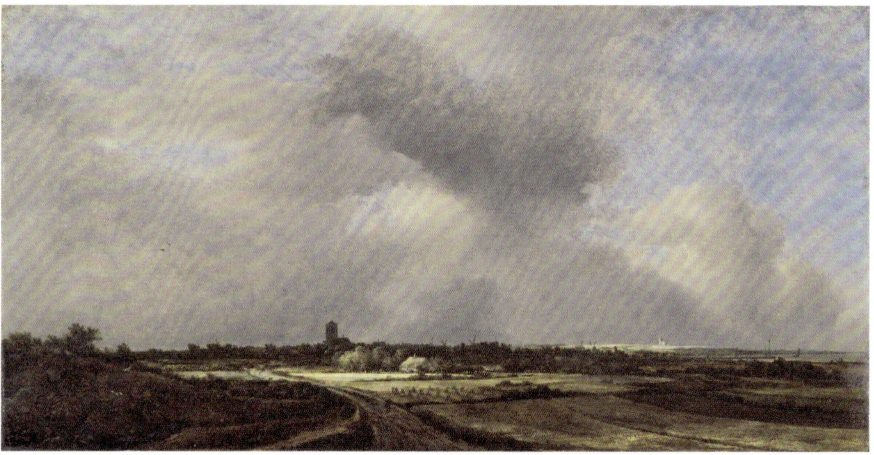

99. Jacob van Ruysdael, *View of Naarden*, 1647, 35 × 67 cm (13⅞ × 26½ in.). Museo Nacional Thyssen-Bornemisza, Madrid.

nondescript-ness, its not having much to do with us... these have become the things to be depicted. Maybe in the case of *Goldweigher's Field* even the word 'uncanny' is appropriate.

◆

I make no apology for putting *Goldweigher's Field* alongside *House near Gardanne*. It seems to me the same shadow companion to Cézanne that *Dream of Joachim* was to *Garden at Issy* (FIGS 90 & 75) – not an 'influence', but a measure. Looking at the road, sea and cities in Rembrandt, we lose our bearings. Looking at Cézanne's house in its solitude, ditto. Landscape painting is given back its strangeness.

There is a kind of landscape practice, we could say, of which *Goldweigher's Field* and *House near Gardanne* are examples, that seems to be interested in the world, or not-quite-world, that crops up between places – where for a moment we find ourselves not 'on the way' to the wood or the town or the distant horizon, but just somewhere...

I crossed a moor, with a name of its own
And a certain use in the world no doubt,
Yet a hand's-breadth of it shines alone
'Mid the blank miles round about:

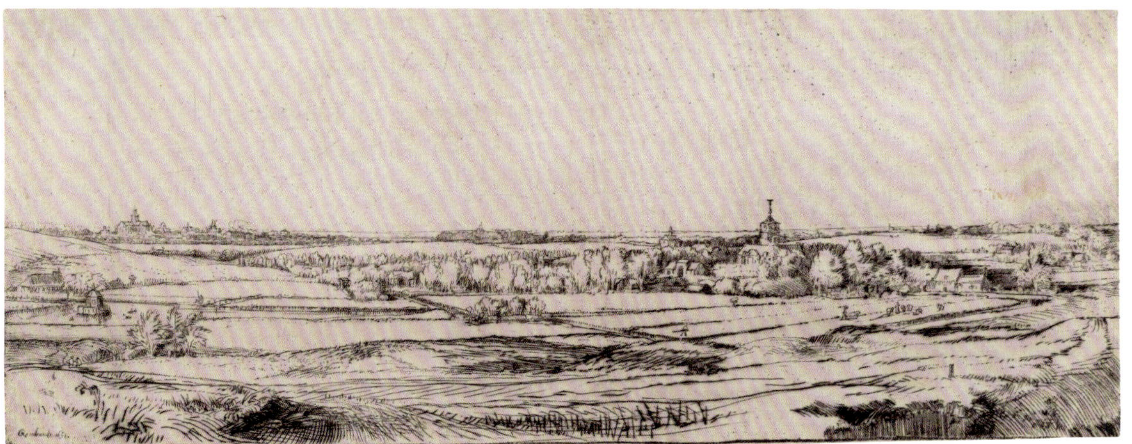

100. Rembrandt Harmensz van Rijn, *The Goldweigher's Field*, etching, 1651, 12 × 32 cm (4¾ × 12⅞ in.). Minneapolis Institute of Art.

For there I picked up on the heather
And there I put inside my breast
A moulted feather, an eagle-feather!
Well, I forget the rest.[5]

Perhaps Robert Browning's tone is too whimsical. The eagle-feather and the exclamation mark are a touch Victorian. But the feeling of contingency in the other seven lines seems apposite – and, in poetry, rare. Haarlem and Saxenburg are in sight.

◆

I'd like to think about the strangeness of *House near Gardanne* world-historically for a moment – putting it back into the 100,000 years (at least) since the beginnings of burial of the dead, control of fire, ochre workshops, trade in high-quality hand-axes, the first shadows of religion. Into the history of the species, that is. Is what we are looking at in Cézanne – what we find chilling and dazzling – simply a vision of Nature from which the gods, at last, have been expelled? The guardians... the ancestors... the totems... the spirits of place. Is this Max Weber's 'disenchantment of the world'?

Maybe. Let us accept, maintaining the 100,000 years as our frame, that human dealings with the realm of necessity have been premised through the millennia on a view of that realm as shaped and animated – made comprehensible – by supernatural beings. The natural world had been *inhabited* – peopled by charged, familiar, more-than-human forces: a pool by a rock with healing powers, a swift or ruthless animal, the wind in a certain quarter, a kind of plant, a poison or a hallucinogen. We should remind ourselves, looking at *House near Gardanne*, that this previous picture of a peopled environment had been central to the species' survival: it had furthered the kind of mapping and memorizing that proved, for the immense majority of *Homo sapiens*'s existence, adaptive – efficient, conducive to the group's passing on of knowledge and action in common.

Several things follow for landscape painting. If there was to be, slowly and painfully, a process of secularization in human life, in which certain kinds of knowledge and action on the world shook themselves free of the frame of religion and battled for primacy with it, this would surely happen most intensely – with the fiercest tug-of-war in the imagination – around the previous *animation* of the object-world. And some such battle – some such tug-of-war – was sensed from the beginning in Cézanne. Critics, whether hostile or admiring, agreed that what was characteristic of his landscapes was that they showed a world without inhabitants. They were 'lifeless'. Inanimate. Stone dead and teeming with sense-data. And isn't this the basic scandal – the aliveness and deadness entwined – that gives a Cézanne its power?

◆

I start again. Let us step back from the foreground of *House near Gardanne* and look at the painting from six feet away – trying to hold onto the impression it makes immediately, seen across a room. Because I believe that it's this apperception, this strange non-totality, that lies at the heart of the Cézanne effect; more than any subsequent local disturbance or nuance. I want to call this first and abiding appearance of *House near Gardanne* the look of a landscape being intercepted. And in order to establish the force of this look – what it does to the landscape genre, why it proved crucial to Cézanne's hold on the subsequent century (to his hold on Matisse, for example) – I have again to speak broadly to the tradition.

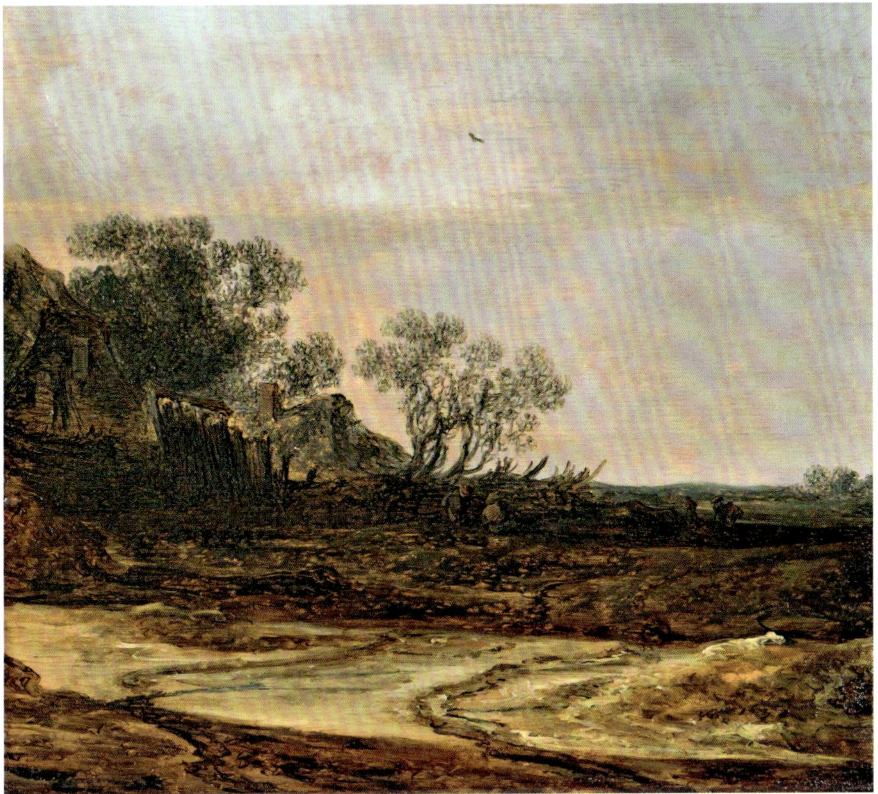

101. Jan van Goyen, *House in the Dunes*, c. 1650, 26.5 × 31 cm (10½ × 12¼ in.). Nivaagaard Collection, Niva, Denmark.

Look once more at the cluster of Dutch landscape paintings that take as their subject just being somewhere, in between places. People have always valued this aspect of the Dutch achievement. The poet Zbigniew Herbert, for example, was an enthusiast in particular for Jan van Goyen (FIG. 101):

> Goyen painted a number of 'Village Lanes'. The outline is simple, beginning at the base of the painting: a narrow canal, a sandy sprawling road, a shed or something that once upon a time was a house and today is a picturesque ruin, a few scrawny trees, and a goat, the heraldic animal of poverty.
>
> All this elicits many questions. Where did the enthusiasts for this subject matter come from in prosperous Holland? Were there many such alleys of poverty in the country?...

> A road through a village, a ferry floating down the river, a hut among dunes, clusters of trees and haystacks, travellers waiting for a ride – these are the typical motifs... Often the topography of Goyen's work is unclear: we are somewhere on the side of a dune, on the banks of some river, at the turn of a road on a certain evening... Canvases with no anecdote, loosely composed, flimsy and slim, with a weak pulse and nervous outline... When I first saw Goyen's canvases I felt I had waited a long time for just this painter, that he filled a gap in the museum of my imagination.[6]

Landscapes like Goyen's or *Goldweigher's Field*, Herbert is saying, are original above all in their way of framing the piece of nature they choose to show: they go in for a new kind of relation between the scene in front of us and the larger reality off-screen. A great deal of landscape painting's persuasiveness and pathos as a genre – it's hard to understand why this has been so little talked about – had always depended on a painting's ability to imply, or seemingly to lead to, the world *not* included in the rectangle. Nature is a continuum. Any picture is an extract, obviously, but the extract an ordinary landscape painter is interested in is given finitude and typicality – this is the claim – by the way the 'scene' appears to do no more than orchestrate (amplify) some familiar organizing accident of nature itself: a clearing (that central word), a glimpse into distance through trees, a stopping place, the shelter of a great tree. In Van Goyen there are no such accidents. Because 'finitude and typicality' are constructs. They aren't true to nature's fits and starts.

Look back at Cézanne. Is it not the least uncanny aspect of *House near Gardanne* that the picture rectangle seems packed with things – fields, paths, mountain ranges – continuing horizontally off frame, but that *why* this particular stretch of the continuum has been chosen, and what the particular stretch does to the very idea of continuity, should leave a viewer floundering? There is a nick of white paint where the mountain meets the picture's edge, top left, echoing a weird nick of blue at the top of the nearby escarpment: the white seems almost a signal that the painting stops – breaks – just where its edge happens to be, and therefore has nothing to say about whether the mountain carries on.

The art historian Fritz Novotny was again pointing to something fundamental when he suggested in the 1920s that one key to Cézanne's painting's strangeness was simply the *section* of the visible – the width of the stretch of terrain presented and the way the terrain related to the rectangle containing it – he saw now as paintable.[7] I come back to the idea of landscape painting as interception. *House near Gardanne* is entirely convincing as a totality: one's eye and mind very soon accept it as a complex fine-tuned artefact, each touch of colour and qualification of line adjusted to the tension of the whole. But it is, exultantly, a *made* thing. Its perfection is internal. The totality it offers is unique – contingent. The feeling of arbitrariness never goes away. Nature takes on an order for us, says Cézanne, not because it *has* one, but because we make one up. Representing is intervening. A picture, to be true to life, ought to be full of the sense that things could have been otherwise.

◆

I proceed to the house itself. The way the building's walls and roof relate to the objects abutting it, and the way the 'faces' of the building are stressed or interrupted, have always appealed to the painter's admirers. Meyer Schapiro writes about them beautifully, in particular the play between trees and windows:

> Very fine is the composition of trees isolating the house from the rest of the landscape. They are broadly symmetrical in pattern, and the edges of the farther group are related to the breaks and shadows on the mountain above... Two foreground trees, superposed to suggest a single tree, mask the joining of the two walls. This bold device strengthens the horizontal of the house and reduces the intensity of convergence of these walls – they seem to merge vaguely, as if at an angle approaching 180 degrees. The placing of the windows and door – oddly, yet in harmony with nearby forms – is an example of Cézanne's great scruple and delicacy in the design of details. See how the tree masks one window, and how the door and the other window form a slightly sloping line with the chimney and the tree above it; imagine the

> dullness of the first window complete and the stiffness of the other openings in a normal alignment and you will admire Cézanne more for his arbitrariness and discretion.[8]

Yet in spite of this the house remains a clearly lit, sharply delineated solid. The left-hand side of the wall without windows could hardly be clearer, for instance; and a tree to the left, which seems to be rooted just in front of the wall, packs its leaves out of sight round the corner so as to leave the straight edge undisturbed. The other front corner, to follow Schapiro, is all but masked by a tree, or maybe two trees pretending to be one. The wall in the sun to the right, with a beautiful wilful geometry of dark windows and door all across it, ends at another straight line; but this one is half lost in among branches, and the whole end of the house at this side – there could be a further low wall to the right, perhaps a pen for animals – reaches out to the strange trapezoid of the ploughed field. The roof is an exquisite floating relative of the hard-edged fields and rock-faces all round.

From the farmhouse chimney (Schapiro sees this immediately) comes a plume of facetious green smoke. Trees crowd along the summit of the house, sealing it in. The house seems half buried in the hill. Grass laps its right side like a wave. A great luminous staircase or waterslide of grass and hay rises to meet its near wall, the hay's yellow humming against the complementary violets in the half-shadow. The hay bale on top of the pile here might as well be a door: it opens the wall as much as casts an equivocal shadow on it. Between the bale and the blind niche up to the left – complete nuance, this niche, but totally sure of itself – there is an interminable to-and-fro of solid and void, yellow and violet, coming forwards and fading away. The wall and bale and the spinning-top of foliage next to them are painting exemplified. Illusionism and its discontents.

What is it these swaps, leakages and substitutions end up *doing* to the house? They are none of them louder than a whisper, but they fix the attention as only a whisper can. Do they make the house part of Nature – folding things into it, analogizing its forms to those in the world at large? Well, maybe – partly. But for every fading and folding there is a hard edge; for every rhyming or merging shape there is one as staccato as a consonant.

Do the leakages end up annihilating the identity 'house' altogether? Surely not. The house stands firm. Its intervention in Nature is implacable. It is where and how the intervention – the identity – ends that Cézanne seems unwilling to decide on. The house's limits are porous. Parts of the world look to be making an appearance inside it, and it seems in turn to be opening into its surroundings (we might almost say, contaminating them) in ways that exceed, or even poke fun at, its man-made foursquare. The chimney puffs its green smoke.

◆

Could we understand *House near Gardanne* as Cézanne's *Allegory of Painting*? Let us look at the house, in other words, not just as the human in the landscape, but specifically as the *picture* – the picture in the world, and maybe of it. The prepositions hereabouts seem to me what the painting is worrying at. Maybe a picture, if it is good enough, 'opens onto the object', as the philosophers say: that's what the play at the edges seems to intimate. But the house's straight sides go on speaking to something else, some contrary logic. A picture is, perhaps necessarily, closed *against* the world and obsessed with its own estrangements – its windows with no view out, its internal orders, its arbitrary shifts. Maybe 'opening onto the object' is always a conjuring trick, a device. Is that what the green smoke and the haystack waterslide are there to tell us?

Sometimes the house looks to me entirely a thing out of Samuel Beckett: I think I hear one of his heroes soliloquizing in an upper room. But then I see the whole thing's – the picture's, the house's – simplicity, and the paradoxes take their place again as accompaniment. Grace notes to the great tune of colour.

◆

Go back to the house as a building. Whether or not humanity's presence in nature is an intrusion, and whether the intrusion is malignant or benign – these have always been landscape painting's questions. When the Milanese Paolo Lomazzo wrote the first broad account of the genre in 1584 – the first for Europeans, that is – he began as follows:

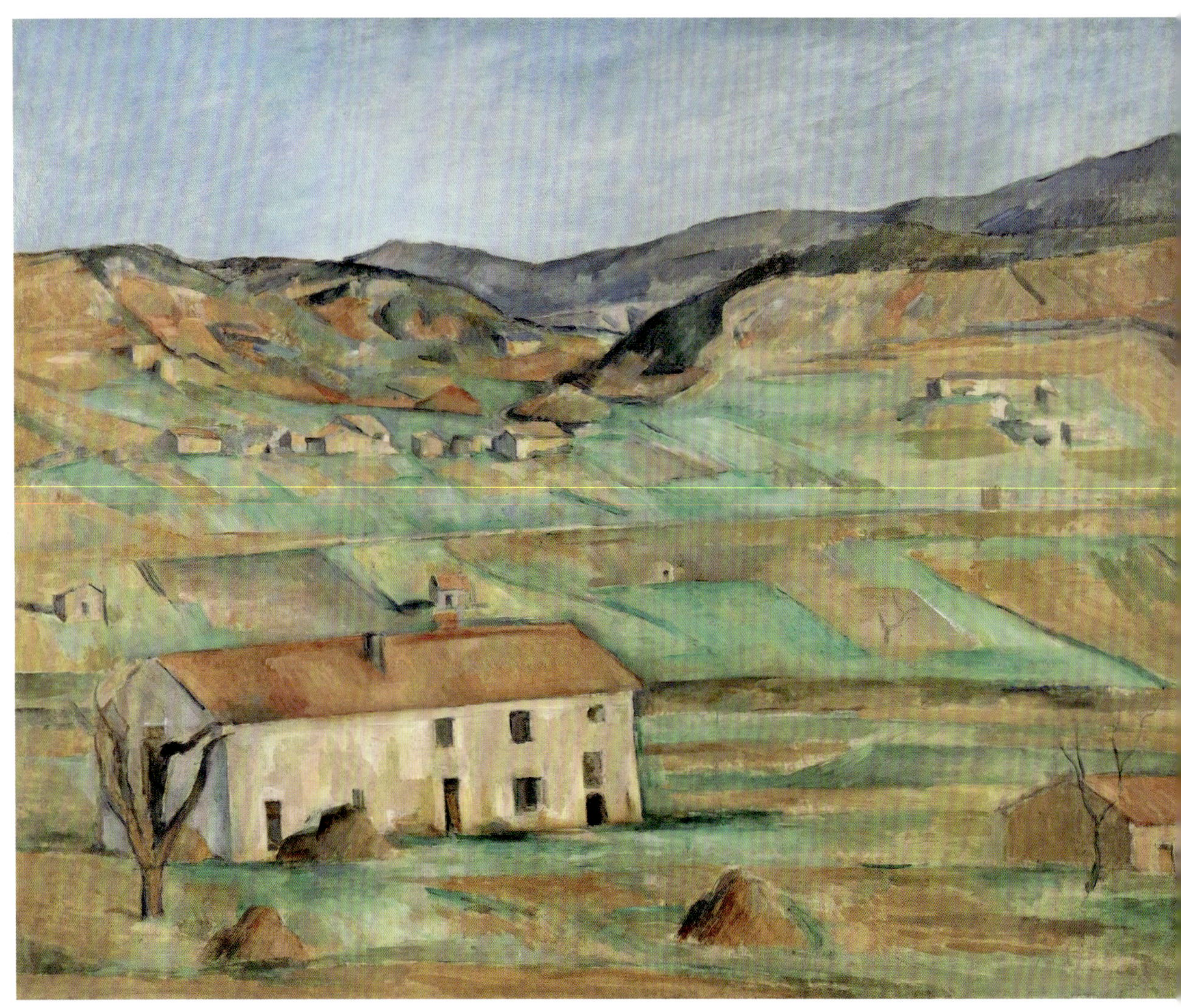

102. *Environs of Gardanne, c.* 1886–90, 58.5 × 72 cm (23 × 28⅜ in.). Private Collection.

> Those who have shown excellence and grace in this branch of painting, both in private and public places [he knows that the genre already has a public dimension], have discovered various ways of setting about it – such as fetid, dark underground places, religious and macabre, where they represent graveyards, tombs, deserted houses, sinister and lonesome sites, caves, dens, ponds and pools…[9]

He goes on to enumerate less strange and dreadful aspects of the landscape world, but it is important that his list begins as it does. And of course it matters – looking at *House near Gardanne* – that the catalogue includes deserted houses and sinister, lonesome sites.

Put *House near Gardanne* next to a Cézanne done at much the same moment, probably no more than a mile or two away – let's call it *Environs of Gardanne* – and enter into the story what historians tell us about the landscape in question: that by the mid-1880s Gardanne, though still asleep on its hill (FIG. 52), was surrounded by coal fields – worked since medieval times – a cement factory, potteries, lime works. The preponderant crop was tobacco.[10]

In the landscape tradition emptiness – an empty building – is most often a figure of ruin or abandonment. And this offers its own kind of reassurance. It seems to put us in the wake of catastrophe, looking back on human occupation from Nature's point of view. Isn't this the message of *House with Cracked Walls* (FIG. 95)? In *Environs of Gardanne*, by contrast, emptiness and overcrowding coincide. Occupation is everywhere, but the picture seems intent on dramatizing the occupation's thinness, its being only a few inches deep. The house in this case – peculiar stretched object – concentrates the general feeling of improvisation, randomness. Ruin is ongoing. Smoke from these chimneys will not be green. We as viewers are not put *after* anything – least of all in a place which Nature has reclaimed. The non-catastrophe called 'farming' is still in un-picturesque mid-flow. In the foreground there are haycocks, in the distance scoured earth – maybe mine diggings and spoil tips. It is as if the image had been stopped by a pause button. I feel the struggle with the realm of necessity in every square inch.

◆

My book could have ended with *Environs of Gardanne*. The picture's inconclusiveness; its dispersal of attention; the feeling in it of the world having retreated to an unnerving mid-distance; and of a clinging to beauty in the face of such a feeling – all of these, I'm convinced, speak deeply to Cézanne's sense of life. Yet to finish on such a note would be wrong. For the beauty *was* clung onto; it was what mattered; it was insisted on, gloried in, apotheosized – in its very uniqueness and improbability, its remoteness from the world we are in.

I end, therefore, with *Montagne Sainte-Victoire seen from Bibémus Quarry* (FIGS 54 & 103).[11]

Don't ask, to begin, where we *are* in the Bibémus quarry – where we're standing, exactly, where we're looking from. That would be like asking, apropos the opening lines of Eliot's *Ash-Wednesday*, who the 'I' is in 'Because I do not hope to turn again/Because I do not hope'. The I of the poem is the I the words create. The thing seen is the thing the *picture* sees. There is no standpoint – no warrant – for the sight of the mountain apart from the chaos within the rectangle. ('Chaos' being one of the names we have for orders whose insistencies we feel – we give in to – but do not understand. The orders of life.)

Yes, of course… The painting also permits us, maybe encourages us, to notice – to be knowing about – the fact that we're 'nowhere' as viewers. Bibémus quarry was a wilderness in Cézanne's day: it was picturesque. It gave one a glimpse of the mountain to the south from a point seemingly underground, ungrounded – in the air, among the treetops, balanced on the edge of a cliff. But ultimately, responding to the stresses and reticences in the scene as Cézanne actually renders it – the quarry is not an abyss, the trees in the foreground hardly detain us, the rocks don't teem with accidental faces – it is the self-evidence, the inevitability, of the view that strikes home. This is how things are. This is the moment – the balance of forces, the distance, the plainness and hyperbole – at which reality asserts itself.

◆

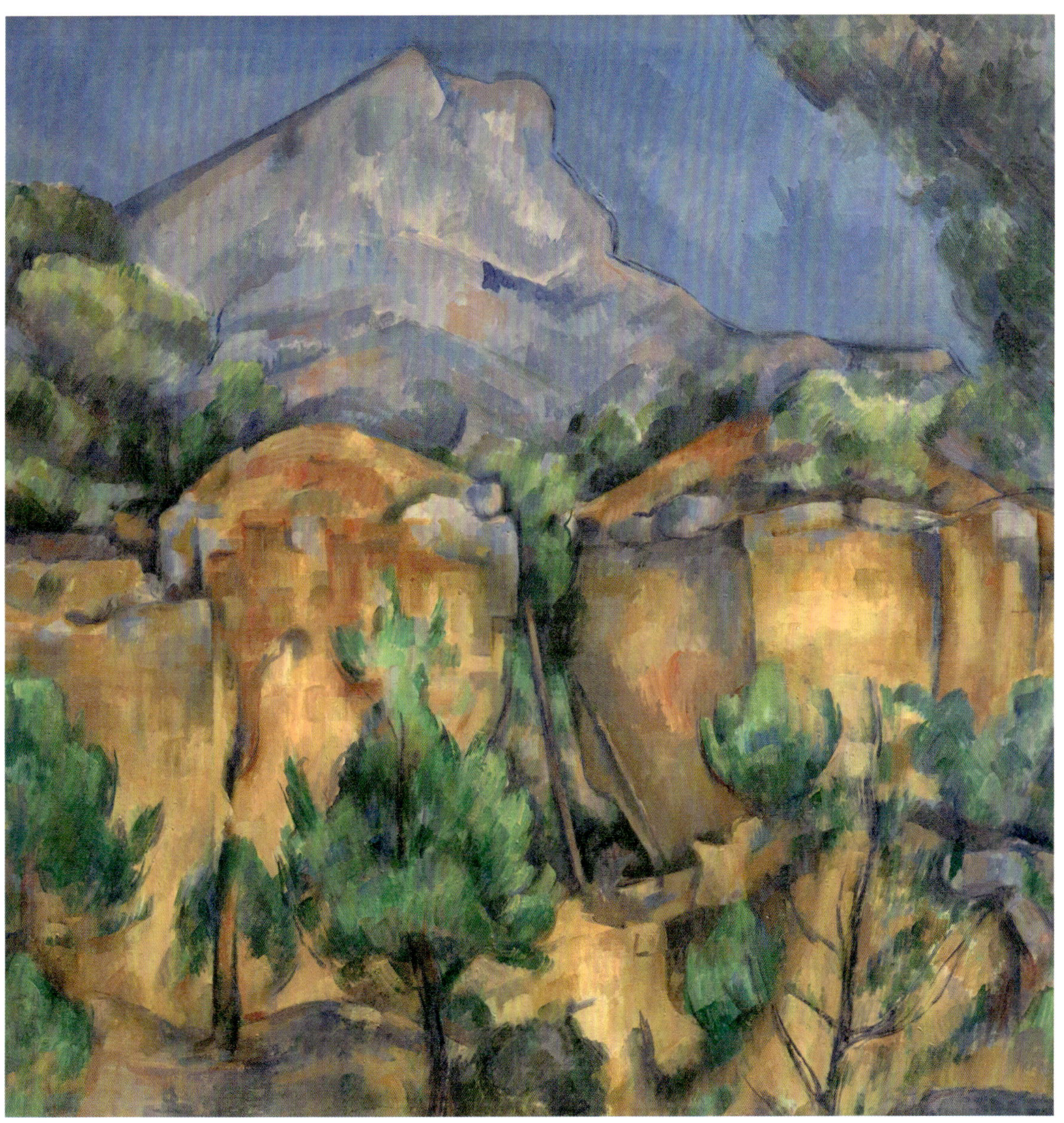

103. Detail from Fig. 54: *Montagne Sainte-Victoire seen from Bibémus Quarry*, *c.* 1895–1900. Baltimore Museum of Art.

A voice in my head, looking over this and assenting, is almost ready to change its mind about the argument – the affect – of the book as a whole. 'Aren't we looking at the *world*, then? Haven't you finally admitted as much?... The world as it is, in all its restlessness and enormity.' 'I may agree', the voice continues, 'that we're not *used* to the world, and that everyday existence seems to depend on us tuning reality down to an almost colourless monotone. But *this* is reality. How can anyone doubt it? You've been calling the quality of the things Cézanne shows us "strangeness", but it's the monotone that's strange, not the mountain.'

Part of me goes along with the voice; maybe I'll end up giving in to it completely. But immediately, indelibly, another voice speaks back – equally sure it has the truth of the picture in its grasp. 'How can you possibly miss seeing that this *isn't* reality?' it says. 'You know full well – the painting could hardly be more insistent – that the scene you're looking at is "out of this world". It is an apparition, a spectacle... as remote from ordinary experience as must have been the first depictions flickering in the torchlight in the darkness of the caves.'

Maybe both voices are right. For didn't the depictions in the cave (and Cézanne following them) speak to what the world *was* – and remains – for the always overeager sensorium? ('It's frightening, life.') The world is an unreality: that is its nature for humans confronting it. Torchlight is its natural element. And from this fact – this enduring, consoling, factitious 'sociality of the image' – stems much of the history of mankind. When Marx reached back to the notion of fetishism in trying to characterize his society's fantasy relation to the world of goods, he spoke to the depth – maybe the intractability – of the subject.

◆

'All the same,' says the previous voice, 'I still don't see that your book concludes on at all the same note as it began. What you said you saw in Cézanne at the beginning, in 1958, was "how it felt to be modern". But where's modernity in *Montagne Sainte-Victoire seen from Bibémus*? You began with history – or you promised us history – but end with metaphysics.'

Just so. I end with an all-or-nothing argument, carried on, interminably, by the work of art itself. The all-or-nothing not as 'background' to the work; not as a frame within which representation might be worked on locally, with a due sense of proportion about what mere depiction might be capable of; but as *the question the picture exists to put* – hectically, desperately, as if for the first and last time. ('If I succeed with this bloke, the theory will be true.') 'Is this reality or phantasmagoria?' 'Is this the world occurring or the world transfigured?' 'Is there even a difference between the two?'

And don't you see that the argument – the absolutism of the alternatives, the beauty of the either/or, the complete conviction that here, in the picture, at last one alternative or the other will be proven – *is* modernity? The view from the quarry is modernity incarnate. The feeling of the present – of presentness, of depthlessness, of a subjectivity flickering interminably between performance and passivity, 'data' overtaking sensation; and of that state as both fabulous and intolerable – has never been stronger.

◆

Sometimes, looking at the mountain, I think I am face to face with another *Allegory of Painting* – maybe a counter-allegory to *House near Gardanne*. The *mountain* is the picture, not the four-square house. And the picture, it follows, is not a closed thing – not an artefact or a 'work'. It is not even an exposure to the world of sense or sensation, opening onto the object if all goes well. The picture is the world we are in.

Such a world is unfamiliar to us, granted. For a moment it registers as a vision, a phantasm. It is framed in a chaos (or held back by a barrier) of yellows and greens. We stare at it from under the earth. But *look* – look at the touches of green and pink on the mountain face, look at the pooling of blue, look at the lines just holding the mountain's right edge. Look at the mountain's whole shape. 'Vision' is the wrong word for it. It is the thing itself.

Acknowledgments

When a book takes as long as this one to write, acknowledging help given along the way is a hopeless task. Too many people's insights have been drawn on. My notes are specific: they are not intended as reports on the 'state of the field' past and present, and they certainly do not register all my debts to a century of scholarship. Many of the texts I've learnt from are not cited. Haven't I spent decades admiring and arguing with Theodore Reff's psychoanalytic 'Cézanne's Bather with Outstretched Arm'? Didn't Richard Shiff's pioneering studies send us all back to the first responses to Cézanne's work in the 1890s? How many times have I read Merleau-Ponty's 'Cézanne's Doubt'? Where are the shadows in the book of Lionello Venturi, John Rewald, Bernard Dorival, Erle Loran, Lawrence Gowing, Susan Sidlauskas, Mary Louise Krumrine, Kurt Badt, Wayne Andersen, Mary Tomkins Lewis, John House, Pavel Machotka, Carol Armstrong, Jean-Claude Lebensztejn, Alex Danchev, even the great nay-sayer Hans Sedlmayr? The shadows are there, and I am happy to acknowledge them. Other writers and curators – Roger Fry, Meyer Schapiro, Fritz Novotny, Clement Greenberg, Michael Doran, John Elderfield, Joachim Pissarro – are addressed explicitly, though often not at the length they deserve. All my chapters began as lectures, given more than once and improving with time: the criticisms and questions of my audiences were vital. Many of the book's ideas were first developed in courses I gave at U C Berkeley over the years, to graduate and undergraduate classes: I am deeply grateful to participants. Finally, my notes do make clear, I hope, an indebtedness to a younger generation of Cézanne scholars: Bridget Alsdorf, Nina Athanassoglou-Kallmyer, André Dombrowski, Aruna D'Souza, Chiao-Mei Liu, Nancy Locke, Paul Smith and Kathryn Tuma. Their ideas and objections have been precious.

I gratefully acknowledge help given along the way by the Getty Research Institute, the Mellon Foundation and the University of California, Berkeley's Humanities Research Fellowships.

ACKNOWLEDGMENTS

This book is mainly an invitation to look again at Cézanne – to look and be taken aback. I was taught that imperative by Fry and Schapiro, and had it confirmed, unforgettably, in classes I took from Robert Ratcliffe in the 1960s in the old Courtauld Gallery, its daylight making the pictures glow. Later on I looked at Cézanne in Michael Fried's company: I remember him standing in front of a *Bay at L'Estaque* on one occasion and saying, characteristically, 'Just look at that blue! You could plunge your arm in it up to the shoulder!' Through the years, the appetite for art of Sherie and Mel Scheer, and their lack of respect for received opinion, have been inspiriting. I owe a great deal to Wendy Lesser's unfailing energy and encouragement. Conversations with Elise Archias, Iain Boal, the late Robert Boardingham, the late Achim Borchardt-Hume, Phil Cohen, Todd Cronan, Brigid Doherty, Nina Dubin, Sarah Evans, Hal Foster, Peter Goulds, Darcy Grimaldo Grigsby, Matthew Jackson, Christina Kiaer, Don Moss, Todd Olson, Richard Rizzo, Lytle Shaw, Daniel Spaulding, Evi Staikou, Ron Walkey, Marnin Young and Lynne Zeavin stick in the mind. I am very grateful to the *London Review of Books*, in particular to editors Mary-Kay Wilmers and Alice Spawls. The comradeship of Joseph Matthews, Donald Nicholson-Smith and Mia Rublowska has been vital – as the man said, 'About modernity they were never wrong…'

At Thames & Hudson, my warm thanks go to Roger Thorp for his support of the book, and to Julie Bosser, Karin Fremer, Nikolas Kotsopoulos, Elisa Merino, Michela Parkin and especially Mohara Gill for their help in making it.

Particular exhibitions mattered greatly: the book would have been entirely different without the curatorial energy and care, at crucial points, of William Rubin, Joseph Rishel, Philip Conisbee, John Elderfield and Joachim Pissarro. And in recent decades I have learned about Cézanne from Bridget Alsdorf, André Dombrowski, Jeremy Melius and Kathryn Tuma; as well as from Nancy Locke and Christopher Campbell – generous friends, passionate *Cézannistes*, always taking me back to the beauty and difficulty of the thing itself. In particular, my thanks go to Christopher Campbell for all his help with the book's illustrations.

This book is an offering to Anne Wagner. She did so much to make it. Among many memories, I treasure a moment when she turned to me from a painting we both had looked at hundreds of times (a fine reproduction kept us company over decades) and said, '*Now* I see the house behind the trees! Now I begin to understand.' Such delight in seeing is good to live with.

Notes

Introduction

1 The dating of Cézanne's paintings is difficult. Documentary evidence is mostly lacking and his stylistic development is often hard to reconstruct. The dates given in my picture captions sometimes disagree with published sources.

2 See especially Kathryn Tuma, 'Cézanne and Lucretius at the Red Rock', *Representations*, 78, no. 1 (2002), pp. 56–85; Ann Byrd, 'The Brush Stroke as Catastrophe: Gasquet's *Cézanne* and the Paintings of the Bibémus Quarry', *Canadian Art Review*, 34, no. 1 (2009), pp. 41–52; and, more generally on Bibémus, John Elderfield, ed., *Cézanne: The Rock and Quarry Paintings* (New Haven and London, 2020), pp. 1–63 (essays by Elderfield and Faya Causey), pp. 103–27. John Elderfield tells me that a 'viewpoint' has now been identified for *Red Rock*. No one disputes that Cézanne made his 'non-givens' – his works of art – from the 'givens', the data. (When we come to his *Bathers* the case is more complicated.) His admirers have done fine work through the decades on those 'givens' and the degree to which Cézanne stayed true to them. My subject, which I think still too little explored, is what the 'non-given' – the 'non-world' – Cézanne actually *made* is like; and what that object means to tell us (or maybe doesn't mean to, but does so all the same) about our relation to the 'world'.

3 Thomas S. Eliot, 'The Burial of the Dead', *The Waste Land*, 1922.

Chapter 1

1 'Quel état faites-vous de Cézanne? Je le vois, dans son art, ce que fut Rimbaud dans la littérature, une mine inépuisable de diamants.' See Charles Morice, 'Enquête sur les Tendances Actuelles des Arts Plastiques', *Mercure de France* (1 August 1905), p. 350. Part of this chapter was first published as 'Strange Apprentice', *London Review of Books* (8 October 2020), pp. 15–21.

2 Identifications of the other sitters vary. The man in the top hat is probably the photographer, and possibly Nicolás Martinéz Valdivieso, a wealthy Cuban who lived in Auvers. The two melancholy youngsters are (again, possibly) Allonso, a medical student and amateur painter from Cuba, and A. Aguiar, established later in Cuba as a doctor and painter. (He may have been born in Puerto Rico.) Pissarro maintained connections with his Caribbean birthplace throughout his life.

3 Cited in William S. Meadmore, *Lucien Pissarro: Un Coeur Simple* (London, 1962), p. 27. For the letter in full, which is translated freely by Meadmore, see Anne Thorold, *Artists, Writers, Politics: Camille Pissarro and his Friends* (Oxford, 1980), pp. 8–9.

4 Maurice Denis, *Journal, Tome 2 (1905–1920)* (Paris, 1957), p. 30, cited in Michael Doran, ed., *Conversations avec Cézanne* (Paris, 1978), p. 94. Karl E. Osthaus, 'Une visite à Paul Cézanne', *Das Feuer* (1920–21), reporting on a visit in 1906, cited *ibid.*, p. 98.

5 See especially Charles H. Kahn, *Plato and the Socratic Dialogue: The Philosophical Use of a Literary Form* (Cambridge, 1997) and Diskin Clay, *Platonic Questions: Dialogues with the Silent Philosopher* (University Park, PA, 2000).

6 Letter to Théodore Duret, 2 May 1873, cited in Janine Bailly-Herzberg, ed., *Correspondance de Camille Pissarro*, 5 vols (Paris, 1980–91), vol. 1, p. 80.

7 See Émile Bernard, 'Paul Cézanne', *L'Occident* (July 1904), cited in Doran *Conversations*, p. 37.

8 Both quotes from Clement Greenberg, 'Review of *Camille Pissarro: Letters to His Son*', in John O'Brian, ed., *Clement Greenberg, The Collected Essays and Criticism*, 4 vols (Chicago, 1986–93), vol. 1, p. 216.

9 Joachim Gasquet, *Cézanne* (Paris, 1926 [first published 1921]), p. 136. Scholars disagree about the trustworthiness of Gasquet's quotes. This one seems compatible with evidence from other sources. For instance, Antoine Guillemet's letter to Francisco Oller, 12 September 1866, rehearsing what is clearly already common ground between Guillemet, Pissarro and Cézanne: 'Seul Pissarro continue à faire des chefs d'oeuvre… Cézanne est à Aix où il a fait des études superbes d'audace: Manet ressemble à Ingres en comparaison… Vois par taches: le métier n'est rien, pâte et justesse: tel doit être le but à poursuivre.' Cited and discussed in Joachim Pissarro, *Pioneering Modern Painting: Cézanne and Pissarro 1865–1885* (New York, 2005), pp. 35–36 and 218. See, on the wider question, Doran, *Conversations*, pp. 192–93, note 20, and Nancy Locke, '*Piquer, Plaquer*: Cézanne, Pissarro, and Palette-Knife Painting', in André Dombrowski, ed., *A Companion to Impressionism* (London, 2021). Locke discusses the use of the palette knife in Pissarro's mid-1870s work.

10 An argument pursued with subtlety throughout Schapiro's writings on modern art, in particular in Meyer Schapiro, *Impressionism: Reflections and*

Perceptions (New York, 1997) and his *Paul Cézanne* (New York, 1952), mentioned in my introduction. On Impressionist 'immediacy', see the classic essay by Robert L. Herbert, 'Method and Meaning in Monet', *Art in America*, 67 (September 1979), pp. 901–8.

11 Cézanne to Émile Bernard, 1905, in John Rewald, ed., *Paul Cézanne: Correspondance* (Paris, 1978), p. 314 [hereafter PCC]. Cézanne seems to be replying to the platitudes on art and anarchism Bernard had produced in an article on Cézanne the previous year: see É. Bernard, 'Paul Cézanne', *L'Occident* (July 1904), cited in Doran, *Conversations*, p. 32. Compare Bernard's letter to his mother, reporting on a first visit to Cézanne, 4 February 1904: 'C'est un brave homme, une sorte de seigneur de la peinture qui retourne d'épais empâtements comme une terre grasse. Il professe les théories du naturalisme et de l'impressionnisme, me parle de Pissarro, qu'il déclare colossal.' Cited in *ibid.*, p. 24.

12 Compare these phrases from Cézanne's letters: 'Le peintre concrète, au moyen du dessin et de la couleur, ses sensations, ses perceptions. On n'est ni trop scrupuleux, ni trop sincère, ni trop soumis à la nature...' (to Bernard, 1904, PCC, p. 303); 'La sensation forte de la nature – et certes, je l'ai vive…' (to Louis Aurenche, 1904, PCC, p. 298); 'En nous ne s'est pas endormie la vibration des sensations répercutées de ce bon soleil de Provence, nos vieux souvenirs de jeunesse, de ces horizons, de ces paysages, de ces lignes inouïes qui laissent en nous tant d'impressions profondes... Pour l'heure présente, je continue à chercher l'expression de ces sensations confuses que nous apportons en naissant.' (To Henri Gasquet, 1899, PCC, pp. 270–71); or even 'Il n'y a que la force initiale id est, le tempérament...' (to Charles Camoin, 1903, PCC, p. 293). See also note 23 in Chapter 5 and note 1 in the Conclusion.

13 On the two *Louveciennes*, see Joachim Pissarro, *Pioneering Modern Painting*, pp. 103–7 and Joachim Pissarro, *Cézanne/Pissarro, Johns/Rauschenberg: The Aesthetics of Collaboration in Modern Art* (Cambridge, 2006), pp. 130–32. On Pissarro in the 1870s more generally, see Rachael Ziady DeLue, 'Pissarro, Landscape, Vision, and Tradition', *Art Bulletin*, 80, no. 4 (1998), pp. 718–36.

14 The few yards alter everything, in fact. Cézanne seems to have moved far enough to the left to leave the tall central tree in the Pissarro out of frame. Or is he 'seeing through it'? Painting it out of the picture? His viewpoint seems closer to the two main houses – they loom larger in his visual field – but the distance across Maubuisson's strips of garden to the wall at the base of the hill registers as greater.

15 See Joachim Pissarro, *Pioneering Modern Painting*, pp. 58–59, 187–201.

16 Louis Le Bail, unpublished reminiscences, circa 1896–97, cited in John Rewald, *Cézanne: sa vie, son oeuvre, son amitié pour Zola* (Paris, 1939), p. 283.

17 John House's datings (unpublished) were arrived at in response to MoMA's 'Pioneering Modern Painting' and several major Cézanne shows in the years following, notably Philip Conisbee's 'Cézanne in Provence', National Gallery of Art, Washington, D.C., 2006.

18 Roger Fry, 'The New Gallery', *The Athenaeum*, no. 4081 (13 January 1906), p. 56.

Chapter 2

1 Émile Bernard, 'Souvenirs sur Paul Cézanne', *Mercure de France*, 69, no. 5 (16 October 1907), p. 160, cited in Doran, *Conversations*, p. 70. 'Personne ne me touchera.' Bernard had just made the mistake of lending the old man a helping hand in the street.

2 Timothy J. Clark, 'Symptoms of Cézannoia', *London Review of Books* (2 December 2010). Inset quote from letter to Bernard, 21 September 1906, PCC, p. 326: '…il n'y a que la preuve à faire de ce qu'on pense qui présente de sérieux obstacles. Je continue donc mes études.'

3 Thadée Natanson, 'Paul Cézanne', *La Revue Blanche*, 9 (1 December 1895), p. 499. 'Il ose être fruste et comme sauvage et ne se laisse entraîner jusqu'au bout, au mépris de tout le reste, que par le seul souci qui mène les initiateurs, de créer quelques signes neufs.' Several critics in 1895, some decidedly sympathetic to Cézanne's art, commented on its solemnity or lugubriousness. For example, the anonymous reviewer, 'Les Expositions', *L'Art Français* (23 November 1895), p. 4: 'M. Césanne [sic], lui, est demeuré aussi farouche qu'il fut au début, aussi lugubre d'aspect, aussi intransigeant dans ses convictions… Mais il y a sur toutes ces choses vraiment fortes, comme un voile de tristesse. L'art lugubre est peut-être l'art de demain.' Compare Désiré Louis, 'Notes d'Art', *La Justice* (13 December 1895), p. 1: 'Peu à peu, la rétine s'habitue, distingue mieux les curiosités, les beautés de cet art un peu heurté, un peu âpre. La hardiesse dans le rapprochement des tons, la simplicité synthétique, la naïveté se dégagent des verts et des ombres qui ont une teinte tendrement funèbre, un peu triste et grandiose.'

4 Pissarro to Lucien, 3 December 1890, PCC, vol. 2, p. 371: 'J'ai reçu une lettre de

Murer me disant qu'il avait rencontré Guillaumin qui lui dit que Cézanne était dans une maison de fous!... tous donc!... c'est navrant!...' Pissarro had written to Theo van Gogh on 30 July offering sympathy after Vincent's suicide, and then on 18 October had reported to Lucien about Theo's state of health: 'Lui qui aimait tant sa femme et son enfant, il a voulu les tuer. Bref, on a dû l'emmener à la maison du Docteur Blanche.' (See John Rewald, ed., *Camille Pissarro, Lettres à son Fils Lucien* [Paris, 1950], p. 189. For some reason this letter is not reprinted in volume 2 of PCC.)

5 'What do you make of Cézanne?' See Charles Morice, 'Enquête sur les Tendances Actuelles des Arts Plastiques', *Mercure de France* (1 and 15 August, 1 September 1905), pp. 346–59, 538–55, 61–85.

6 Madame Marval, 'Enquête sur les Tendances Actuelles', *Mercure de France* (1 August 1905), p. 353.

7 Kurt Badt, *The Art of Cézanne*, trans. Sheila Ogilvie (London, 1965 [German edition 1956]), p. 181.

8 György Lukács, 'Georg Simmel (Nachruf)', *Pester Lloyd* (2 October 1918), in K. Gassen and M. Landmann, eds, *Buch des Dankes an Georg Simmel* (Berlin, 1958), p. 173.

9 Ernst Bloch, *The Spirit of Utopia*, trans. Anthony Nassar (Stanford, 2000), p. 31. (First published 1918, written in 1916.)

10 Clement Greenberg, 'Cézanne and the Unity of Modern Art', *Partisan Review*, May–June 1951, in John O'Brian, ed., *Clement Greenberg: The Collected Essays and Criticism* (Chicago and London, 1986–93), vol. 3, pp. 82–91. The best writing on Cézanne in the 1960s and 1970s was most often in dialogue with Greenberg's emphases: see, for instance, John Elderfield, 'Drawing in Cézanne', *Artforum*, 9 (June 1971), pp. 51–57, and Elderfield, 'The World Whole: Color in Cézanne', *Arts Magazine* (April 1978), pp. 148–53.

11 Among previous literature, see in particular Bridget Alsdorf, 'Interior Landscapes: Metaphor and Meaning in Cézanne's Late Still Lifes', *Word & Image*, 26, no. 4 (1 November 2010), pp. 314–23, for a fine extended treatment, treating aspects of the painting I give short shrift. On Cézanne's still lifes more generally, see Carol Armstrong, *Cézanne in the Studio: Still Life in Watercolor* (Los Angeles, 2004) and Benedict Leca, ed., *The World is an Apple: The Still Lifes of Paul Cézanne* (Hamilton, Ontario, 2014). My chapter is also deeply indebted to (though in many ways at odds with) Meyer Schapiro's 'The Apples of Cézanne: An Essay on the Meaning of Still-life', in Schapiro, *Modern Art: 19th and 20th Centuries* (New York, 1978), pp. 1–38.

12 Georges Lecomte, 'L'Impressionisme', *Revue de l'Évolution Sociale* (May 1892), p. 217: 'Au temps héroïques du naturalisme, on se plut à exalter l'équilibre incertain de quelques-unes d'entre [ses études de la nature], leur bizarrerie fortuite, comme si l'art pouvait s'accommoder de disproportion et de déséquilibre.' Lecomte is struggling in the early 1890s to understand the taste for Cézanne's disequilibrium among the young artists of his day. Compare his hostile verdict a month earlier, in 'L'Art Contemporain', *La Revue Indépendante* (April 1892), p. 16: 'Ce qui séduit les peintres idéistes, ce ne sont pas les toiles belles par la logique ordonnance et la très saine harmonie des tons... mais bien d'incomplètes compositions que chacun s'accorde, avec l'assentiment de M. Cézanne lui-même, à juger inférieures, en raison de leur arrangement déséquilibré et d'un coloris vraiment trop confus.' On the persistence of these concerns in early Cézanne criticism, see Richard Shiff, 'Seeing Cézanne', *Critical Inquiry* (Summer 1978), pp. 769–808.

13 Cézanne to Zola, 4 April 1886, PCC, p. 225.

14 Lecomte, 'L'Impressionisme', *Revue de l'Évolution Sociale*, p. 217. Lecomte is unsure how to value or characterize the disarray, and about what gave rise to it. Compare, in the same article: 'ses synthèses et ses simplifications de couleurs, si surprenantes chez un peintre particulièrement épris de réalité et d'analyse.'

15 Reported in C. Zervos, 'Conversation avec Picasso', *Cahiers d'art* (special issue, 1935), cited in Pablo Picasso, *Propos sur l'art* (Paris, 1998), p. 36.

16 Dante Alighieri, *Paradiso*, ed. and trans. Charles S. Singleton (Princeton, 1982), p. 268.

17 See Fritz Novotny, *Cézanne und das Ende der wissenschaftlichen Perspektive* (Vienna, 1938); extracts translated in Christopher Wood, ed., *The Vienna School Reader* (New York, 2000), pp. 379–433; and discussion below in Chapters 3 and 4. The brief essay by Novotny translated in the Phaidon book, *Cézanne* (London, 1937), pp. 7–21, is also useful.

18 Karl Marx, *Capital: A Critical Analysis of Capitalist Production*, trans. Samuel Moore and Edward Aveling (Moscow, 1961 [first published 1887]), vol. 1, p. 47. Compare the text in Karl Marx, *Das Capital: Kritik der politischen Ökonomie, erster Band*, 4th edition (Berlin, 1991), p. 49. Daniel Spaulding, in helpful comments on the German, confirms that the translation of 'Werthgegenständlichkeit' as 'value of commodities' rather than 'value-objectivity' flattens the contrast with 'Gegenständlichkeit', 'coarse objectivity'. Marx clearly

wants to suggest that two full forms of 'objectivity' are at issue. Likewise, translating 'Waarenkörper' ('commodity-body') as 'substance' loses the force of Marx's Shakespearean–Hegelian heavy dancing. 'Werthding', the final word of the passage, is yet another weird portmanteau. 'I would hazard', writes Spaulding, 'that what Marx wants to convey is not so much that a thing possesses value as the reverse: value possesses the thing, or rather, value has somehow made itself into or precipitated a thing.' Pity the poor translators!

19 Rainer Maria Rilke, *Letters on Cézanne*, trans. Joel Agee (New York, 1985 [German edition 1952]), p. 96.

20 Martha Fehsenfeld and Lois Overbeck, eds, *The Letters of Samuel Beckett, Vol. 1, 1929–1940* (Cambridge, 2009), letter to Thomas McGreevy, 8 September 1934, p. 223.

21 *Ibid.*, p. 222.

22 Gasquet, *Cézanne*, p. 132, cited in Merleau-Ponty, 'Cézanne's Doubt', in Maurice Merleau-Ponty, *Sense and Non-Sense*, trans. Herbert and Patricia Dreyfus (Evanston, IL, 1964), p. 17: 'The landscape thinks itself in me, he said, and I am its consciousness.' The original form of words in Gasquet: 'Le paysage se reflète, s'humanise, se pense en moi. Je l'objective, le projette, le fixe sur ma toile… L'autre jour, vous me parliez de Kant. Je vais bafouiller, peut-être, mais il me semble que je serais la conscience subjective de ce paysage, comme ma toile en serait la conscience objective.' Whatever one's scepticism about Gasquet's reformulations, his pages 130–38 are a dazzling, and in many ways plausible, rendering of the whole reach of Cézanne's ambitions. See also Michael Podro, 'The Landscape Thinks Itself In Me', *The International Review of Psycho-Analysis*, 17 (1990), pp. 401–8.

23 Marx, *Capital*, p. 35, note 2.

24 *Ibid.*, p. 72. It is entirely possible to argue, as Daniel Spaulding did to me after an earlier lecture, that Marx is not putting forth a 'phenomenology' at all, but describing a purely economic form. He may indeed have intended to; but in practice (as Spaulding's later comments suggest) his language, and his argument, shift all the time between the realms of 'experience' and 'behaviour'; and necessarily so.

25 Cézanne to his son Paul, 15 October 1906, PCC, p. 332.

Chapter 3

1 Denis, *Journal, Tome 2*, p. 30, cited in Doran, *Conversations*, p. 94: 'La nature, jai voulu la copier, je n'arrivais pas.' This chapter started life as 'Phenomenality and Materiality in Cézanne', in Tom Cohen et al., eds, *Material Events: Paul de Man and the Afterlife of Theory* (Minneapolis and London, 2001), pp. 93–113. As the title indicates, the article was addressed to an academic audience and mobilized concepts and concerns associated with Paul de Man and his version of (and challenge to) 'materialism'. I have revised the text of the article extensively, particularly its opening sections, with a view to making the issues involved clearer – they will never be entirely clear – for non-specialist readers. This has meant dismantling or rephrasing much of the 'de-Manian' machinery. It is sad that I may seem here to be following the academic tide, which has swept a disgraced de Man into oblivion. The disgrace is merited (de Man's youthful collaboration with the Nazi regime in Belgium, and subsequent concealments and duplicities, speak for themselves); the oblivion, in my view, not. De Man's reworking of materialism remains fundamental, like it or not, and informs my chapter throughout. For a different 'de Manian' account of Cézanne, see Fred Orton, '(Painting) Out Of Time', *parallax*, 3 (September 1996), pp. 99–112. Pervasive in my chapter, though in a way that doesn't lend itself to footnoting, are Maurice Merleau-Ponty's great essay 'Cézanne's Doubt' and his 'Eye and Mind', trans. Carleton Dallery, in Merleau-Ponty, *The Primacy of Perception* (Evanston, IL, 1964), pp. 159–90. They are the most eloquent statement of the 'phenomenality' case.

2 To put the question in de Man's terms: Is it the case, as we usually assume in thinking about the signs we manufacture (whether using the voice box, the paint brush or the letters of the alphabet) that these material events are aligned 'by an infinite variety of devices or turns… with the phenomenality, as knowledge (meaning) or sensory experience, of the signified toward which they are directed'? (Citation from Paul de Man, 'Hegel on the Sublime', in Paul de Man, *Aesthetic Ideology* [Minneapolis and London, 1996], p. 111.) Or does the sign – the mere materiality of the sign, the sequences and detours thrown up by its behaviour as *stuff* – constantly threaten 'the undoing of cognition and its replacement by the uncontrollable power of the letter as inscription'? (Paul de Man, 'Hypogram and Inscription', in Paul de Man, *The Resistance to Theory* [Minneapolis, 1986], p. 37.)

3 My thanks to Maureen Devine and Josephine Shea, then head and assistant curators of the Edsel and Eleanor Ford House in Grosse Pointe Shores, for their patience and helpfulness during my visit.

4 Richard Wollheim, 'Cézanne

and the Object', paper presented at a conference, *Cézanne and the Aesthetic*, National Gallery, London, 1996.

5 Paul de Man, 'Phenomenality and Materiality in Kant', in de Man, *Aesthetic Ideology*, p. 88.

6 Roger Fry, 'Art. The Post-Impressionists. – II', *The Nation* (3 December 1910), p. 402.

7 See p. 74 and Chapter 2, note 14.

8 See Theodore Reff, 'Cézanne's Constructive Stroke', *Art Quarterly* (Autumn 1962), pp. 214–27.

9 Fry, 'The Post-Impressionists. – II', p. 402.

10 *Ibid.*

11 Among more recent treatments of Cézanne's relation to the positivist culture of his times, see Kathryn Tuma, 'Cézanne and Lucretius', *Representations* (2002); the remarkable series of articles on Cézanne's debts to nineteenth-century colour theory by Paul Smith, especially his 'Cézanne's Color Lab: Not-so-Still Life', in Leca, *The World is an Apple*, pp. 92–144, and 'Vermilion, or why Cézanne took the shine off things', *Word & Image*, 36, no. 1 (2019), pp. 64–79; and André Dombrowski, *Cézanne, Murder, and Modern Life* (Berkeley, 2013), pp. 45–52 (on Cézanne and the naturalist Marion). The pioneer study is Robert Ratcliffe, 'Cézanne's Working Methods and Their Theoretical Background' (Ph.D dissertation, University of London, 1960). Cézanne, my chapter argues, was a positivist in much the same way that the great (agonized) nineteenth-century destroyers of religious certainty were Christians. For a recent attempt to define Cézanne's relation to the wider culture of modernism, see Carol Armstrong, *Cézanne's Gravity* (New Haven and London, 2018).

12 See for instance, Clement Greenberg, 'Cézanne and the Unity of Modern Art', in *Collected Essays*, vol. 3, p. 88 (summing up the argument): 'No wonder he complained to the day of his death of his inability to "realize." The aesthetic effect toward which his means urged was not that which his mind had conceived out of the desire for the organized maximum of an illusion of solidity and depth. Every brushstroke that followed a fictive plane into fictive depth harked back by reason of its abiding, unequivocal character as a mark made by a brush, to the physical fact of the medium; the shape and placing of that mark recalled the shape and position of the flat rectangle that was the original canvas, now covered with pigments that came from pots and tubes. Cézanne made no bones about the tangibility of the medium: there it was in all its grossness of matter.'

13 Fry, 'The Post-Impressionists. – II', p. 402

14 Compare Paul Smith, 'Cézanne's Late Landscapes, or The Prospect of Death', in Philip Conisbee and Dennis Coutagne, eds, *Cézanne in Provence* (New Haven and London, 2006), pp. 59–74.

15 Emily Dickinson, 'I died for Beauty', *The Complete Poems of Emily Dickinson*, ed. Thomas Johnson (Boston, 1961), p. 216.

16 The first phrase from Keats's 'The Fall of Hyperion', the second from Wordsworth's 'Prelude'.

Chapter 4

1 R. P. Rivière and J. F. Schnerb, 'L'atelier de Cézanne', *La Grande Revue* (25 December 1907), cited in Doran, *Conversations*, p. 91. 'Si je réussis ce bonhomme, c'est que la théorie sera vraie.' The French implies causation – almost that the truth of the theory will be what *makes* the painting succeed. But it could be the other way round. Doran suggests that Cézanne is referring to one of his portraits of the gardener Vallier.

2 The best brief accounts remain Roger Fry, *Cézanne, A Study of his Development* (London, 1927), pp. 71–74 and Meyer Schapiro, *Paul Cézanne*, pp. 16 and 88. Bernard Dorival, *Cézanne* (Paris, 1948), pp. 62–65, is good on colour, but has reservations about composition: the Barnes and Metropolitan pictures lean heavily on 'la pyramide qui s'accuse… avec un insistance un peu naïve et pédantesque'. See Nancy Ireson and Barnaby Wright, eds, *Cézanne's Card Players* (London, 2010) for a book-length treatment. A first version of this chapter was published as 'A House of Cards', in Satish Padiyar, ed., *Modernist Games: Cézanne and his Card Players* (London, 2013) [online publication, Courtauld Institute of Art], n. p., alongside essays by André Dombrowski, Gavin Parkinson, Charlotte de Mille, Satish Padiyar and Margaret Iversen.

3 See Pissarro to Lucien, 19 and 21 November 1895, PCC, vol. 4, pp. 116, 119 for mention of the purchases.

4 The small *Card Player* in Worcester Art Museum, which is linked to the Metropolitan Museum's picture, was included in a Vollard show in 1898 (see Walter Feilchenfeldt, Jayne Warman and David Nash, eds, *The Paintings, Watercolors, and Drawings of Paul Cézanne: An Online Catalogue Raisonné*, FWN 679). The Metropolitan picture was first shown and illustrated in 1904 at Cassirer's in Berlin, then in Paris in 1910 and London in 1914; the Barnes Foundation picture is first illustrated in 1907, then regularly up to and even after Barnes's acquisition (there is no evidence of exhibition before 1923 and even then the identification is unsure – could it have been the *Card Players* shown in 1899?); the Pellerin picture was shown

in the 1907 retrospective and illustrated the same year; the Courtauld painting was first shown at Cassirer's in 1904 but not illustrated till 1918; the Musée d'Orsay painting entered the Louvre in 1911 with the Camondo bequest, and is illustrated from 1910 on.

5 Paul Alexis to Émile Zola, February 1891, in PCC, p. 235.

6 See John Rewald, *The Paintings of Paul Cézanne: A Catalogue Raisonné*, 2 vols (New York, 1996), vol. 1, p. 461.

7 See e.g. Theodore Reff, 'Cézanne's "Card Players" and Their Sources', *Arts Magazine* (November 1980), pp. 104–17; Rewald, *Paintings of Cézanne*, vol. 1, pp. 443–48; and Ireson and Wright, *Cézanne's Card Players*, especially Aviva Burnstock, Charlotte Hale, Caroline Campbell and Gabriella Macaro, 'Cézanne's Development of the *Card Players*', pp. 35–53 (interesting new technical evidence: still, in my view, not settling the question of which picture followed which). On the Courtauld painting, see John House's entry in Stephanie Buck, John House, Ernst Vegelin van Claerbergen and Barnaby Wright, eds, *The Courtauld Cézannes* (London, 2008), pp. 90–93.

8 Schapiro, *Paul Cézanne*, p. 88.

9 See Novotny, 'Cézanne und das Ende der wissenschaftlichen Perspektive', in *Vienna School Reader*, pp. 379–425, especially pp. 393–99. Novotny's view of Cézanne's essential purpose is clearest on p. 414: 'This is how it must be in a pictorial space that no longer signifies an actual space accessible to empathy… In view of all the other characteristics of his art, it is only natural that the emotional values of perspective are suppressed… In the disenchanted world of his paintings, there was no room for them.'

10 Roger Fry says of the *Card Players*: 'They are almost the only definite "genre" pieces of his that exist, if we omit the early *Two Men Playing Cards* [by which he means *Alexis and Zola*]', see Fry, *Cézanne*, p. 71; but he makes nothing of the connection. For a fine extended account of the two Alexis and Zola paintings, see Dombrowski, *Cézanne, Murder, and Modern Life*, pp. 99–137.

11 See *Madame Cézanne in a Red Dress*, *c.* 1888–90, in the Metropolitan Museum of Art, New York (FWN 493).

12 Compare Roger Fry on *Alexis and Zola* (for him, *Two Men Playing Cards*): 'Here the reminiscence of Pieter de Hoogh seems unmistakable': see Fry, *Cézanne*, p. 25.

13 For *The Raising of Jairus's Daughter*, see William Rearick, *The Art of Paolo Veronese 1528–1588* (Washington, D.C., 1988), pp. 28–29 and Xavier Salomon, *Veronese* (London, 2014), p. 249 and plate 31. For Desplaces's engraving of *Respect*, see Nicholas Penny, *The Sixteenth-Century Italian Paintings: Volume II: Venice 1540–1600 (National Gallery Catalogues)* (New Haven and London, 2008), p. 426.

14 See Rearick, *The Art of Paolo Veronese*, pp. 136–37 and Terisio Pignatti and Filippo Pedrocco, *Veronese* (Milan, 1995), vol. 2, pp. 381–82. Rearick thinks the Edinburgh painting is studio work (on unconvincing grounds). As usual with Veronese, discussions in the literature are superficial.

15 See p. 82 and Chapter 2, note 16.

16 See Dorival, *Cézanne*, p. 63, and Ireson and Wright, *Cézanne's Card Players*, pp. 26–27.

17 Badt, *The Art of Cézanne*, pp. 92–123.

18 Or the link is rejected, see Reff, 'Cézanne's "Card Players"', pp. 114–16, and John House, 'Cézanne's *Card Players*: Art Without Anecdote', in Ireson and Wright, *Cézanne's Card Players*, p. 67. I find Reff's grounds for dismissal too commonsensical: they would have made Freud smile.

19 Jules Borely, 'Cézanne à Aix', July 1902, in Doran, *Conversations*, p. 21; for Doran's translation, see Michael Doran, ed. and trans., *Conversations with Cézanne* (Berkeley, 2001), p. 23. If Nina Athanassoglou-Kallmyer is right (she admits the fragility of the evidence) that the *Card Players* series coincided with moves in the 1890s to regulate gambling and tax the production of playing cards, then the remarks to Borely may even have had a topical undertow: see Nina Athanassoglou-Kallmyer, *Cézanne and Provence, The Painter in His Culture* (Chicago, 2003), pp. 210–15.

20 Roger Fry was confident that the café surroundings were real: 'The subject is a group of card players which he evidently studied in some humble café in Aix… He could rely no doubt on the fact that the peasants took no notice of him – he was just an "original", an odd old man whom most people thought rather mad but harmless', see Fry, *Cézanne*, pp. 71–72. Given the inconclusive nature of Alexis's 1891 letter, Fry's vision of Cézanne painting in the *cabaret* cannot be dismissed (or proven). In Fry it coexists easily with the idea of Cézanne's absolute aesthetic concentration: 'The simplicity of disposition is such as might even have made Giotto hesitate to adopt it.'

21 On Pissarro's painting, see 'We Field Women', in Timothy J. Clark, *Farewell to an Idea: Episodes from a History of Modernism* (New Haven and London, 1999), pp. 55–137. I try there to situate

Pissarro's anarchism in the early 1890s world of Ravachol, Reclus, Kropotkin, *La Révolte* and *Le Père Peinard*, and to think of the 'peasant subject' in relation to the late-nineteenth-century politics of agricultural protectionism, and the idea (the cult) of the peasant as protector and mainstay of the Republic.

22 On Cézanne's Provence, see Jean Arrouyé, *La Provence de Cézanne* (Aix-en-Provence, 1982) and Athanassoglou-Kallmyer's more substantial *Cézanne and Provence*. On Cézanne's relation to the Provençal intelligentsia (he had one, but it is fiercely difficult to reconstruct), see, for example, Paul Smith, 'Joachim Gasquet, Virgil and Cézanne's Landscape: "My Beloved Golden Age"', *Apollo*, 147, no. 439 (October 1998), pp. 11–23, and Athanassoglou-Kallmyer, *Cézanne and Provence*, especially pp. 215–31. André Dombrowski kindly alerts me to the afterlife of 'Third Republic' readings of the *Card Players* in the early-twentieth-century Cézanne books. See, for example, Gustave Coquiot, *Paul Cézanne* (Paris, 1919), pp. 223–24: 'C'est un émouvant hommage à ceux de la glèbe, qui gardent tout en jouant aux cartes – un jeu pour roi fou! – la gravité de ceux qui labourent, qui moissonnent en silence, en peinant, en suant tant qu'ils peuvent, tandis que pour eux les oiseaux chantent, concert du ciel accordé à ces taciturnes, dont la langue ne se délie que sous les rasades du vin!' A comprehensive rehearsal, I think, of the tropes Cézanne's paintings were bound to live with and tried to defuse.

Chapter 5

1 First reported by Bernard, letter to his mother, 5 February 1904, cited in Doran, *Conversations*, p. 24. 'C'est effrayant, la vie.' Taken up in various later texts. Bernard says Cézanne repeated it to him 'a hundred times'.

2 Hilary Spurling, *Matisse the Master: A Life of Henri Matisse, Volume 2* (London, 2005), p. 202.

3 For connected discussion, see Alastair Wright, *Matisse and the Subject of Modernism* (Princeton, 2004) and (putting in question the established reading of Matisse's art in terms of 'emotion' and 'subjectivity') Todd Cronan, *Against Affective Formalism: Matisse, Bergson, Modernism* (Minnesota, 2014).

4 Baudelaire to Fernand Desnoyers [late 1853?], in Baudelaire, *Correspondance*, ed. Claude Pichois (Paris, 1973), vol. 1, p. 248.

5 Spurling, *Matisse the Master*, p. 217.

6 Like many boasts, possibly apocryphal. See Jean Renoir, *Renoir, My Father*, trans. Randolph and Dorothy Weaver (Boston, 1962), p. 185. One story is that Renoir threw off the remark, impatiently, to a journalist asking him how he painted with such arthritic hands.

7 See Aleksandr Lavrentiev and John Bowlt, *Varvara Stepanova* (London, 1988), pp. 76–77 for illustrations (incorrectly captioned) and Christina Kiaer, *Imagine No Possessions: The Socialist Objects of Russian Constructivism* (Cambridge, MA and London, 2005), pp. 114–17. For the performance in relation to Soviet feminism, see Kiaer, 'The short life of the equal woman', *Tate Etc.* (20 October 2017), n. p.

8 See Stephanie D'Alessandro and John Elderfield, *Matisse: Radical Invention, 1913–1917* (New Haven and London, 2011), pp. 338–41: they make the case for dating the picture to 1917 (it seems to have been begun in winter 1916 and finished the following year) and have the most searching discussion of the painting as a whole.

9 For the Matisse–Immendorff comparison, see my response to 'Art and Scholarship in Moments of Historical Danger', *Art Margins* (November 2021), pp. 173–75.

10 D'Alessandro and Elderfield, *Matisse: Radical Invention*, pp. 344–45. My thanks to John Elderfield for responding generously to further questions.

11 Henri Matisse, *Écrits et propos sur l'art* (Paris, 1972), p. 44, note 7.

12 *Ibid.*, p. 49, note 15.

13 A remark made in a seminar at Berkeley. See Caroline Arscott, *William Morris and Edward Burne-Jones: Interlacings* (New Haven and London, 2008) for the results.

14 Gertrude Stein, *The Autobiography of Alice B. Toklas* (London, 1966 [first published 1933]), p. 102.

15 See Colin Bailey, *Renoir's Portraits: Impressions of an Age* (National Gallery, Ottawa, 1997), cat. no. 11, cited in D'Alessandro and Elderfield, *Matisse: Radical Invention*, p. 337.

16 Compare Matisse's apology for his 1920s Odalisques: 'Je fais des *Odalisques* pour faire du nu. Mais comment faire du nu sans qu'il soit factice?' See Tériade (Stratis Eleftheriadis), 'Visite à Henri Matisse', in Matisse, *Écrits et propos*, p. 99.

17 My thanks to Jennifer Scappettone for pointing this out after a lecture in Chicago.

18 For Monet's hesitations about the visit, and Matisse's eventual trip in 1917, see Paul Tucker et al., *Monet in the 20th Century* (London and Boston, 1998), pp. 70–71, and Jack Cowart and Dominique Foucart, *Henri Matisse: The Early Years in Nice* (National Gallery, Washington, D.C., 1986), pp. 19, 42, note 14.

19 Hilary Spurling, *The Unknown Matisse: A Life of Henri Matisse, Volume 1* (London, 1998), p. 285, letter of Henri Edmond Cross

to Théo van Rysselberghe, 7 September 1904.

20 Michel Puy, 'Les Fauves', *La Phalange* 2 (15 November 1907), reprinted in Puy, *L'effort des peintres modernes* (Paris, 1933), p. 67, cited in Spurling, *The Unknown Matisse*, p. 397.

21 Schapiro, *Cézanne*, p. 106, argues for the house's integration into the landscape: 'The one human object, the house, set in the fork between earth and rock, rests on a point, like the agitated trees, and repeats their branching form. The lines of the building, accented by the red tiles, are adjusted to the slope of the ground.' And so on for two more sentences. All true, and characteristic of Schapiro's feeling for the play of analogy in Cézanne, but the house still seems to me a heroic, alien presence.

22 See, for instance, Matisse's famous homage to Cézanne, written on donating a *Bathers*, bought on credit from Vollard in 1899, to the Petit Palais: 'Depuis trente-sept ans que je la possède, je connais assez bien cette toile, pas entièrement, je l'espère; elle m'a soutenu moralement dans des moments critiques de mon aventure d'artiste; j'y ai puisé ma foi et ma persévérance...', cited in Matisse, *Écrits et propos*, p. 134.

23 Cézanne to Gasquet, 13 June 1896, PCC, p. 251. Hard to translate: Cézanne is refusing to take part in the launching of a new magazine. 'I make a principle [almost, a fetish] of my individuality.' Or maybe just: 'I hold my individuality apart.'

24 A remark of Gail Day, responding to the painting after a lecture at the Open University.

Conclusion

1 François Jourdain, *Cézanne* (Paris, 1950), p. 11 (reporting on a conversation of 1904), cited in Doran, *Conversations*, p. 84. '"D'ailleurs," ajouta-t-il en se frappant le front, "la peinture... c'est là-dedans!"'

2 See Pavel Machotka, *Cézanne: Landscape into Art* (New Haven and London, 1996), pp. 125–27 for the attempts by himself, Rewald and Erle Loran to tie the painting to a specific motif. Machotka concludes that Cézanne probably 'suppressed' a whole intermediate band of foothills, moving the house and mountain much closer together on the picture plane.

3 Fehsenfeld and Overbeck, eds, *The Letters of Samuel Beckett, Vol. 1*, p. 223.

4 See Christopher White, *The Late Etchings of Rembrandt* (British Museum, 1969), p. 14, for a slightly different description of the motif.

5 Robert Browning, 'Memorabilia', *The Poems, Volume 1* (Harmondsworth, 1981), p. 643.

6 Zbigniew Herbert, *Still Life with Bridle: Essays and Apocryphas*, trans. John and Bogdana Carpenter (New York, 1991), pp. 14–15. For subtle treatment of connected issues, see Lytle Shaw, *New Grounds for Dutch Landscape* (Stockholm, 2021).

7 See Novotny, *Cézanne und das Ende der wissenschaftlichen Perspektive*, pp. 30–33, its closing page translated in *Vienna School Reader*, p. 379. 'Section', as the translator points out, is a rendering of Novotny's non-standard term 'Ausschnidt', with its suggestion of 'cutting away'.

8 Schapiro, *Cézanne*, p. 70.

9 Paolo Lomazzo, 'Trattato dell'arte della pittura, scoltura et architettura' [Milan 1584], book 6, chap. 62, cited in Ernst Gombrich, *Norm and Form: Studies in the Art of the Renaissance* (London, 1966), p. 120.

10 Athanassoglou-Kallmyer, *Cézanne and Provence*, pp. 116–21 (a fine piece of disenchanting art history); Pavel Machotka, ed., *P. Cézanne: Les sites provençaux* (Marseille, 2005), pp. 59–60; and Bruno Ely, 'Gardanne, Montbriand and Bellevue', in Conisbee and Coutagne, eds, *Cézanne in Provence*, especially pp. 150–53 (in the wake of Athanassoglou-Kallmyer, still approving of the way Cézanne 'made no particular references to human activity and deliberately avoided superfluous detail').

11 The finest discussion remains Schapiro, *Cézanne*, p. 110. On Cézanne's quarry viewpoint, see John Elderfield and Ariel Kline, 'Bibémus', in Elderfield, *Cézanne: The Rock and Quarry Paintings*, pp. 111–12. Compare the brief remarks in John Golding, 'Cézanne, Braque and Pictorial Space', in Joseph Rishel and Katherine Sachs, eds, *Cézanne and Beyond* (New Haven and London, 2009), pp. 259, 268: 'The space... envelopes us totally and reassures us.'

Picture Credits

Works are oil on panel or oil on canvas unless otherwise specified.

1 Art Institute of Chicago. Helen Birch Bartlett Memorial Collection
2 Norton Simon Art Foundation, Pasadena, CA. Gift of Mr Norton Simon
3 The National Gallery, London. Bought, Courtauld Fund, 1926
4 Musée de l'Orangerie, Paris. Photo RMN-Grand Palais (Musée de l'Orangerie)/Hervé Lewandowski
5 Private Collection
6 Private Collection
7 The J. Paul Getty Museum, Los Angeles
8 Private Collection. Photo Christopher Campbell
9 Kunstmuseum St Gallen. Photo Sebastian Stadler, 2014
10 The Metropolitan Museum of Art, New York. The Walter H. and Leonore Annenberg Collection. Gift of Walter H. and Leonore Annenberg, 1997, bequest of Walter H. Annenberg, 2002
11 The Henry and Rose Pearlman Foundation. On loan since 1976 to the Princeton University Art Museum. Photo Christopher Campbell
12 Private Collection. Photo Christopher Campbell
13 Ashmolean Museum, Oxford. Bequeathed by Montague Shearman through the Contemporary Art Society, 1940
14, 15 Carmen Thyssen-Bornemisza Collection on loan at the Museo Nacional Thyssen-Bornemisza, Madrid. Photo Colección Carmen Thyssen-Bornemisza en depósito en el Museo Nacional Thyssen-Bornemisza/Scala, Florence
16, 17 Private Collection. Photo Christopher Campbell
18 The J. Paul Getty Museum, Los Angeles
19 The National Gallery, London. Presented by C.S. Carstairs to the Tate Gallery through the Art Fund, 1926; transferred, 1950
20 Private Collection. Photo Christie's Images/Bridgeman Images
21 Musée d'Orsay, Paris. Photo Christopher Campbell
22 Museo d'arte della Svizzera italiana, Lugano. Collection Cantone Ticino. Donation Carla Milich-Fassbind. Photo Christopher Campbell
23 Private Collection
24 Private Collection
25 Musée d'Orsay, Paris. Photo RMN-Grand Palais (Musée d'Orsay)/Hervé Lewandowski
26 Private Collection. Photo Christopher Campbell
27 Wadsworth Atheneum Museum of Art, Hartford, CT. The Ella Gallup Sumner and Mary Catlin Sumner Collection Fund, 1966.315. Photo Allen Phillips/ Wadsworth Atheneum
28, 29 The J. Paul Getty Museum, Los Angeles
30 Private Collection
31 The Metropolitan Museum of Art, New York. Bequest of Stephen C. Clark, 1960
32 Nationalmuseum, Stockholm
33 Musée de l'Orangerie, Paris. Photo RMN-Grand Palais (Musée de l'Orangerie)/Hervé Lewandowski
34 Sammlung Oskar Reinhart 'Am Römerholz', Winterthur
35 Private Collection. Photo Christopher Campbell
36 Barnes Foundation, Philadelphia
37 Private Collection
38 Sammlung Oskar Reinhart 'Am Römerholz', Winterthur
39 Fondation Beyeler, Riehen/ Basel, Sammlung Beyeler. Photo Robert Bayer
40 Private Collection
41 The Samuel Courtauld Trust, The Courtauld Gallery, London. Courtauld Bequest 1948. Photo Courtauld Gallery/Bridgeman Images
42 National Gallery of Art, Washington, D.C. Chester Dale Collection
43 Neue Pinakothek, Bayerische Staatsgemäldesammlungen, Munich. Photo Scala, Florence/ bpk, Bildagentur für Kunst, Kultur und Geschichte, Berlin
44 The State Hermitage Museum, St Petersburg. Photo The State Hermitage Museum/Pavel Demidov
45 Pola Museum of Art, Kanagawa
46, 48 Private Collection
47 The Phillips Collection, Washington, D.C
49 Philadelphia Museum of Art. The Mr and Mrs Carroll S. Tyson, Jr, Collection, 1963
50, 51 Musée de l'Orangerie, Paris. Collection Jean Walter et Paul Guillaume. Photo RMN-Grand Palais (Musée de l'Orangerie)/ Franck Raux
52 Brooklyn Museum, New York. Ella C. Woodward Memorial Fund and Alfred T. White Fund, 23.105. Photo Brooklyn Museum
53 National Gallery of Art, Washington, D.C. Chester Dale Collection
54, 103 The Baltimore Museum of Art. Photo Christopher Campbell
55 Private Collection
56 Barnes Foundation, Philadelphia
57 Saint Louis Art Museum. Funds given by Mrs Mark C. Steinberg
58 The Metropolitan Museum of Art, New York. Bequest of

Stephen C. Clark, 1960
59 Kunsthalle Mannheim. Photo Scala, Florence/bpk, Bildagentur für Kunst, Kultur und Geschichte, Berlin/Cem Yücetas
60 Barnes Foundation, Philadelphia
61 Private Collection
62 Musée d'Orsay, Paris. Photo Musée d'Orsay, Dist. RMN-Grand Palais/Patrice Schmidt
63, 73 The Samuel Courtauld Trust, The Courtauld Gallery, London. Courtauld Gift. Photo Courtauld Gallery/Bridgeman Images
64 Neue Pinakothek, Bayerische Staatsgemäldesammlungen, Munich. Photo Scala, Florence/bpk, Bildagentur für Kunst, Kultur und Geschichte, Berlin
65 Private Collection
66 Museu de Arte de São Paulo Assis Chateaubriand
67 Abegg-Stiftung, CH-3132 Riggisberg, inv. no. 14.8.66. Photo Abegg-Stiftung, CH-3132 Riggisberg, 2011/SIK-ISEA Zürich
68 Pushkin Museum, Moscow
69 Scottish National Gallery, Edinburgh
70 Pushkin Museum, Moscow. Photo akg-images
71 Private Collection
72 Barnes Foundation, Philadelphia
74 The Metropolitan Museum of Art, New York. Gift of Mr and Mrs Charles Wrightsman, 1973
75 Fondation Beyeler, Riehen/Basel, Sammlung Beyeler. Photo Robert Bayer. © Succession H. Matisse/DACS 2022
76 Private Collection. Photo Christie's Images/Bridgeman Images. © Succession H. Matisse/DACS 2022
77 Centre Pompidou, Paris. Photo Centre Pompidou, MNAM-CCI, Dist. RMN-Grand Palais/Philippe Migeat. © Succession H. Matisse/DACS 2022
78 The Cleveland Museum of Art. Purchase from the J. H. Wade Fund 1939.269
79 Rodchenko Stepanova Archive, Moscow. © Rodchenko & Stepanova Archive, DACS, RAO 2022
80 The Phillips Collection, Washington, D.C. © Succession H. Matisse/DACS 2022
81 Musée d'Art Moderne de la Ville de Paris. Gift of Michael Werner, 2012. © The Estate of Jörg Immendorff, Courtesy Galerie Michael Werner, Cologne and New York
82 Private Collection. Photo Peter Willi/SuperStock. © Succession H. Matisse/DACS 2022
83 Barnes Foundation, Philadelphia. Photo The Barnes Foundation/Bridgeman Images. © Succession H. Matisse/DACS 2022
84 Private Collection. Photo Archives Henri Matisse. © Succession H. Matisse/DACS 2022
85 The Museum of Modern Art, New York. Gift of Mr and Mrs Samuel A. Marx. Photo The Museum of Modern Art, New York/Scala, Florence. © Succession H. Matisse/DACS 2022
86 Centre Pompidou, Paris. Photo Centre Pompidou, MNAM-CCI, Dist. RMN-Grand Palais/Philippe Migeat. © Succession H. Matisse/DACS 2022
87 Private Collection
88 Private Collection. Photo Archives Henri Matisse. © Succession H. Matisse/DACS 2022
89 The White House Collection, Washington D.C
90 Arena Chapel, Padua. Photo Joseph Martin/Album/Superstock
91 Carnegie Museum of Art. Acquired through the generosity of Mrs Alan M. Scaife. Photo Heritage Images/Fine Art Images/akg-images
92 Musée d'Orsay, Paris. Photo Musée d'Orsay, Dist. RMN-Grand Palais/Patrice Schmidt
93 Musée d'Orsay, Paris. Photo Musée d'Orsay, Dist. RMN-Grand Palais/Patrice Schmidt
94, 97 Indianapolis Museum of Art. Gift of Mrs James W. Fesler in memory of Daniel W. and Elizabeth C. Marmon
95 The Metropolitan Museum of Art, New York. The Walter H. and Leonore Annenberg Collection, Gift of Walter H. and Leonore Annenberg, 1993, Bequest of Walter H. Annenberg, 2002
96 The Museum of Modern Art, New York. Mrs Simon Guggenheim Fund. Photo The Museum of Modern Art, New York/Scala, Florence. © Succession H. Matisse/DACS 2022
98 Kunsthistorisches Museum, Vienna
99 Museo Nacional Thyssen-Bornemisza, Madrid
100 Minneapolis Institute of Art. Bequest of Herschel V. Jones by exchange, The Putnam Dana McMillan Fund, The Edith and Norman Garmezy Prints and Drawings Acquisitions Fund and Gift of funds from the Print and Drawing Council
101 Nivaagaard Collection, Niva
102 Private Collection

Index

Page numbers in *italic* refer to the illustrations

Frontispiece: Detail from Fig. 28, Paul Cézanne, *Still Life with Apples*, *c.* 1893–95. The J. Paul Getty Museum, Los Angeles.

First published in the United Kingdom in 2022 by
Thames & Hudson Ltd, 181A High Holborn, London WC1V 7QX

First published in the United States of America in 2022 by
Thames & Hudson Inc., 500 Fifth Avenue, New York, New York 10110

Reprinted 2023

Designed by Karin Fremer

British Library Cataloguing-in-Publication Data
A catalogue record for this book is available from the British Library

Library of Congress Control Number 2022931259

ISBN 978-0-500-02528-4

Printed and bound in China by C&C Offset Printing Co, Ltd

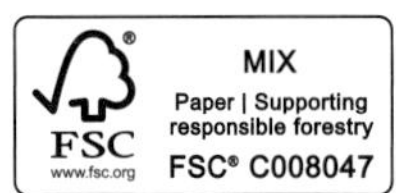